ASSASSINATION CLASSROOM

YUSEI MATSUI

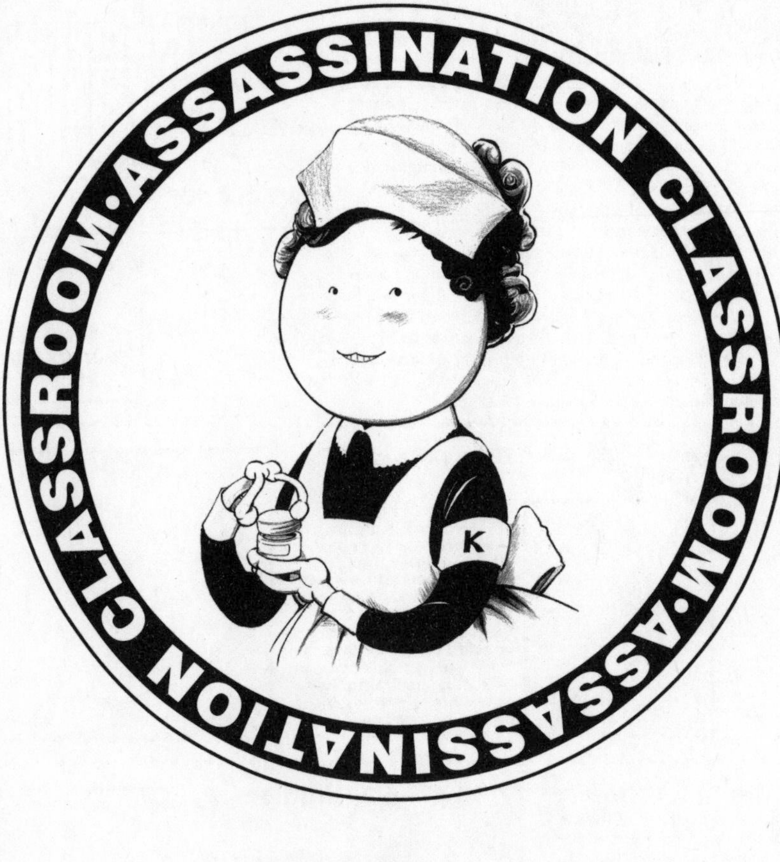
ASSASSINATION CLASSROOM·ASSASSINATION CLASSROOM·
K

19

TIME TO GO TO SCHOOL

SHONEN JUMP ADVANCED

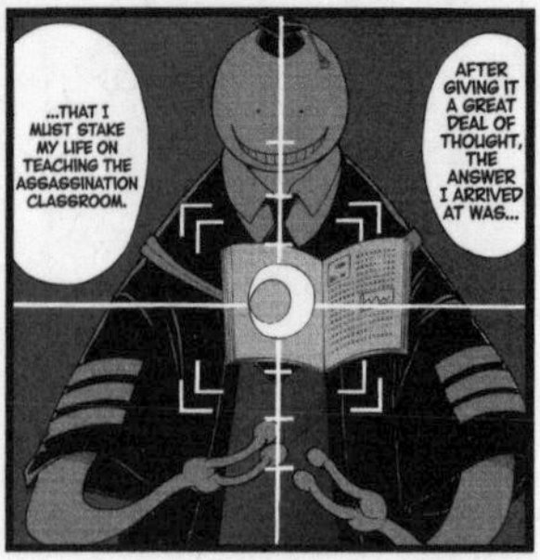
AFTER GIVING IT A GREAT DEAL OF THOUGHT, THE ANSWER I ARRIVED AT WAS...
...THAT I MUST STAKE MY LIFE ON TEACHING THE ASSASSINATION CLASSROOM.

Koro Tribune

February Issue

Published by: Class 3-E Newspaper Staff

Story Thus Far

Kunugigaoka Junior High Class 3-E is taught by a monster who even the armies of the world with all their state-of-the-art technology can't kill. That monster, Koro Sensei, is fated to self-destruct and take the planet Earth with him, so...

Nice work on your entrance exams! Now let's concentrate on the assassination until graduation!

...a bounty has been placed on his head. It comes down to his students in 3-E, the so-called "End Class." Once looked down upon by the rest of the school, this class of misfits is now respected for the athleticism and powers of concentration they have developed thanks to the dedicated instruction of Koro Sensei and Mr. Karasuma of the Ministry of Defense. A strong bond has formed between the students and Koro Sensei, transcending their relationship as assassins and target. After learning the truth about Koro Sensei's past (that he is the result of a mad scientist's experiments and is fated to explode against his will) and after an unorthodox decision-making process, the students have begun to search for a way to save their teacher...

We promise to find a way to save you, Koro-Sensei!

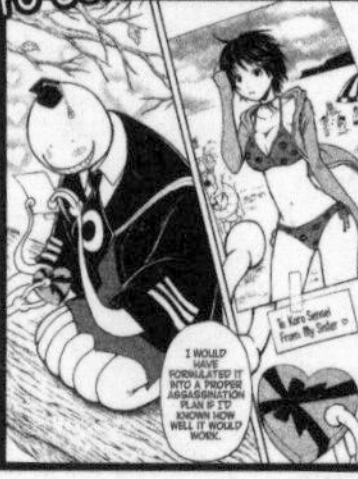
To Koro Sensei From My Sister
I WOULD HAVE FORMULATED IT INTO A PROPER ASSASSINATION PLAN IF I'D KNOWN HOW WELL IT WOULD WORK.

Koro Sensei

A mysterious, man-made, octopus-like creature whose name is a play on the words "koro senai," which means "can't kill." He is capable of flying at Mach 20 and his versatile tentacles protect him from attacks and aid him in everyday activities. He followed in the footsteps of Aguri, the woman who saved his humanity, by becoming the teacher of Class 3-E.

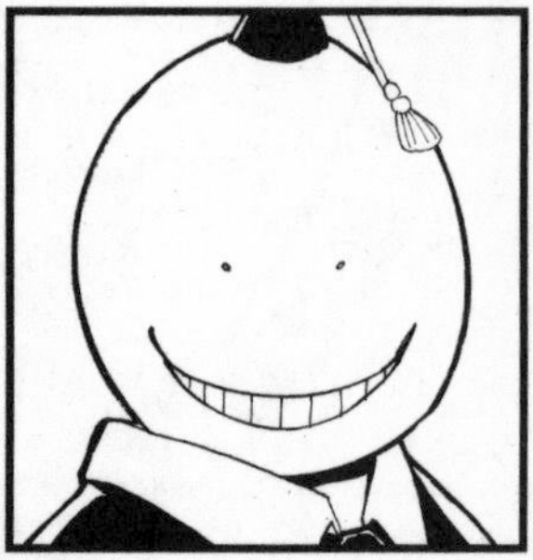

Kaede Kayano

Class E student. Class E student. She enrolled in Class E to avenge her sister's death by killing Koro Sensei. Her tentacles have since been removed. Does she have special feelings for Nagisa now...?!

You mustered up the courage! Well done!

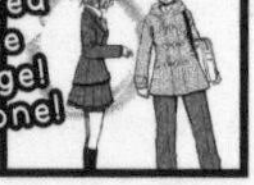

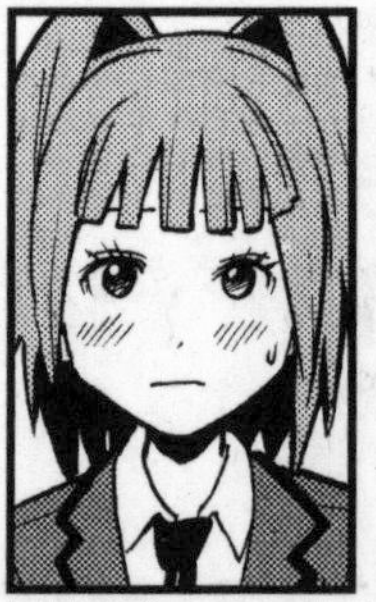

Nagisa Shiota

Class E student. He has a hidden talent for assassinations and decides to hone those skills to help others. He's a good kisser too.

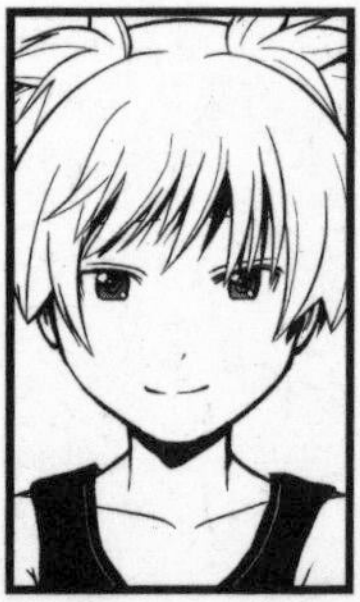

Meg Kataoka

pick up!

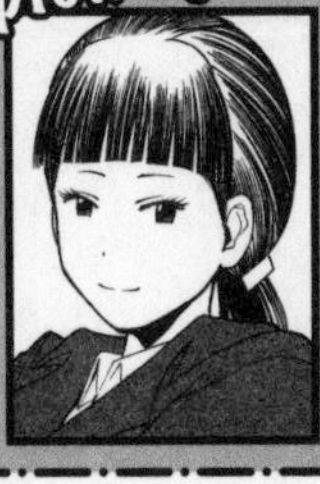

She received 18 Valentine's Day chocolate gifts this year. She couldn't figure out how to refuse them, so before she knew it, she was the recipient of unwelcome handshakes and hugs. These awkward occurrences have been escalating over the years.

Karma Akabane

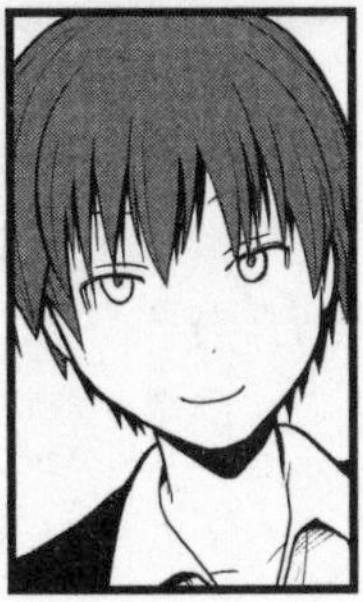

Class E student. He learned to take his studies a bit more seriously after some initial failures and earned first place in the overall school scores on the second semester midterm.

Tadaomi Karasuma

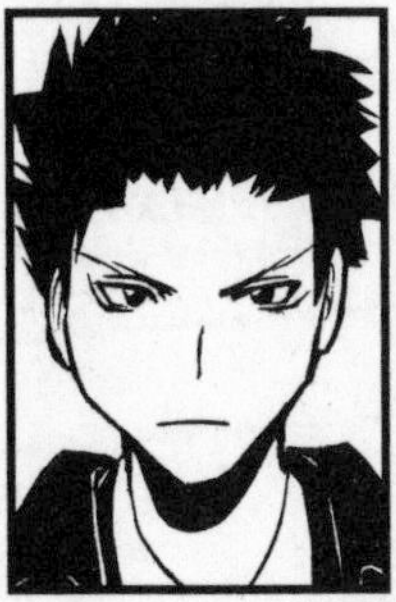

Member of the Ministry of Defense and the Class E students' P.E. teacher. Though serious about his duties, he has successfully built good relationships with his students.

Itona Horibe

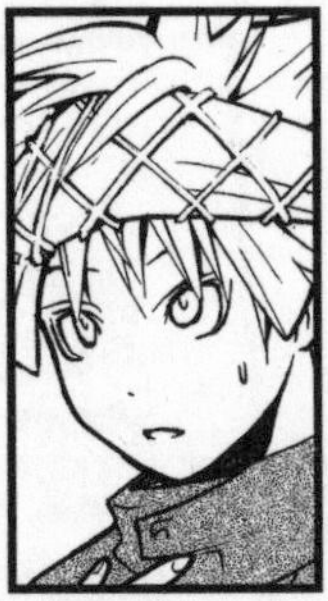

Class E student. His hostile attitude from when he was possessed by tentacles has disappeared, and he has found his place in Class E. The assassination technology he creates is above and beyond the level of a hobby and has greatly increased the range of Class E's assassinations.

February is almost over...!

Everyone is preoccupied lately. We want to play more and assassinate more, but in the back of our minds we know we're all about to go our separate ways after we graduate. It's the season for melancholic thoughts like that.

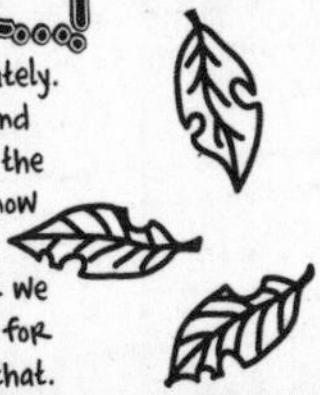

Irina Jelavich

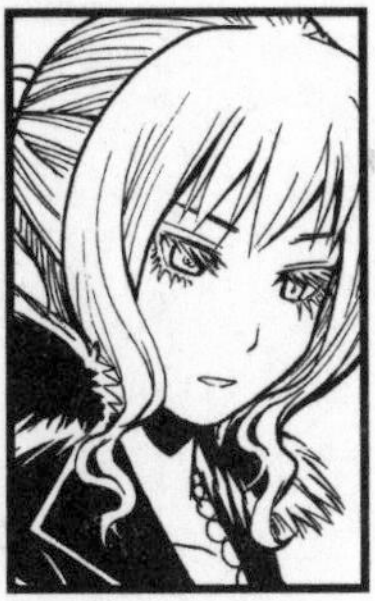

A sexy assassin hired as an English teacher. She's known for using her "womanly charms" to get close to a target. Karasuma has finally admitted that he reciprocates her feelings for him and they have moved in together.

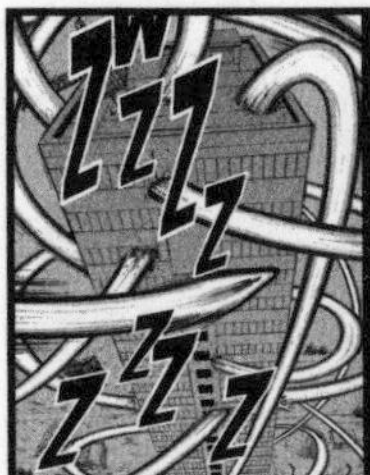

Demolish buildings in the blink of an eye!

Call Shiro Construction for estimates! Guaranteed safe and secure!

Kotaro Yanagisawa

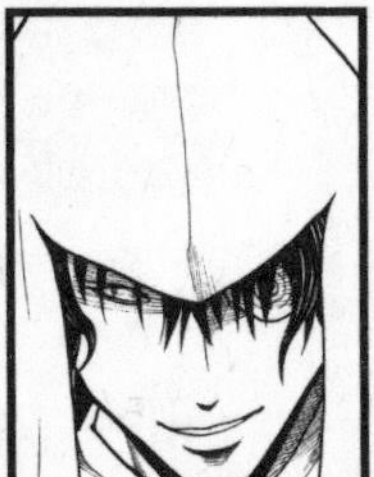

This scientific genius who created Koro Sensei hates his experimental subject for stealing everything from him and has vowed revenge.

ASSASSINATION CLASSROOM 19 CONTENTS

on 1): Answer the following
ns about the relationships
n the following organisms.

lage on the right depicts the
of the food chain. The lowest
is the producer organisms, the
d stage is the herbivores that
e producer organisms, the
stage is the carnivores and the
n stage is the tentacle creature.

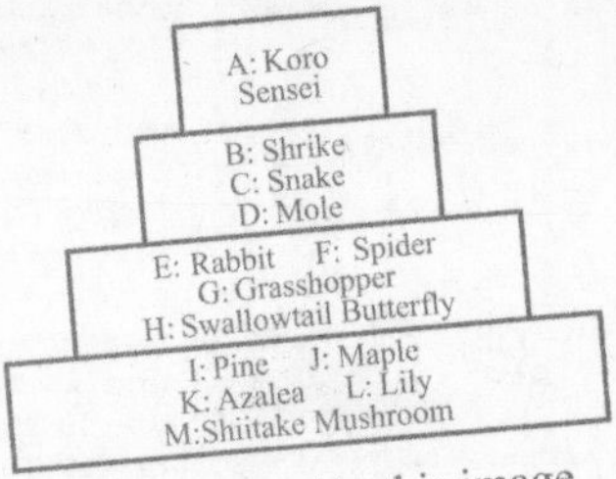
A: Koro Sensei
B: Shrike
C: Snake
D: Mole
E: Rabbit F: Spider
G: Grasshopper
H: Swallowtail Butterfly
I: Pine J: Maple
K: Azalea L: Lily
M:Shiitake Mushroom

There are two organisms that ... misplaced in this image.
e the letter corresponding to ... explain.

er: ( ) Reason:

er: ( ) Reason:

Choose the correct answer

example, if for some reas
n ③ will decline in number
sulting in more producer
ganisms. Therefore, certai
e maintained in constant
umbers.

A: Producer Organisms
B: Herbivorous Organisms

(Question 2): Chemical re

(1): Magnesium and Oxy

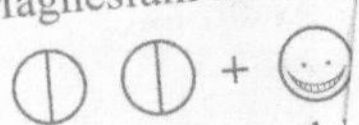

In the same manner, 1
choose the correct ans
and respond below.

① Natural Gas (Carbo

② Copper oxide due

(ANSWER SHEET)

Grade	3	Class	E	Name	CONTENTS	Score	

You're Reading in the Wrong Direction!!

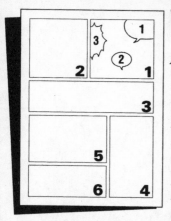

Whoops! Guess what? You're starting at the wrong end of the comic!

...It's true! In keeping with the original Japanese format, **Assassination Classroom** is meant to be read from right to left, starting in the upper-right corner.

Unlike English, which is read from left to right, Japanese is read from right to left, meaning that action, sound effects and word-balloon order are completely reversed... something which can make readers unfamiliar with Japanese feel pretty backwards themselves. For this reason, manga or Japanese comics published in the U.S. in English have sometimes been published "flopped"—that is, printed in exact reverse order, as though seen from the other side of a mirror.

By flopping pages, U.S. publishers can avoid confusing readers, but the compromise is not without its downside. For one thing, a character in a flopped manga series who once wore in the original Japanese version a T-shirt emblazoned with "M A Y" (as in "the merry month of") now wears one which reads "Y A M"! Additionally, many manga creators in Japan are themselves unhappy with the process, as some feel the mirror-imaging of their art skews their original intentions.

We are proud to bring you Yusei Matsui's **Assassination Classroom** in the original unflopped format.

For now, though, turn to the other side of the book and let the adventure begin...!

—Editor

Seraph of the End

—VAMPIRE REIGN—

STORY BY **Takaya Kagami**   ART BY **Yamato Yamamoto**

STORYBOARDS BY **Daisuke Furuya**

Vampires reign— humans revolt!

Yuichiro's dream of killing every vampire is near-impossible, given that vampires are seven times stronger than humans, and the only way to kill them is by mastering Cursed Gear, advanced demon-possessed weaponry. Not to mention that humanity's most elite Vampire Extermination Unit, the Moon Demon Company, wants nothing to do with Yuichiro unless he can prove he's willing to work in a team—which is the last thing he wants!

THE LATEST CHAPTERS SERIALIZED IN **WEEKLY SHONEN JUMP**

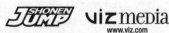

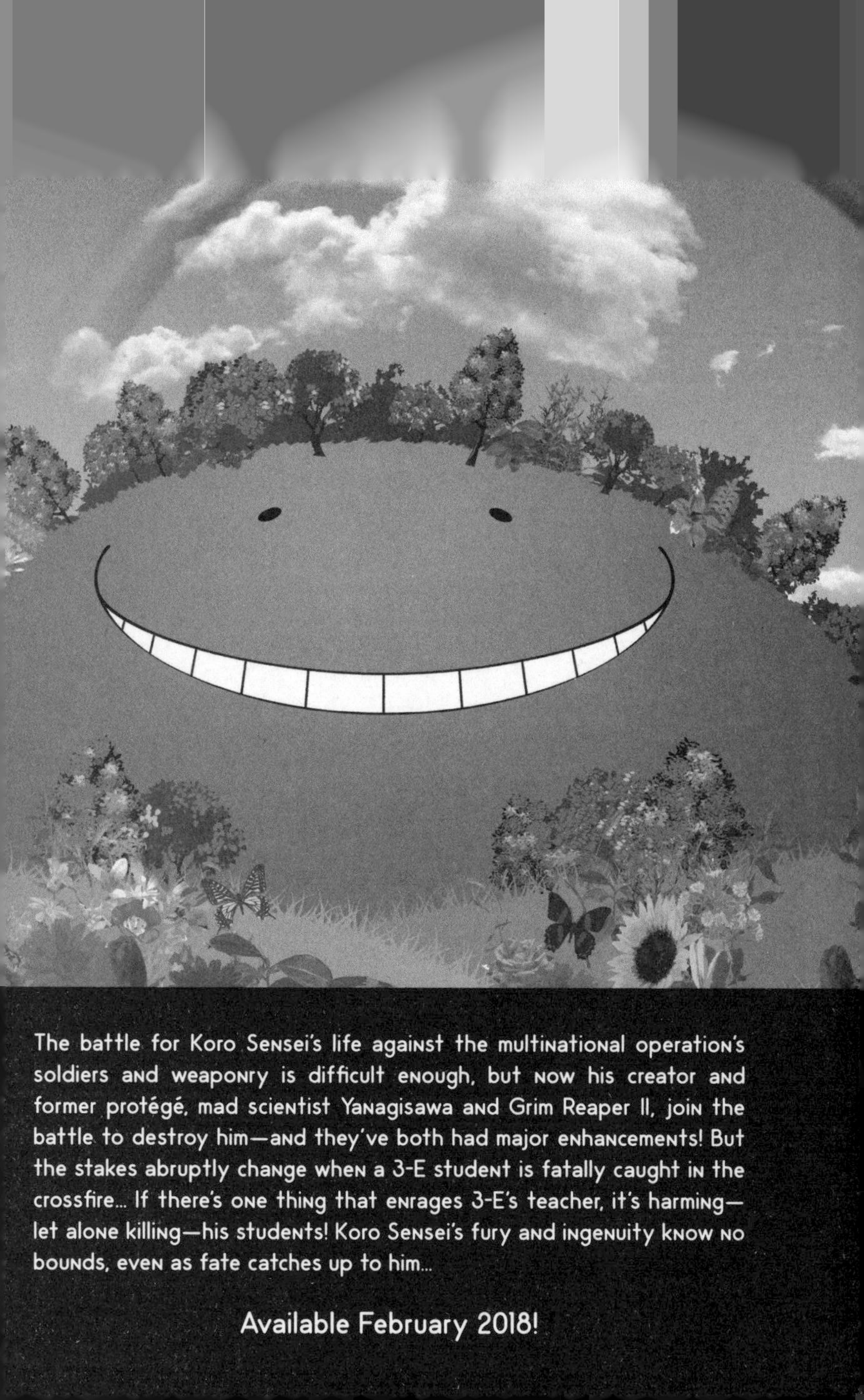

The battle for Koro Sensei's life against the multinational operation's soldiers and weaponry is difficult enough, but now his creator and former protégé, mad scientist Yanagisawa and Grim Reaper II, join the battle to destroy him—and they've both had major enhancements! But the stakes abruptly change when a 3-E student is fatally caught in the crossfire... If there's one thing that enrages 3-E's teacher, it's harming—let alone killing—his students! Koro Sensei's fury and ingenuity know no bounds, even as fate catches up to him...

Available February 2018!

ASSASSINATION CLASSROOM

Volume 19
SHONEN JUMP ADVANCED Manga Edition

Story and Art by YUSEI MATSUI

Translation/Tetsuichiro Miyaki
English Adaptation/Bryant Turnage
Touch-up Art & Lettering/Stephen Dutro
Cover & Interior Design/Sam Elzway
Editor/Annette Roman

ANSATSU KYOSHITSU © 2012 by Yusei Matsui
All rights reserved.
First published in Japan in 2012 by SHUEISHA Inc., Tokyo.
English translation rights arranged by SHUEISHA Inc.

Published by VIZ Media, LLC
P.O. Box 77010
San Francisco, CA 94107

10 9 8 7 6 5 4 3 2 1
First printing, December 2017

www.viz.com

www.shonenjump.com

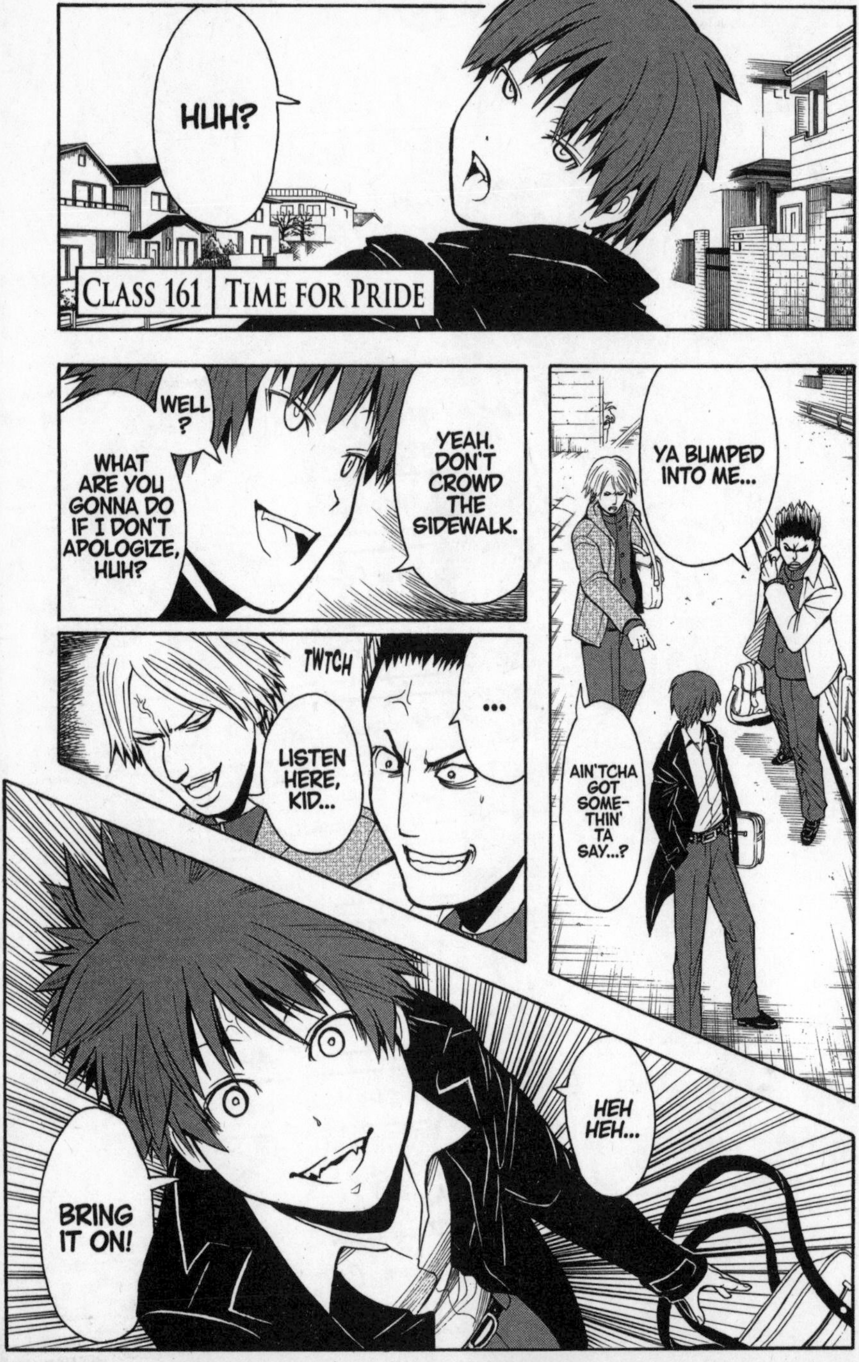
HUH?
CLASS 161 | TIME FOR PRIDE
YA BUMPED INTO ME...
AIN'TCHA GOT SOME-THIN' TA SAY...?
YEAH. DON'T CROWD THE SIDEWALK.
WELL?
WHAT ARE YOU GONNA DO IF I DON'T APOLOGIZE, HUH?
...
TWTCH
LISTEN HERE, KID...
HEH HEH...
BRING IT ON!

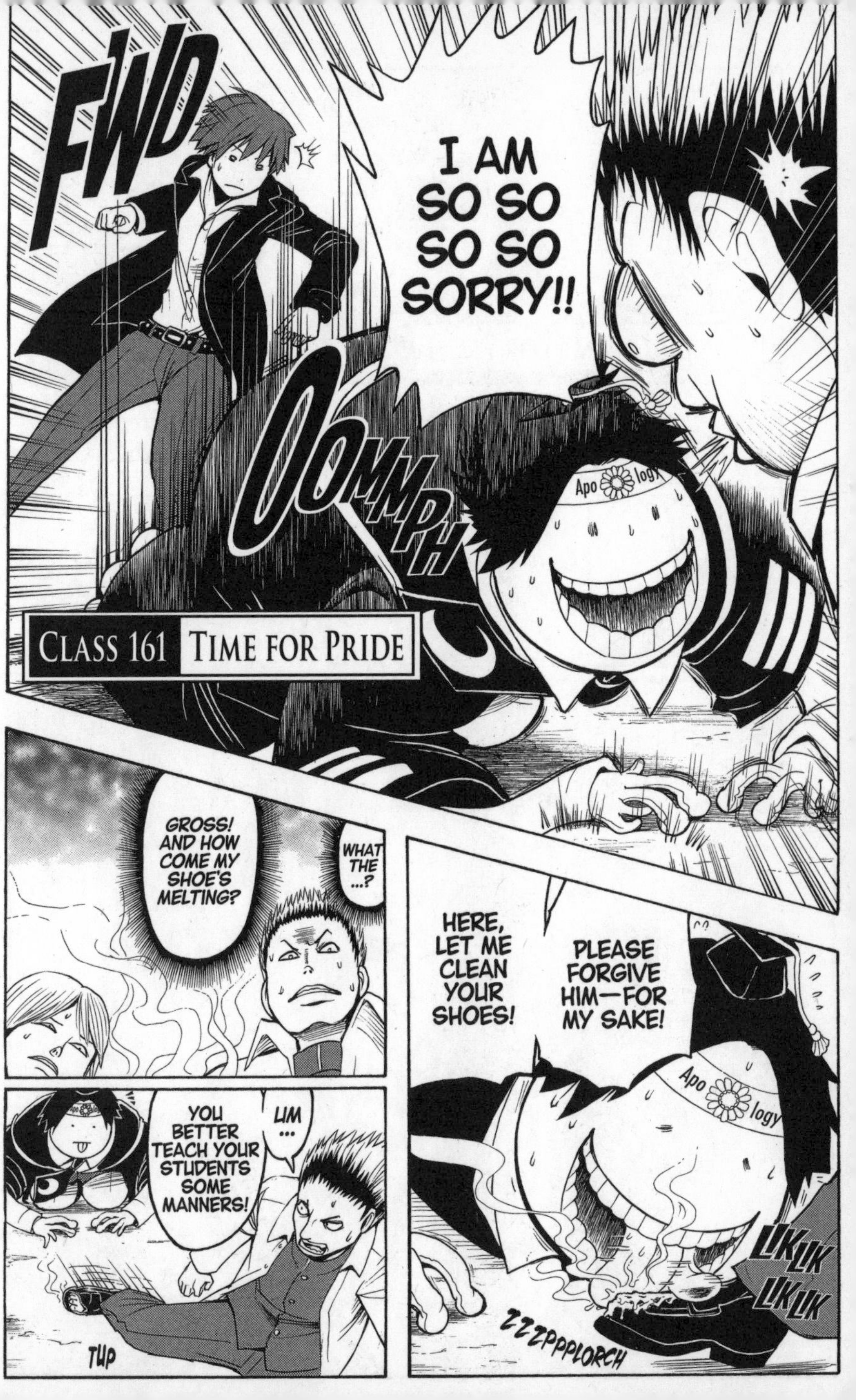
I AM SO SO SO SO SORRY!!
FWD
OOMMPH
CLASS 161 TIME FOR PRIDE
PLEASE FORGIVE HIM—FOR MY SAKE!
HERE, LET ME CLEAN YOUR SHOES!
LIK LIK LIK LIK
ZZZZPPPLORCH
WHAT THE ...?
GROSS! AND HOW COME MY SHOE'S MELTING?
UM ...
YOU BETTER TEACH YOUR STUDENTS SOME MANNERS!
TUP

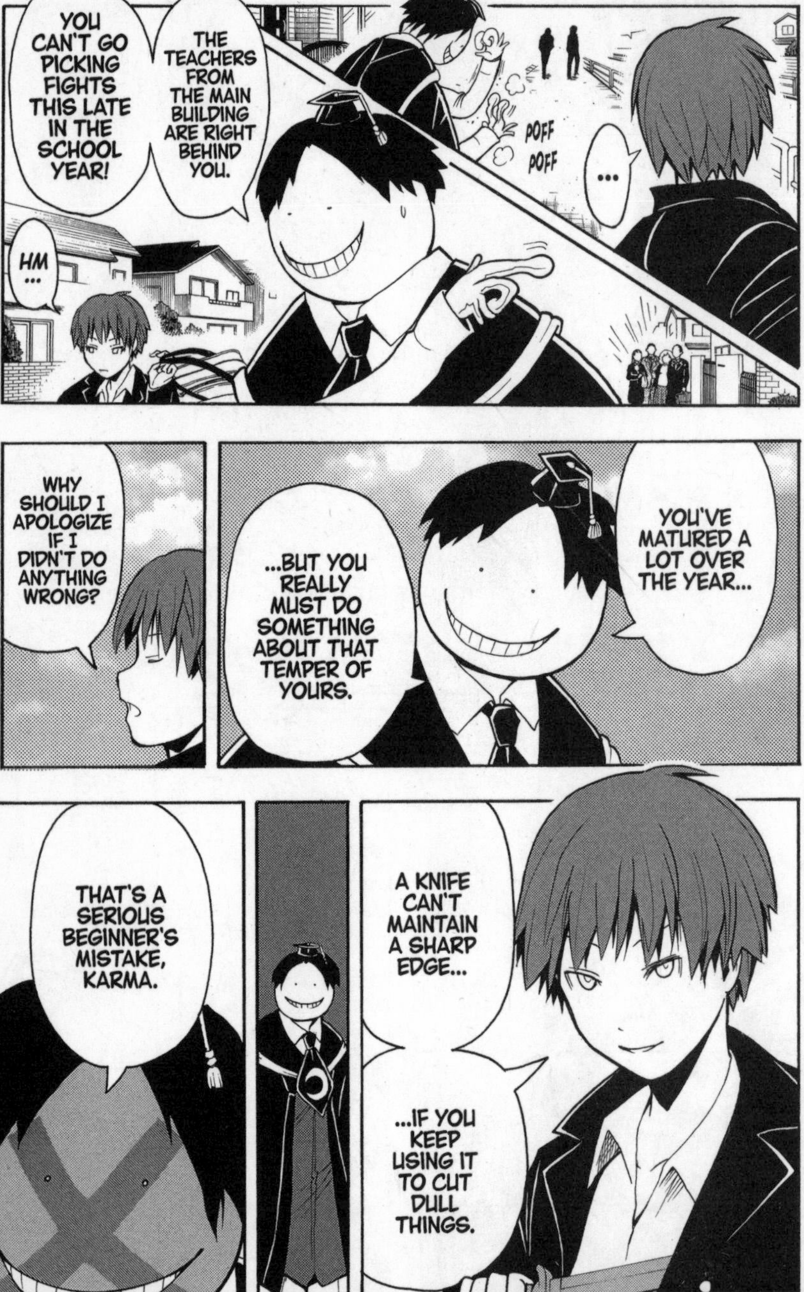
...
POFF POFF
THE TEACHERS FROM THE MAIN BUILDING ARE RIGHT BEHIND YOU.
YOU CAN'T GO PICKING FIGHTS THIS LATE IN THE SCHOOL YEAR!
HM ...
YOU'VE MATURED A LOT OVER THE YEAR...
...BUT YOU REALLY MUST DO SOMETHING ABOUT THAT TEMPER OF YOURS.
WHY SHOULD I APOLOGIZE IF I DIDN'T DO ANYTHING WRONG?
A KNIFE CAN'T MAINTAIN A SHARP EDGE...
...IF YOU KEEP USING IT TO CUT DULL THINGS.
THAT'S A SERIOUS BEGINNER'S MISTAKE, KARMA.

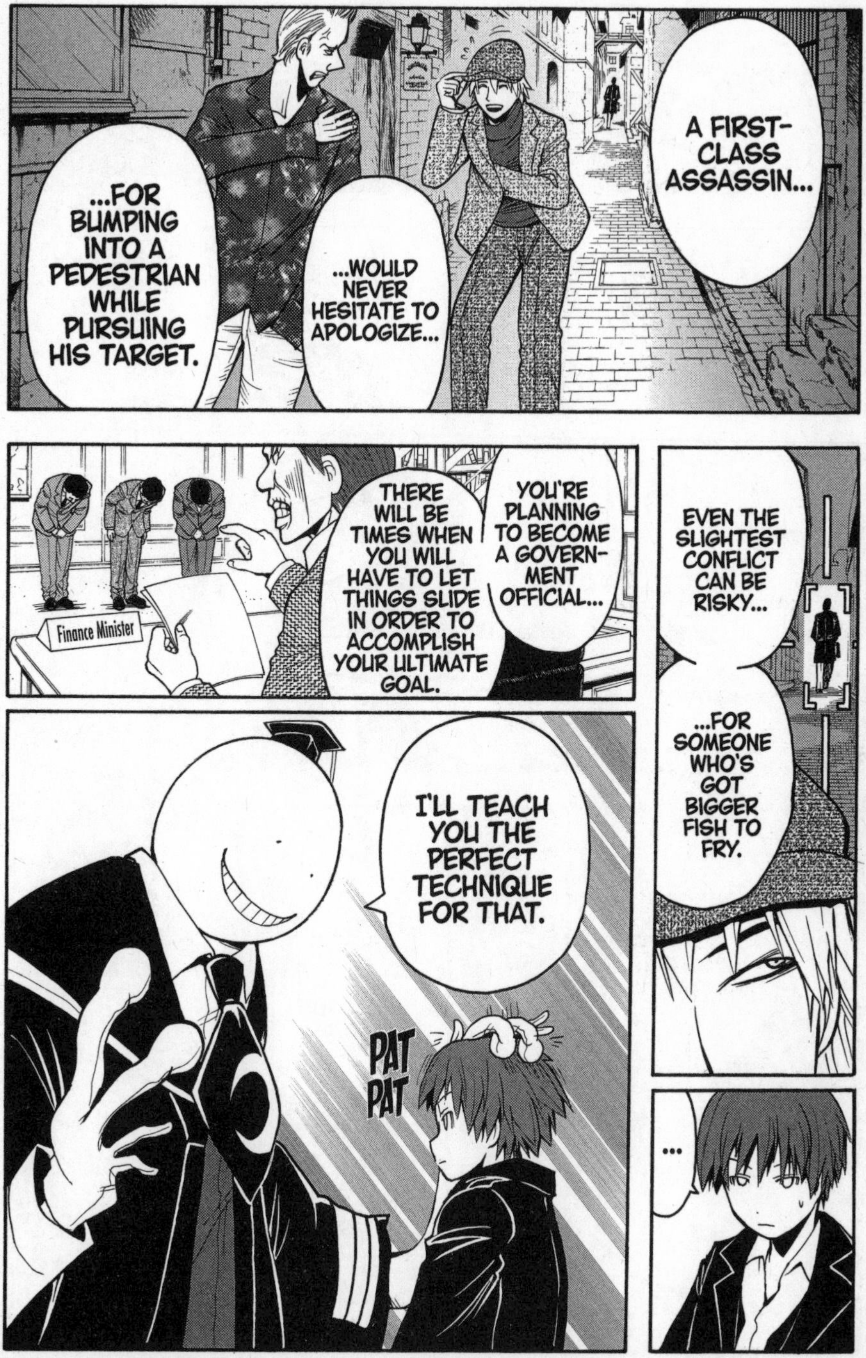
A FIRST-CLASS ASSASSIN...
...WOULD NEVER HESITATE TO APOLOGIZE...
...FOR BUMPING INTO A PEDESTRIAN WHILE PURSUING HIS TARGET.
EVEN THE SLIGHTEST CONFLICT CAN BE RISKY...
...FOR SOMEONE WHO'S GOT BIGGER FISH TO FRY.
...
YOU'RE PLANNING TO BECOME A GOVERNMENT OFFICIAL...
THERE WILL BE TIMES WHEN YOU WILL HAVE TO LET THINGS SLIDE IN ORDER TO ACCOMPLISH YOUR ULTIMATE GOAL.
Finance Minister
I'LL TEACH YOU THE PERFECT TECHNIQUE FOR THAT.
PAT PAT

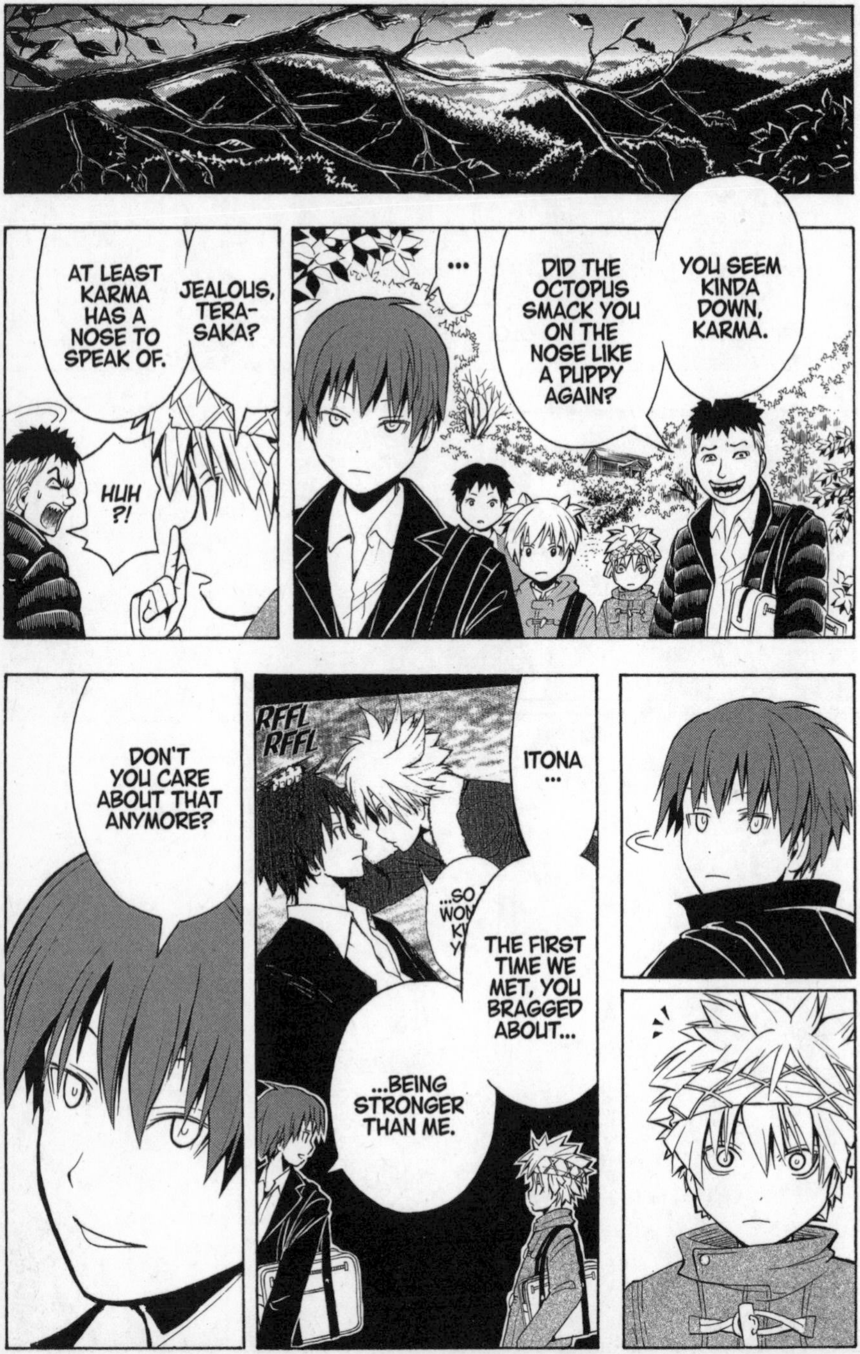
YOU SEEM KINDA DOWN, KARMA.
DID THE OCTOPUS SMACK YOU ON THE NOSE LIKE A PUPPY AGAIN?
...
JEALOUS, TERA-SAKA?
AT LEAST KARMA HAS A NOSE TO SPEAK OF.
HUH?!
RFFL RFFL
ITONA...
THE FIRST TIME WE MET, YOU BRAGGED ABOUT...
...BEING STRONGER THAN ME.
DON'T YOU CARE ABOUT THAT ANYMORE?

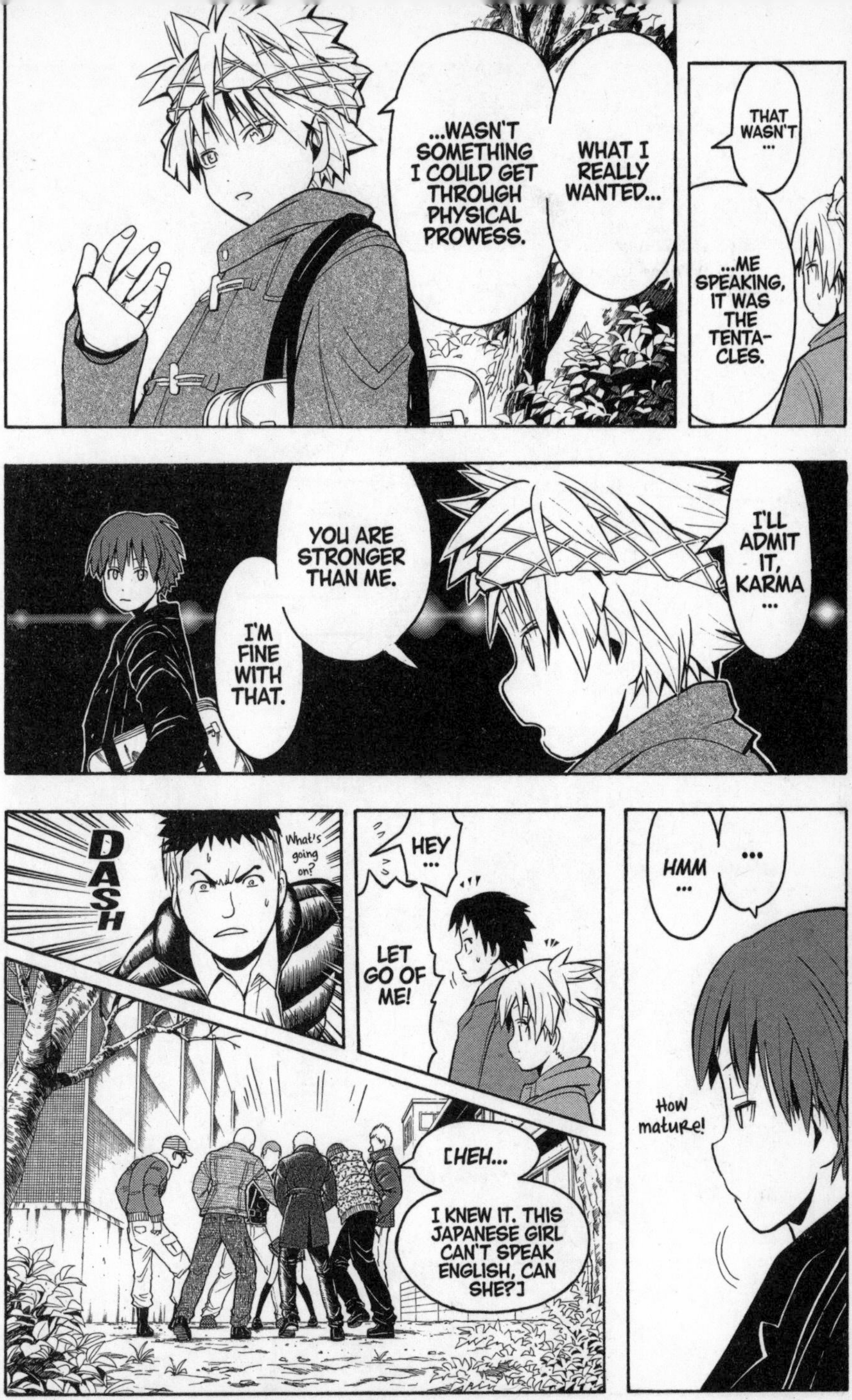
THAT WASN'T ...
...ME SPEAKING, IT WAS THE TENTA-CLES.
WHAT I REALLY WANTED...
...WASN'T SOMETHING I COULD GET THROUGH PHYSICAL PROWESS.
I'LL ADMIT IT, KARMA ...
YOU ARE STRONGER THAN ME.
I'M FINE WITH THAT.
...
HMM ...
How mature!
HEY ...
LET GO OF ME!
DASH
What's going on?
[HEH...
I KNEW IT. THIS JAPANESE GIRL CAN'T SPEAK ENGLISH, CAN SHE?]

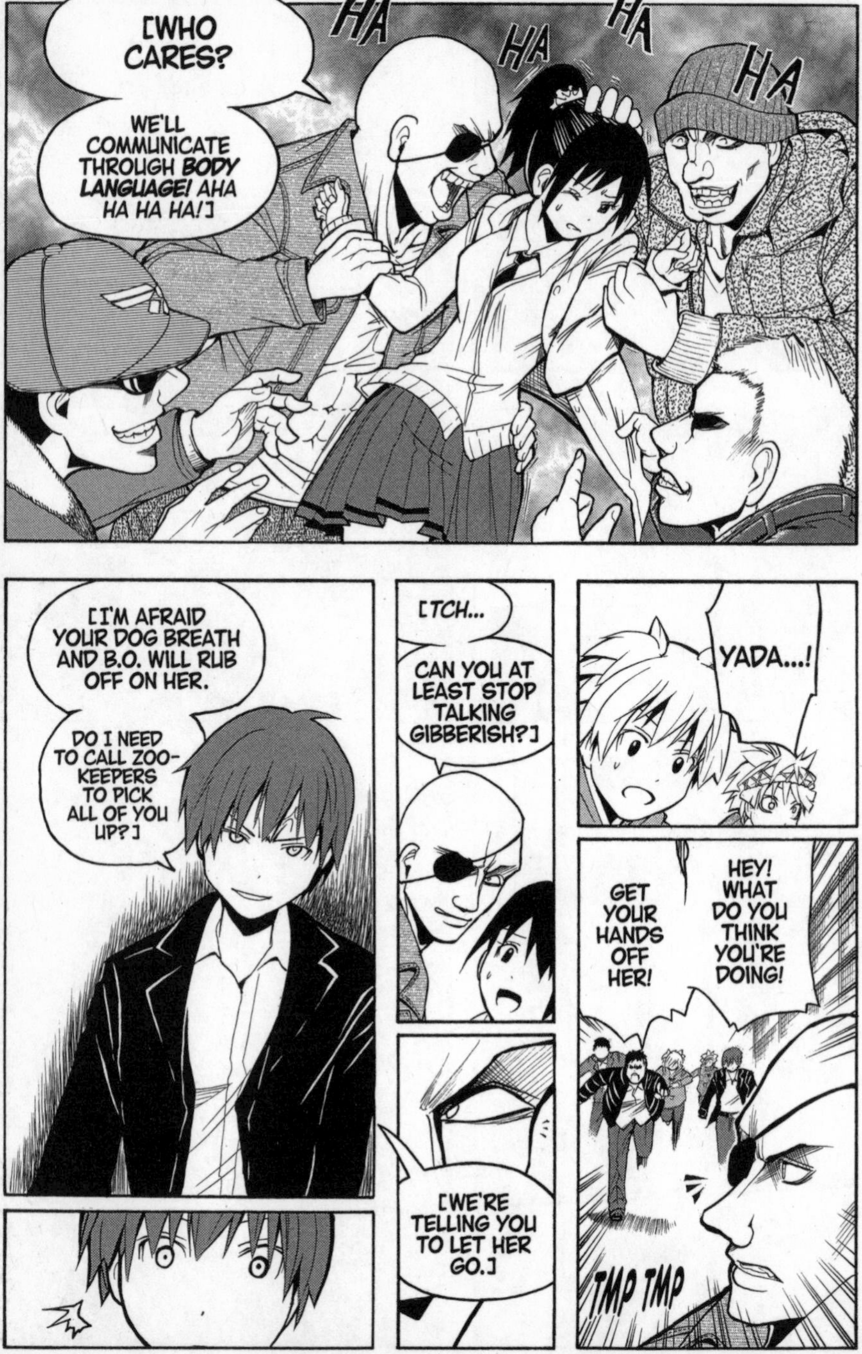
HA
HA
HA
HA
[WHO CARES?
WE'LL COMMUNICATE THROUGH BODY LANGUAGE! AHA HA HA HA!]
YADA...!
HEY! WHAT DO YOU THINK YOU'RE DOING!
GET YOUR HANDS OFF HER!
TMP TMP
[TCH...
CAN YOU AT LEAST STOP TALKING GIBBERISH?]
[WE'RE TELLING YOU TO LET HER GO.]
[I'M AFRAID YOUR DOG BREATH AND B.O. WILL RUB OFF ON HER.
DO I NEED TO CALL ZOO-KEEPERS TO PICK ALL OF YOU UP?]

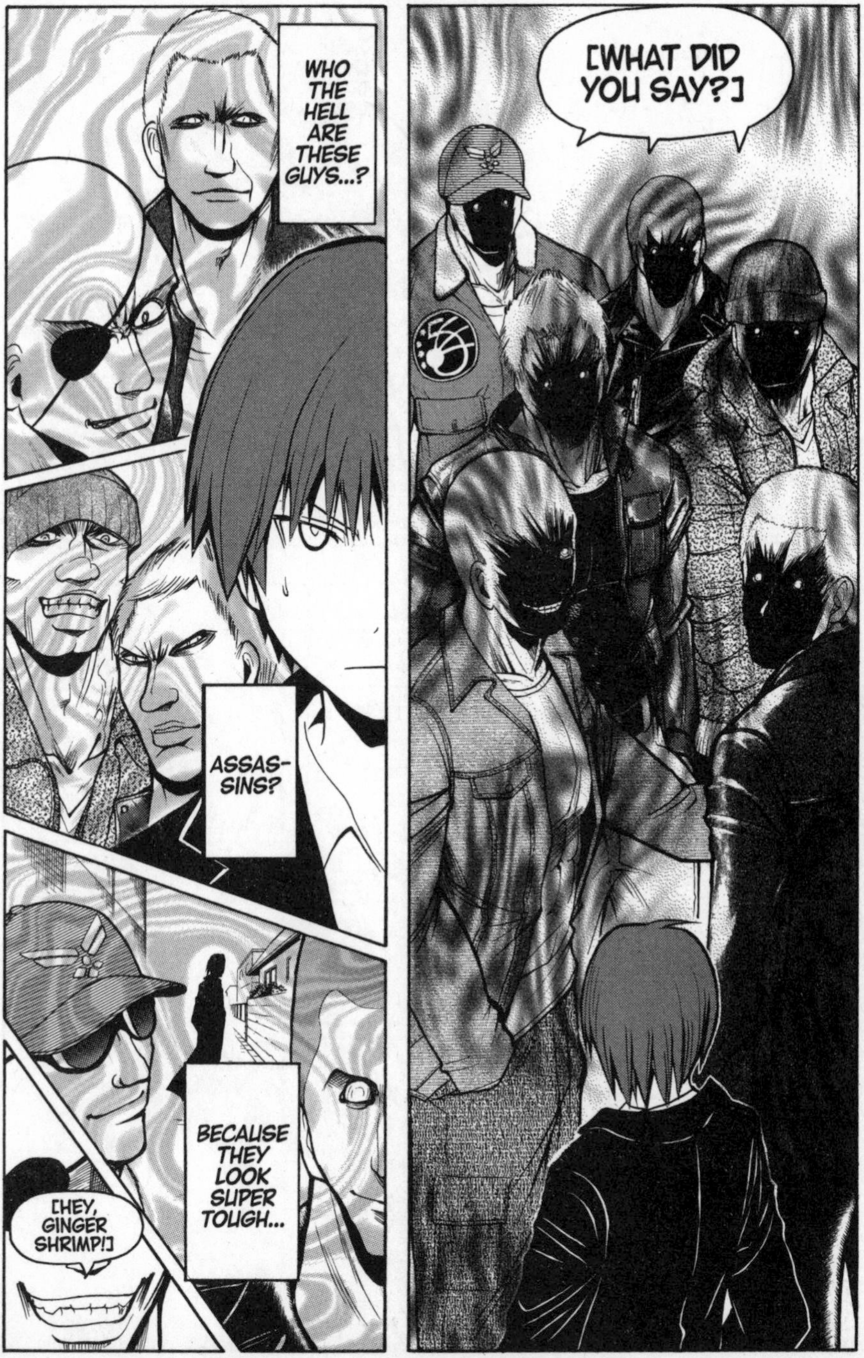

[WHAT DID YOU SAY?]
WHO THE HELL ARE THESE GUYS...?
ASSAS-SINS?
BECAUSE THEY LOOK SUPER TOUGH...
[HEY, GINGER SHRIMP!]

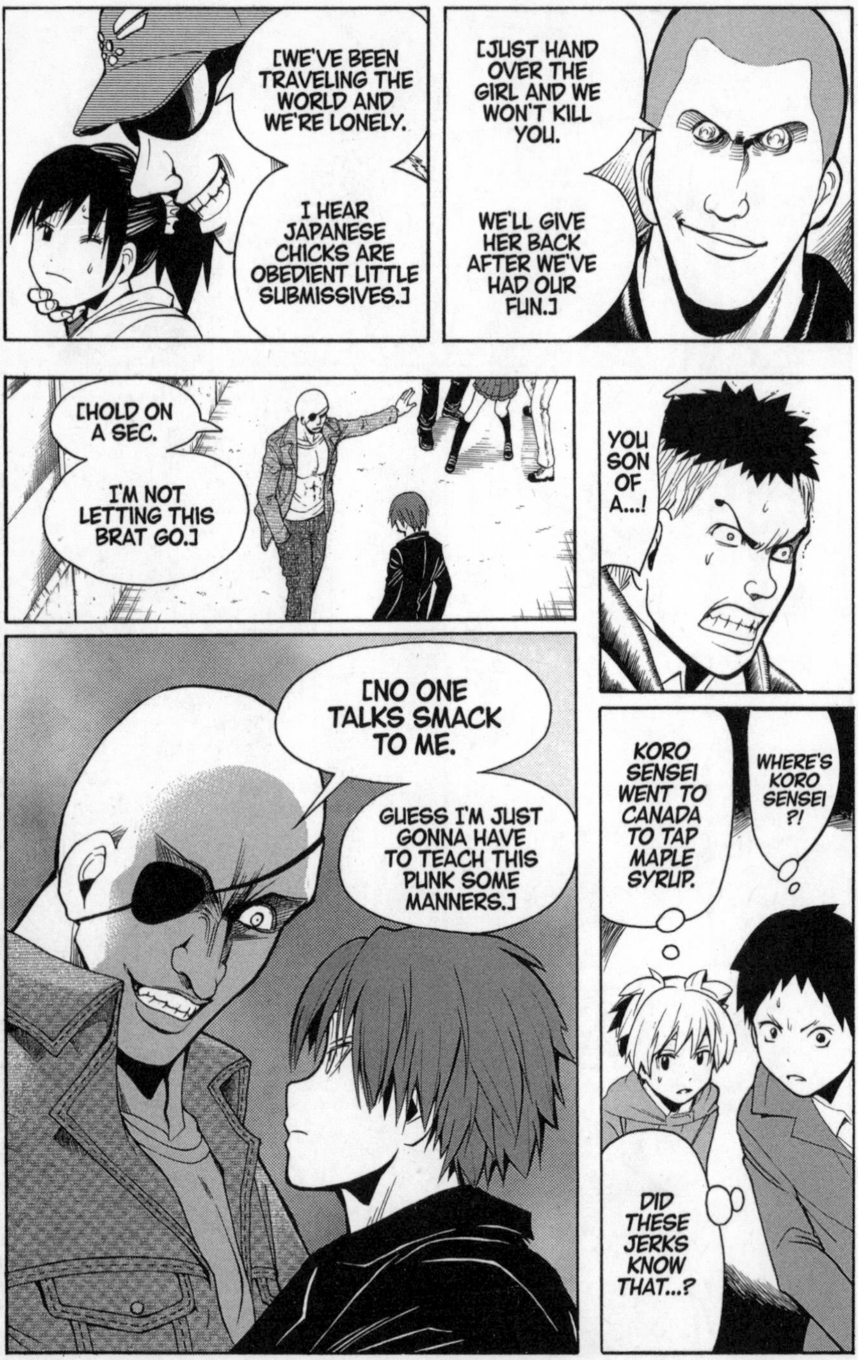
[JUST HAND OVER THE GIRL AND WE WON'T KILL YOU.
WE'LL GIVE HER BACK AFTER WE'VE HAD OUR FUN.]
[WE'VE BEEN TRAVELING THE WORLD AND WE'RE LONELY.
I HEAR JAPANESE CHICKS ARE OBEDIENT LITTLE SUBMISSIVES.]
YOU SON OF A...!
[HOLD ON A SEC.
I'M NOT LETTING THIS BRAT GO.]
[NO ONE TALKS SMACK TO ME.
GUESS I'M JUST GONNA HAVE TO TEACH THIS PUNK SOME MANNERS.]
WHERE'S KORO SENSEI ?!
KORO SENSEI WENT TO CANADA TO TAP MAPLE SYRUP.
DID THESE JERKS KNOW THAT...?

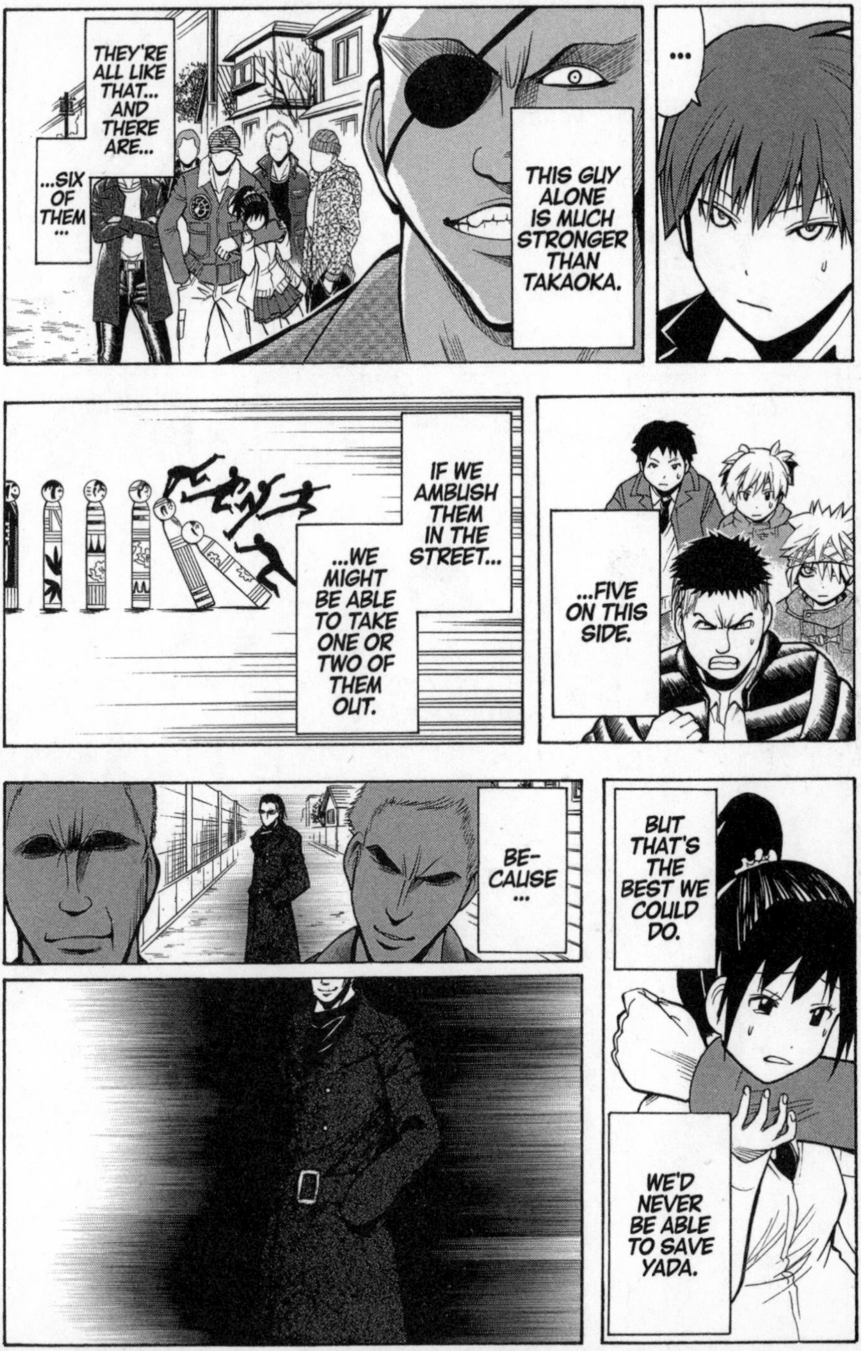

...
THIS GUY ALONE IS MUCH STRONGER THAN TAKAOKA.
THEY'RE ALL LIKE THAT... AND THERE ARE...
...SIX OF THEM ...
...FIVE ON THIS SIDE.
IF WE AMBUSH THEM IN THE STREET...
...WE MIGHT BE ABLE TO TAKE ONE OR TWO OF THEM OUT.
BUT THAT'S THE BEST WE COULD DO.
WE'D NEVER BE ABLE TO SAVE YADA.
BE-CAUSE ...

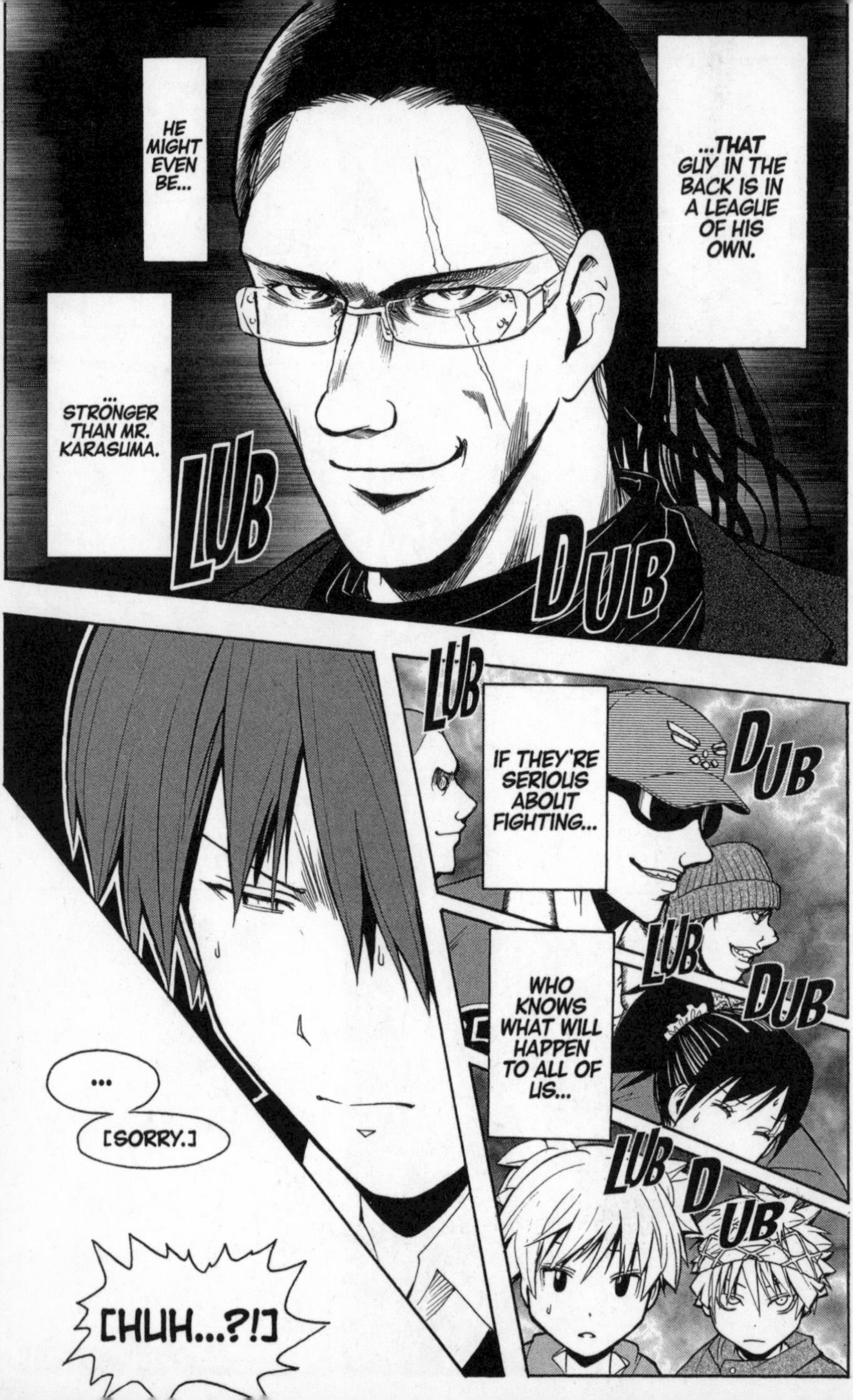
...THAT GUY IN THE BACK IS IN A LEAGUE OF HIS OWN.
HE MIGHT EVEN BE...
...STRÖNGER THAN MR. KARASUMA.
LUB
DUB
LUB
DUB
IF THEY'RE SERIOUS ABOUT FIGHTING...
LUB
DUB
WHO KNOWS WHAT WILL HAPPEN TO ALL OF US...
LUB
DUB
...
[SORRY.]
[HUH...?!]

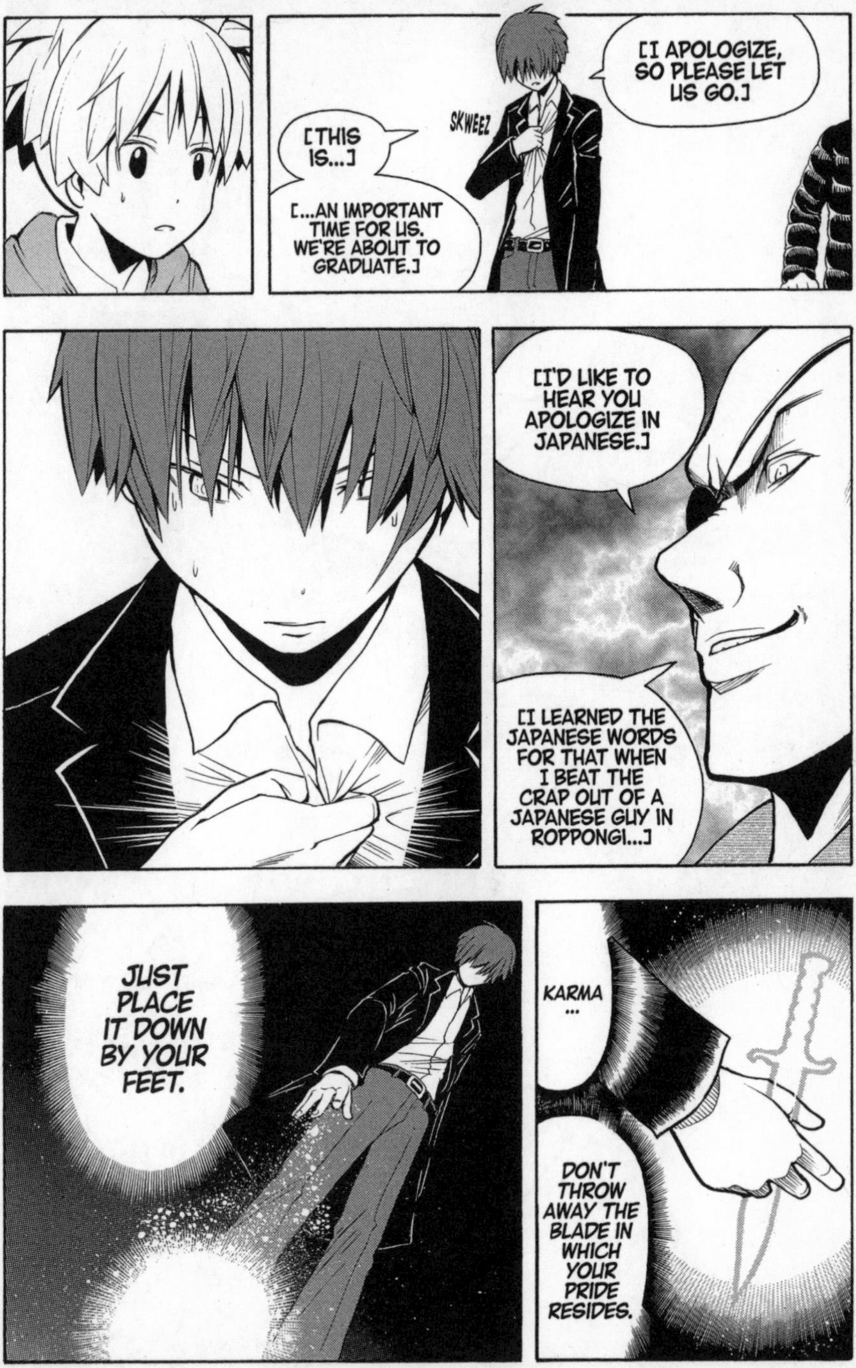
[I APOLOGIZE, SO PLEASE LET US GO.]
SKWEEZ
[THIS IS...]
[...AN IMPORTANT TIME FOR US. WE'RE ABOUT TO GRADUATE.]
[I'D LIKE TO HEAR YOU APOLOGIZE IN JAPANESE.]
[I LEARNED THE JAPANESE WORDS FOR THAT WHEN I BEAT THE CRAP OUT OF A JAPANESE GUY IN ROPPONGI...]
KARMA...
DON'T THROW AWAY THE BLADE IN WHICH YOUR PRIDE RESIDES.
JUST PLACE IT DOWN BY YOUR FEET.

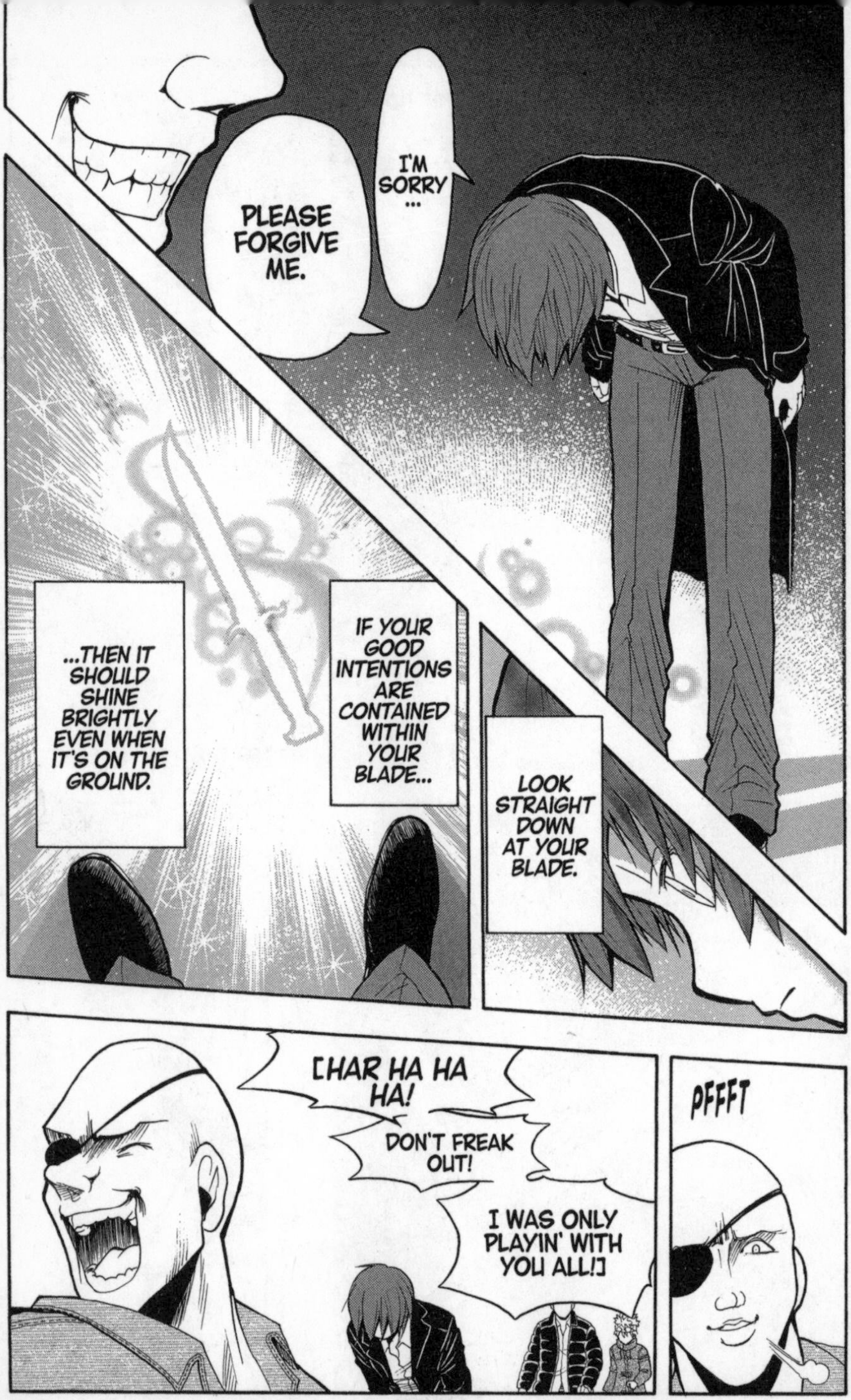
I'M SORRY...
PLEASE FORGIVE ME.
LOOK STRAIGHT DOWN AT YOUR BLADE.
IF YOUR GOOD INTENTIONS ARE CONTAINED WITHIN YOUR BLADE...
...THEN IT SHOULD SHINE BRIGHTLY EVEN WHEN IT'S ON THE GROUND.
PFFFT
[HAR HA HA HA!
DON'T FREAK OUT!
I WAS ONLY PLAYIN' WITH YOU ALL!]

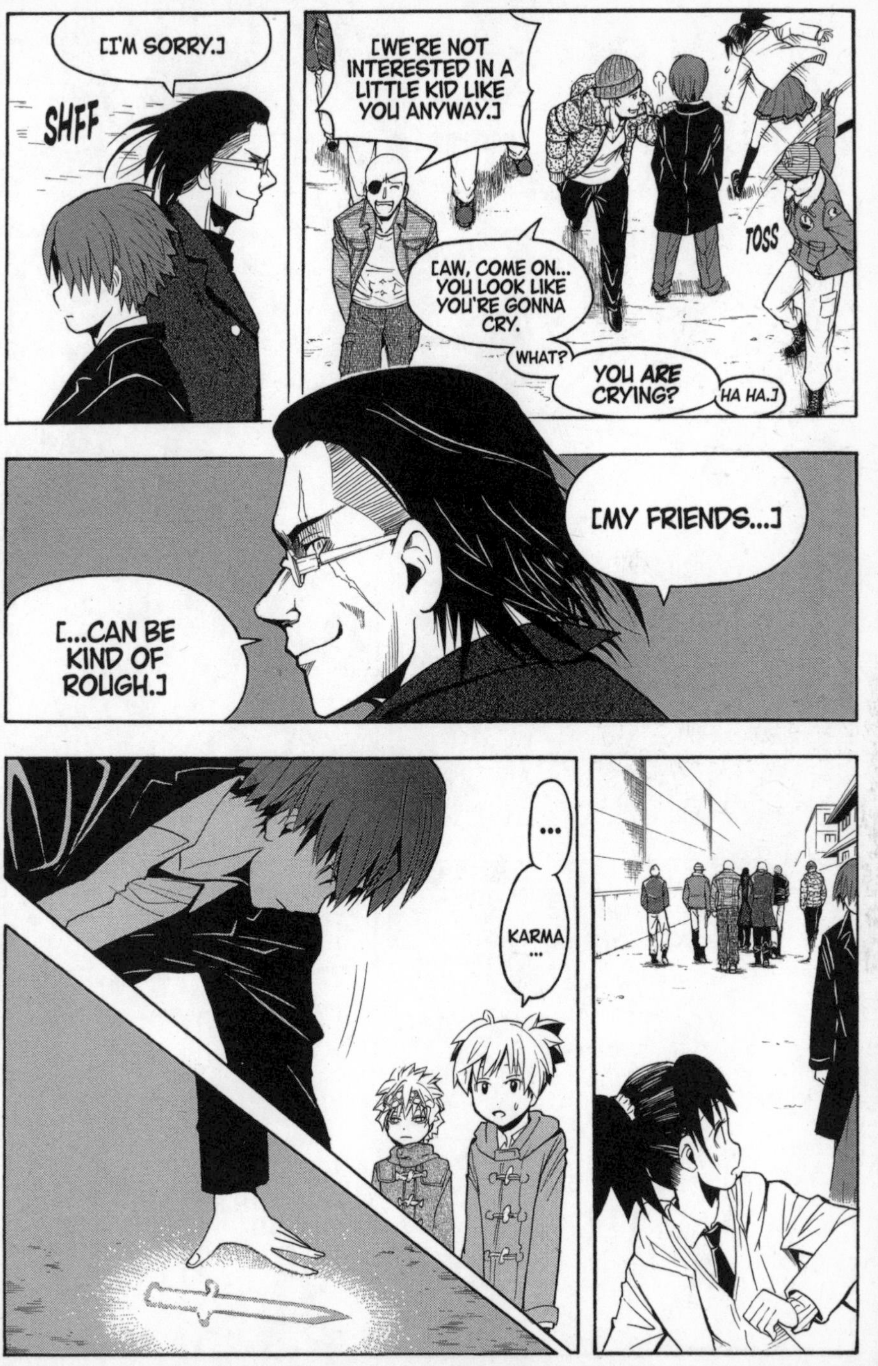
[WE'RE NOT INTERESTED IN A LITTLE KID LIKE YOU ANYWAY.]
TOSS
[AW, COME ON... YOU LOOK LIKE YOU'RE GONNA CRY.
WHAT?
YOU ARE CRYING?
HA HA.]
[I'M SORRY.]
SHFF
[MY FRIENDS...]
[...CAN BE KIND OF ROUGH.]
...
KARMA ...

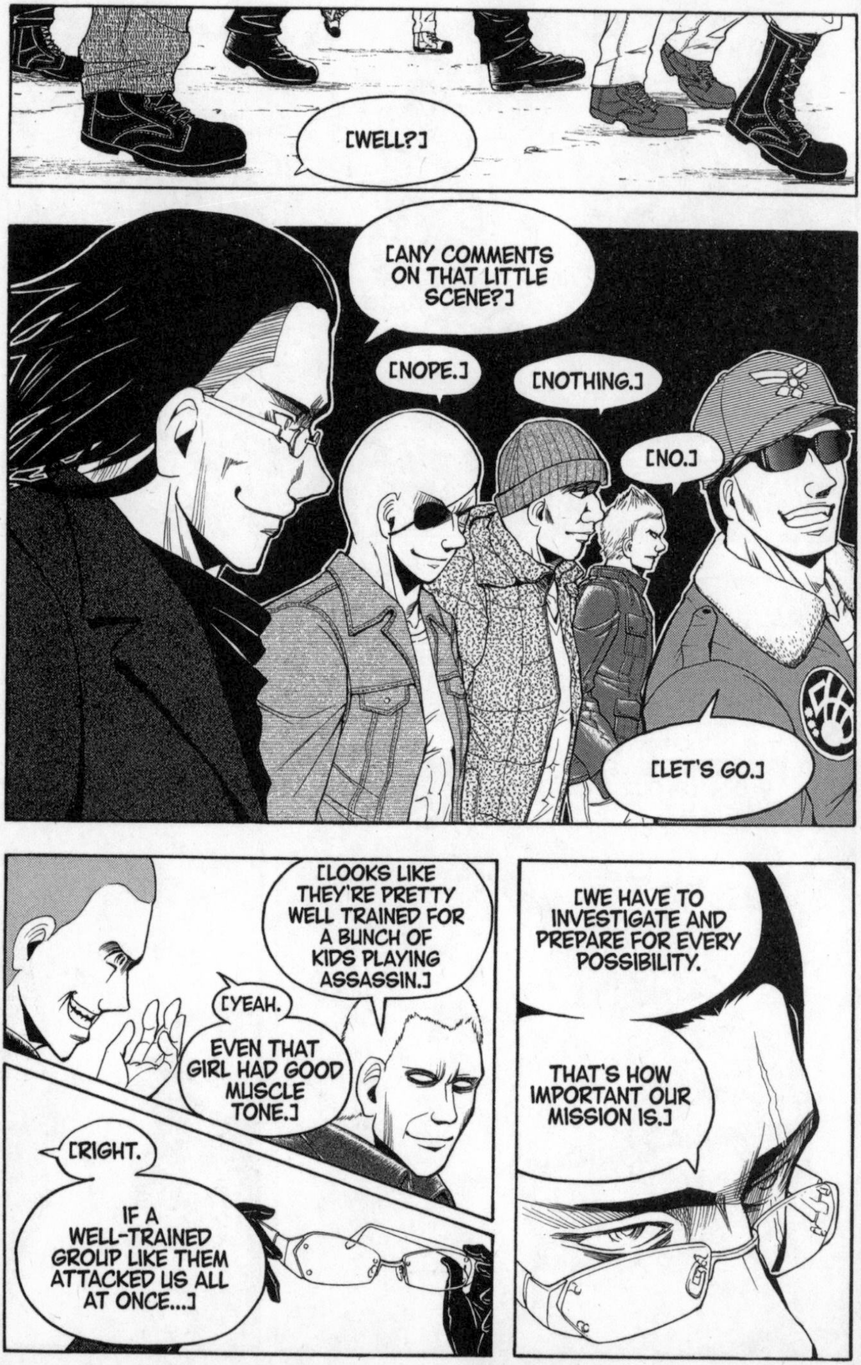
[WELL?]
[ANY COMMENTS ON THAT LITTLE SCENE?]
[NOTHING.]
[NOPE.]
[NO.]
[LET'S GO.]
[WE HAVE TO INVESTIGATE AND PREPARE FOR EVERY POSSIBILITY.
THAT'S HOW IMPORTANT OUR MISSION IS.]
[LOOKS LIKE THEY'RE PRETTY WELL TRAINED FOR A BUNCH OF KIDS PLAYING ASSASSIN.]
[YEAH.
EVEN THAT GIRL HAD GOOD MUSCLE TONE.]
[RIGHT.
IF A WELL-TRAINED GROUP LIKE THEM ATTACKED US ALL AT ONCE...]

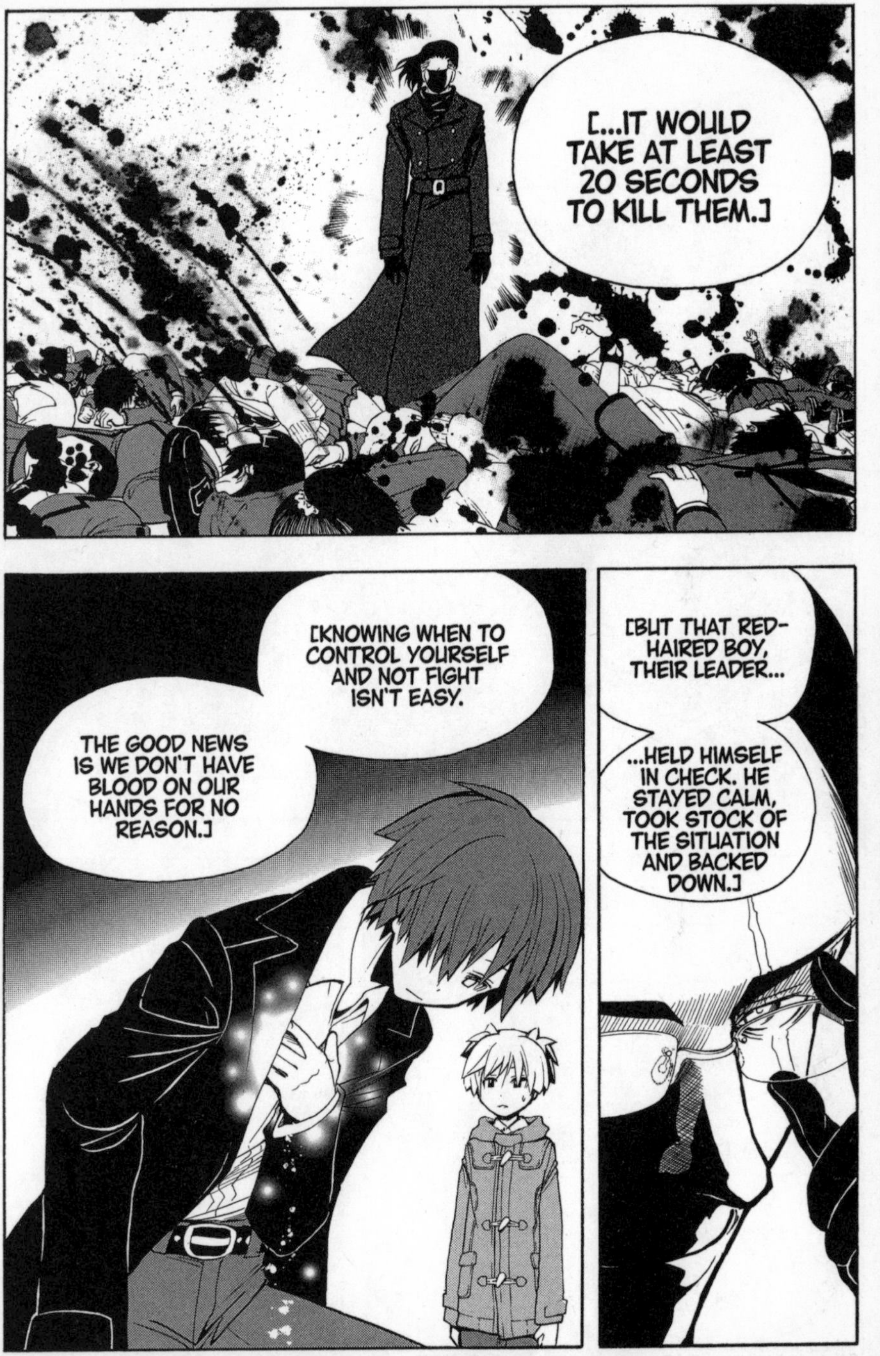
[...IT WOULD TAKE AT LEAST 20 SECONDS TO KILL THEM.]
[BUT THAT RED-HAIRED BOY, THEIR LEADER...
...HELD HIMSELF IN CHECK. HE STAYED CALM, TOOK STOCK OF THE SITUATION AND BACKED DOWN.]
[KNOWING WHEN TO CONTROL YOURSELF AND NOT FIGHT ISN'T EASY.
THE GOOD NEWS IS WE DON'T HAVE BLOOD ON OUR HANDS FOR NO REASON.]

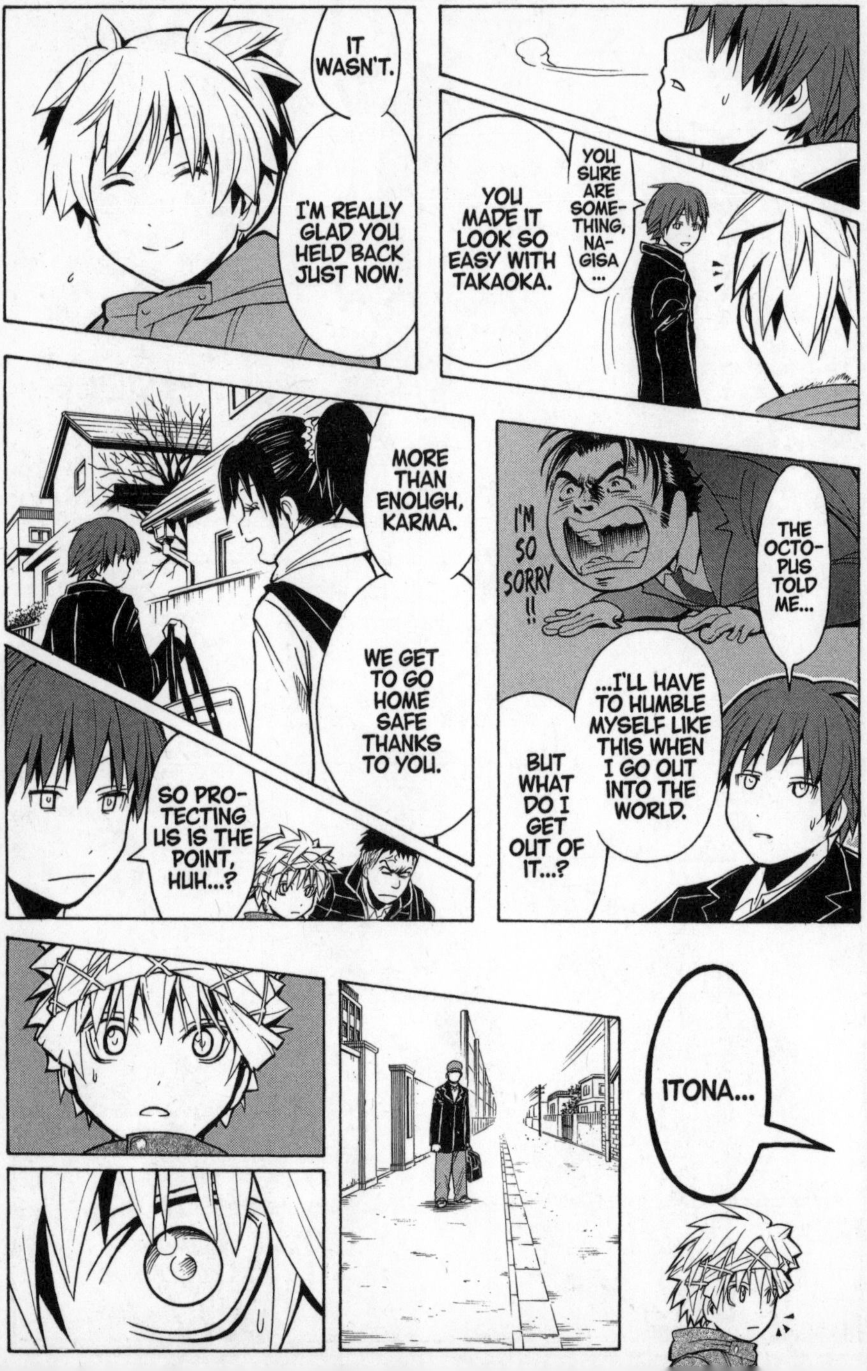

YOU SURE ARE SOMETHING, NAGISA...
YOU MADE IT LOOK SO EASY WITH TAKAOKA.
IT WASN'T.
I'M REALLY GLAD YOU HELD BACK JUST NOW.
THE OCTOPUS TOLD ME...
...I'LL HAVE TO HUMBLE MYSELF LIKE THIS WHEN I GO OUT INTO THE WORLD.
I'M SO SORRY!!
BUT WHAT DO I GET OUT OF IT...?
MORE THAN ENOUGH, KARMA.
WE GET TO GO HOME SAFE THANKS TO YOU.
SO PROTECTING US IS THE POINT, HUH...?
ITONA...

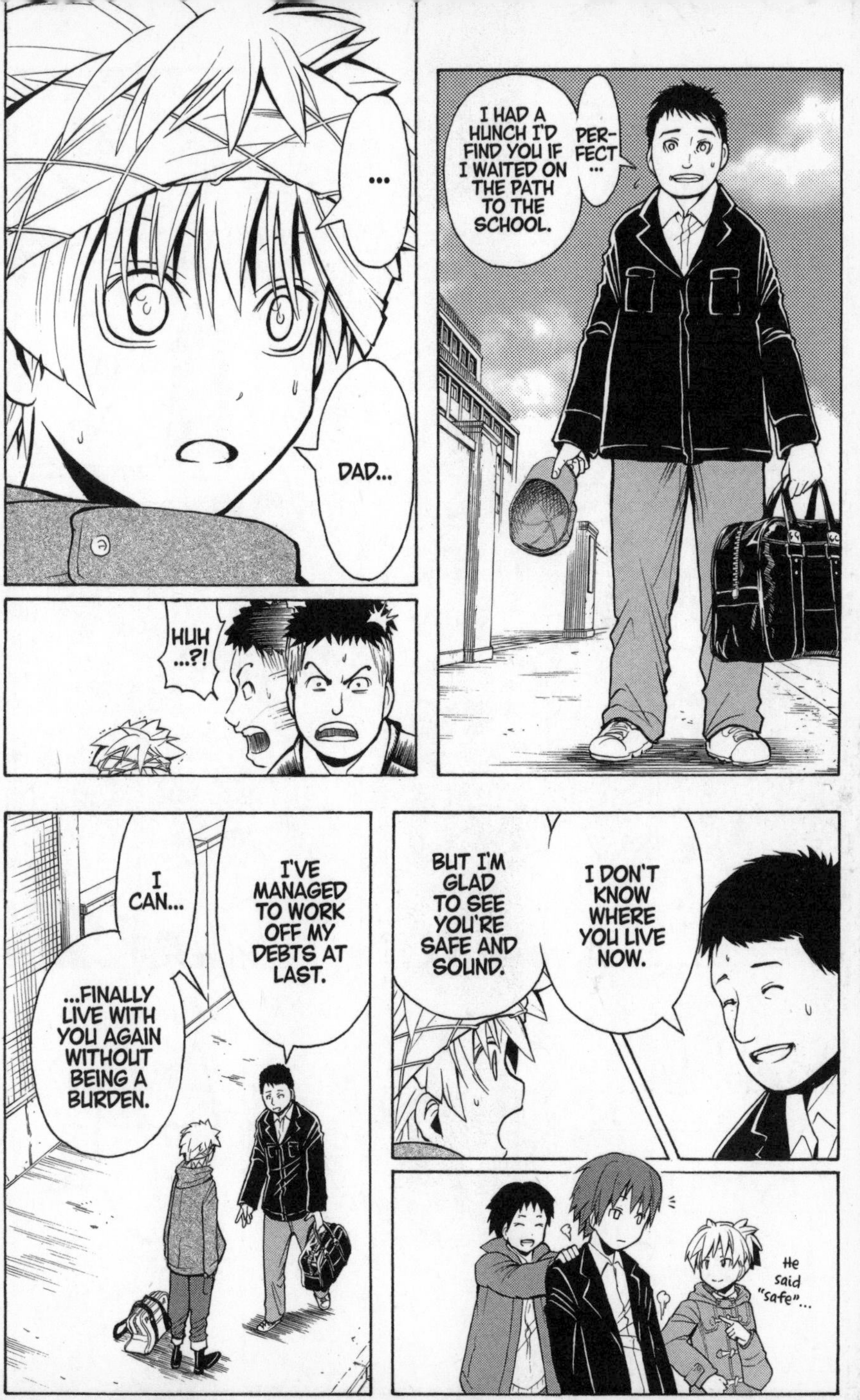
PER-FECT...
I HAD A HUNCH I'D FIND YOU IF I WAITED ON THE PATH TO THE SCHOOL.
...
DAD...
HUH ...?!
I DON'T KNOW WHERE YOU LIVE NOW.
BUT I'M GLAD TO SEE YOU'RE SAFE AND SOUND.
He said "safe"...
I'VE MANAGED TO WORK OFF MY DEBTS AT LAST.
I CAN...
...FINALLY LIVE WITH YOU AGAIN WITHOUT BEING A BURDEN.

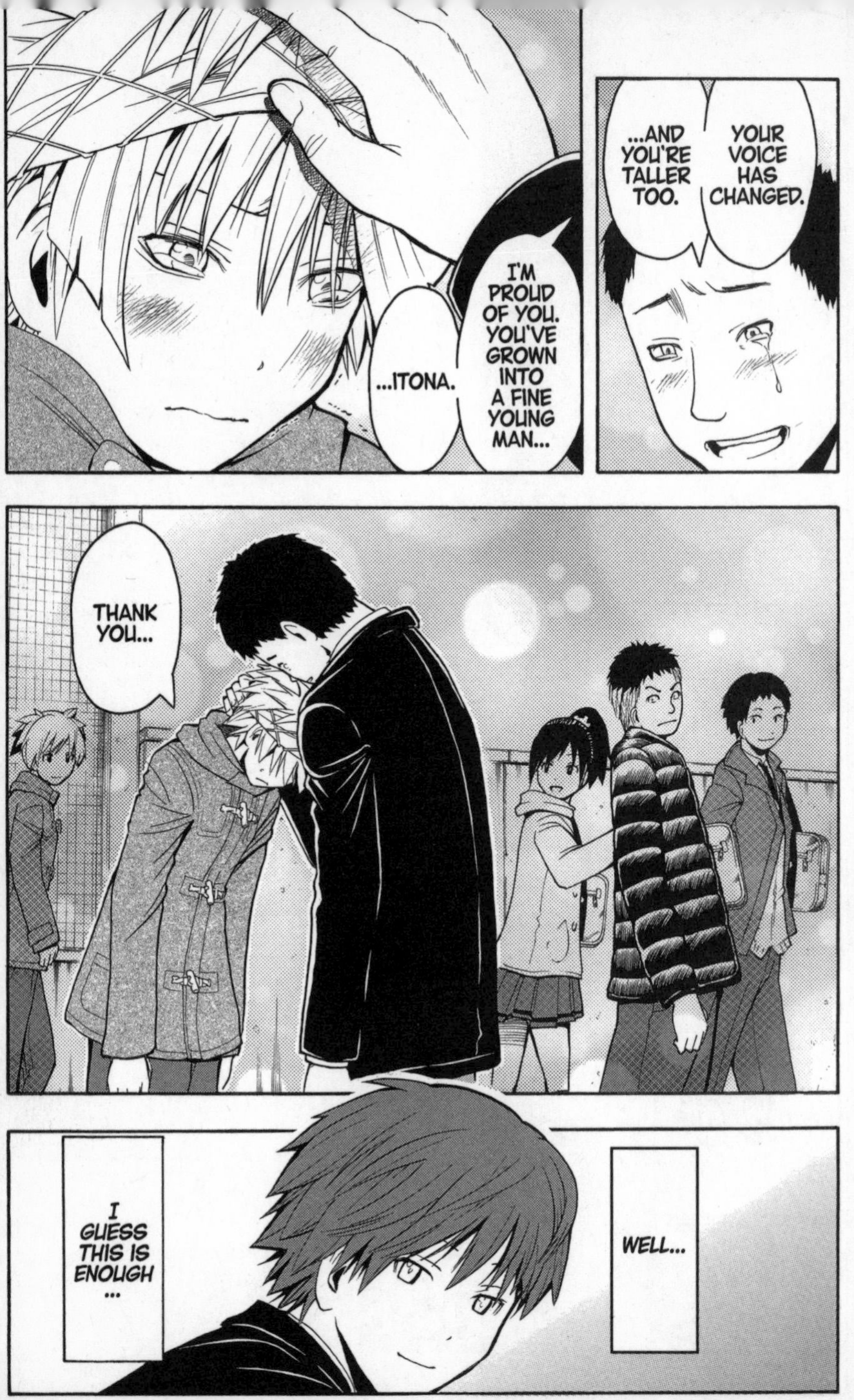
YOUR VOICE HAS CHANGED.
...AND YOU'RE TALLER TOO.
I'M PROUD OF YOU. YOU'VE GROWN INTO A FINE YOUNG MAN...
...ITONA.
THANK YOU...
WELL...
I GUESS THIS IS ENOUGH...

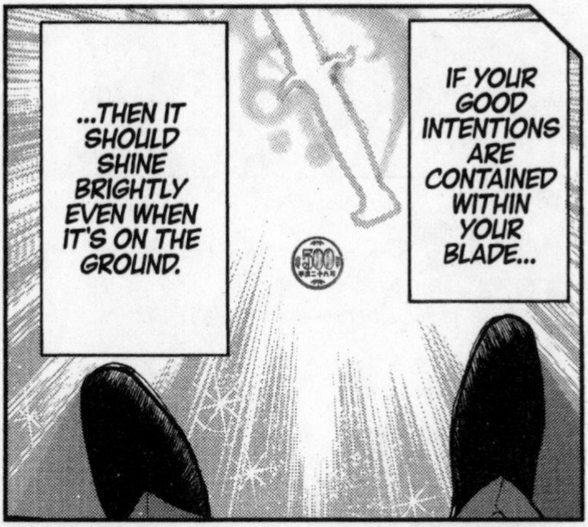
IF YOUR GOOD INTENTIONS ARE CONTAINED WITHIN YOUR BLADE...
...THEN IT SHOULD SHINE BRIGHTLY EVEN WHEN IT'S ON THE GROUND.

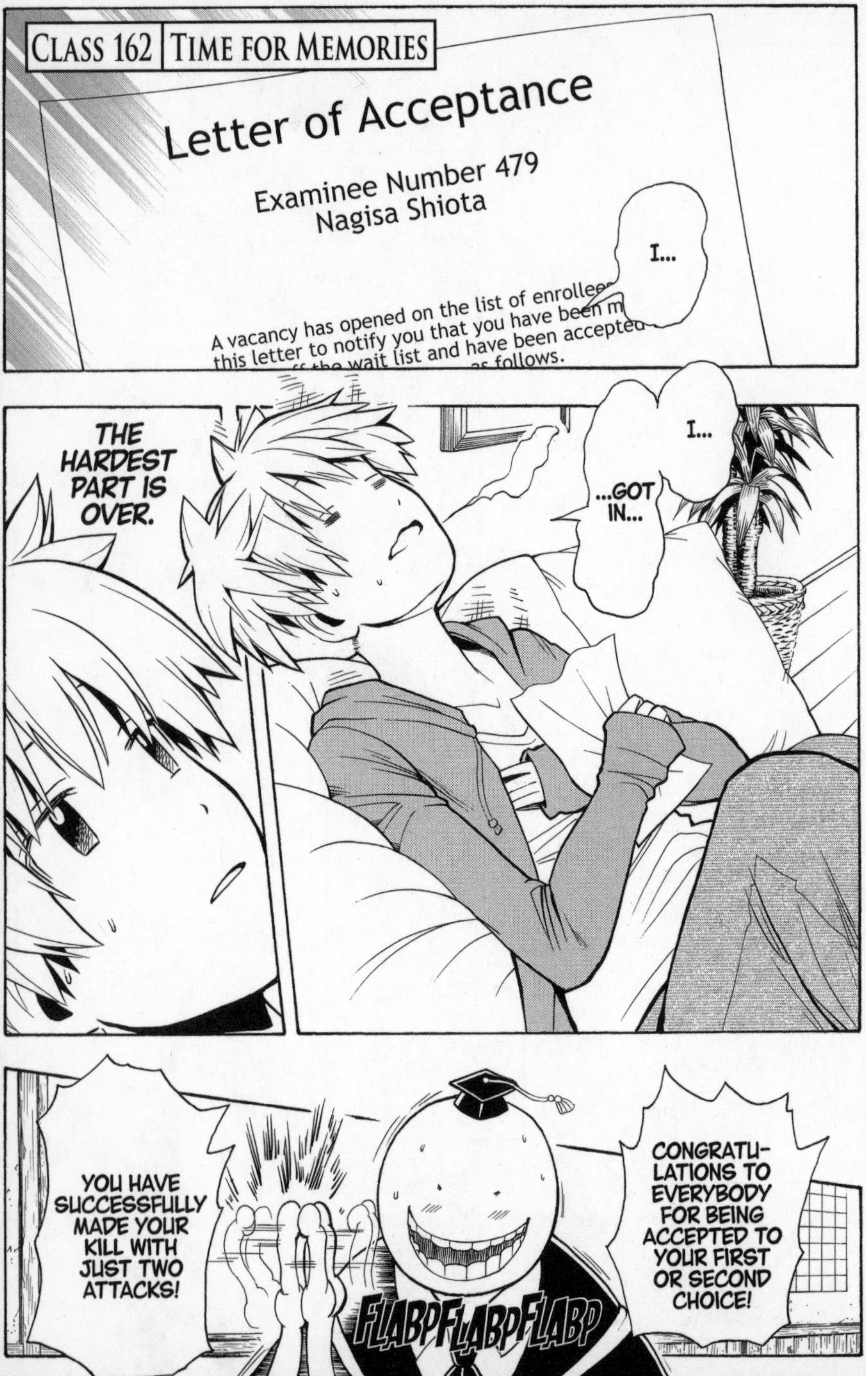
CLASS 162 TIME FOR MEMORIES
Letter of Acceptance
Examinee Number 479
Nagisa Shiota
A vacancy has opened on the list of enrollee
this letter to notify you that you have been m
list and have been accepted
I...
I...
...GOT IN...
THE HARDEST PART IS OVER.
CONGRATULATIONS TO EVERYBODY FOR BEING ACCEPTED TO YOUR FIRST OR SECOND CHOICE!
YOU HAVE SUCCESSFULLY MADE YOUR KILL WITH JUST TWO ATTACKS!
FLABP FLABP FLABP

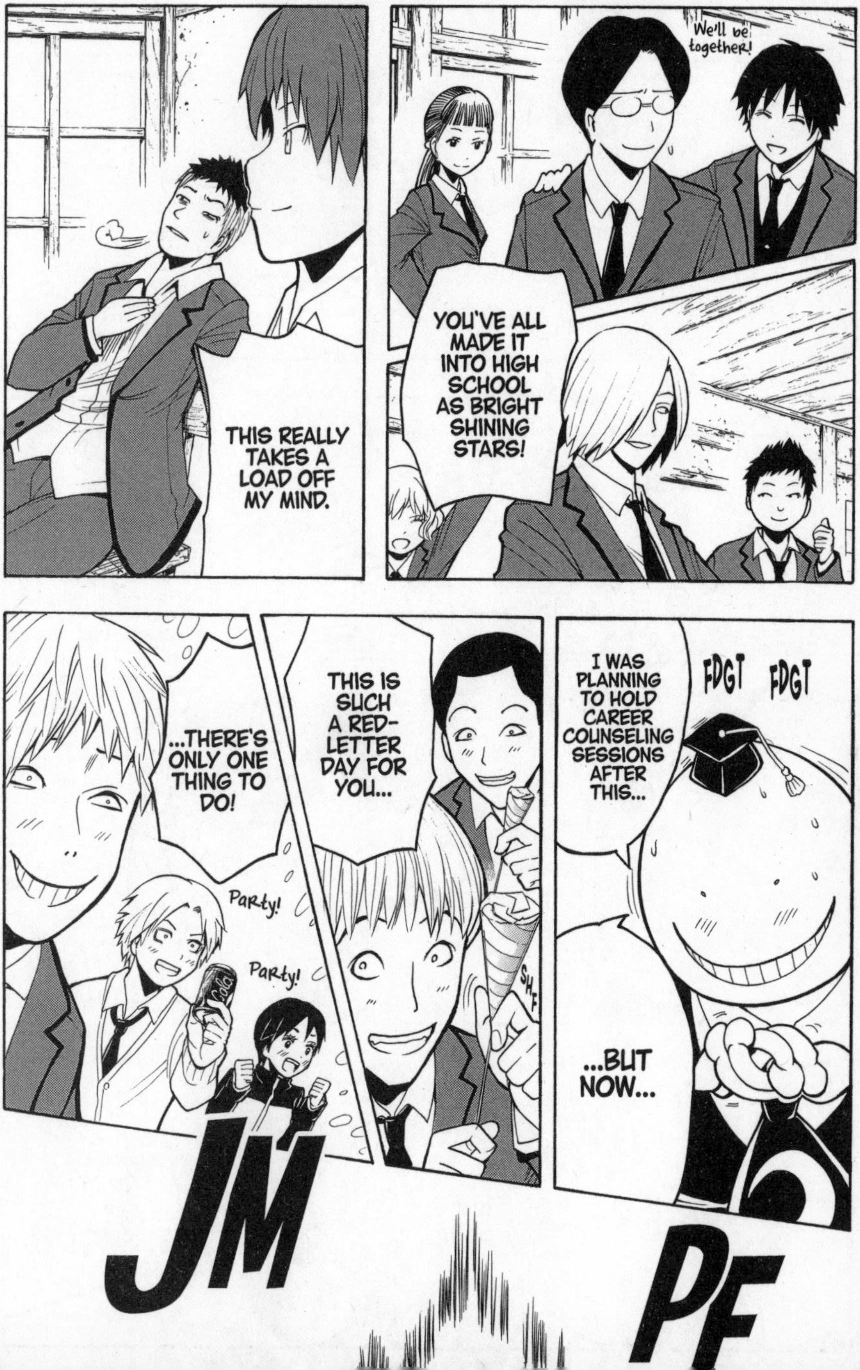
We'll be together!
YOU'VE ALL MADE IT INTO HIGH SCHOOL AS BRIGHT SHINING STARS!
THIS REALLY TAKES A LOAD OFF MY MIND.
FDGT
FDGT
I WAS PLANNING TO HOLD CAREER COUNSELING SESSIONS AFTER THIS...
...BUT NOW...
THIS IS SUCH A RED-LETTER DAY FOR YOU...
SHF
...THERE'S ONLY ONE THING TO DO!
Party!
Party!
Cola
JM
PF

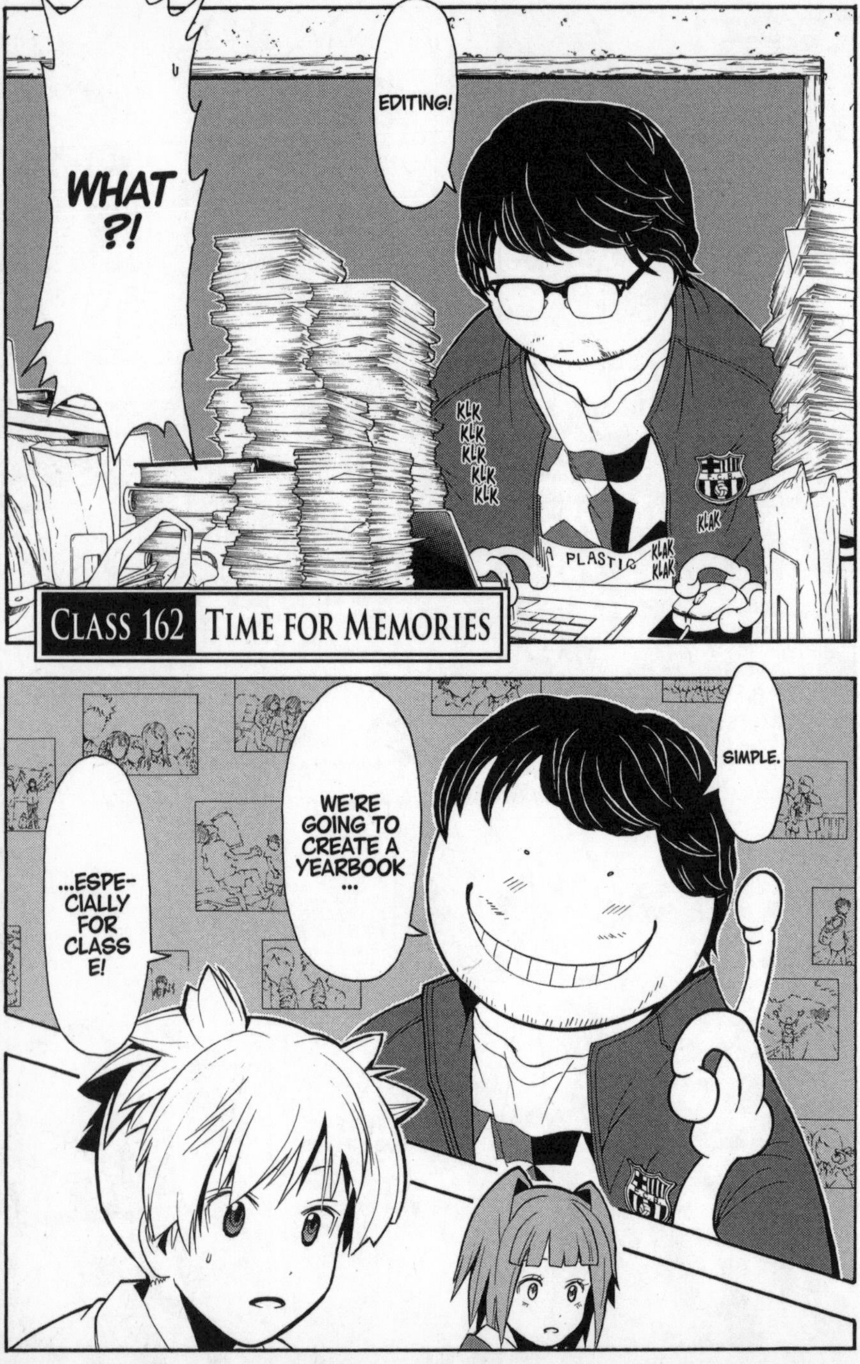
EDITING!
WHAT?!
KLK KLK KLK KLK KLK
KLAK
KLAK KLAK
A PLASTIC
CLASS 162 TIME FOR MEMORIES
SIMPLE.
WE'RE GOING TO CREATE A YEARBOOK...
...ESPECIALLY FOR CLASS E!

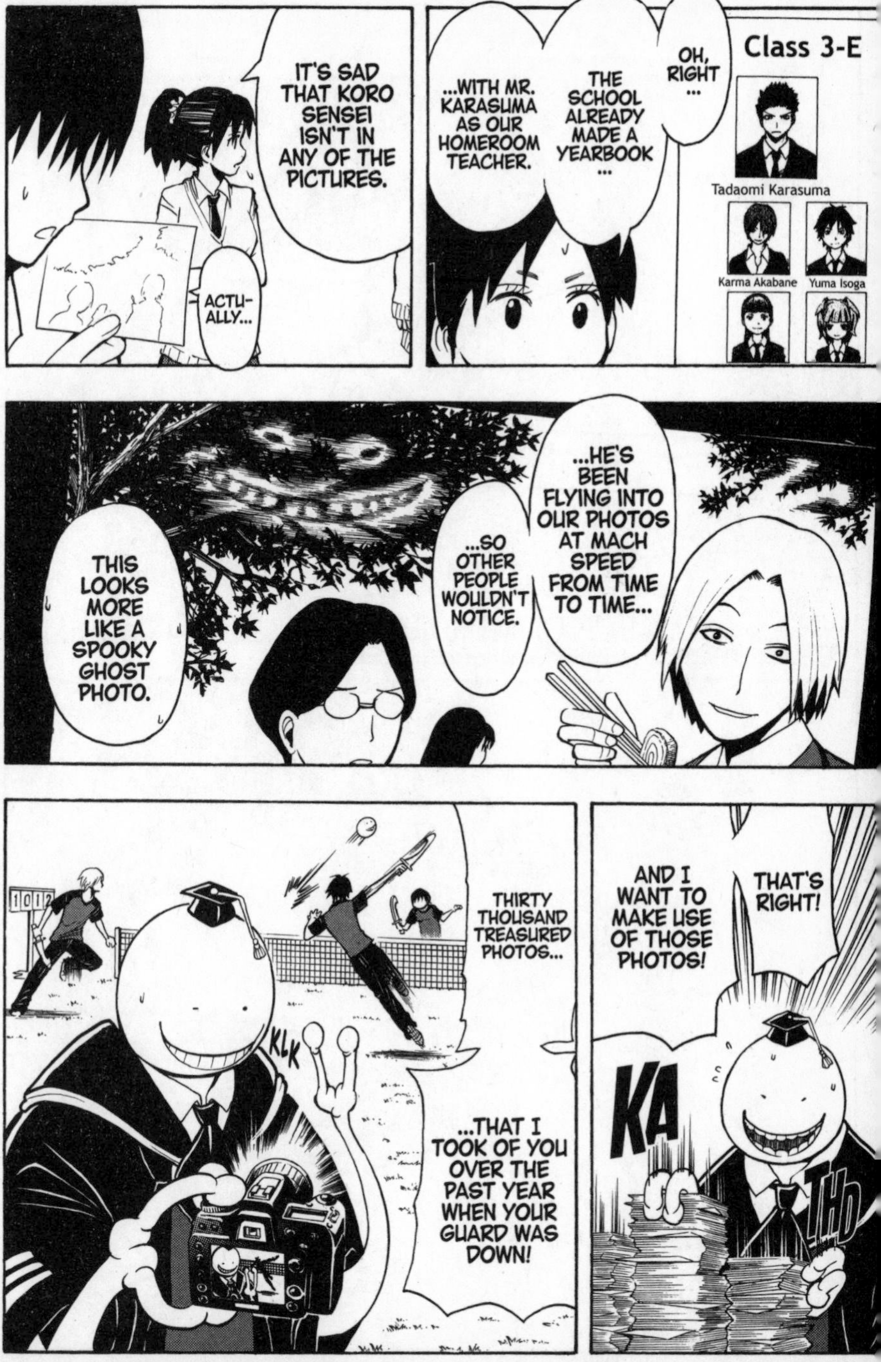
Class 3-E
Tadaomi Karasuma
Karma Akabane
Yuma Isoga
OH, RIGHT...
THE SCHOOL ALREADY MADE A YEARBOOK...
...WITH MR. KARASUMA AS OUR HOMEROOM TEACHER.
IT'S SAD THAT KORO SENSEI ISN'T IN ANY OF THE PICTURES.
ACTUALLY...
...HE'S BEEN FLYING INTO OUR PHOTOS AT MACH SPEED FROM TIME TO TIME...
...SO OTHER PEOPLE WOULDN'T NOTICE.
THIS LOOKS MORE LIKE A SPOOKY GHOST PHOTO.
THAT'S RIGHT!
AND I WANT TO MAKE USE OF THOSE PHOTOS!
KA
THD
THIRTY THOUSAND TREASURED PHOTOS...
KLK
...THAT I TOOK OF YOU OVER THE PAST YEAR WHEN YOUR GUARD WAS DOWN!

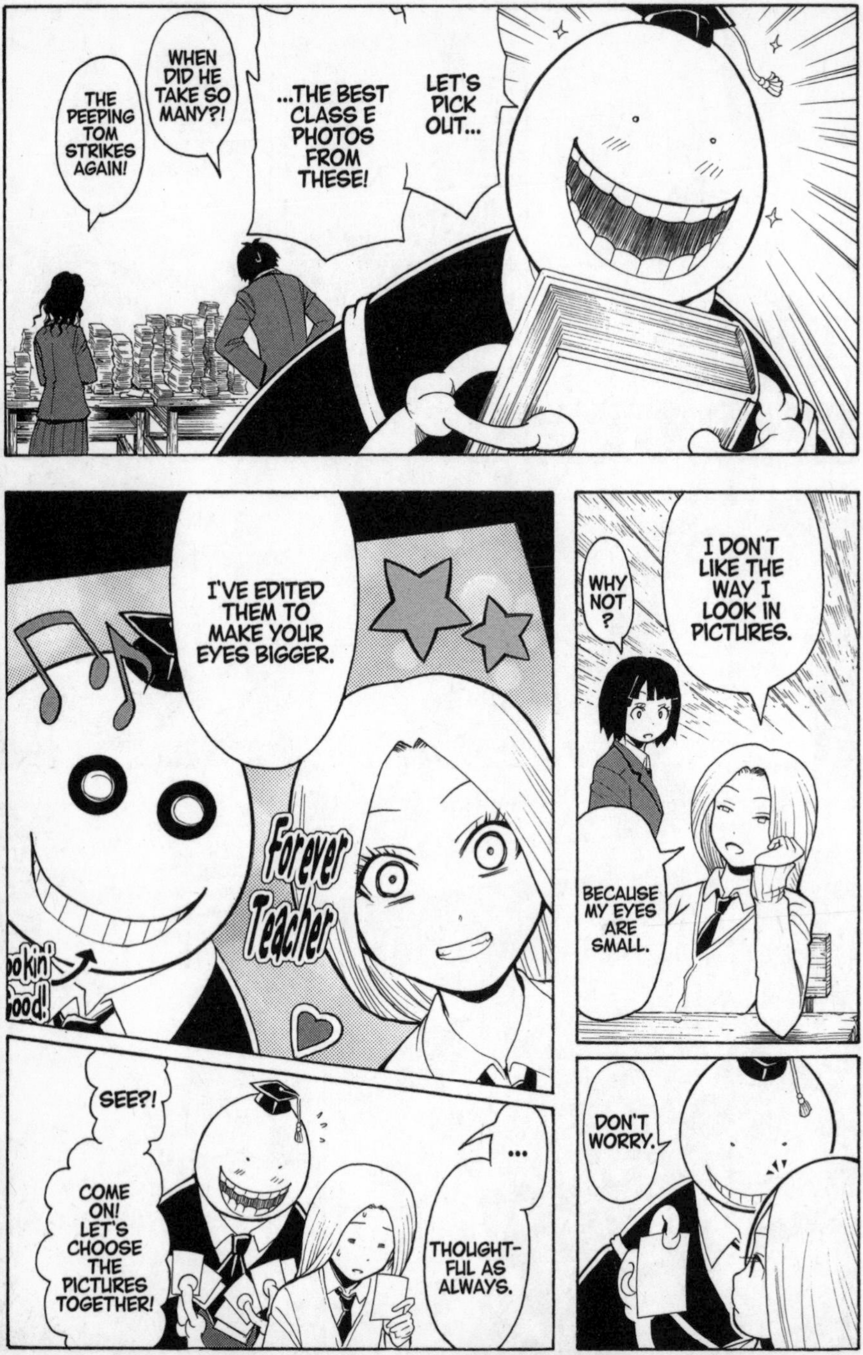
LET'S PICK OUT...
...THE BEST CLASS E PHOTOS FROM THESE!
WHEN DID HE TAKE SO MANY?!
THE PEEPING TOM STRIKES AGAIN!
I DON'T LIKE THE WAY I LOOK IN PICTURES.
WHY NOT?
BECAUSE MY EYES ARE SMALL.
DON'T WORRY.
I'VE EDITED THEM TO MAKE YOUR EYES BIGGER.
Forever Teacher
ookin' Good!
...
THOUGHT-FUL AS ALWAYS.
SEE?!
COME ON! LET'S CHOOSE THE PICTURES TOGETHER!

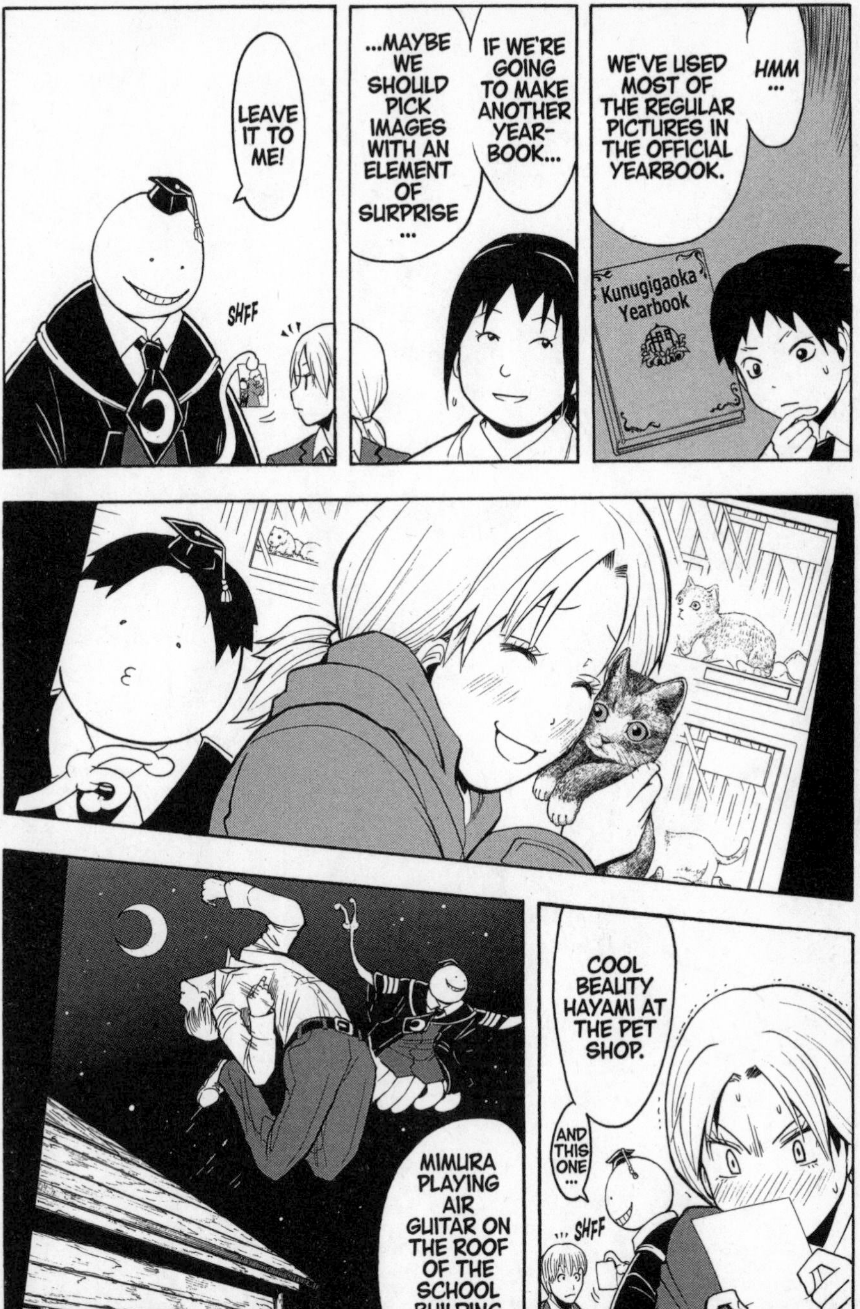
HMM...
WE'VE USED MOST OF THE REGULAR PICTURES IN THE OFFICIAL YEARBOOK.
Kunugigaoka Yearbook
IF WE'RE GOING TO MAKE ANOTHER YEAR-BOOK...
...MAYBE WE SHOULD PICK IMAGES WITH AN ELEMENT OF SURPRISE...
LEAVE IT TO ME!
SHFF
COOL BEAUTY HAYAMI AT THE PET SHOP.
AND THIS ONE...
SHFF
MIMURA PLAYING AIR GUITAR ON THE ROOF OF THE SCHOOL BUILDING AT NIGHT.

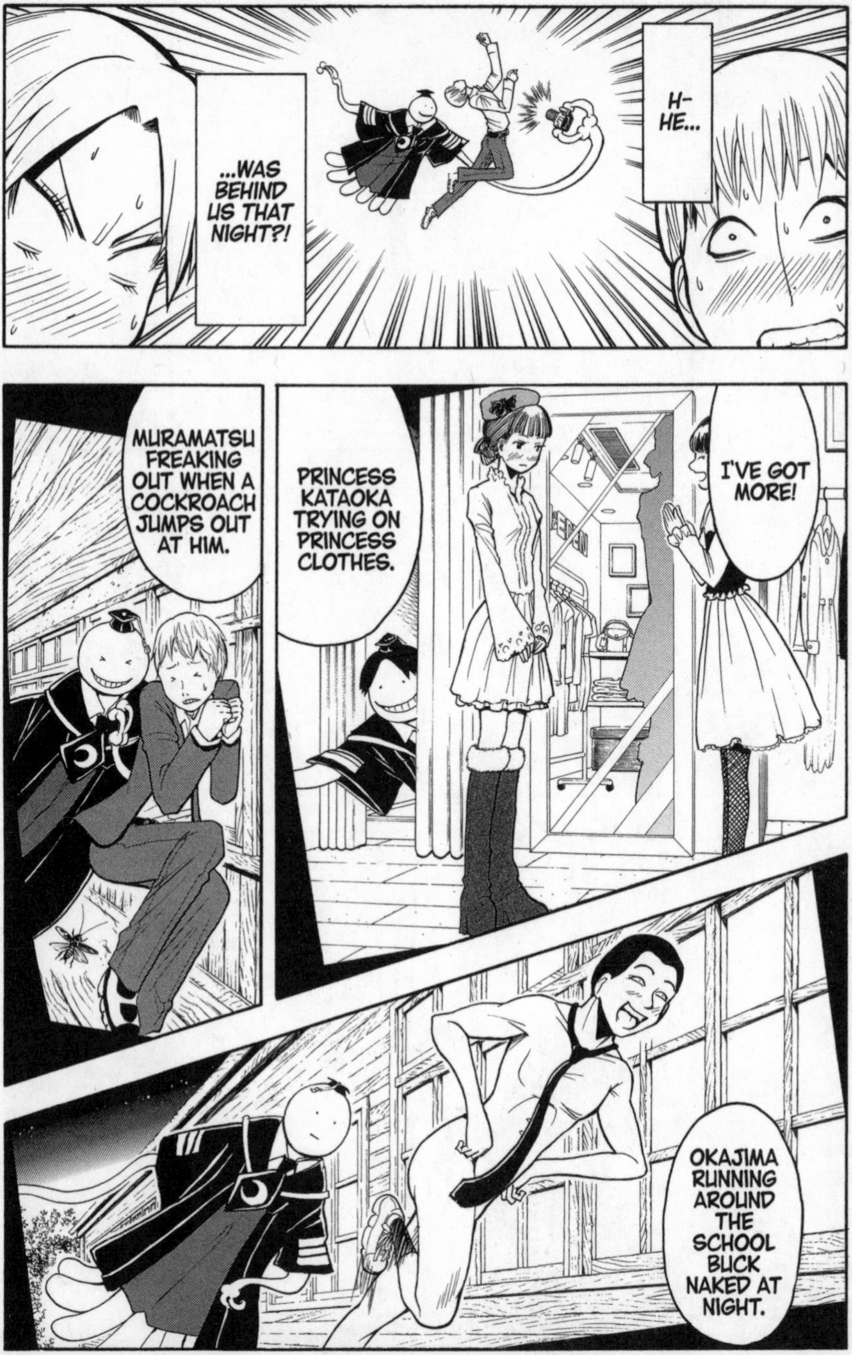
H-HE...
...WAS BEHIND US THAT NIGHT?!
I'VE GOT MORE!
PRINCESS KATAOKA TRYING ON PRINCESS CLOTHES.
MURAMATSU FREAKING OUT WHEN A COCKROACH JUMPS OUT AT HIM.
OKAJIMA RUNNING AROUND THE SCHOOL BUCK NAKED AT NIGHT.

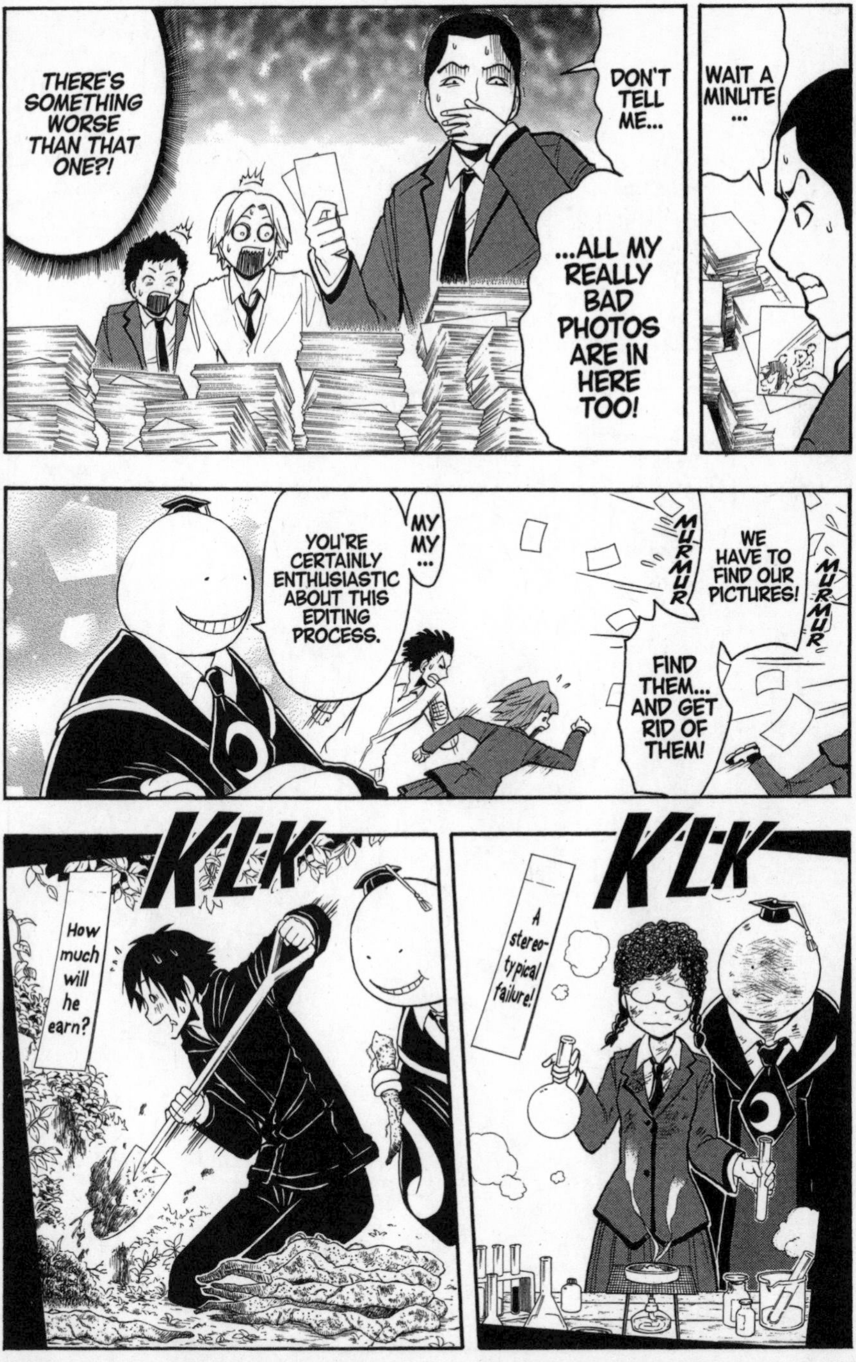
WAIT A MINUTE ...
DON'T TELL ME...
...ALL MY REALLY BAD PHOTOS ARE IN HERE TOO!
THERE'S SOMETHING WORSE THAN THAT ONE?!
MURMUR
WE HAVE TO FIND OUR PICTURES!
FIND THEM... AND GET RID OF THEM!
MURMUR
MY MY ...
YOU'RE CERTAINLY ENTHUSIASTIC ABOUT THIS EDITING PROCESS.
KLIK
A stereo-typical failure!
KLIK
How much will he earn?

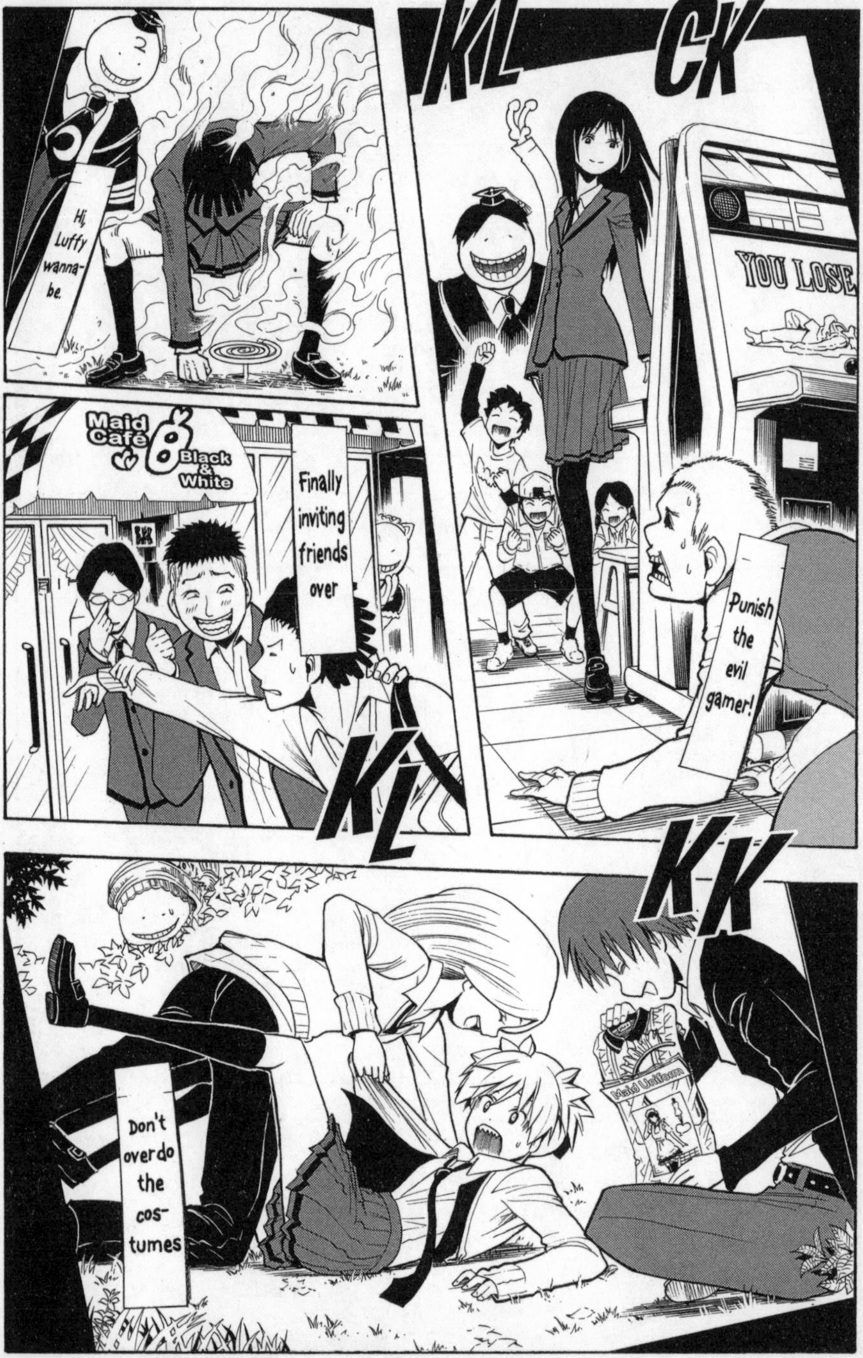

KL CK
YOU LOSE
Punish the evil gamer!
Hi, Luffy wanna-be.
Maid Café Black & White
Finally inviting friends over
KL
KK
Maid Uniform
Don't overdo the costumes

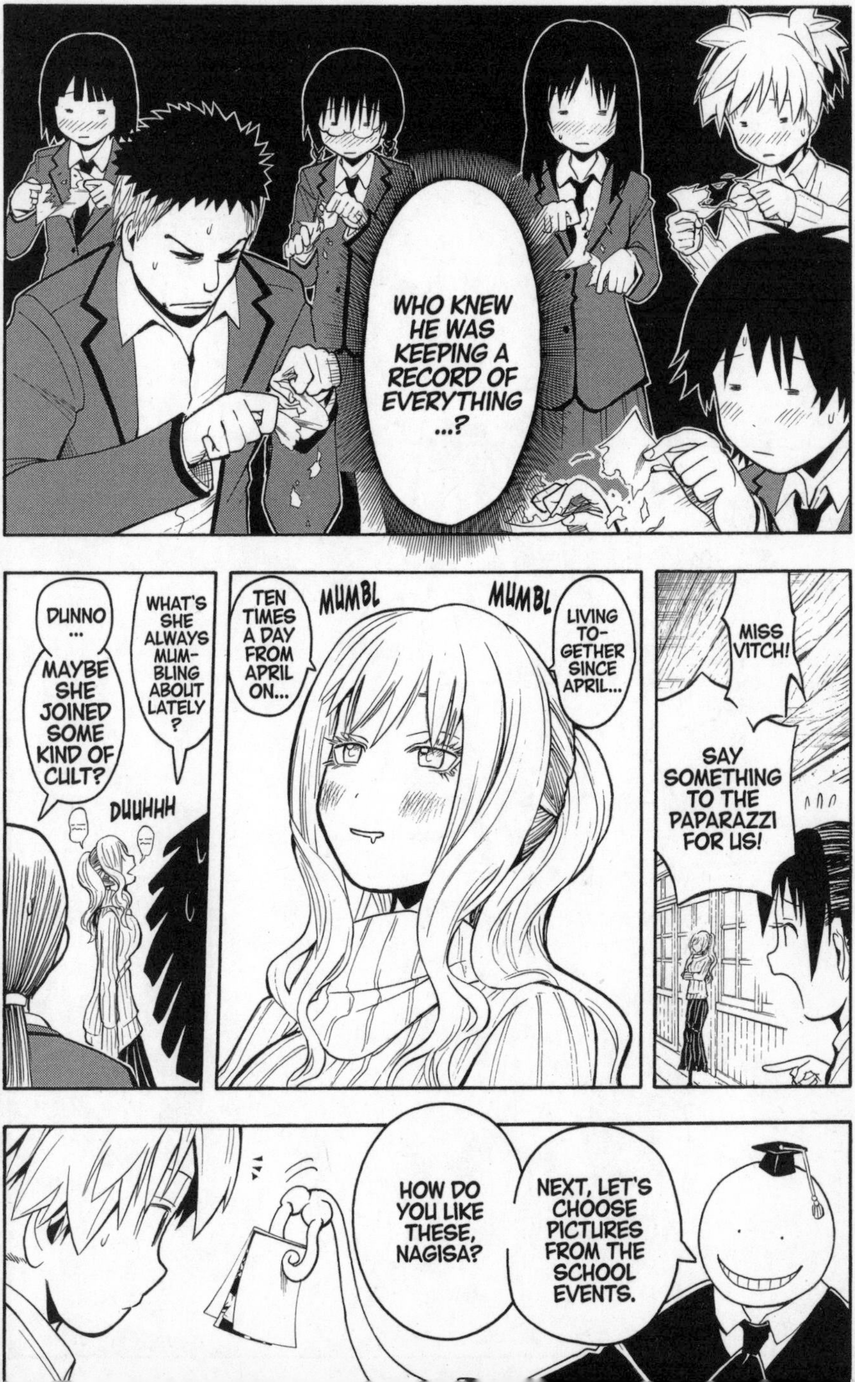
WHO KNEW HE WAS KEEPING A RECORD OF EVERYTHING ...?
MISS VITCH!
SAY SOMETHING TO THE PAPARAZZI FOR US!
MUMBL
LIVING TO-GETHER SINCE APRIL...
MUMBL
TEN TIMES A DAY FROM APRIL ON...
WHAT'S SHE ALWAYS MUM-BLING ABOUT LATELY ?
DUNNO ...
MAYBE SHE JOINED SOME KIND OF CULT?
DUUHHH
NEXT, LET'S CHOOSE PICTURES FROM THE SCHOOL EVENTS.
HOW DO YOU LIKE THESE, NAGISA?

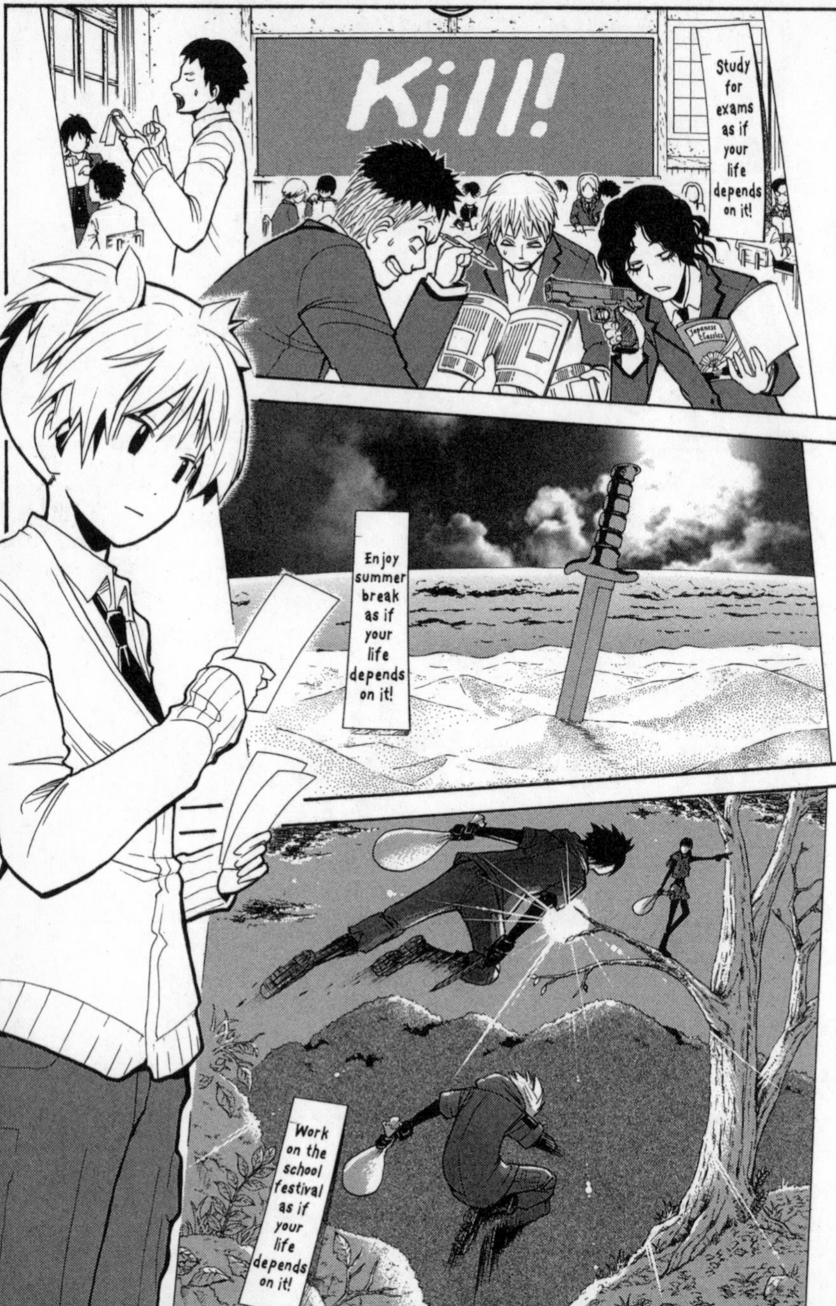
Study for exams as if your life depends on it!
Kill!
Japanese Classics
Enjoy summer break as if your life depends on it!
Work on the school festival as if your life depends on it!

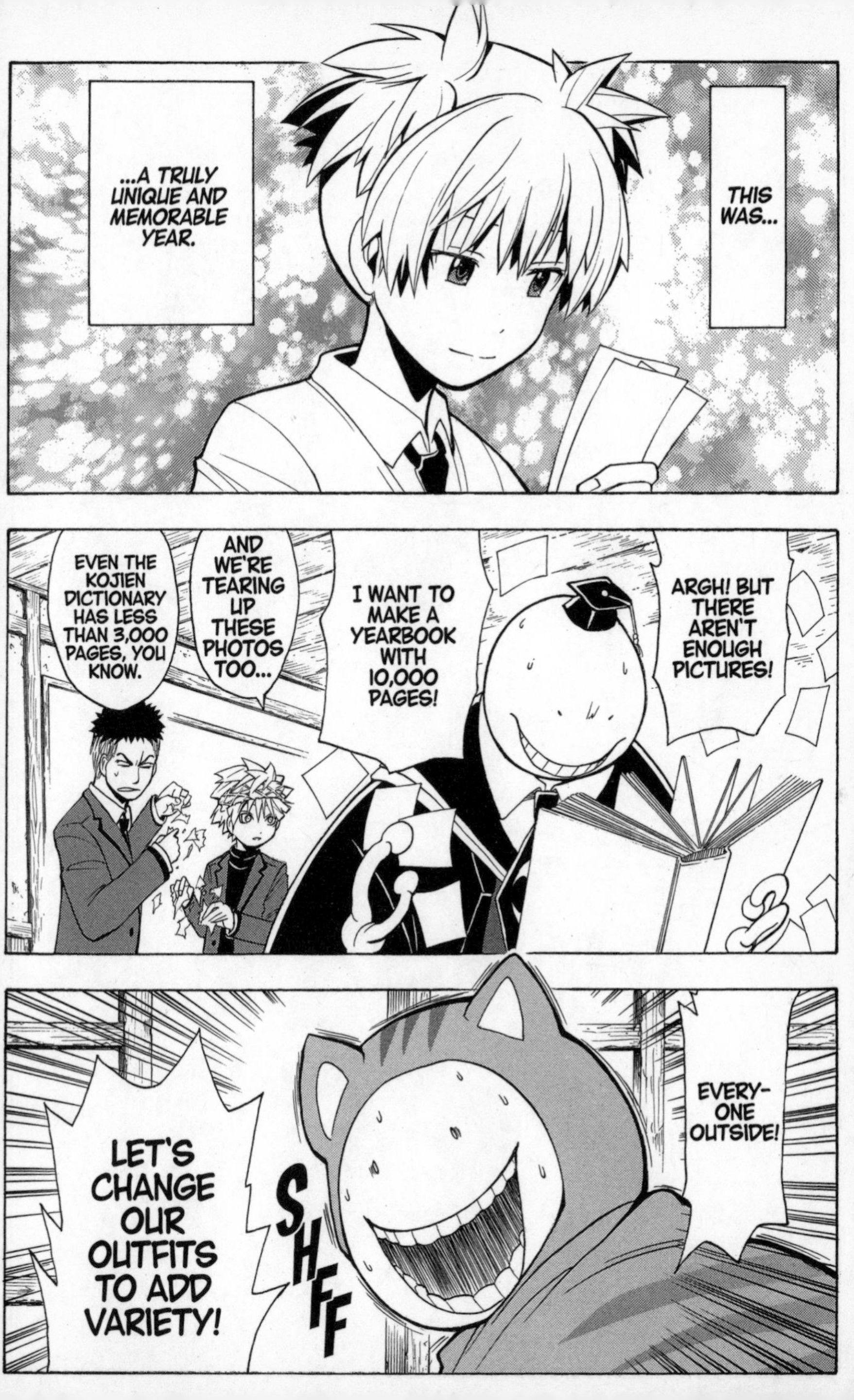
THIS WAS...
...A TRULY UNIQUE AND MEMORABLE YEAR.
ARGH! BUT THERE AREN'T ENOUGH PICTURES!
I WANT TO MAKE A YEARBOOK WITH 10,000 PAGES!
AND WE'RE TEARING UP THESE PHOTOS TOO...
EVEN THE KOJIEN DICTIONARY HAS LESS THAN 3,000 PAGES, YOU KNOW.
EVERY-ONE OUTSIDE!
SHFF
LET'S CHANGE OUR OUTFITS TO ADD VARIETY!

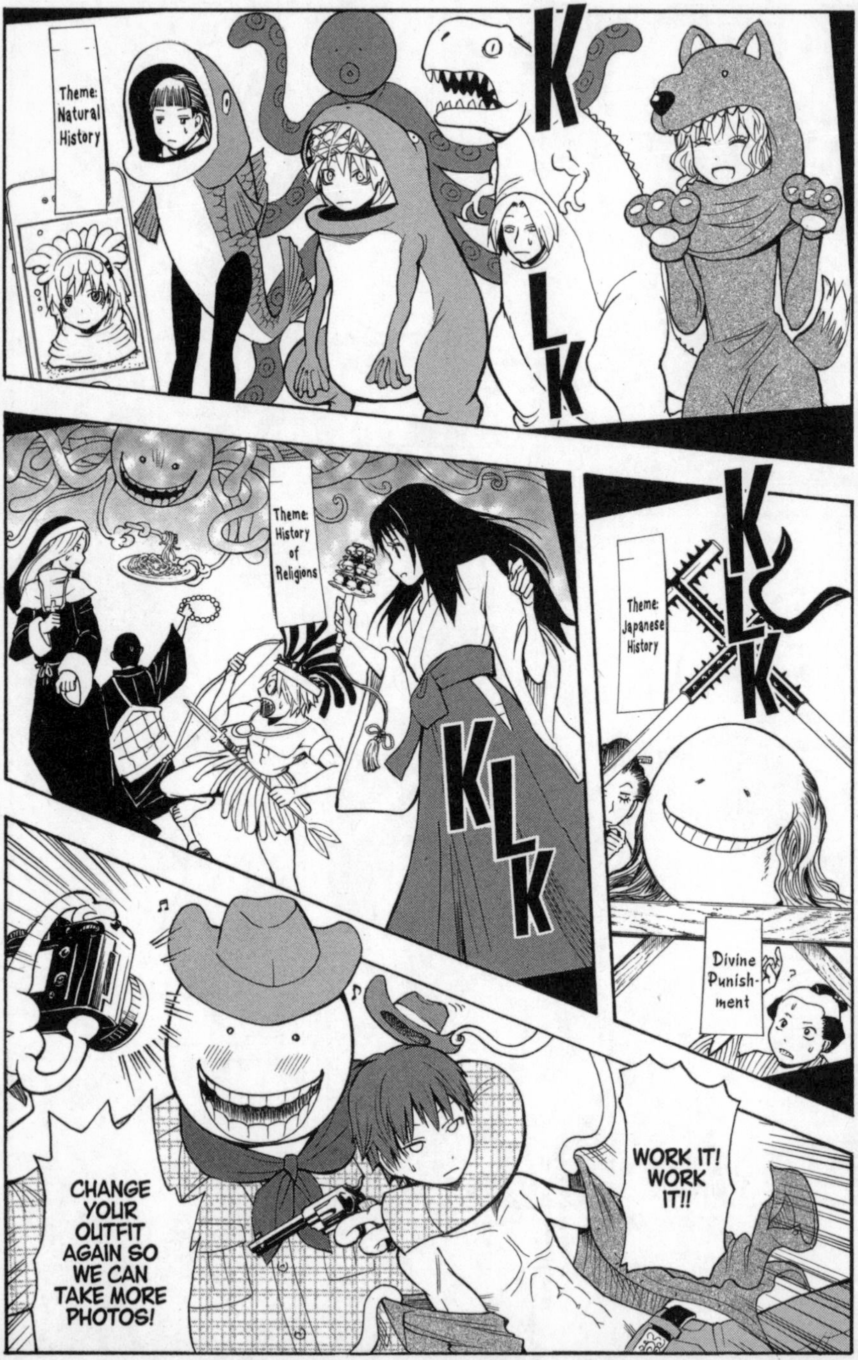
KLK
Theme: Natural History
KLK
Theme: Japanese History
Divine Punishment
KLK
Theme: History of Religions
WORK IT! WORK IT!!
CHANGE YOUR OUTFIT AGAIN SO WE CAN TAKE MORE PHOTOS!

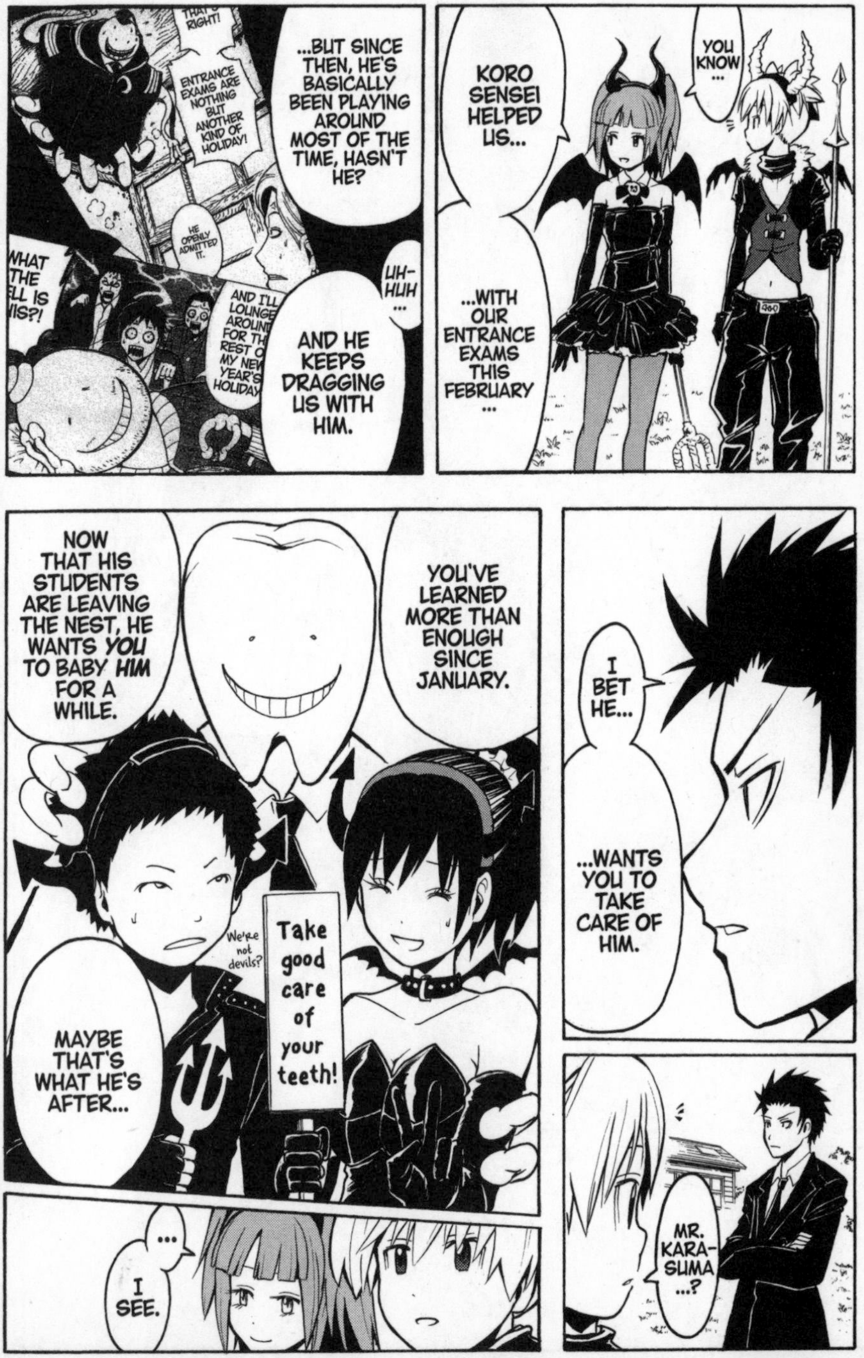
YOU KNOW...
KORO SENSEI HELPED US...
...WITH OUR ENTRANCE EXAMS THIS FEBRUARY...
...BUT SINCE THEN, HE'S BASICALLY BEEN PLAYING AROUND MOST OF THE TIME, HASN'T HE?
UH-HUH...
AND HE KEEPS DRAGGING US WITH HIM.
RIGHT!
ENTRANCE EXAMS ARE NOTHING BUT ANOTHER KIND OF HOLIDAY!
HE OPENLY ADMITTED IT.
WHAT THE
AND I'LL FOR THE REST MY NEW
I BET HE...
...WANTS YOU TO TAKE CARE OF HIM.
YOU'VE LEARNED MORE THAN ENOUGH SINCE JANUARY.
NOW THAT HIS STUDENTS ARE LEAVING THE NEST, HE WANTS *YOU* TO BABY *HIM* FOR A WHILE.
Take good care of your teeth!
We're not devils?
MAYBE THAT'S WHAT HE'S AFTER...
MR. KARASUMA...?
...
I SEE.

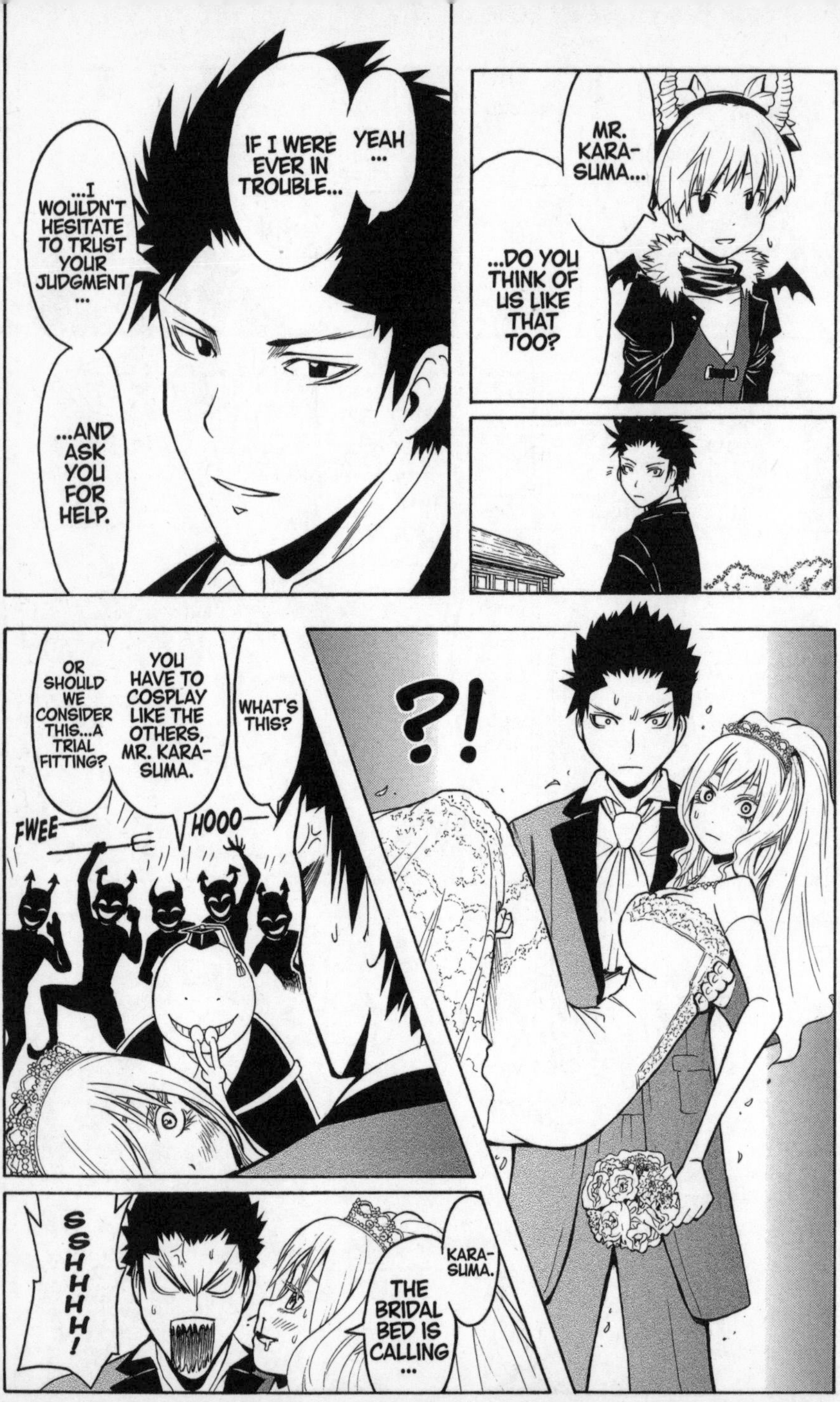
MR. KARA-SUMA...
...DO YOU THINK OF US LIKE THAT TOO?
YEAH...
IF I WERE EVER IN TROUBLE...
...I WOULDN'T HESITATE TO TRUST YOUR JUDGMENT...
...AND ASK YOU FOR HELP.
?!
WHAT'S THIS?
YOU HAVE TO COSPLAY LIKE THE OTHERS, MR. KARA-SUMA.
OR SHOULD WE CONSIDER THIS...A TRIAL FITTING?
HOOO—
FWEE—
KARA-SUMA.
THE BRIDAL BED IS CALLING...
SSHHHH!

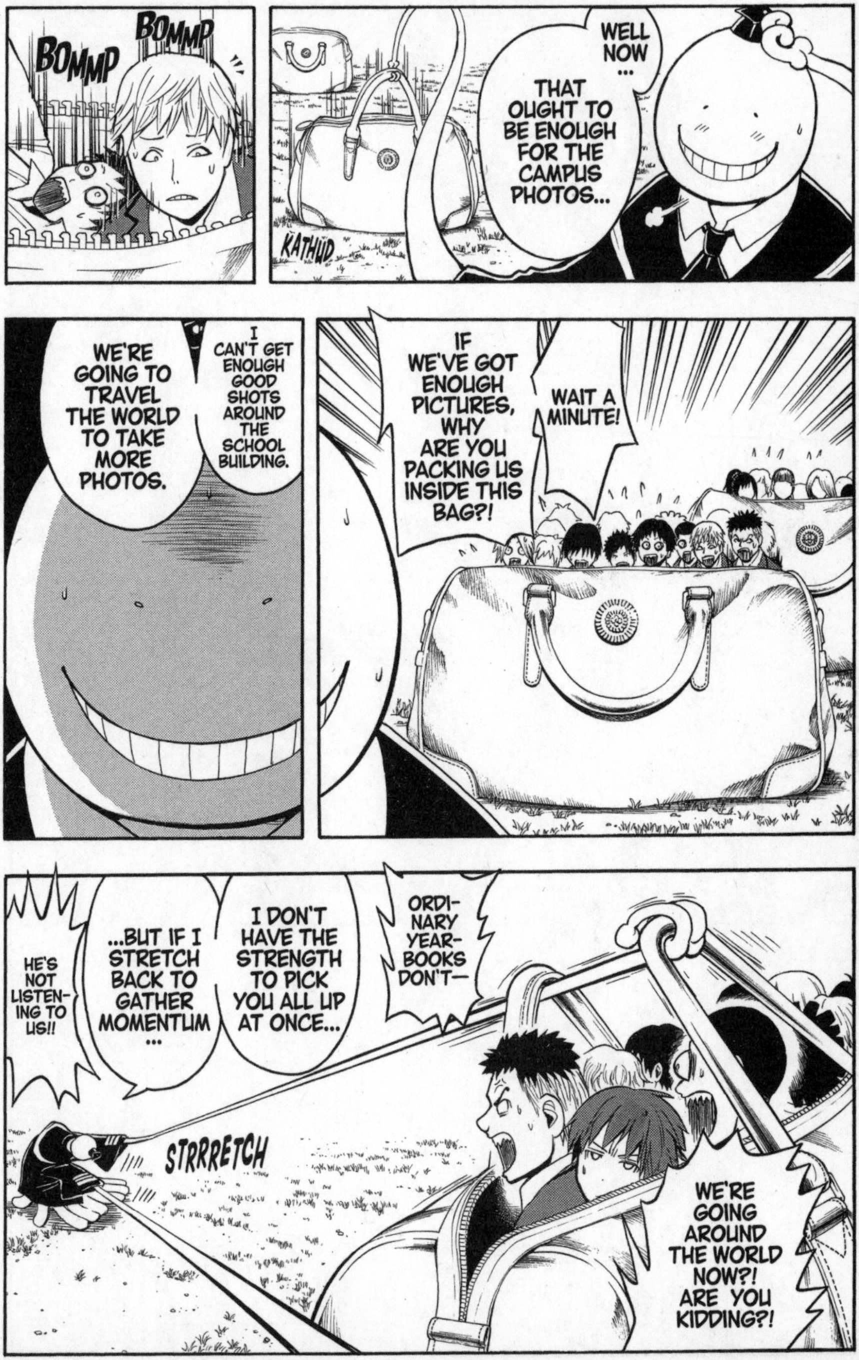
WELL NOW ...
THAT OUGHT TO BE ENOUGH FOR THE CAMPUS PHOTOS...
KATHÜD
BOMMP
BOMMP
WAIT A MINUTE!
IF WE'VE GOT ENOUGH PICTURES, WHY ARE YOU PACKING US INSIDE THIS BAG?!
I CAN'T GET ENOUGH GOOD SHOTS AROUND THE SCHOOL BUILDING.
WE'RE GOING TO TRAVEL THE WORLD TO TAKE MORE PHOTOS.
ORDINARY YEARBOOKS DON'T—
I DON'T HAVE THE STRENGTH TO PICK YOU ALL UP AT ONCE...
...BUT IF I STRETCH BACK TO GATHER MOMENTUM ...
HE'S NOT LISTENING TO US!!
STRRRETCH
WE'RE GOING AROUND THE WORLD NOW?! ARE YOU KIDDING?!

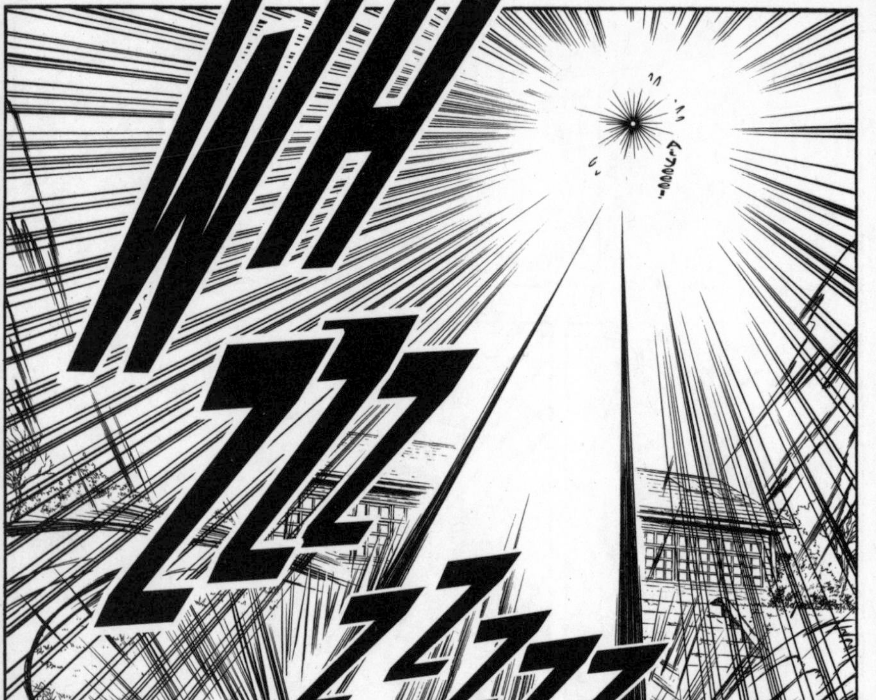
WHZZZZZZZ
Aiyeee!
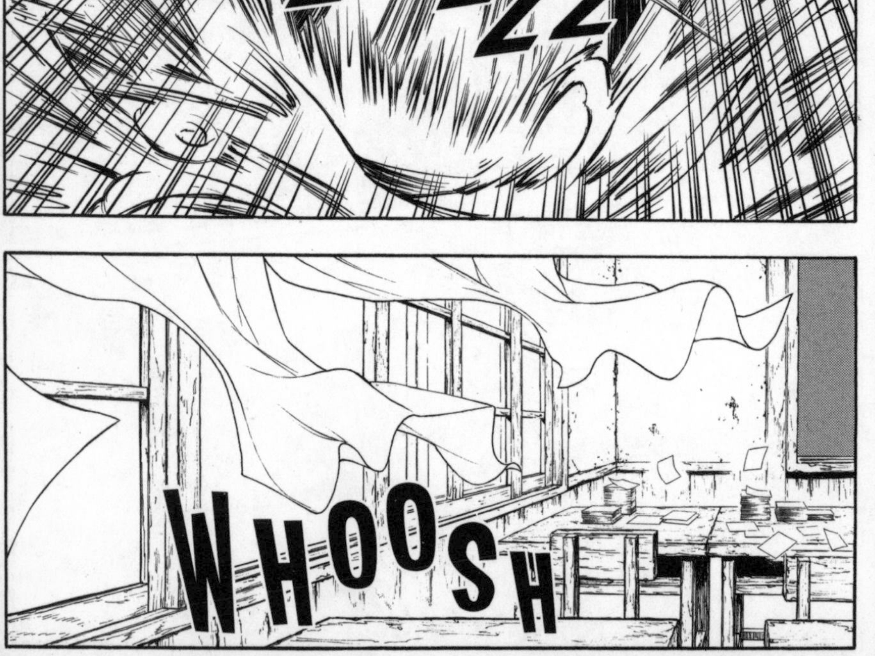
WHOOSH

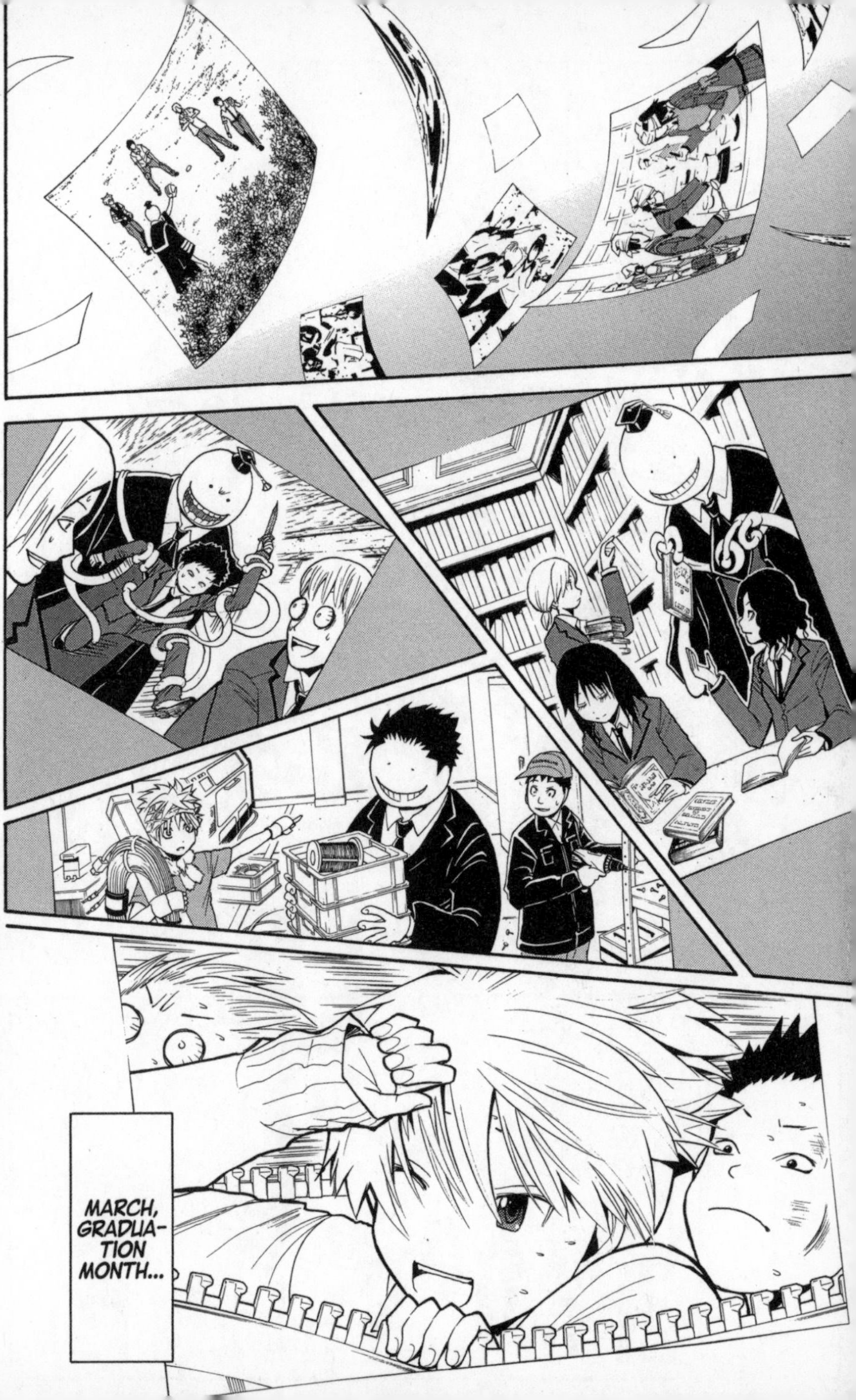
MARCH, GRADUA-TION MONTH...

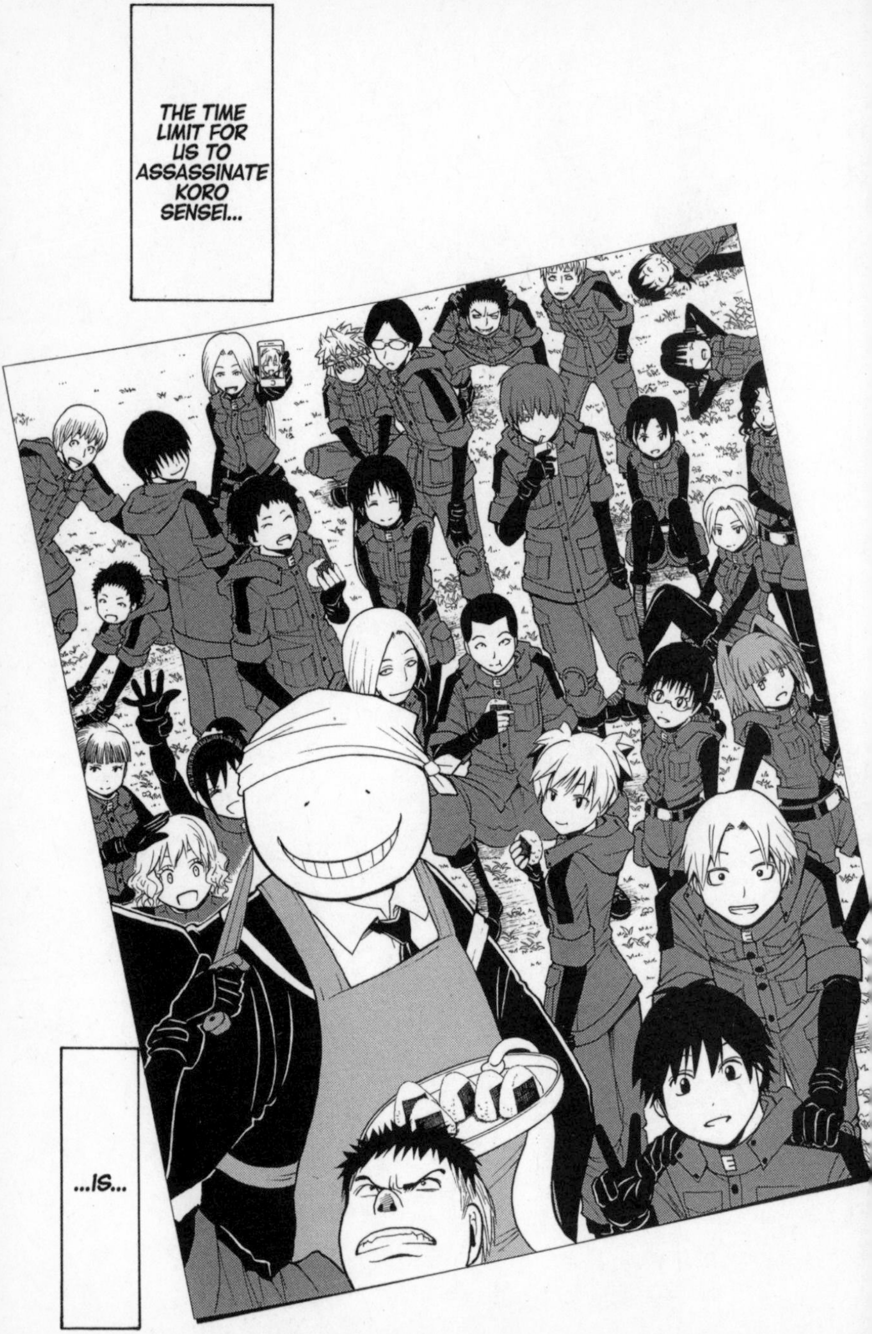
THE TIME LIMIT FOR US TO ASSASSINATE KORO SENSEI...
...IS...

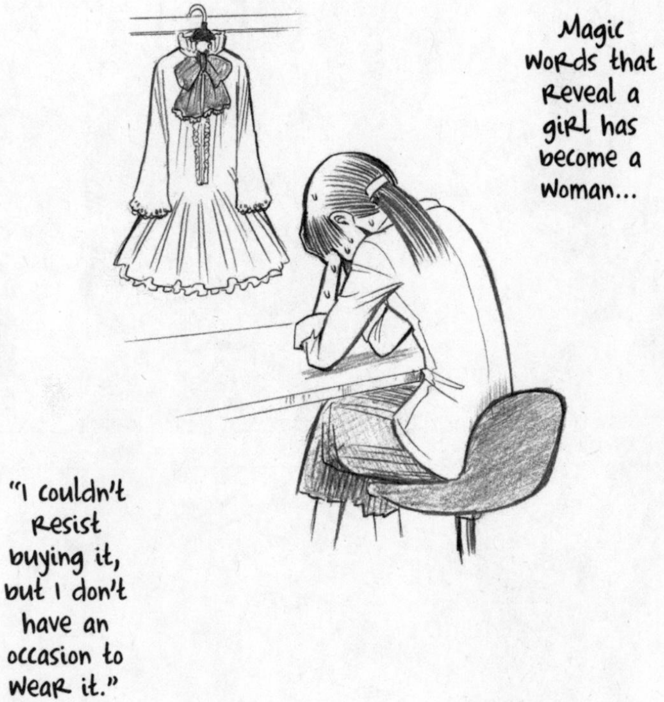
Magic words that reveal a girl has become a woman...
"I couldn't resist buying it, but I don't have an occasion to wear it."

CLASS 163 TIME FOR DECISIONS

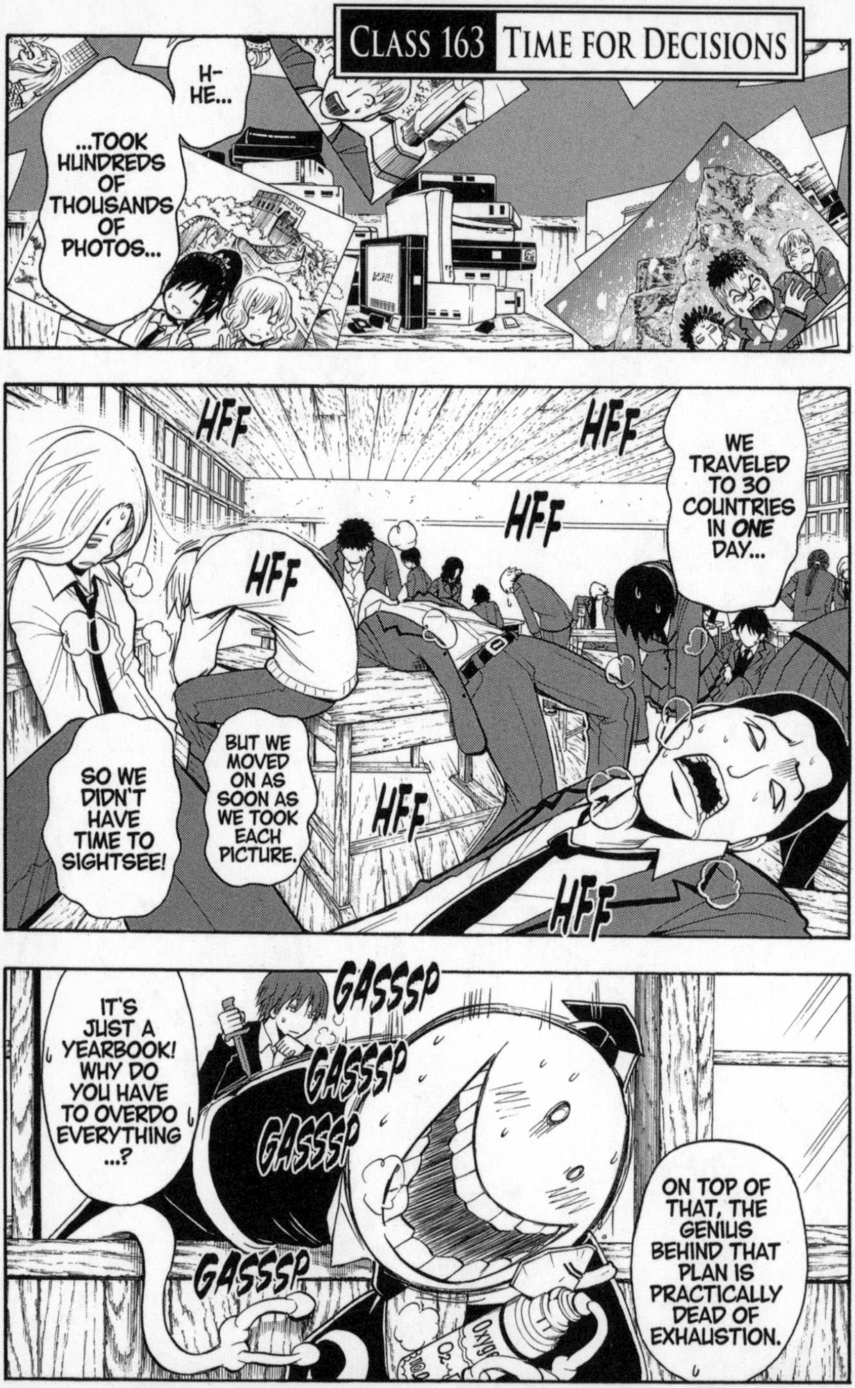
H-
HE...
...TOOK HUNDREDS OF THOUSANDS OF PHOTOS...
HFF
HFF
WE TRAVELED TO 30 COUNTRIES IN ONE DAY...
HFF
HFF
BUT WE MOVED ON AS SOON AS WE TOOK EACH PICTURE.
SO WE DIDN'T HAVE TIME TO SIGHTSEE!
HFF
HFF
GASSSP
GASSSP
GASSSP
IT'S JUST A YEARBOOK! WHY DO YOU HAVE TO OVERDO EVERYTHING ...?
GASSSP
ON TOP OF THAT, THE GENIUS BEHIND THAT PLAN IS PRACTICALLY DEAD OF EXHAUSTION.

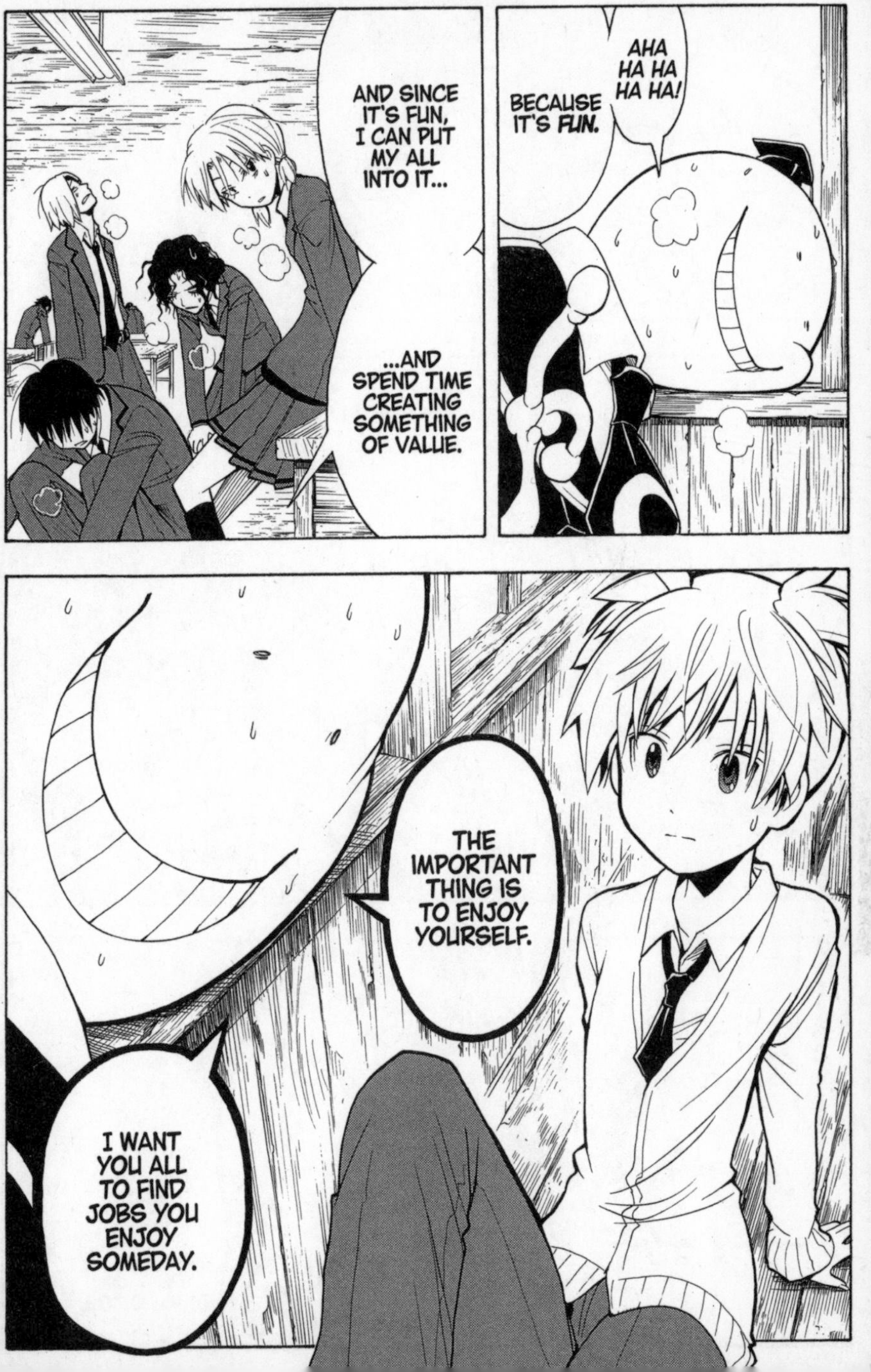
AHA HA HA HA HA!
BECAUSE IT'S FUN.
AND SINCE IT'S FUN, I CAN PUT MY ALL INTO IT...
...AND SPEND TIME CREATING SOMETHING OF VALUE.
THE IMPORTANT THING IS TO ENJOY YOURSELF.
I WANT YOU ALL TO FIND JOBS YOU ENJOY SOMEDAY.

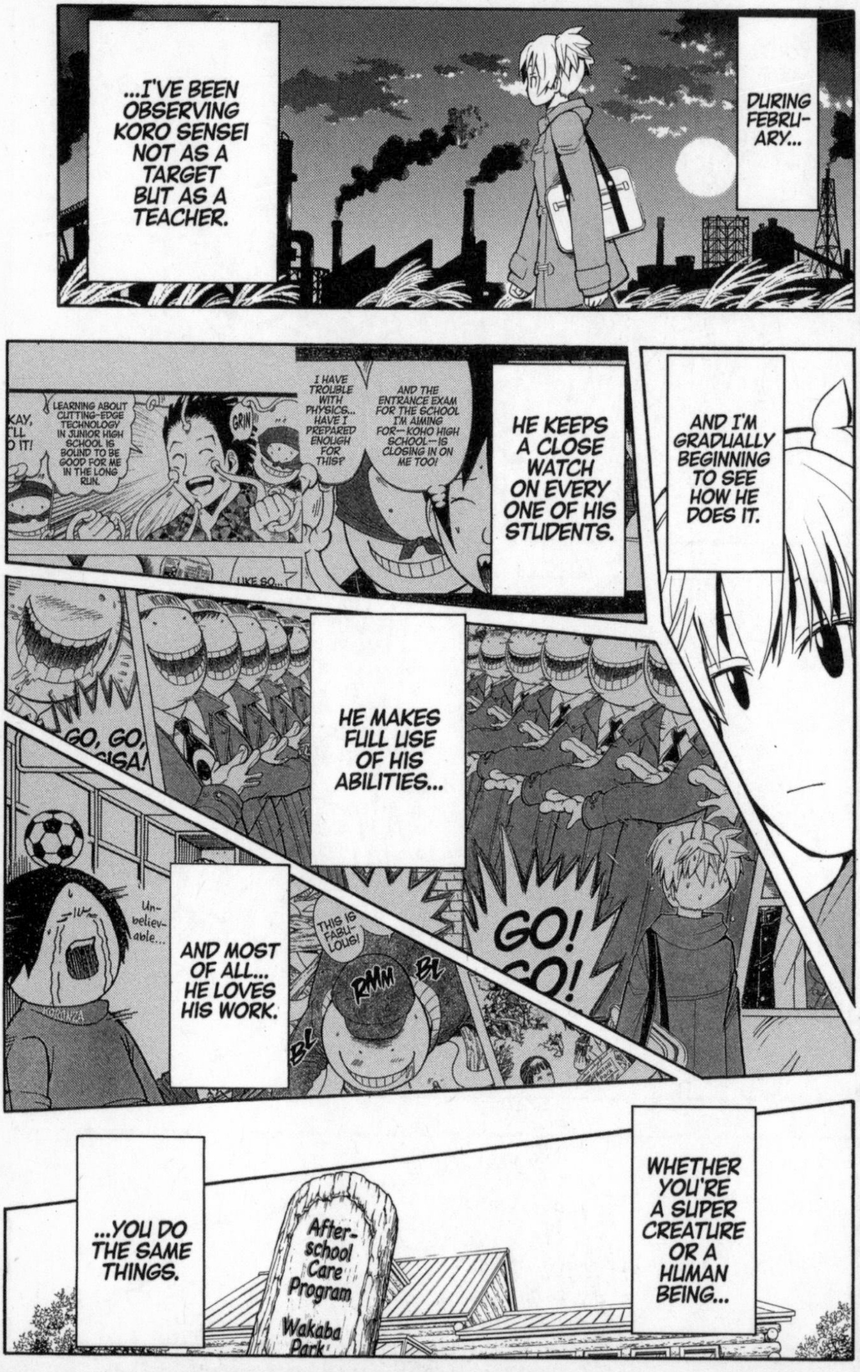
DURING FEBRU-ARY...
...I'VE BEEN OBSERVING KORO SENSEI NOT AS A TARGET BUT AS A TEACHER.
AND I'M GRADUALLY BEGINNING TO SEE HOW HE DOES IT.
HE KEEPS A CLOSE WATCH ON EVERY ONE OF HIS STUDENTS.
AND THE ENTRANCE EXAM FOR THE SCHOOL I'M AIMING FOR—KOHO HIGH SCHOOL—IS CLOSING IN ON ME TOO!
I HAVE TROUBLE WITH PHYSICS... HAVE I PREPARED ENOUGH FOR THIS?
GRIN
LEARNING ABOUT CUTTING-EDGE TECHNOLOGY IN JUNIOR HIGH SCHOOL IS BOUND TO BE GOOD FOR ME IN THE LONG RUN.
LIKE SO...
HE MAKES FULL USE OF HIS ABILITIES...
GO! GO!
GO, GO,
AND MOST OF ALL... HE LOVES HIS WORK.
THIS IS FABU-LOUS!
RMM
BL
BL
Un-believ-able...
WHETHER YOU'RE A SUPER CREATURE OR A HUMAN BEING...
...YOU DO THE SAME THINGS.
After-school Care Program
Wakaba Park

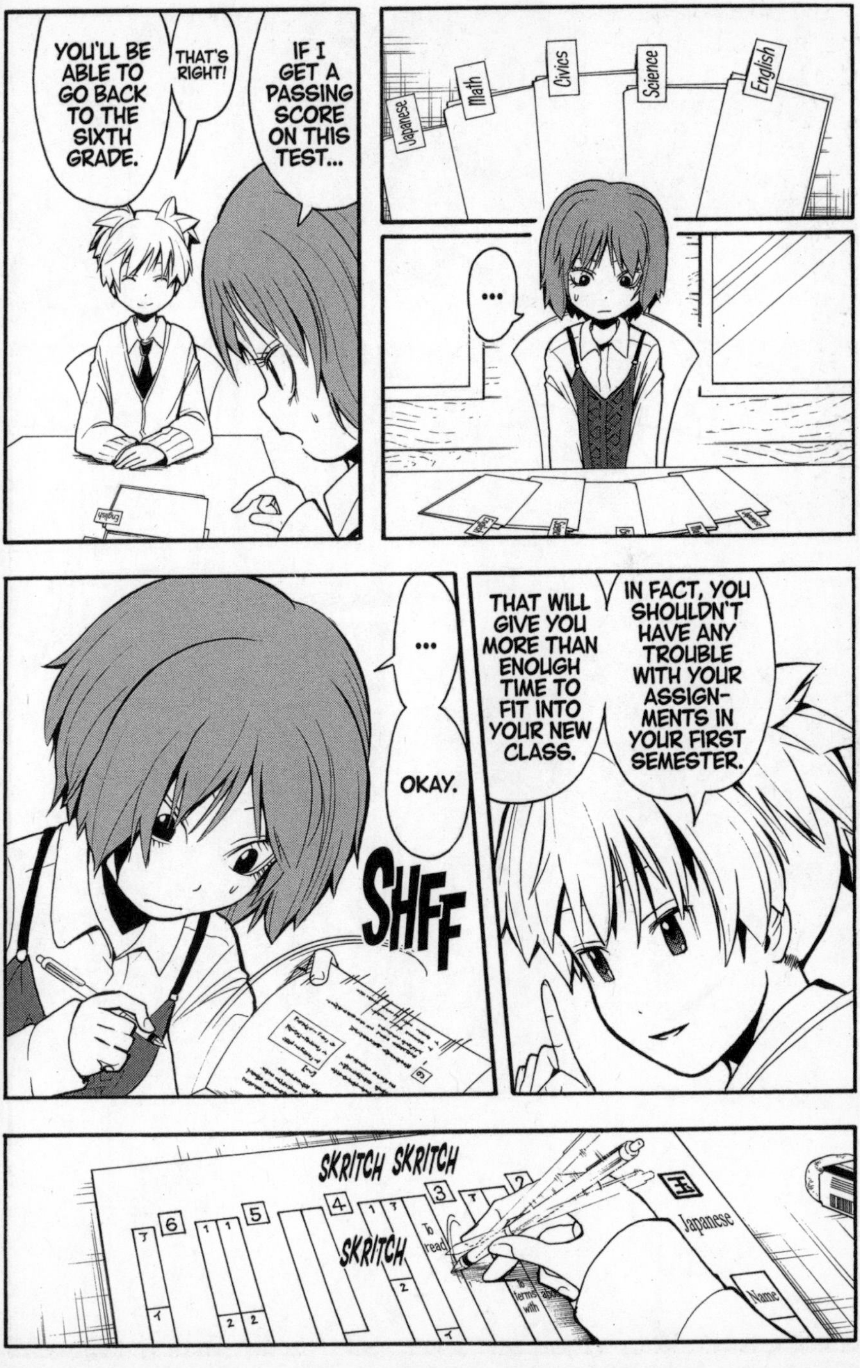
Japanese
Math
Civics
Science
English
...
IF I GET A PASSING SCORE ON THIS TEST...
THAT'S RIGHT!
YOU'LL BE ABLE TO GO BACK TO THE SIXTH GRADE.
IN FACT, YOU SHOULDN'T HAVE ANY TROUBLE WITH YOUR ASSIGNMENTS IN YOUR FIRST SEMESTER.
THAT WILL GIVE YOU MORE THAN ENOUGH TIME TO FIT INTO YOUR NEW CLASS.
...
OKAY.
SHFF
SKRITCH SKRITCH
SKRITCH
Japanese
Name

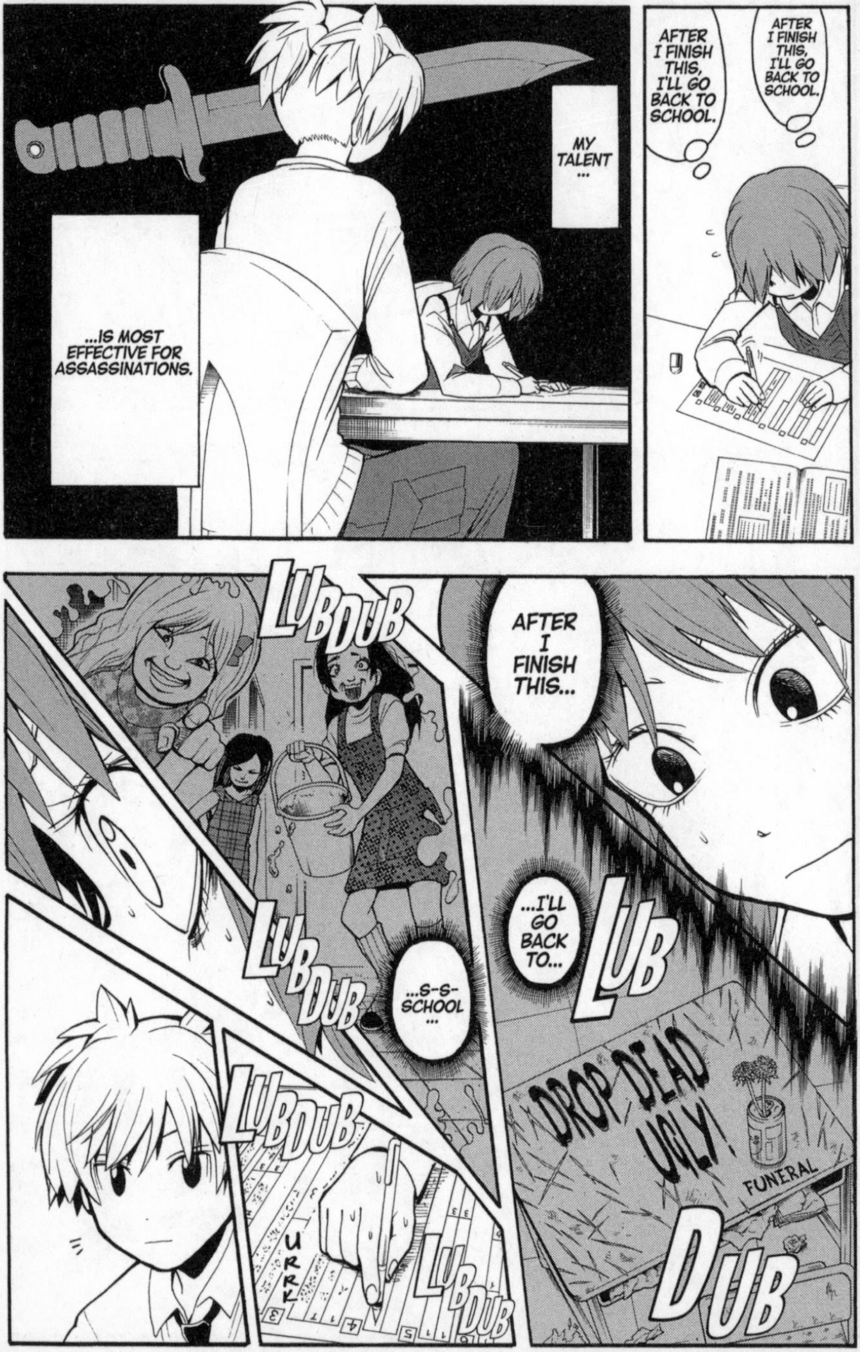
AFTER I FINISH THIS, I'LL GO BACK TO SCHOOL.
AFTER I FINISH THIS, I'LL GO BACK TO SCHOOL.
MY TALENT...
...IS MOST EFFECTIVE FOR ASSASSINATIONS.
AFTER I FINISH THIS...
...I'LL GO BACK TO...
LUB
DUB
DROP DEAD UGLY!
FUNERAL
LUBDUB
LUBDUB
...S-S-SCHOOL...
LUBDUB
URRK
LUBDUB

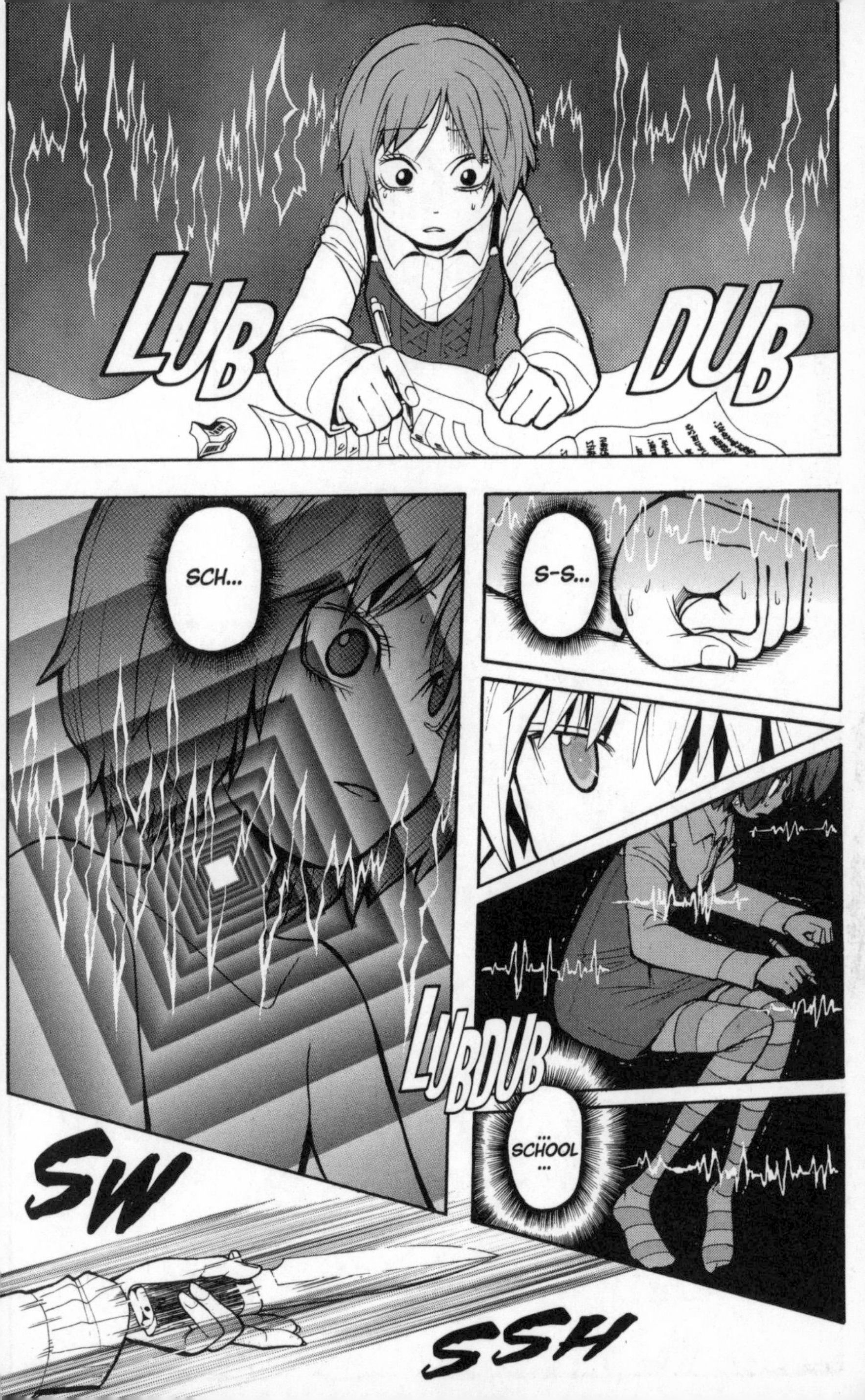
LUB
DUB
S-S...
LUBDUB
... SCHOOL ...
SCH...
SW
SSH

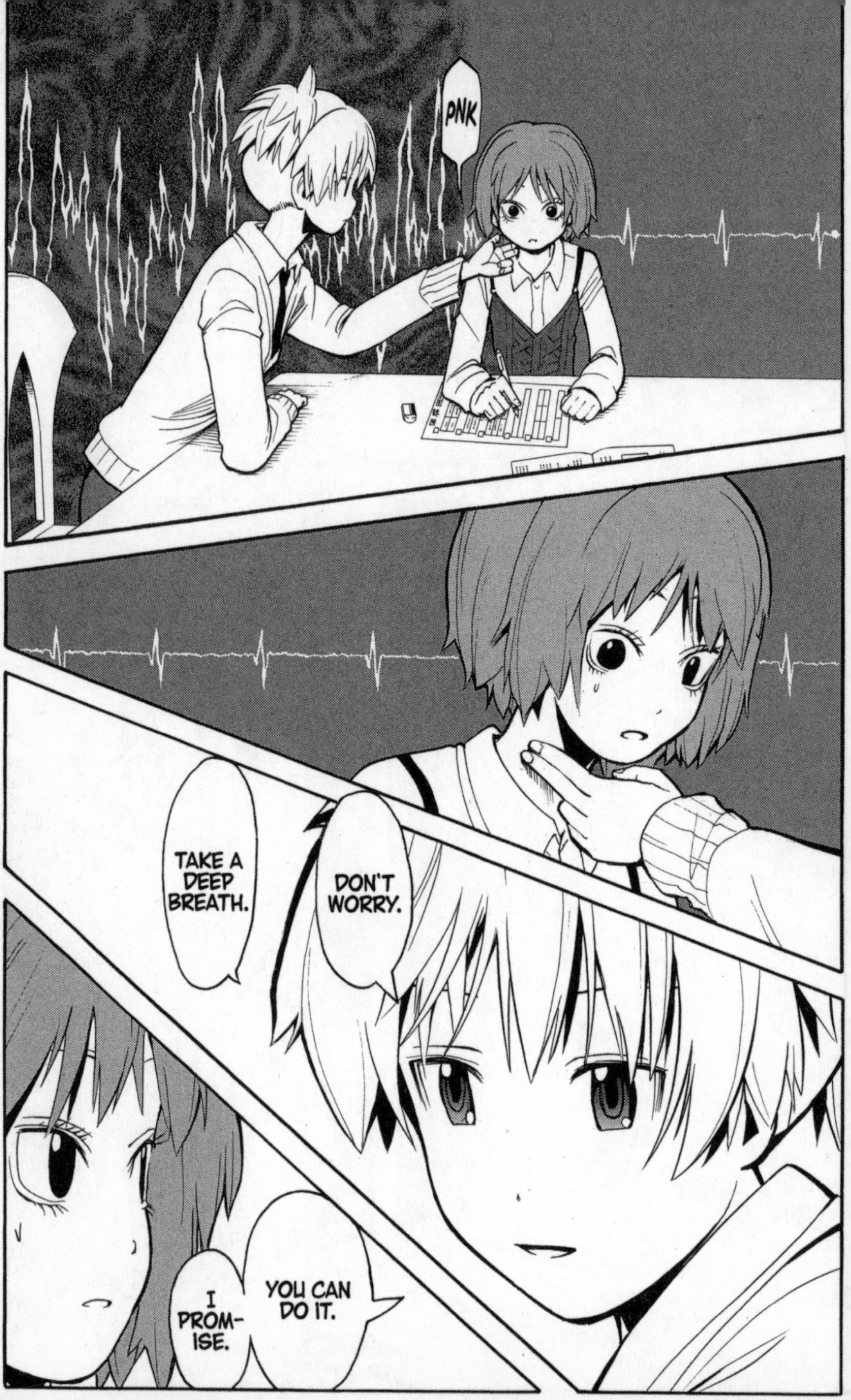
PNK
DON'T WORRY.
TAKE A DEEP BREATH.
YOU CAN DO IT.
I PROMISE.

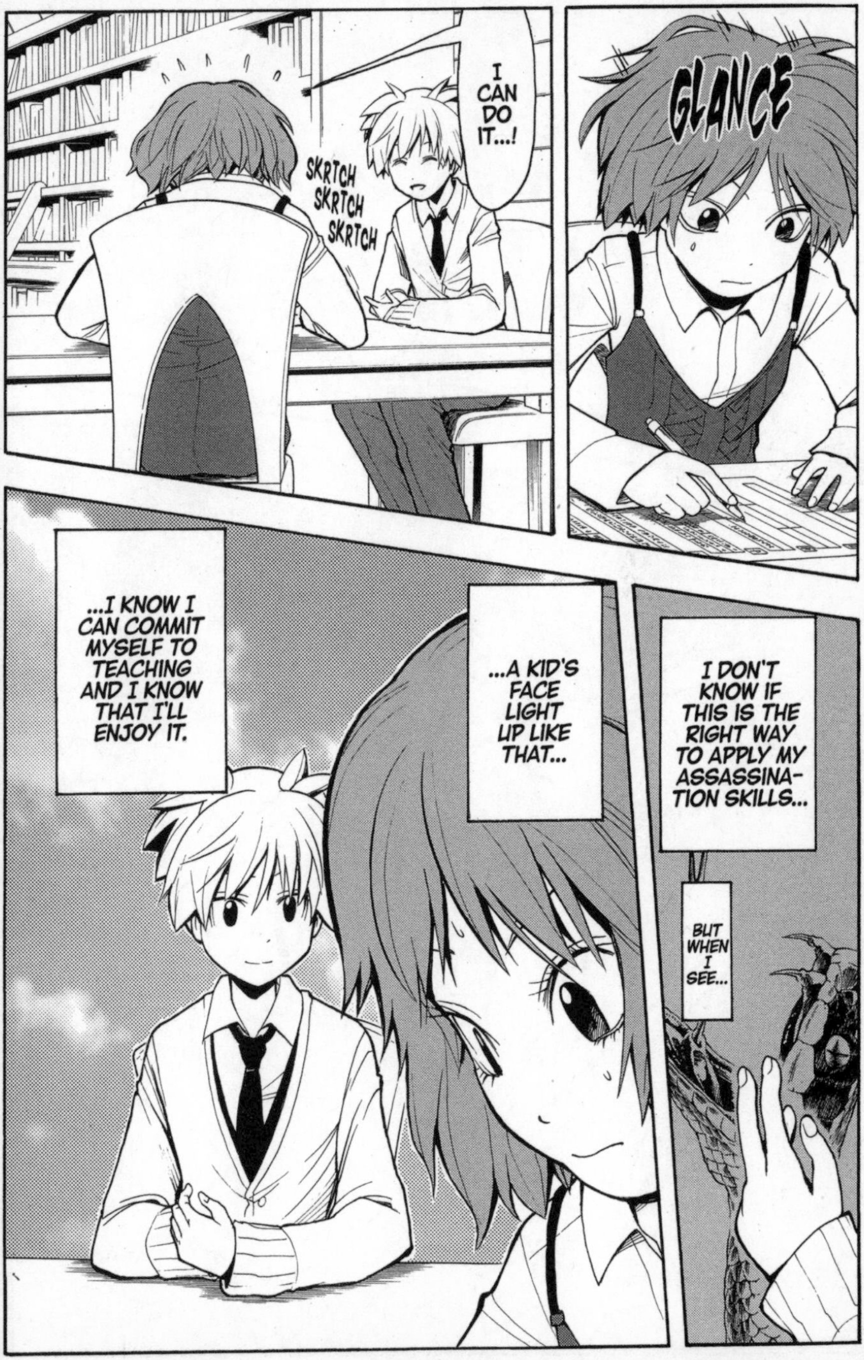
GLANCE
I CAN DO IT...!
SKRTCH SKRTCH SKRTCH
I DON'T KNOW IF THIS IS THE RIGHT WAY TO APPLY MY ASSASSINATION SKILLS...
BUT WHEN I SEE...
...A KID'S FACE LIGHT UP LIKE THAT...
...I KNOW I CAN COMMIT MYSELF TO TEACHING AND I KNOW THAT I'LL ENJOY IT.

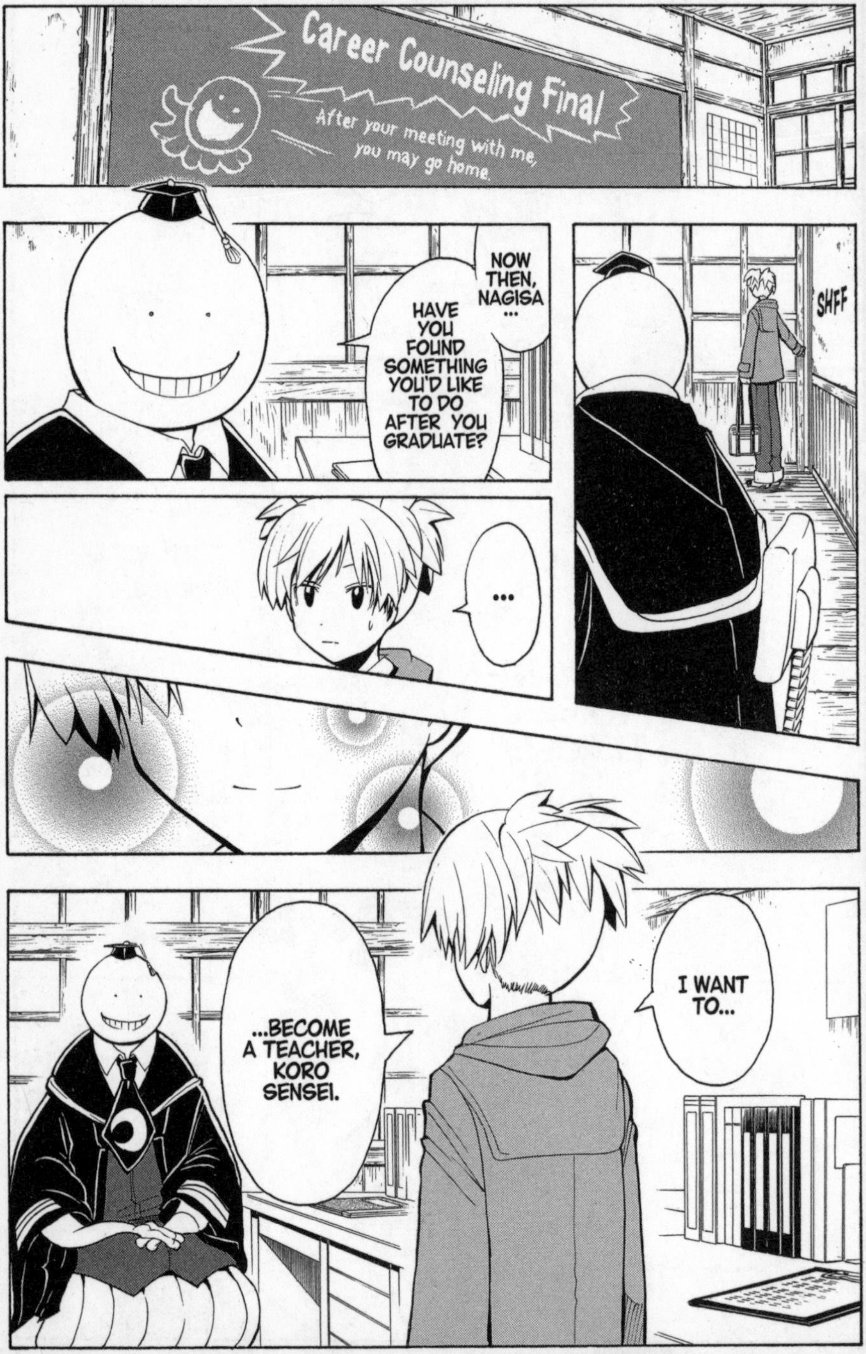
Career Counseling Final
After your meeting with me, you may go home.
SHFF
NOW THEN, NAGISA...
HAVE YOU FOUND SOMETHING YOU'D LIKE TO DO AFTER YOU GRADUATE?
...
I WANT TO...
...BECOME A TEACHER, KORO SENSEI.

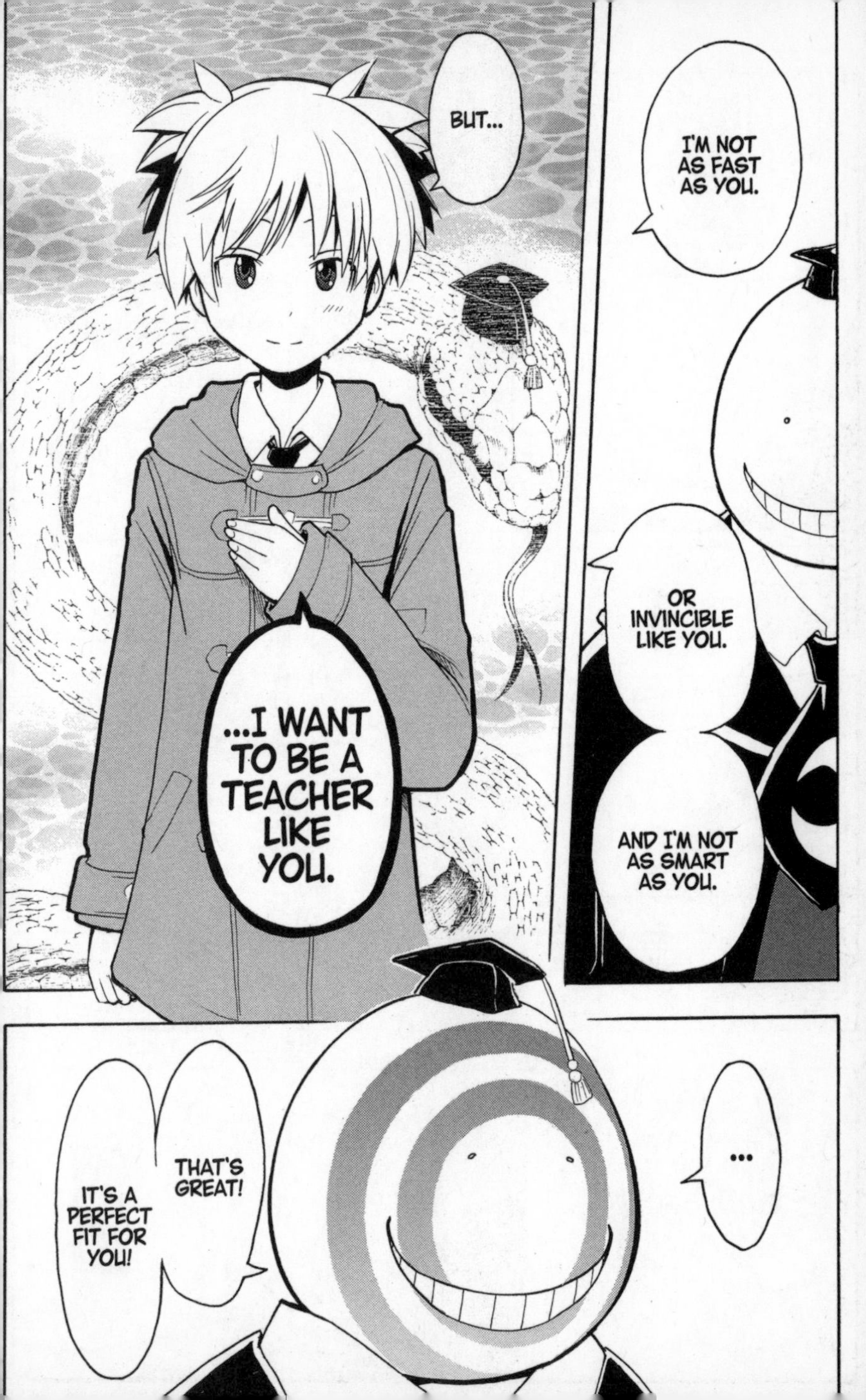
I'M NOT AS FAST AS YOU.
OR INVINCIBLE LIKE YOU.
AND I'M NOT AS SMART AS YOU.
BUT...
...I WANT TO BE A TEACHER LIKE YOU.
...
THAT'S GREAT!
IT'S A PERFECT FIT FOR YOU!

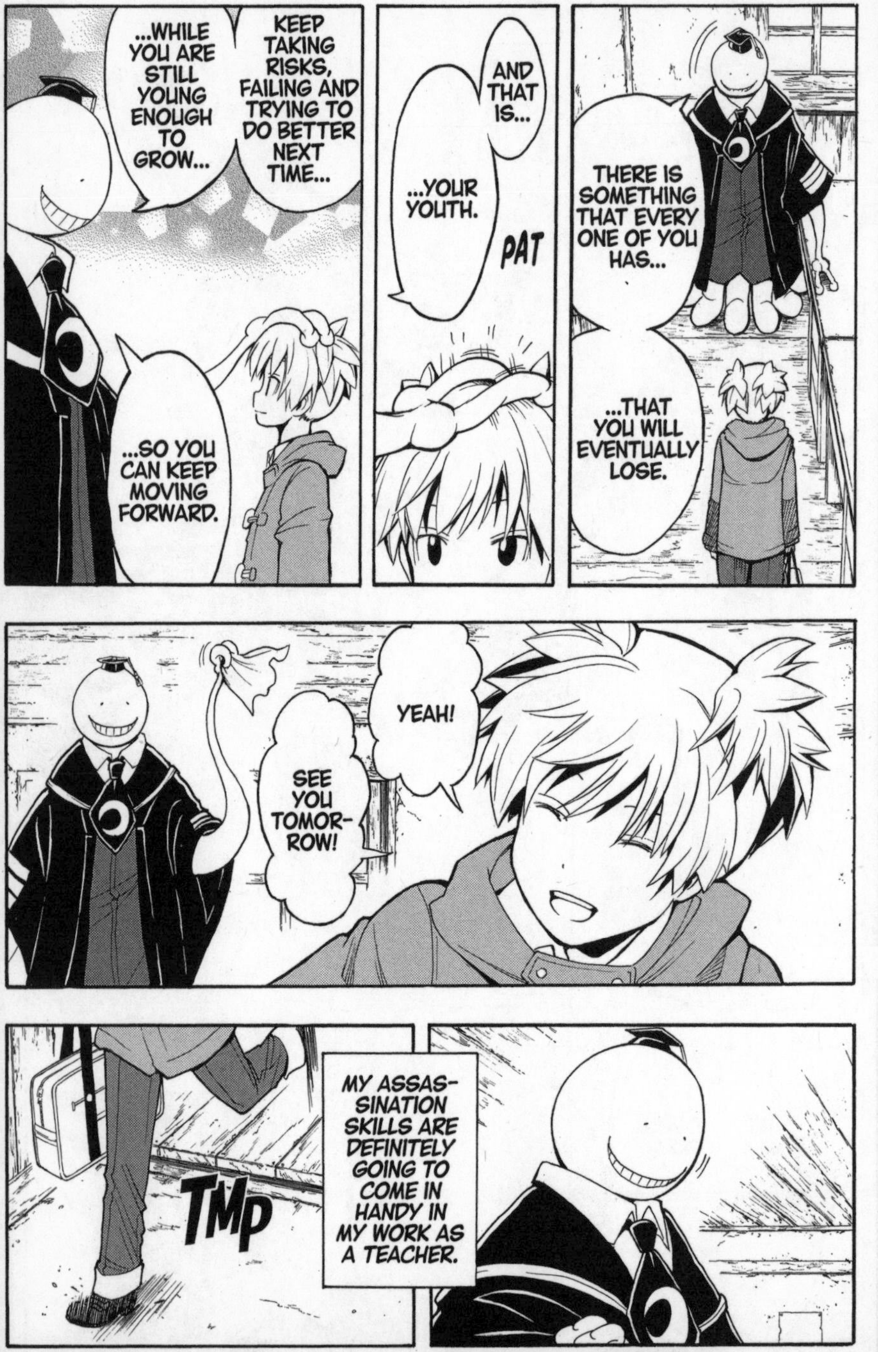
THERE IS SOMETHING THAT EVERY ONE OF YOU HAS...
...THAT YOU WILL EVENTUALLY LOSE.
AND THAT IS...
...YOUR YOUTH.
PAT
KEEP TAKING RISKS, FAILING AND TRYING TO DO BETTER NEXT TIME...
...WHILE YOU ARE STILL YOUNG ENOUGH TO GROW...
...SO YOU CAN KEEP MOVING FORWARD.
YEAH!
SEE YOU TOMOR-ROW!
MY ASSAS-SINATION SKILLS ARE DEFINITELY GOING TO COME IN HANDY IN MY WORK AS A TEACHER.
TMP

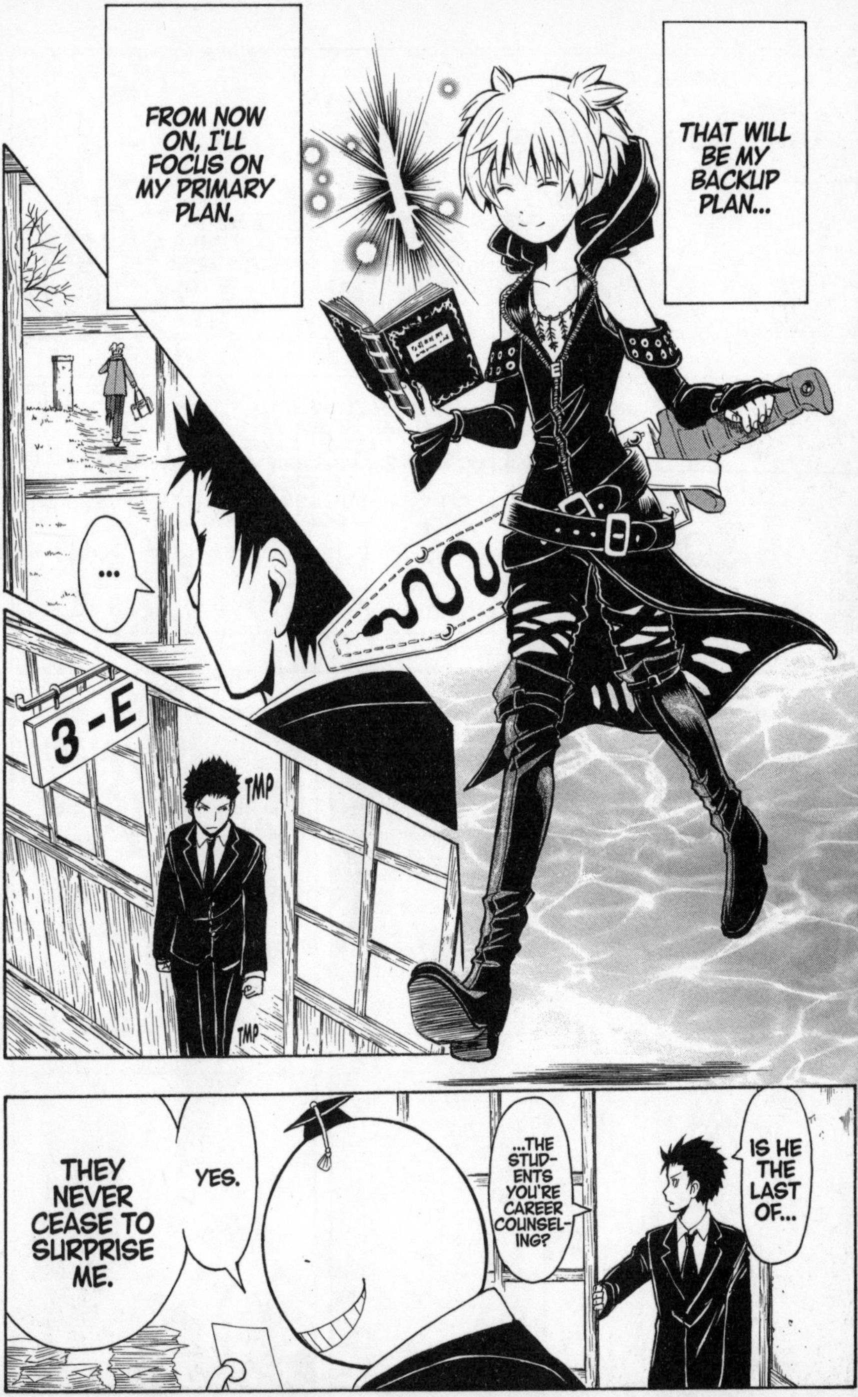
THAT WILL BE MY BACKUP PLAN...
FROM NOW ON, I'LL FOCUS ON MY PRIMARY PLAN.
3-E
...
TMP
TMP
IS HE THE LAST OF...
...THE STUD-ENTS YOU'RE CAREER COUNSEL-ING?
YES.
THEY NEVER CEASE TO SURPRISE ME.

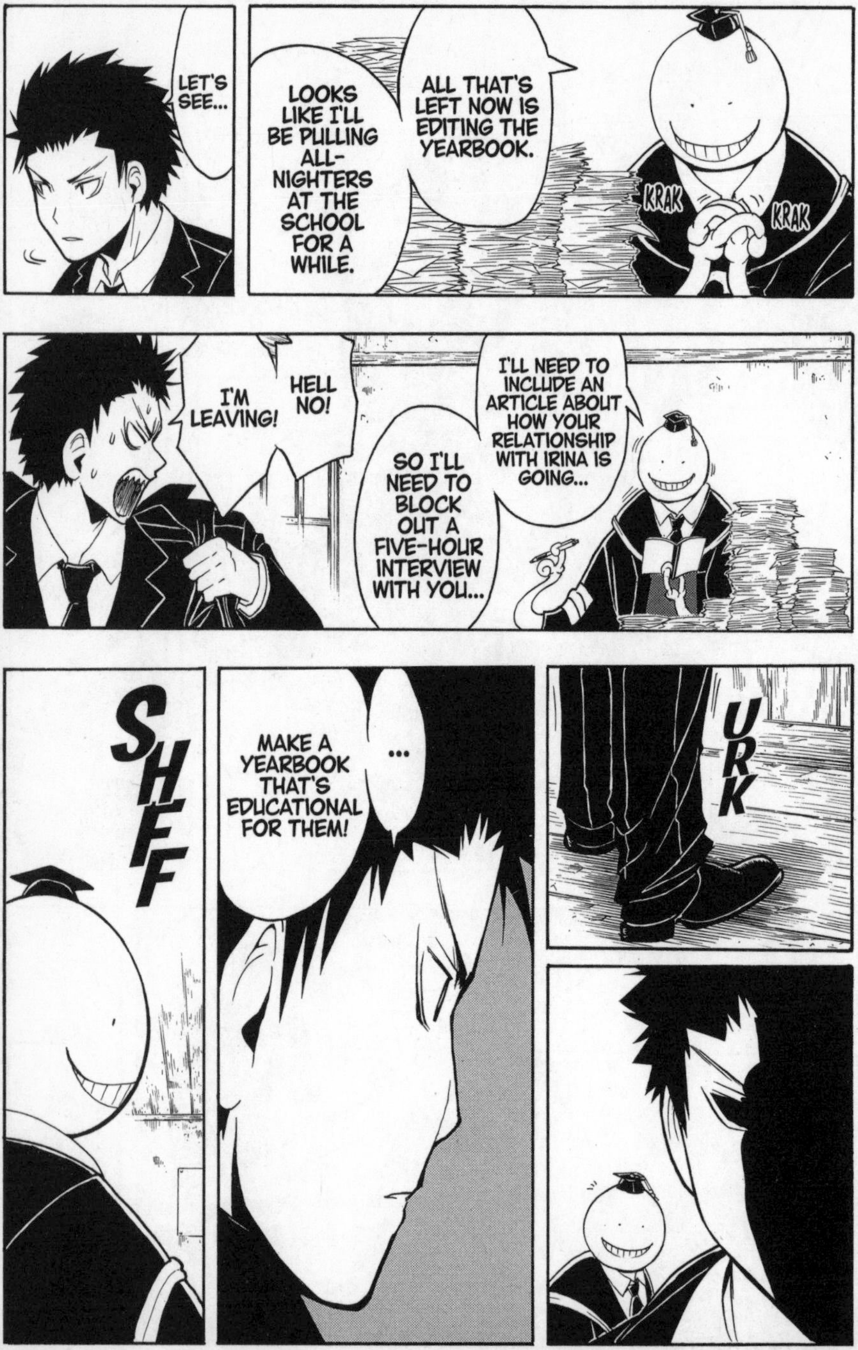
ALL THAT'S LEFT NOW IS EDITING THE YEARBOOK.
KRAK
KRAK
LOOKS LIKE I'LL BE PULLING ALL-NIGHTERS AT THE SCHOOL FOR A WHILE.
LET'S SEE...
I'LL NEED TO INCLUDE AN ARTICLE ABOUT HOW YOUR RELATIONSHIP WITH IRINA IS GOING...
SO I'LL NEED TO BLOCK OUT A FIVE-HOUR INTERVIEW WITH YOU...
HELL NO!
I'M LEAVING!
URK
...
MAKE A YEARBOOK THAT'S EDUCATIONAL FOR THEM!
SHFF

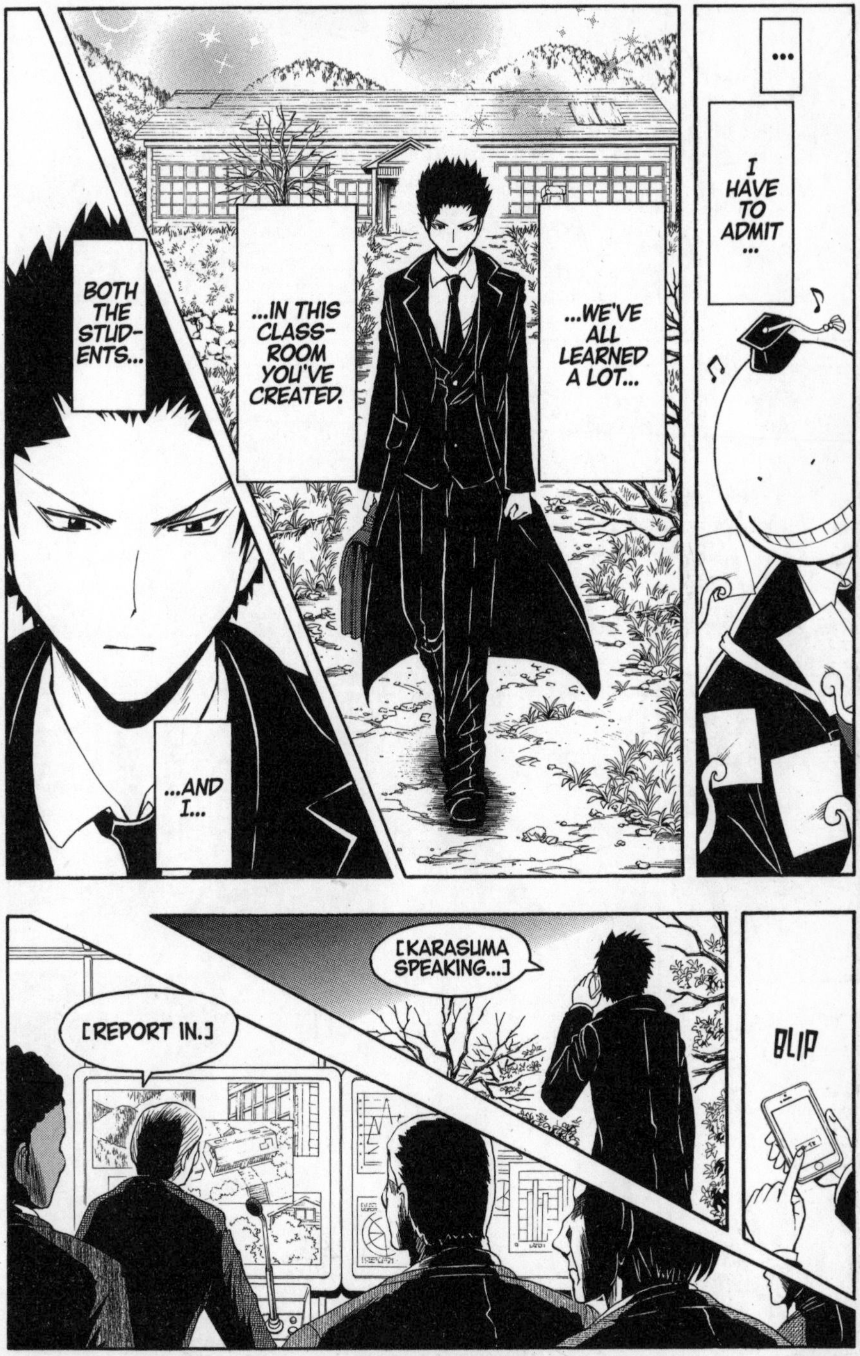
...
I HAVE TO ADMIT...
...WE'VE ALL LEARNED A LOT...
...IN THIS CLASSROOM YOU'VE CREATED.
BOTH THE STUDENTS...
...AND I...
BLIP
[KARASUMA SPEAKING...]
[REPORT IN.]

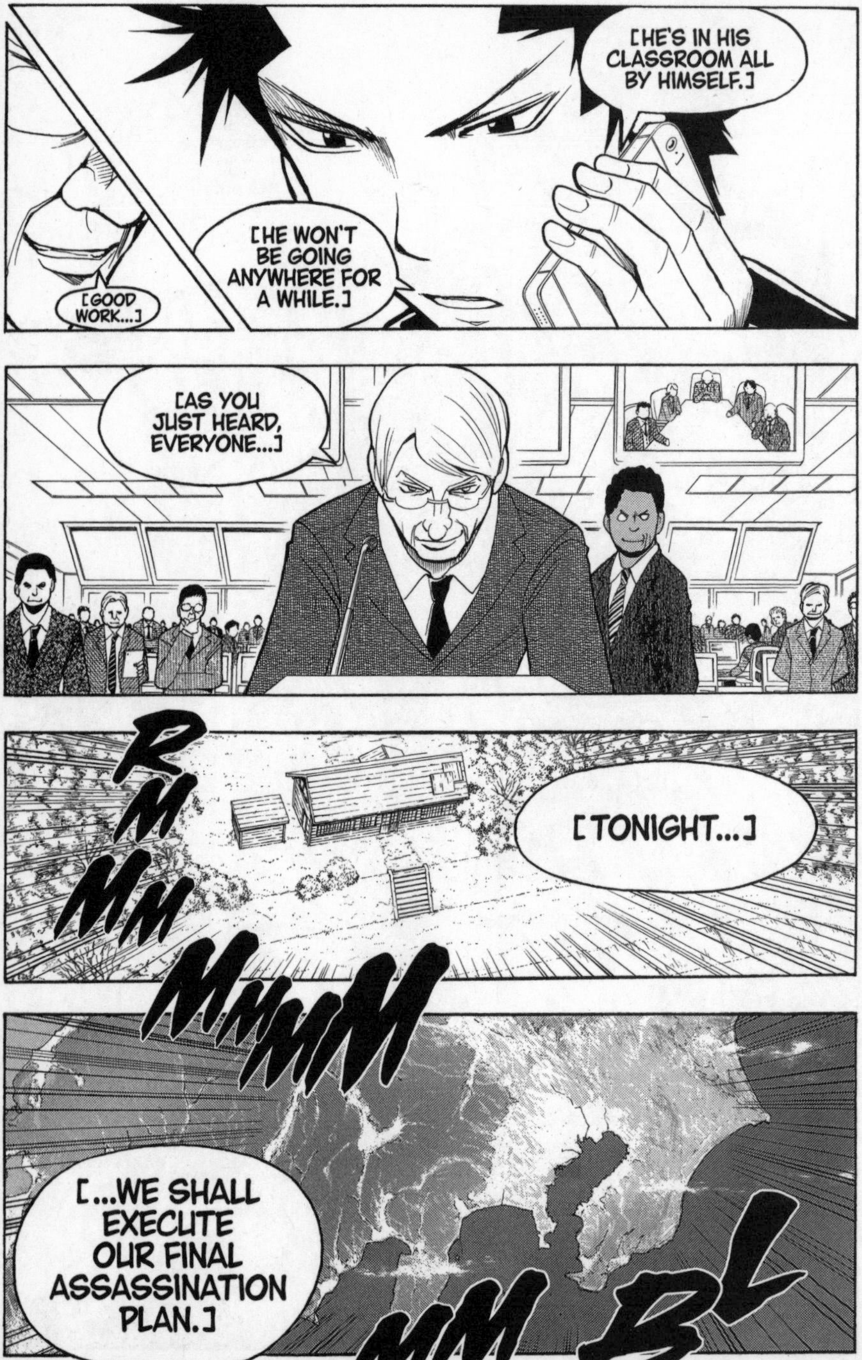
[HE'S IN HIS CLASSROOM ALL BY HIMSELF.]
[HE WON'T BE GOING ANYWHERE FOR A WHILE.]
[GOOD WORK...]
[AS YOU JUST HEARD, EVERYONE...]
[TONIGHT...]
[...WE SHALL EXECUTE OUR FINAL ASSASSINATION PLAN.]

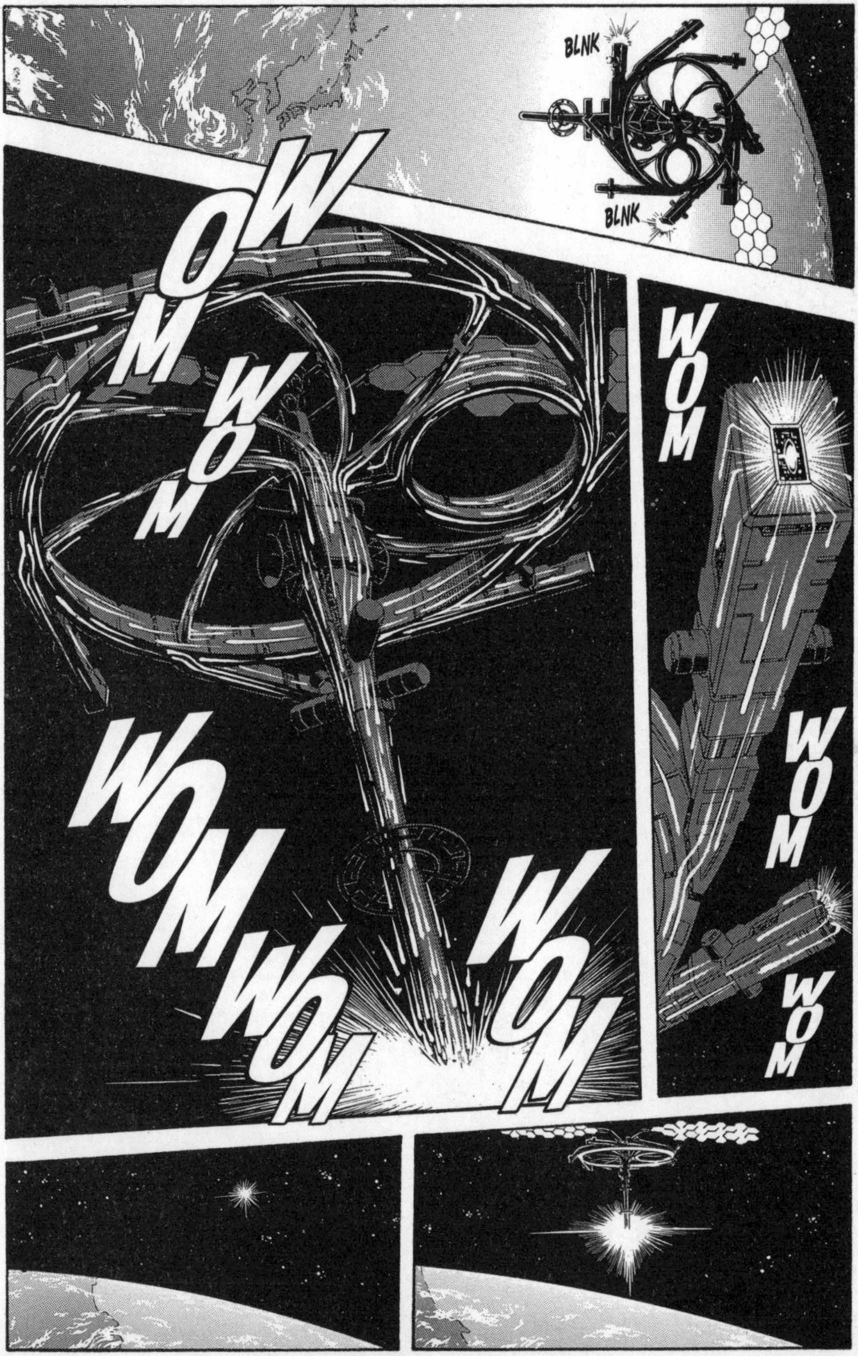
BLNK
BLNK
WOM
WOM
WOM
WOM
WOM
WOM
WOM
WOMWOMWOM

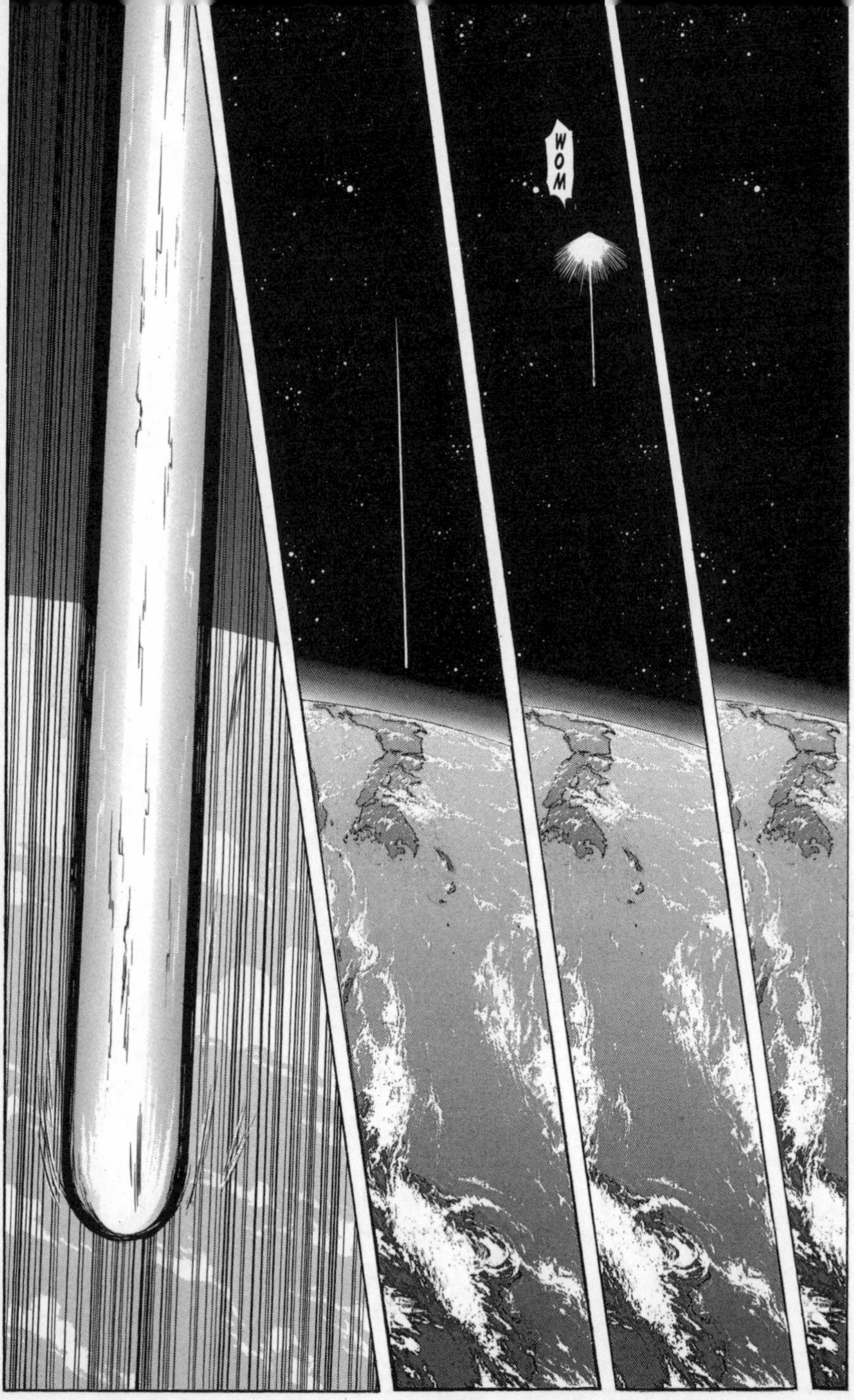
WOM

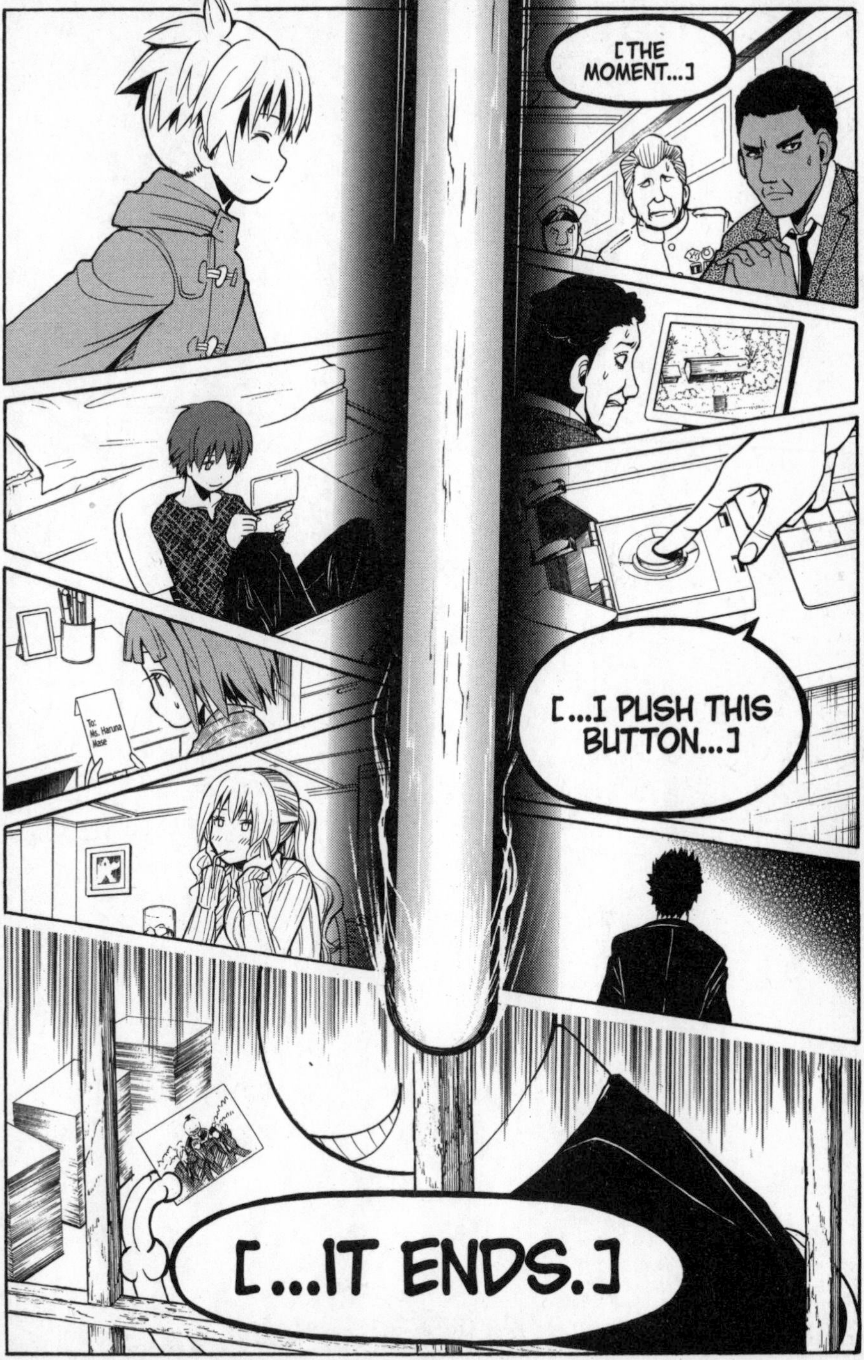
[THE MOMENT...]
To: Ms. Haruna Mase
[...I PUSH THIS BUTTON...]
[...IT ENDS.]

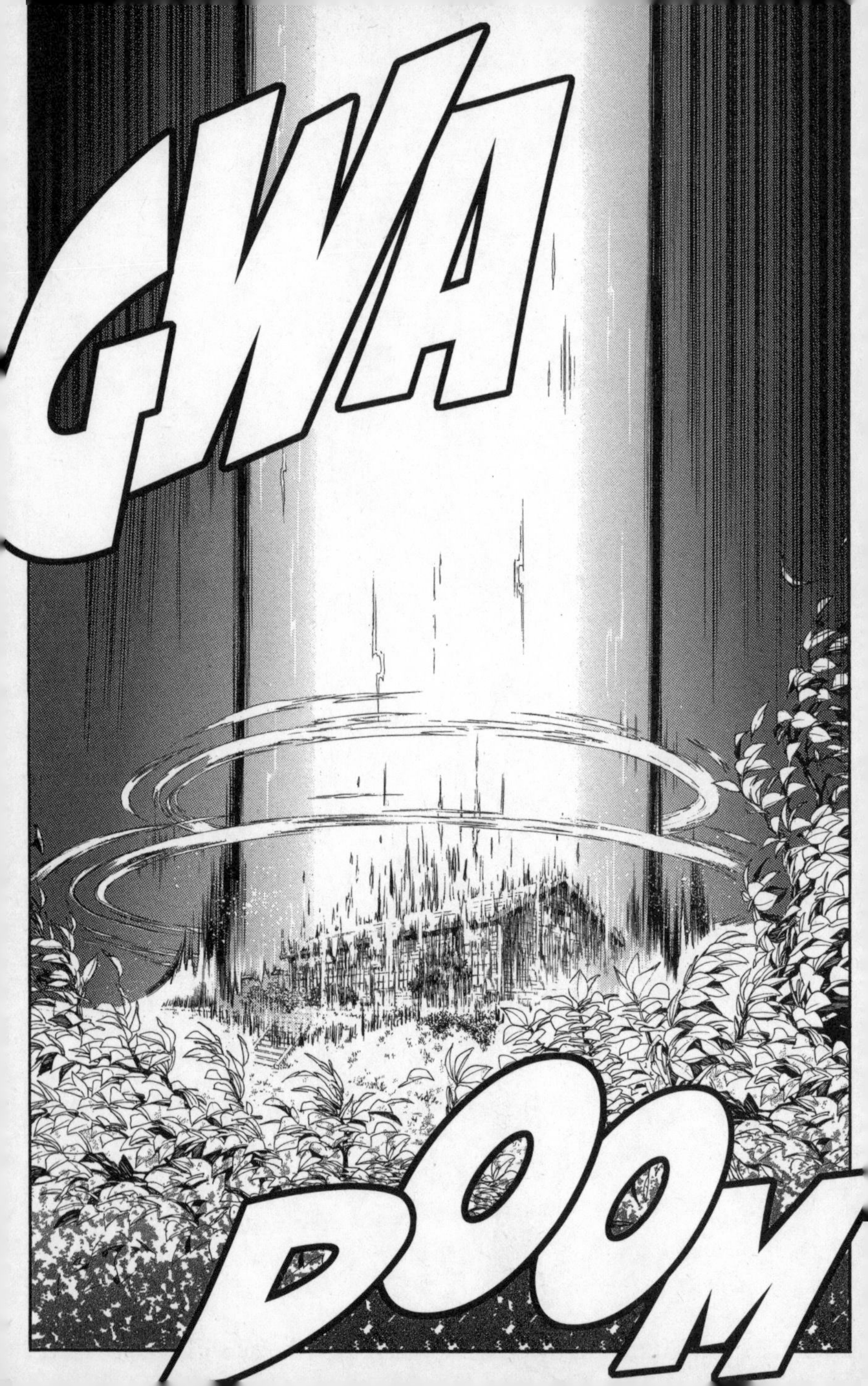
GWA
DOOM

—ASSASSINATION CLASSROOM
FINAL CHAPTER—

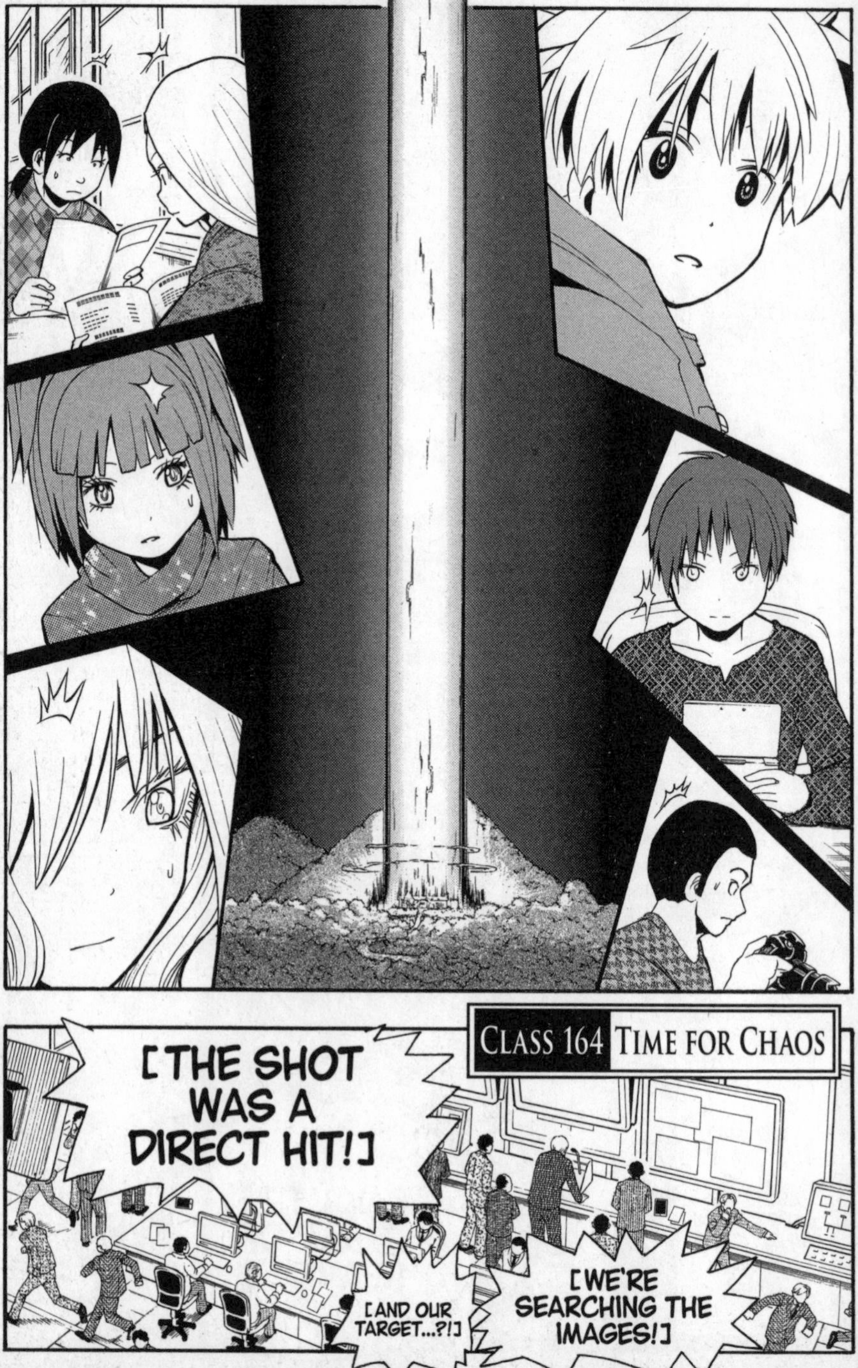
CLASS 164 TIME FOR CHAOS
[THE SHOT WAS A DIRECT HIT!]
[AND OUR TARGET...?!]
[WE'RE SEARCHING THE IMAGES!]

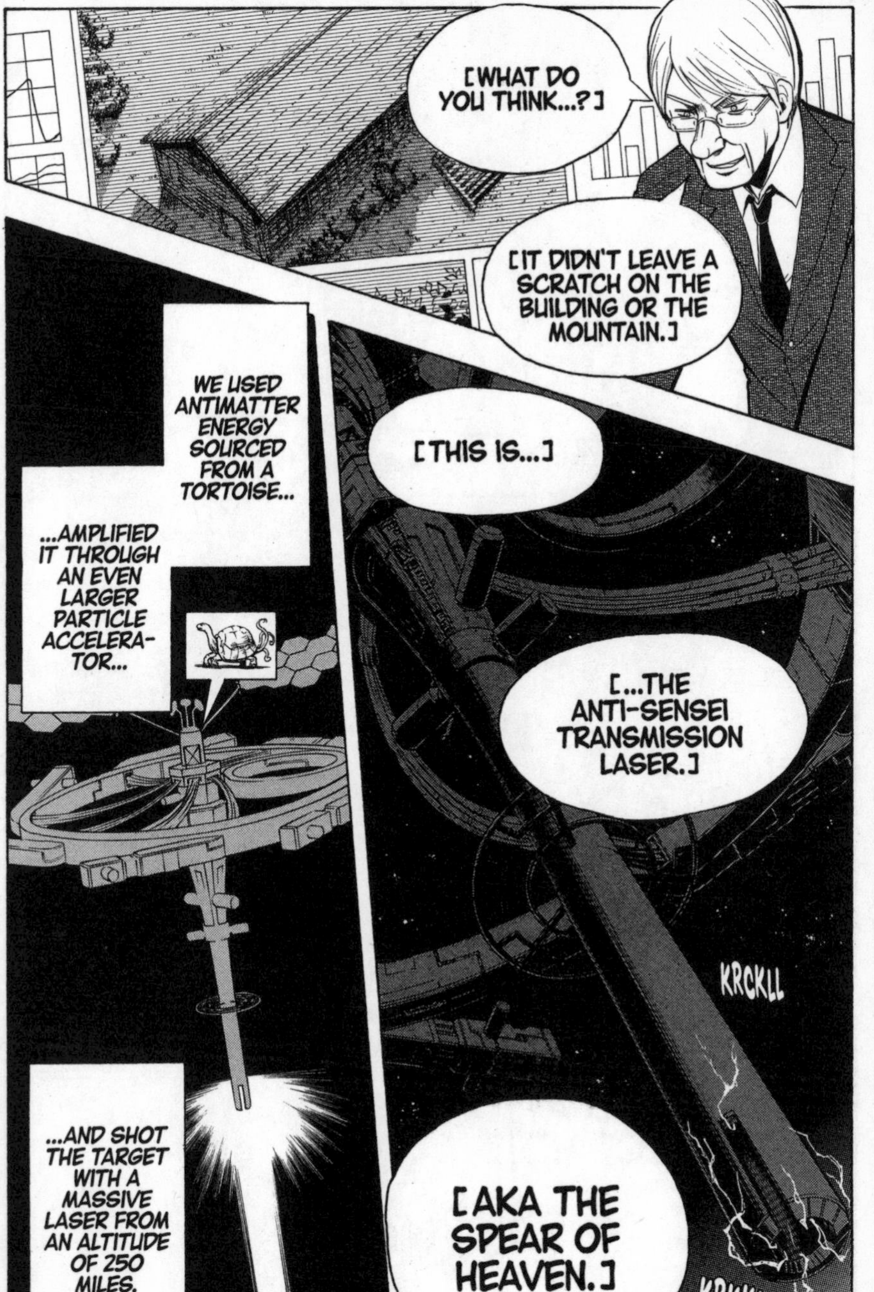
[WHAT DO YOU THINK...?]
[IT DIDN'T LEAVE A SCRATCH ON THE BUILDING OR THE MOUNTAIN.]
[THIS IS...]
[...THE ANTI-SENSEI TRANSMISSION LASER.]
KRCKLL
[AKA THE SPEAR OF HEAVEN.]
KRKKL
WE USED ANTIMATTER ENERGY SOURCED FROM A TORTOISE...
...AMPLIFIED IT THROUGH AN EVEN LARGER PARTICLE ACCELERA-TOR...
...AND SHOT THE TARGET WITH A MASSIVE LASER FROM AN ALTITUDE OF 250 MILES.

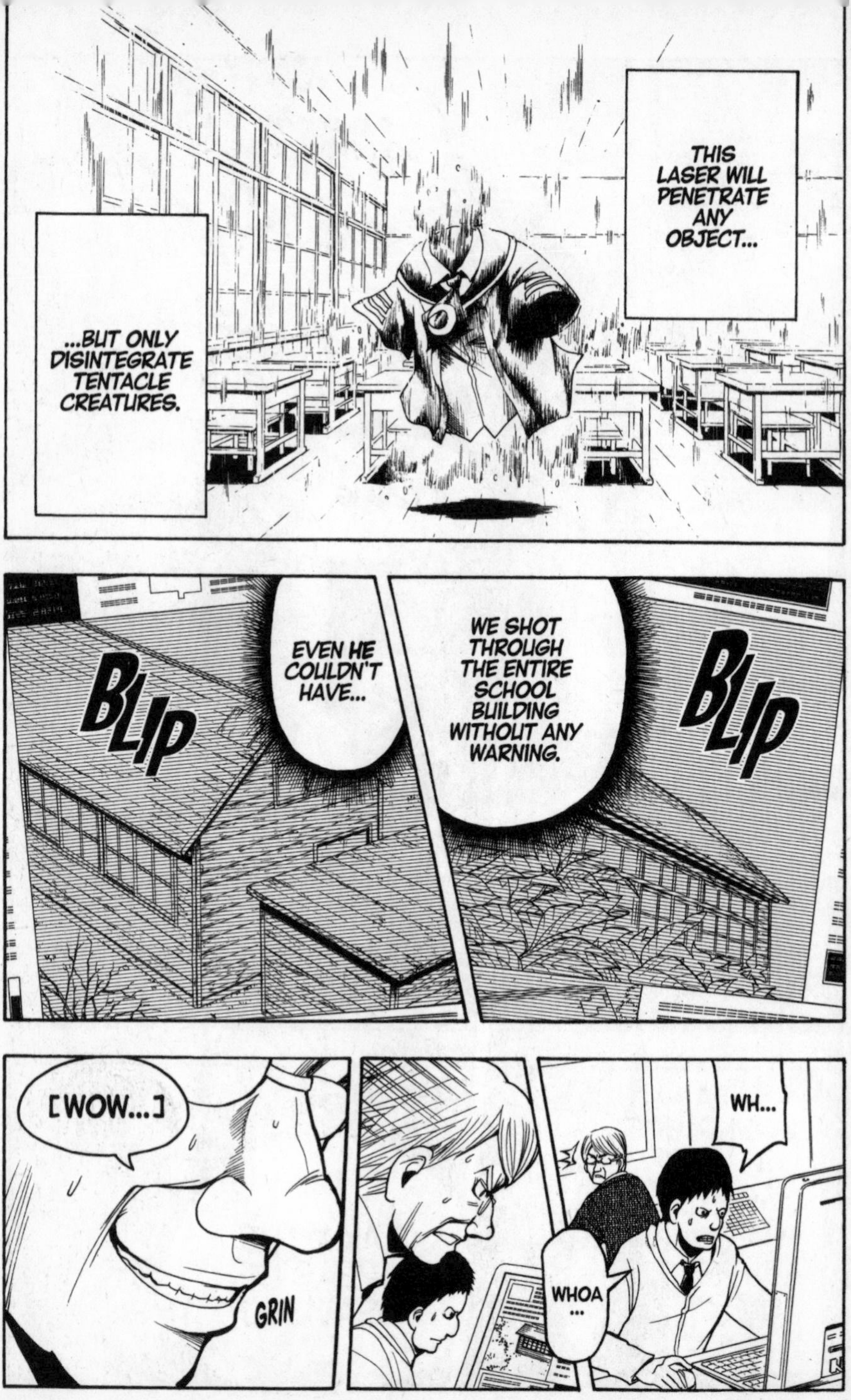
THIS LASER WILL PENETRATE ANY OBJECT...
...BUT ONLY DISINTEGRATE TENTACLE CREATURES.
BLIP
WE SHOT THROUGH THE ENTIRE SCHOOL BUILDING WITHOUT ANY WARNING.
EVEN HE COULDN'T HAVE...
BLIP
WH...
WHOA ...
[WOW...]
GRIN

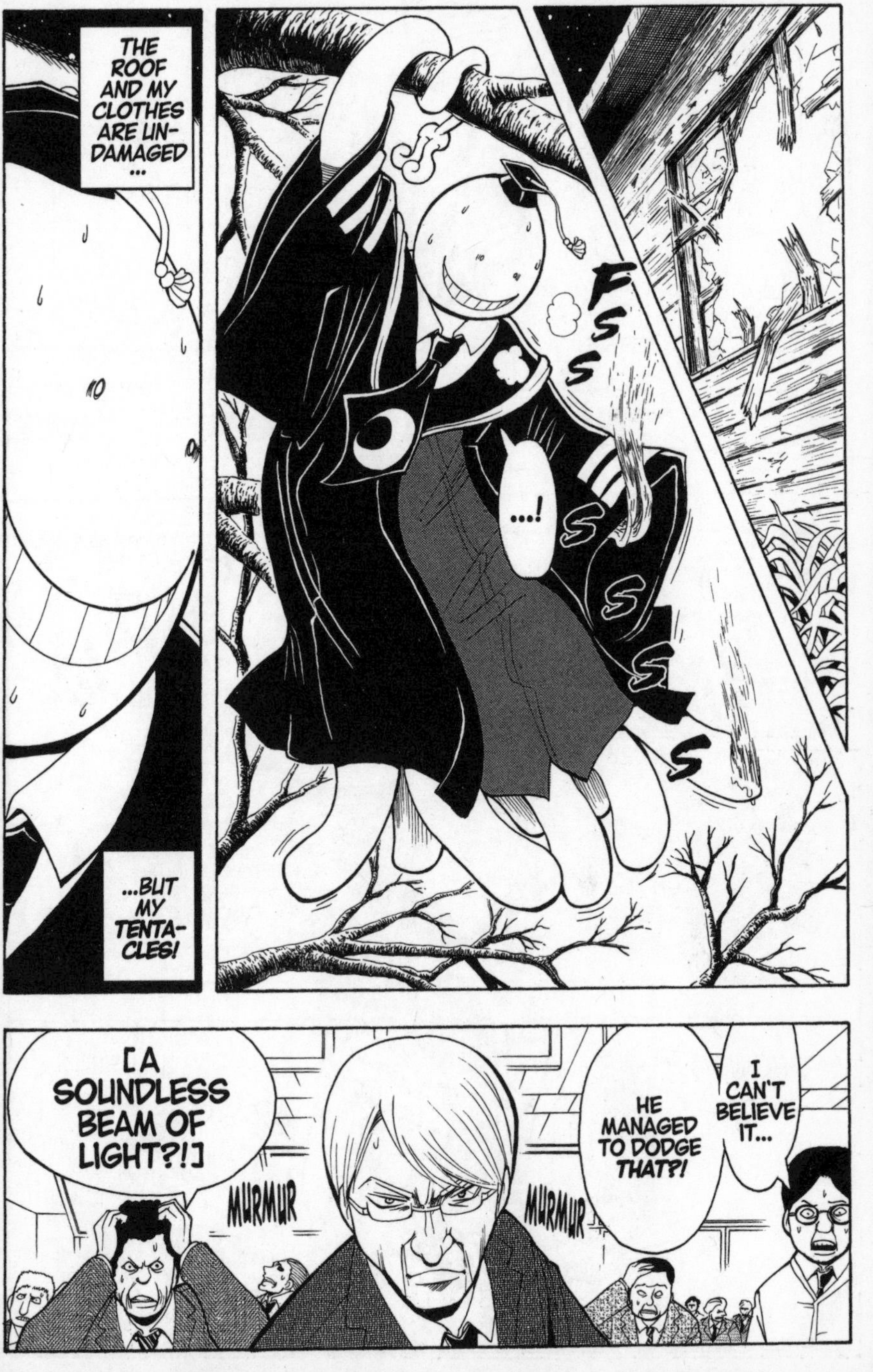
FSSS
...!
SSSSS
THE ROOF AND MY CLOTHES ARE UN-DAMAGED ...
...BUT MY TENTA-CLES!
I CAN'T BELIEVE IT...
HE MANAGED TO DODGE *THAT*?!
MURMUR
MURMUR
[A SOUNDLESS BEAM OF LIGHT?!]

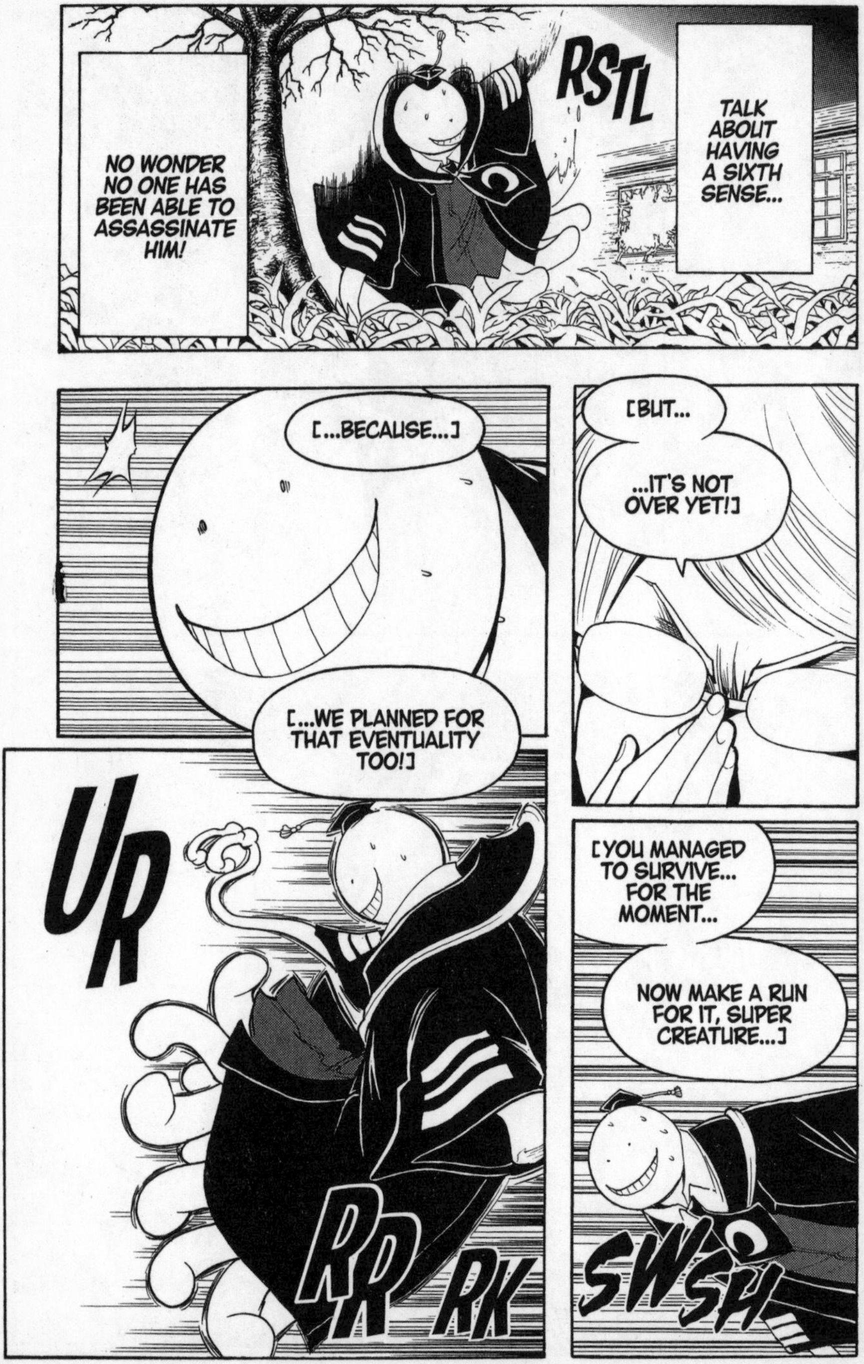
TALK ABOUT HAVING A SIXTH SENSE...
RSTL
NO WONDER NO ONE HAS BEEN ABLE TO ASSASSINATE HIM!
[BUT...
...IT'S NOT OVER YET!]
[...BECAUSE...]
[...WE PLANNED FOR THAT EVENTUALITY TOO!]
[YOU MANAGED TO SURVIVE... FOR THE MOMENT...
NOW MAKE A RUN FOR IT, SUPER CREATURE...]
SWSH
UR
RRRK

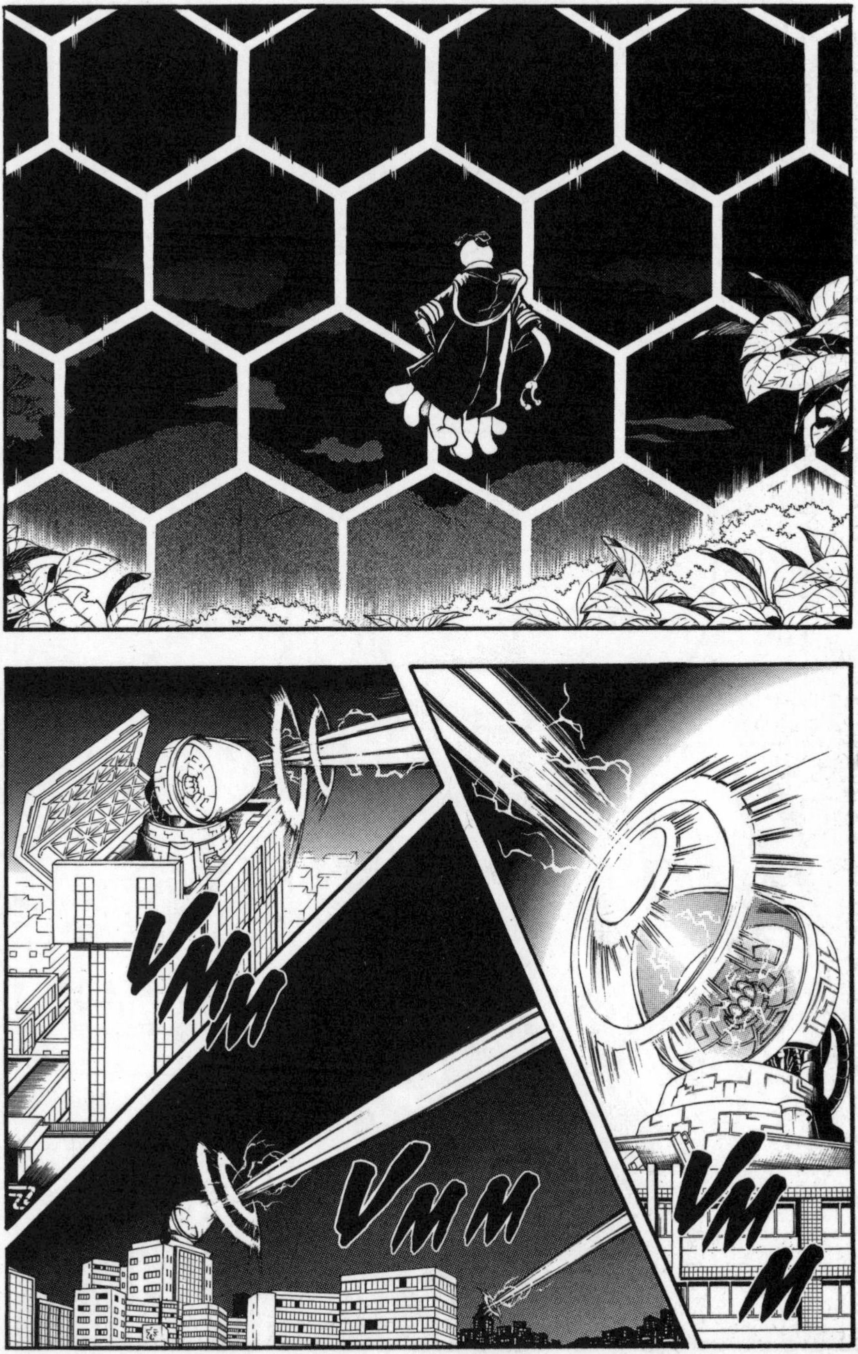
VMM
VMM
VMM

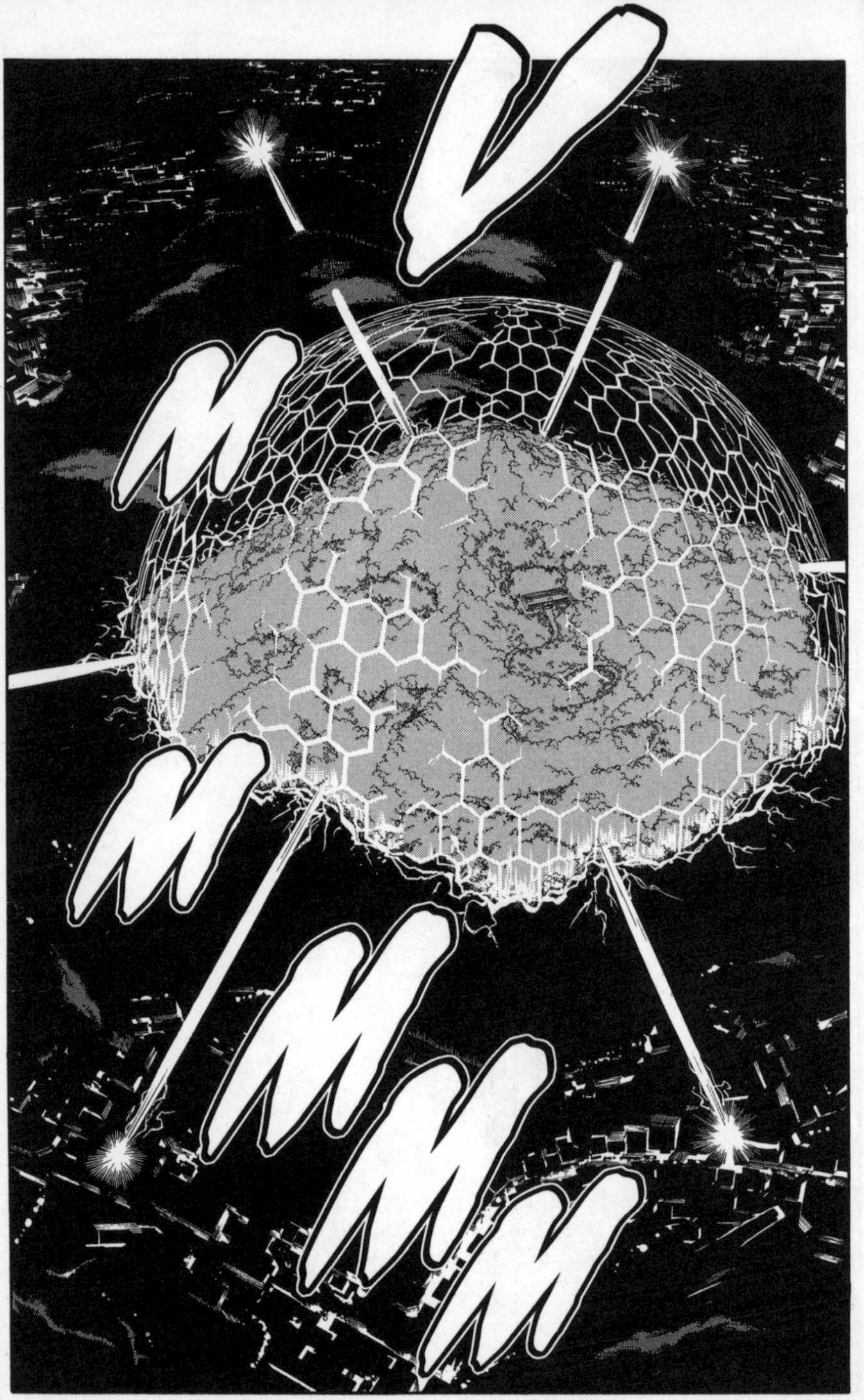
VMMMMM

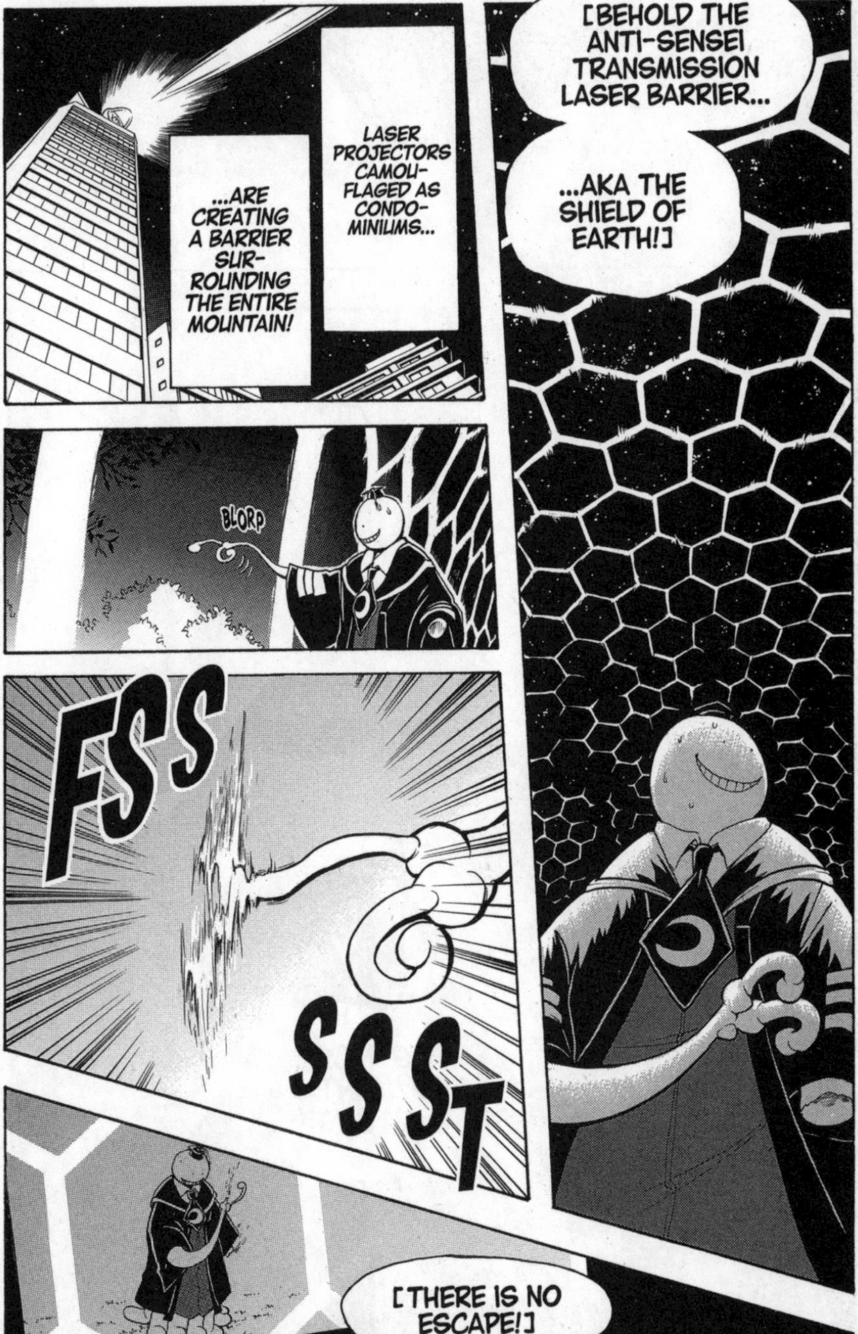
[BEHOLD THE ANTI-SENSEI TRANSMISSION LASER BARRIER...
...AKA THE SHIELD OF EARTH!]
LASER PROJECTORS CAMOU-FLAGED AS CONDO-MINIUMS...
...ARE CREATING A BARRIER SUR-ROUNDING THE ENTIRE MOUNTAIN!
BLORP
FSS
SSST
[THERE IS NO ESCAPE!]

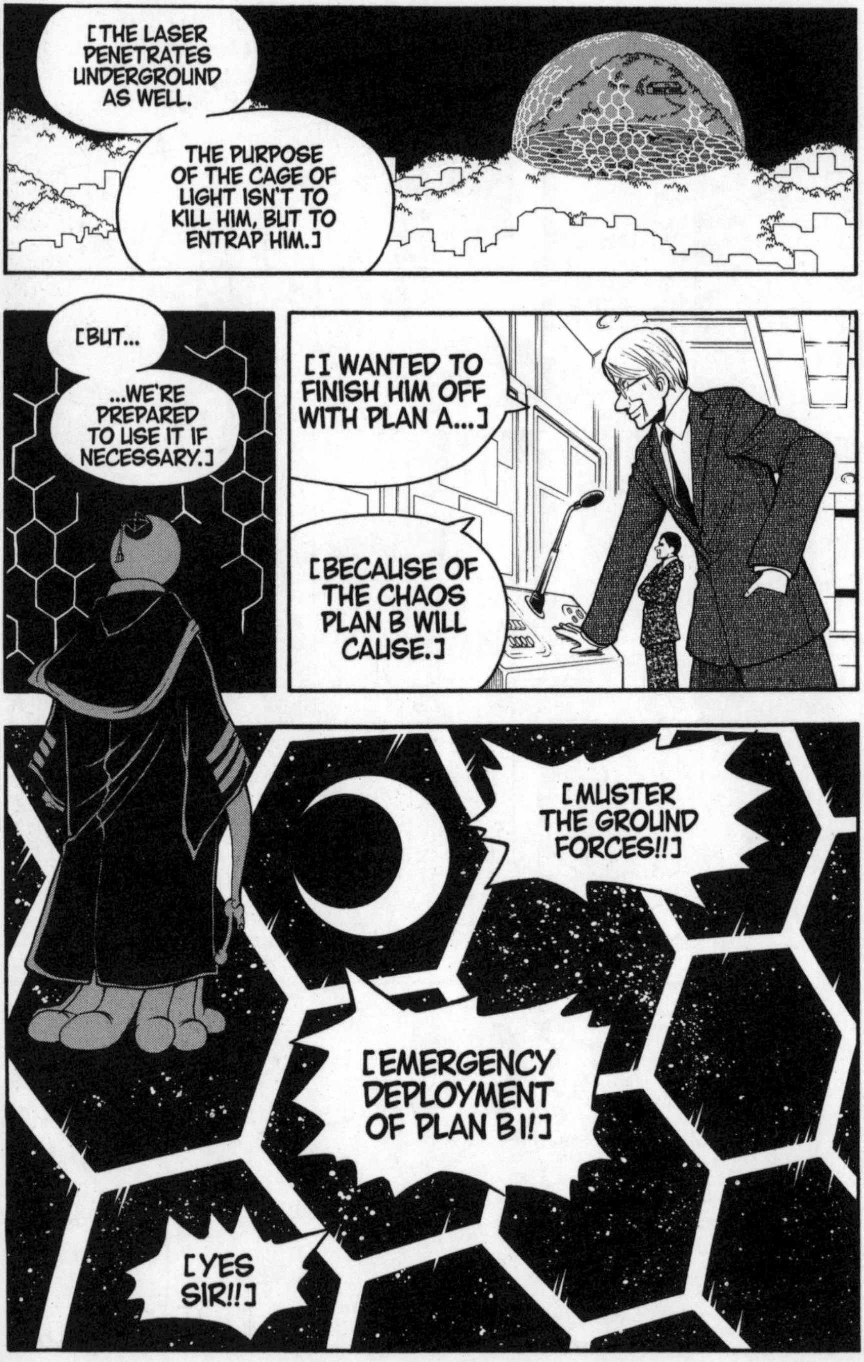
[THE LASER PENETRATES UNDERGROUND AS WELL.
THE PURPOSE OF THE CAGE OF LIGHT ISN'T TO KILL HIM, BUT TO ENTRAP HIM.]
[I WANTED TO FINISH HIM OFF WITH PLAN A...]
[BECAUSE OF THE CHAOS PLAN B WILL CAUSE.]
[BUT...
...WE'RE PREPARED TO USE IT IF NECESSARY.]
[MUSTER THE GROUND FORCES!!]
[EMERGENCY DEPLOYMENT OF PLAN B!!]
[YES SIR!!]

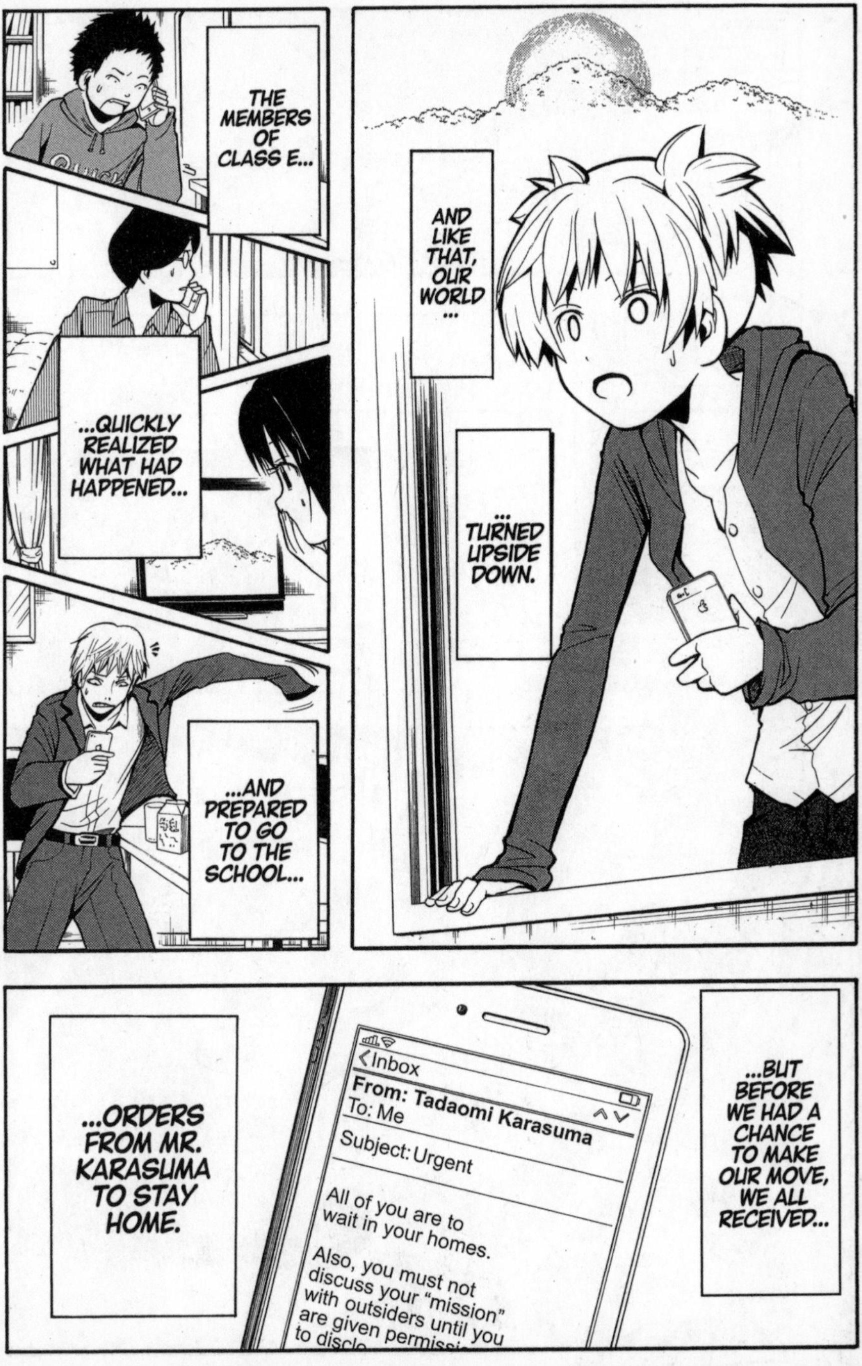
AND LIKE THAT, OUR WORLD...
...TURNED UPSIDE DOWN.
THE MEMBERS OF CLASS E...
...QUICKLY REALIZED WHAT HAD HAPPENED...
...AND PREPARED TO GO TO THE SCHOOL...
...BUT BEFORE WE HAD A CHANCE TO MAKE OUR MOVE, WE ALL RECEIVED...
Inbox
From: Tadaomi Karasuma
To: Me
Subject: Urgent
All of you are to wait in your homes.
Also, you must not discuss your "mission" with outsiders until you are given
...ORDERS FROM MR. KARASUMA TO STAY HOME.

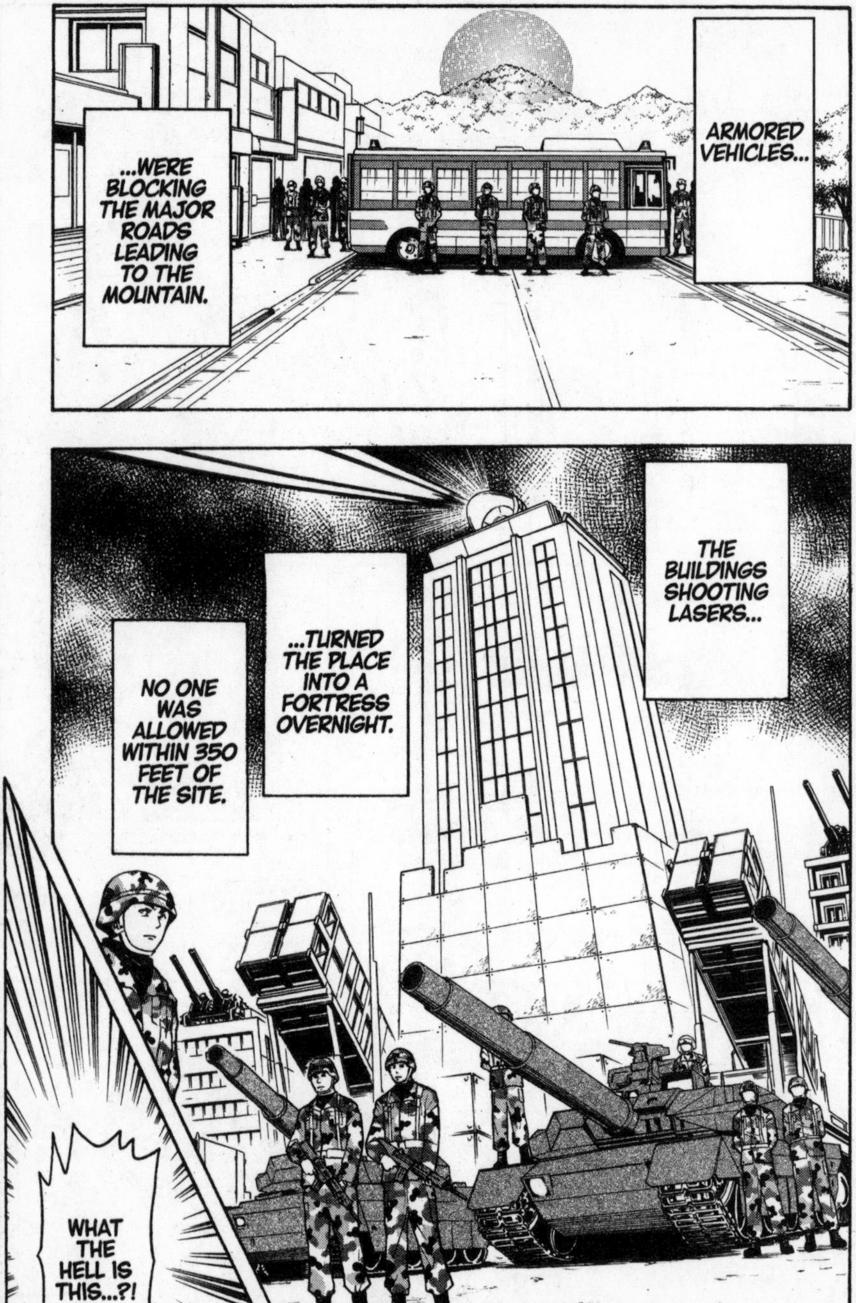
ARMORED VEHICLES...
...WERE BLOCKING THE MAJOR ROADS LEADING TO THE MOUNTAIN.
THE BUILDINGS SHOOTING LASERS...
...TURNED THE PLACE INTO A FORTRESS OVERNIGHT.
NO ONE WAS ALLOWED WITHIN 350 FEET OF THE SITE.
WHAT THE HELL IS THIS...?!

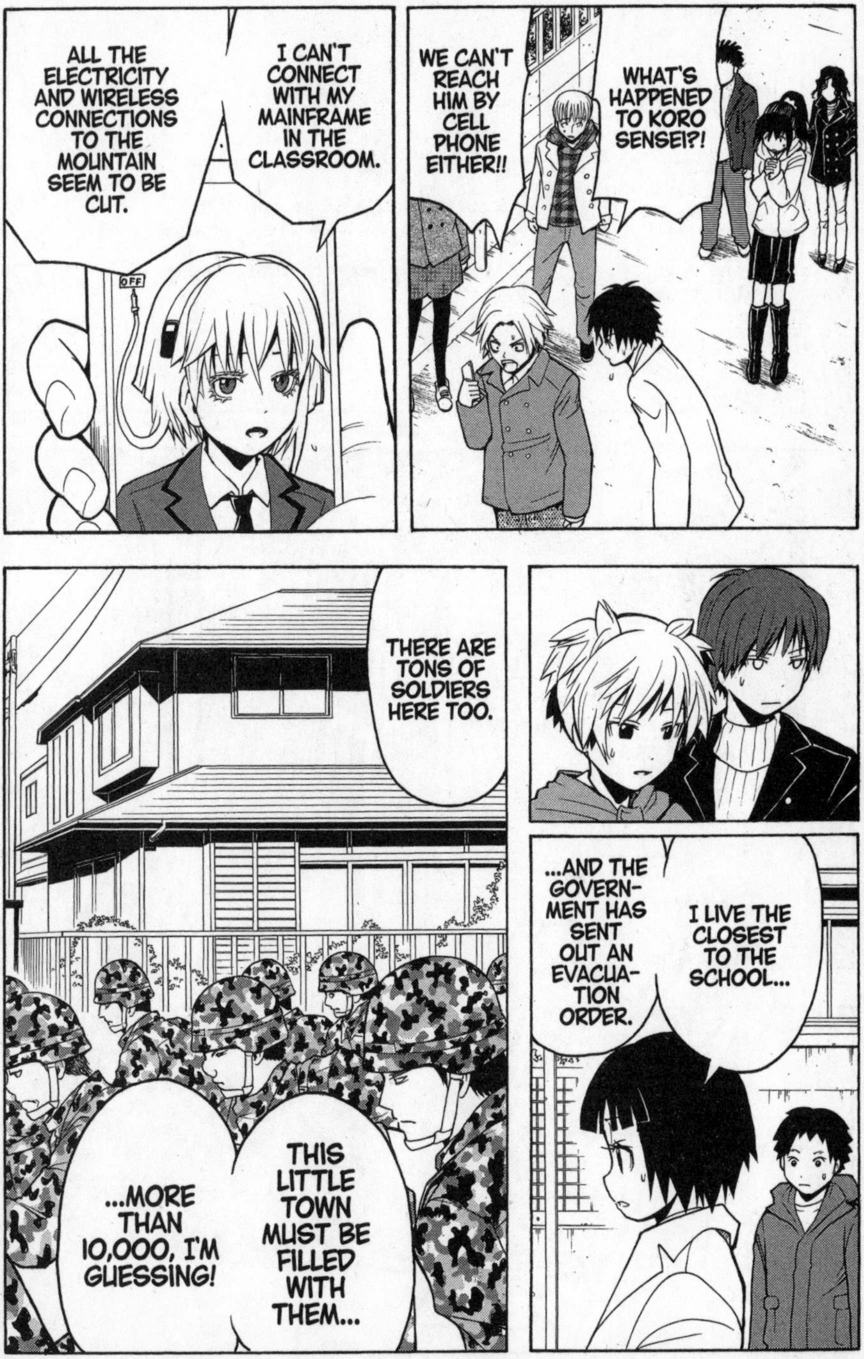
WHAT'S HAPPENED TO KORO SENSEI?!
WE CAN'T REACH HIM BY CELL PHONE EITHER!!
I CAN'T CONNECT WITH MY MAINFRAME IN THE CLASSROOM.
ALL THE ELECTRICITY AND WIRELESS CONNECTIONS TO THE MOUNTAIN SEEM TO BE CUT.
OFF
I LIVE THE CLOSEST TO THE SCHOOL...
...AND THE GOVERNMENT HAS SENT OUT AN EVACUATION ORDER.
THERE ARE TONS OF SOLDIERS HERE TOO.
THIS LITTLE TOWN MUST BE FILLED WITH THEM...
...MORE THAN 10,000, I'M GUESSING!

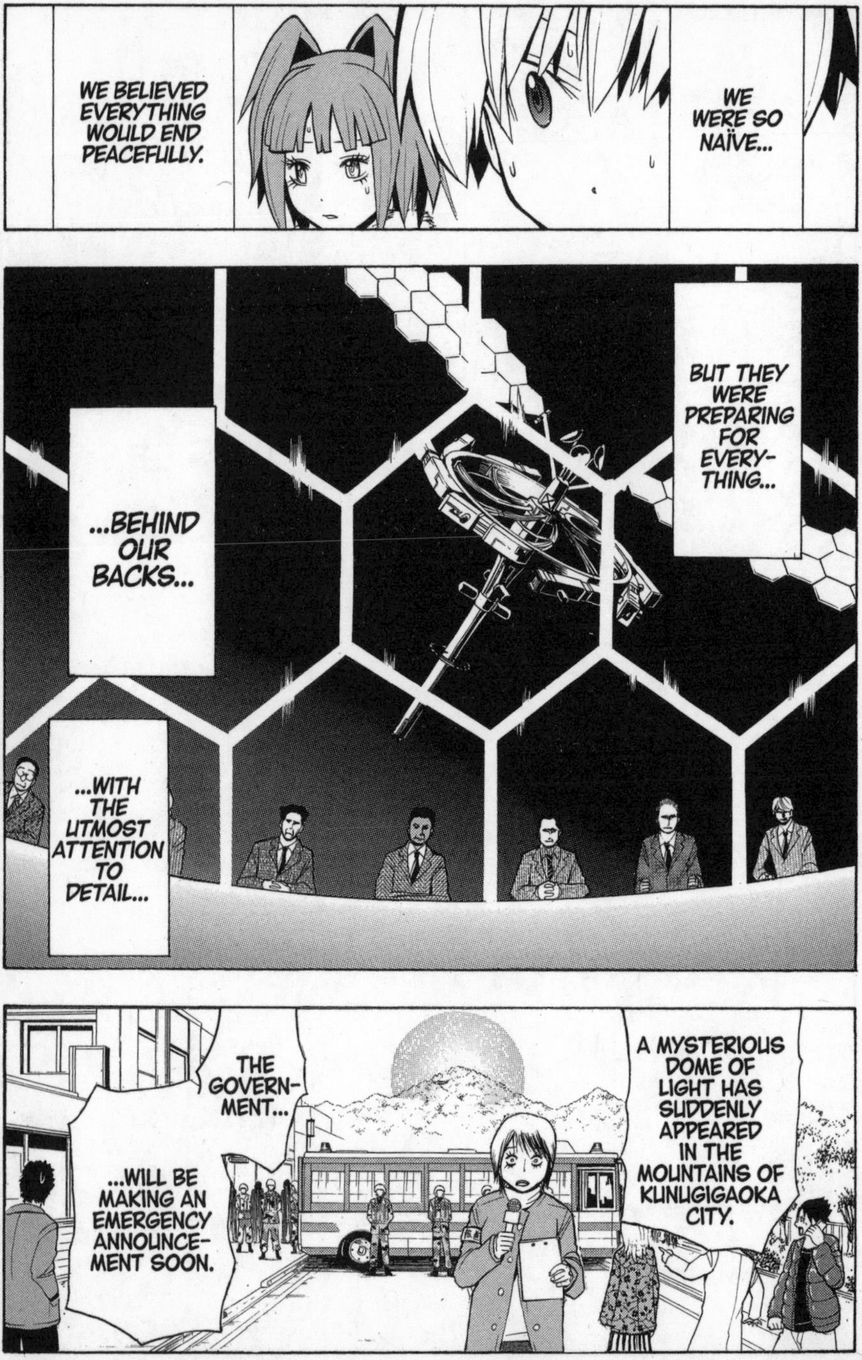
WE WERE SO NAÏVE...
WE BELIEVED EVERYTHING WOULD END PEACEFULLY.
BUT THEY WERE PREPARING FOR EVERYTHING...
...BEHIND OUR BACKS...
...WITH THE UTMOST ATTENTION TO DETAIL...
A MYSTERIOUS DOME OF LIGHT HAS SUDDENLY APPEARED IN THE MOUNTAINS OF KUNUGIGAOKA CITY.
THE GOVERNMENT...
...WILL BE MAKING AN EMERGENCY ANNOUNCEMENT SOON.

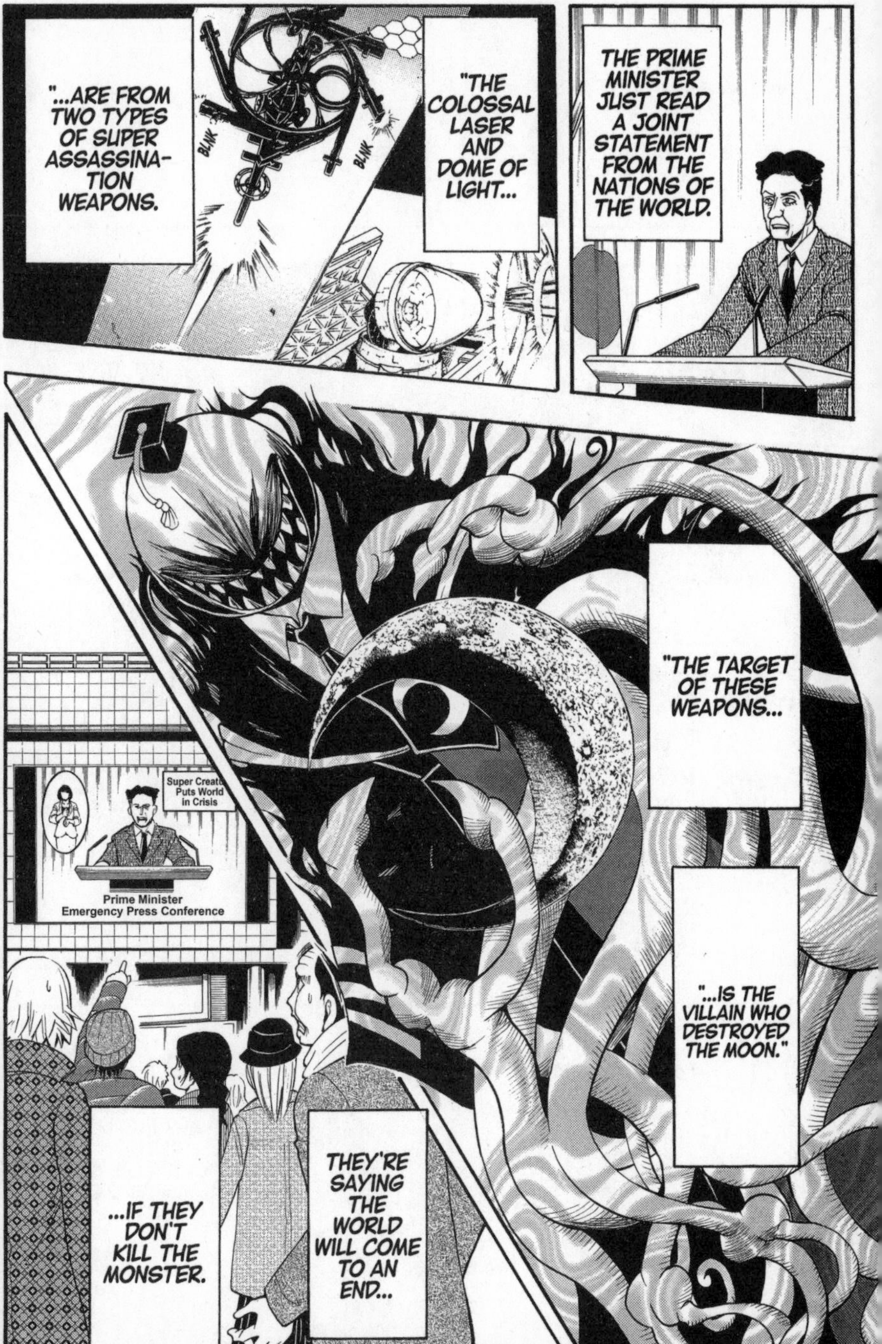
THE PRIME MINISTER JUST READ A JOINT STATEMENT FROM THE NATIONS OF THE WORLD.
"THE COLOSSAL LASER AND DOME OF LIGHT...
BLINK
BLINK
"...ARE FROM TWO TYPES OF SUPER ASSASSINATION WEAPONS.
"THE TARGET OF THESE WEAPONS...
"...IS THE VILLAIN WHO DESTROYED THE MOON."
Super Creat
Puts World in Crisis
Prime Minister Emergency Press Conference
THEY'RE SAYING THE WORLD WILL COME TO AN END...
...IF THEY DON'T KILL THE MONSTER.

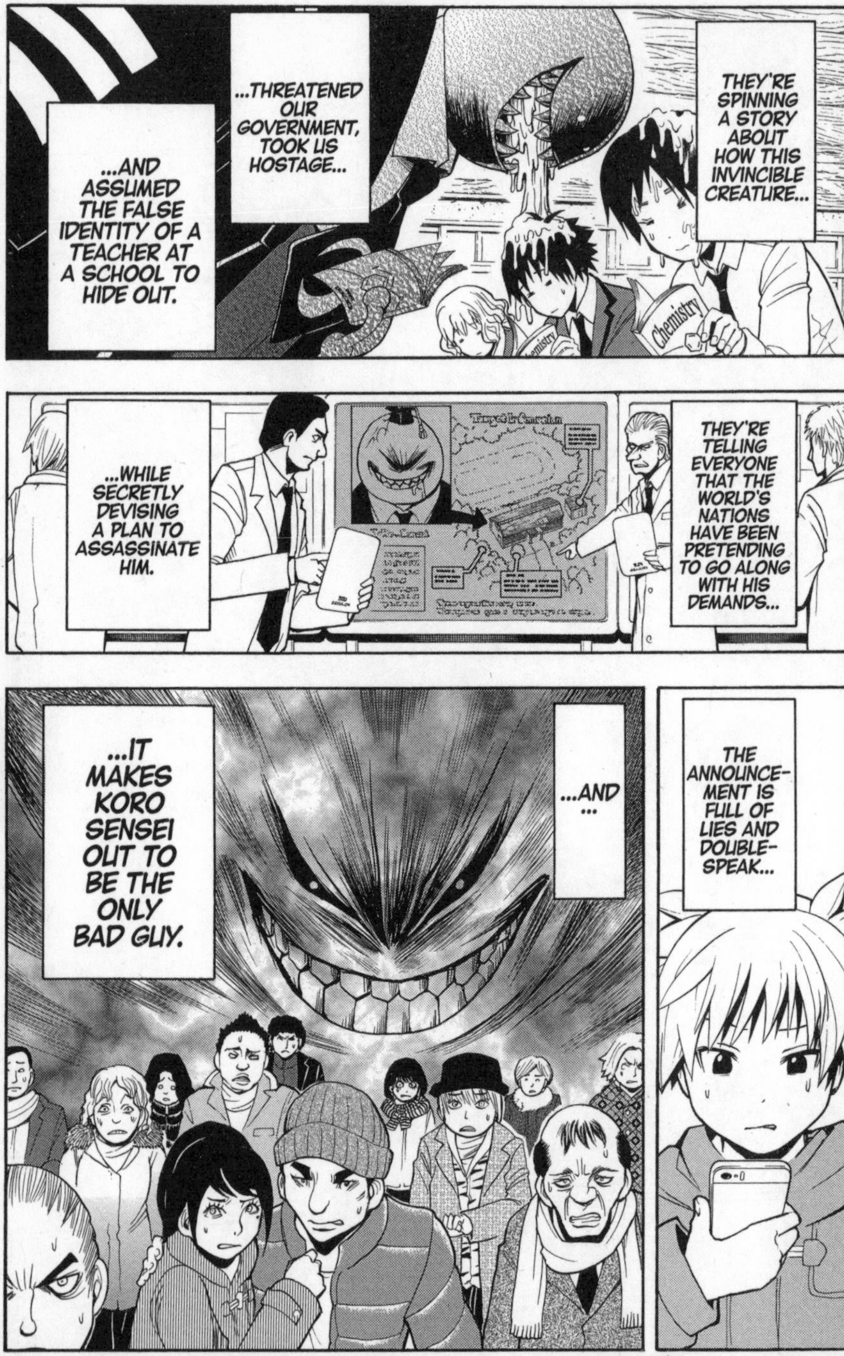
THEY'RE SPINNING A STORY ABOUT HOW THIS INVINCIBLE CREATURE...
Chemistry
...THREATENED OUR GOVERNMENT, TOOK US HOSTAGE...
...AND ASSUMED THE FALSE IDENTITY OF A TEACHER AT A SCHOOL TO HIDE OUT.
THEY'RE TELLING EVERYONE THAT THE WORLD'S NATIONS HAVE BEEN PRETENDING TO GO ALONG WITH HIS DEMANDS...
...WHILE SECRETLY DEVISING A PLAN TO ASSASSINATE HIM.
THE ANNOUNCEMENT IS FULL OF LIES AND DOUBLE-SPEAK...
...AND ...
...IT MAKES KORO SENSEI OUT TO BE THE ONLY BAD GUY.

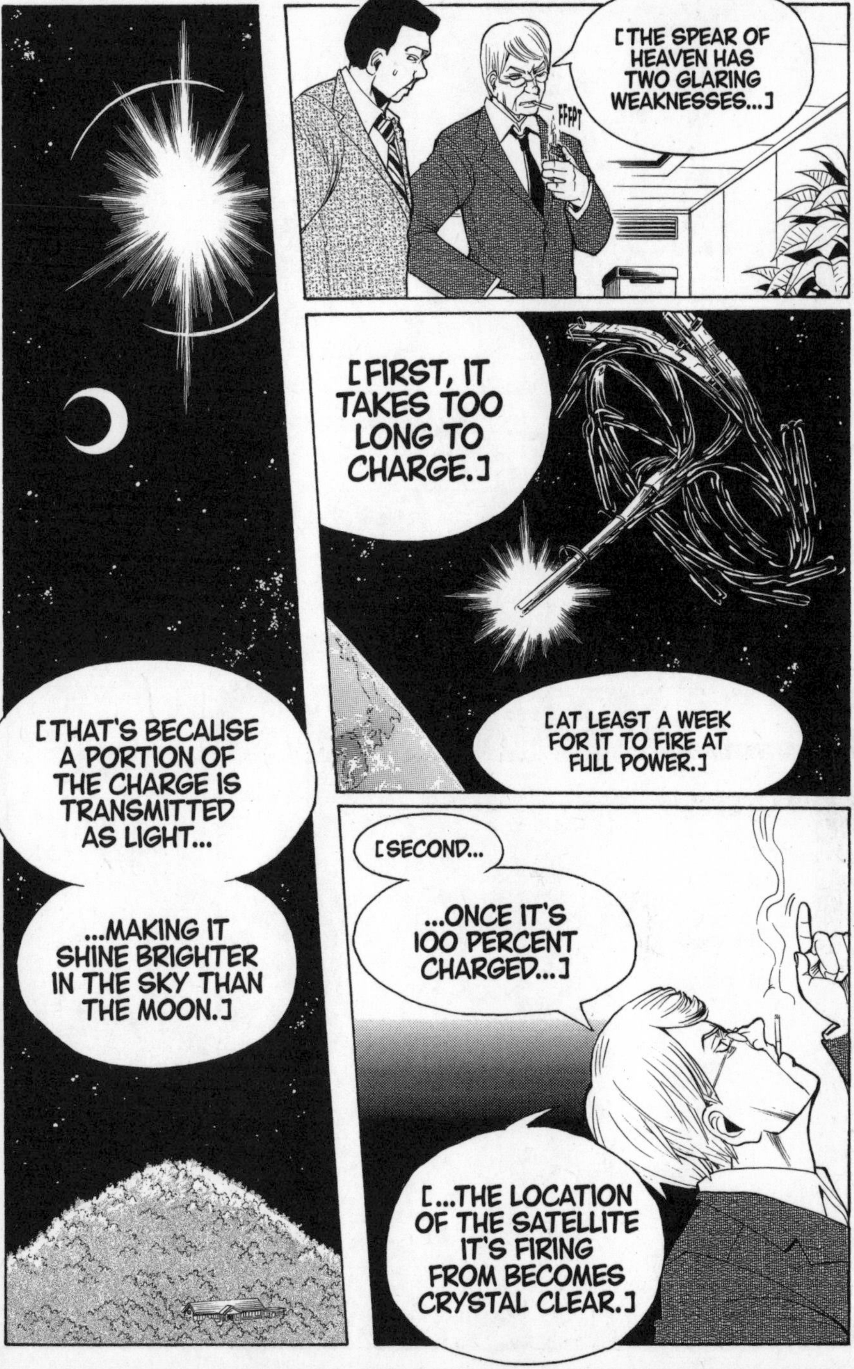
[THE SPEAR OF HEAVEN HAS TWO GLARING WEAKNESSES...]
FFFPT
[FIRST, IT TAKES TOO LONG TO CHARGE.]
[AT LEAST A WEEK FOR IT TO FIRE AT FULL POWER.]
[SECOND...
...ONCE IT'S 100 PERCENT CHARGED...]
[...THE LOCATION OF THE SATELLITE IT'S FIRING FROM BECOMES CRYSTAL CLEAR.]
[THAT'S BECAUSE A PORTION OF THE CHARGE IS TRANSMITTED AS LIGHT...
...MAKING IT SHINE BRIGHTER IN THE SKY THAN THE MOON.]

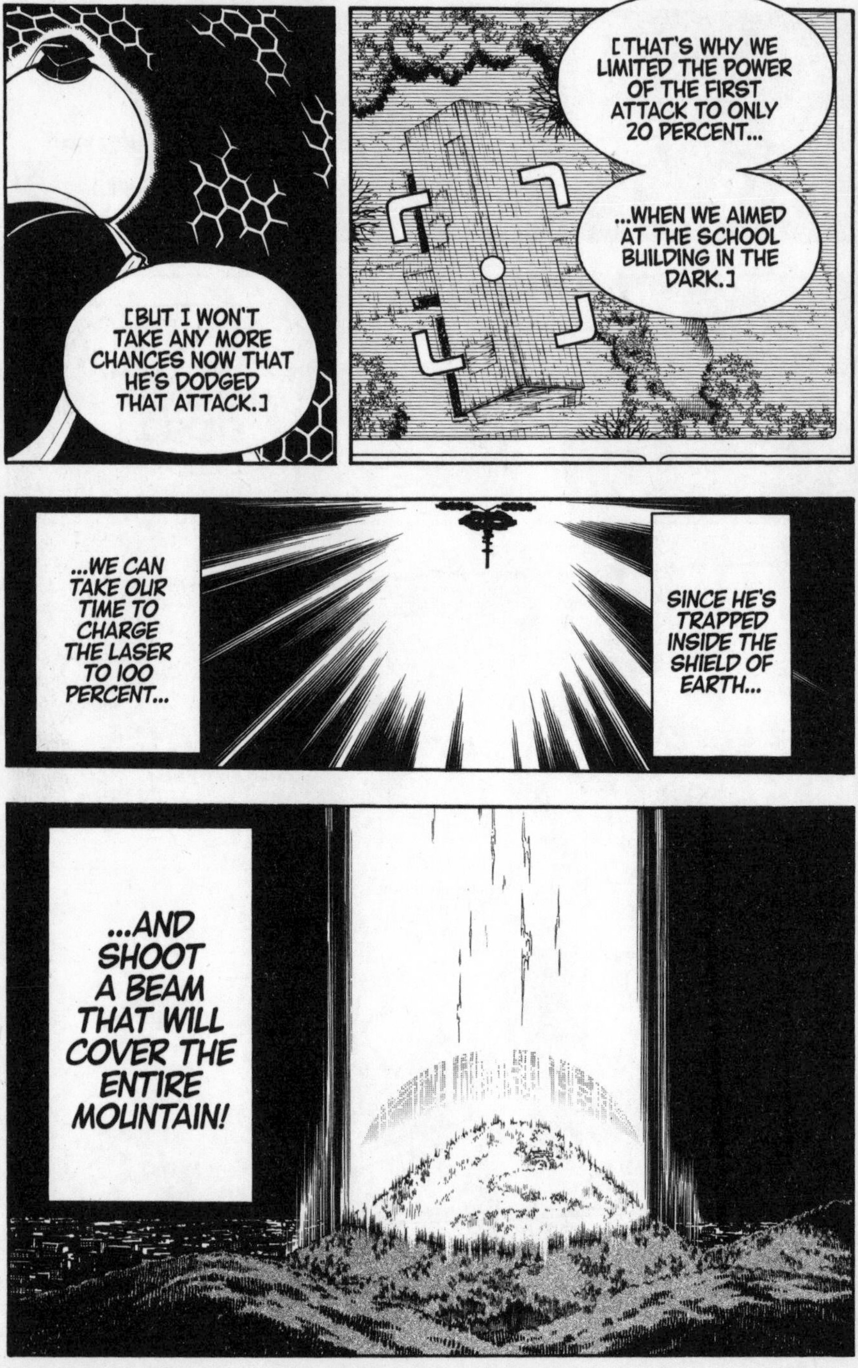
[THAT'S WHY WE LIMITED THE POWER OF THE FIRST ATTACK TO ONLY 20 PERCENT...
...WHEN WE AIMED AT THE SCHOOL BUILDING IN THE DARK.]
[BUT I WON'T TAKE ANY MORE CHANCES NOW THAT HE'S DODGED THAT ATTACK.]
SINCE HE'S TRAPPED INSIDE THE SHIELD OF EARTH...
...WE CAN TAKE OUR TIME TO CHARGE THE LASER TO 100 PERCENT...
...AND SHOOT A BEAM THAT WILL COVER THE ENTIRE MOUNTAIN!

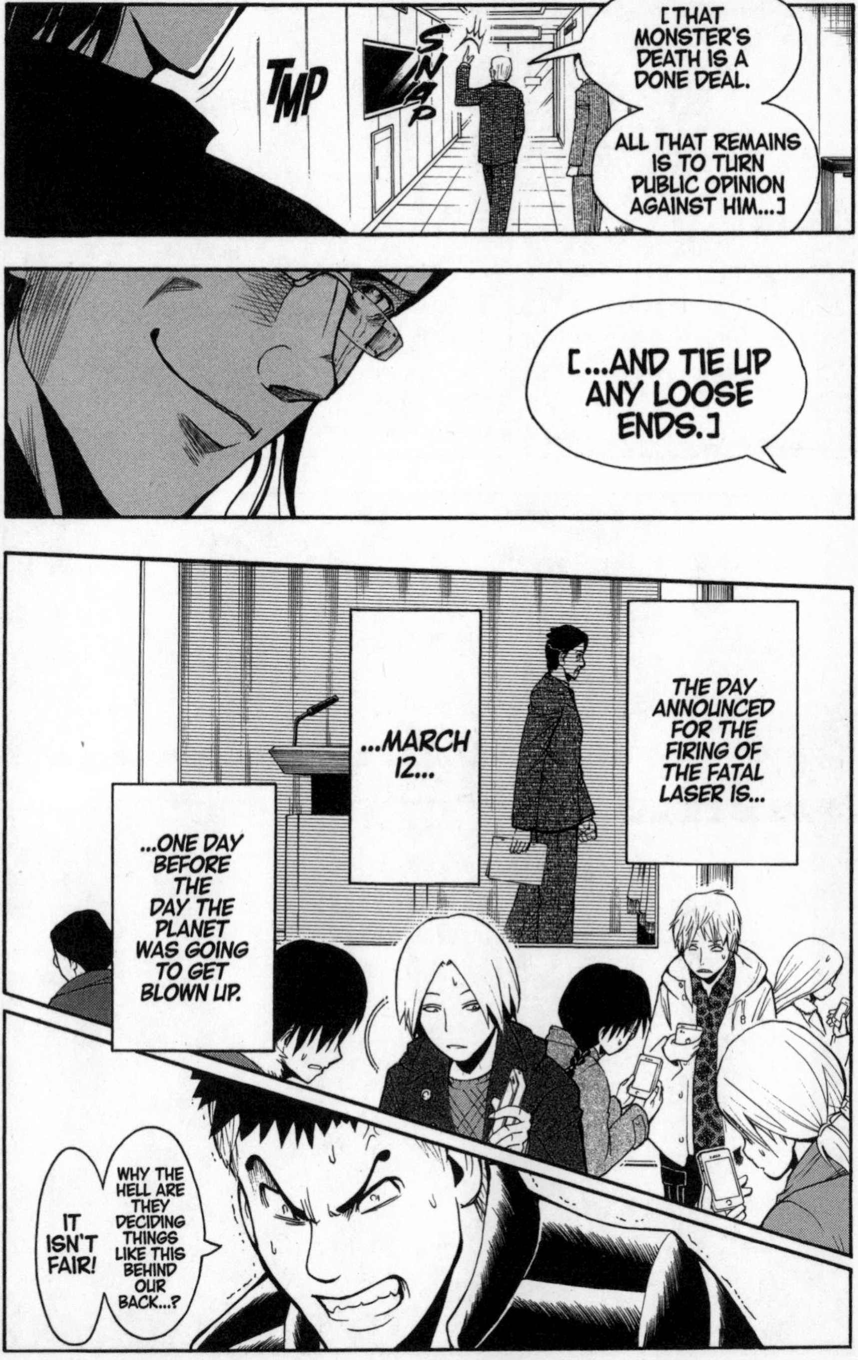
[THAT MONSTER'S DEATH IS A DONE DEAL.
ALL THAT REMAINS IS TO TURN PUBLIC OPINION AGAINST HIM...]
SNAP
TMP
[...AND TIE UP ANY LOOSE ENDS.]
THE DAY ANNOUNCED FOR THE FIRING OF THE FATAL LASER IS...
...MARCH 12...
...ONE DAY BEFORE THE DAY THE PLANET WAS GOING TO GET BLOWN UP.
WHY THE HELL ARE THEY DECIDING THINGS LIKE THIS BEHIND OUR BACK...?
IT ISN'T FAIR!

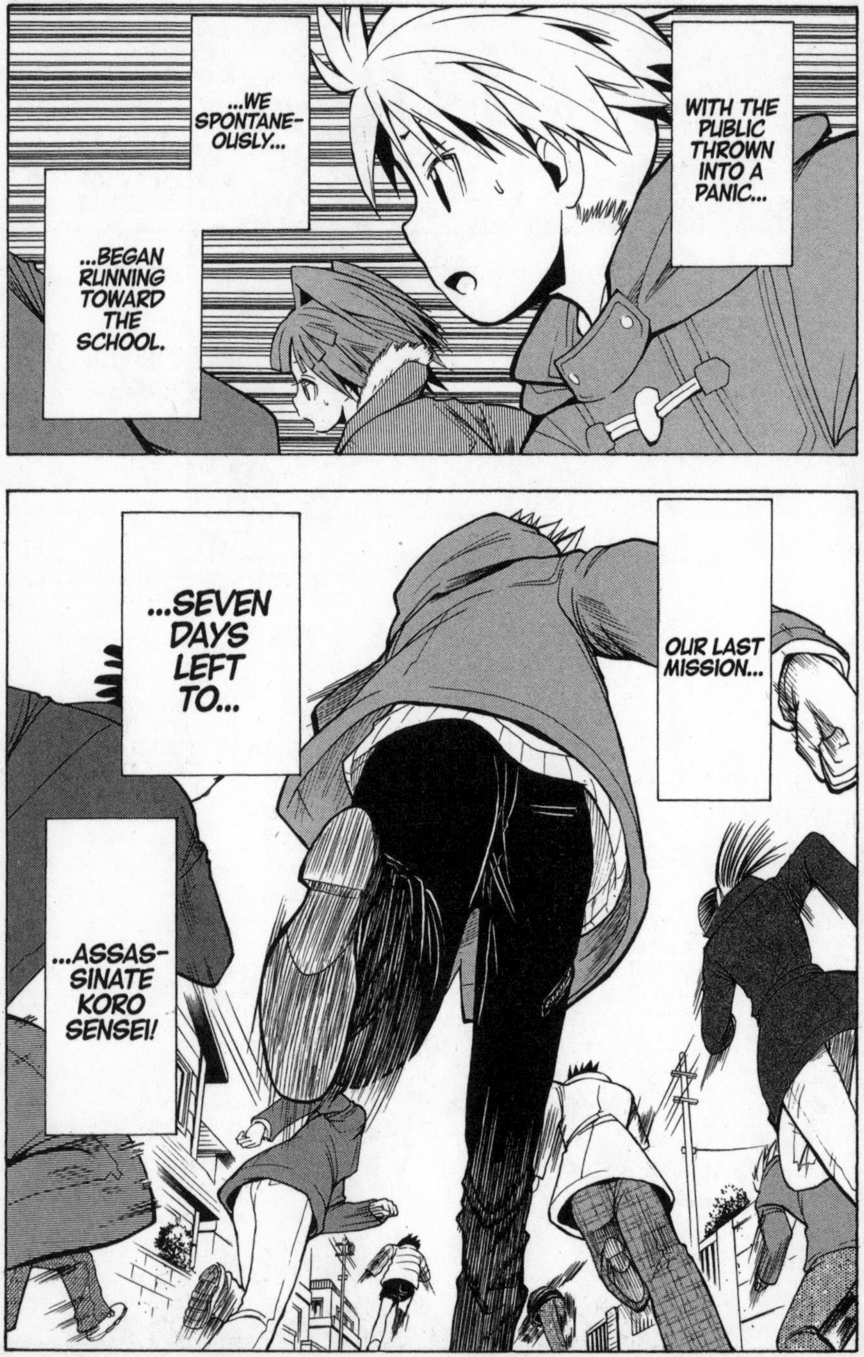
WITH THE PUBLIC THROWN INTO A PANIC...
...WE SPONTANE-OUSLY...
...BEGAN RUNNING TOWARD THE SCHOOL.
OUR LAST MISSION...
...SEVEN DAYS LEFT TO...
...ASSAS-SINATE KORO SENSEI!

The image
the public
has of
KORO
Sensei.

KORO Sensei's
image of
the public
image of him.
Assassination
CLassRoom 19

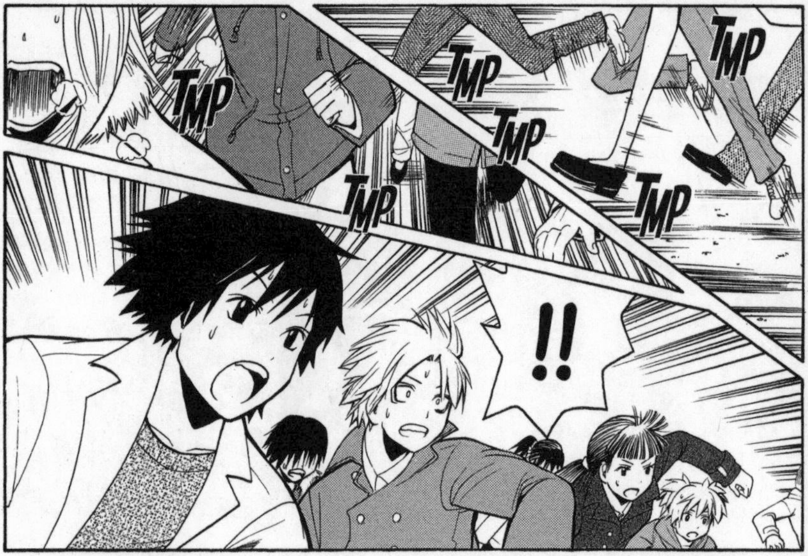
TMP
TMP
TMP
TMP
TMP
TMP
!!

CLASS 165 TIME FOR CONVINCING ARGUMENTS

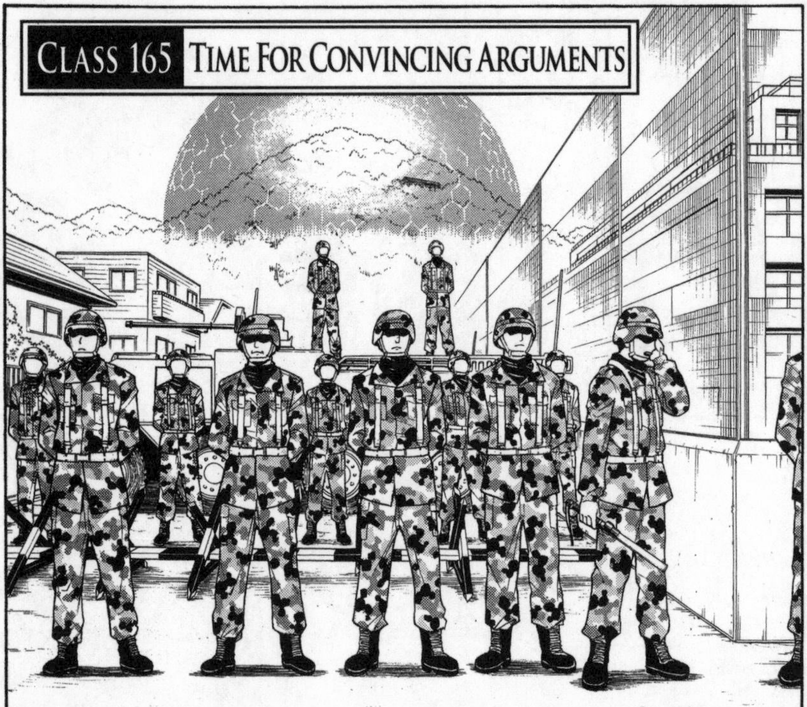

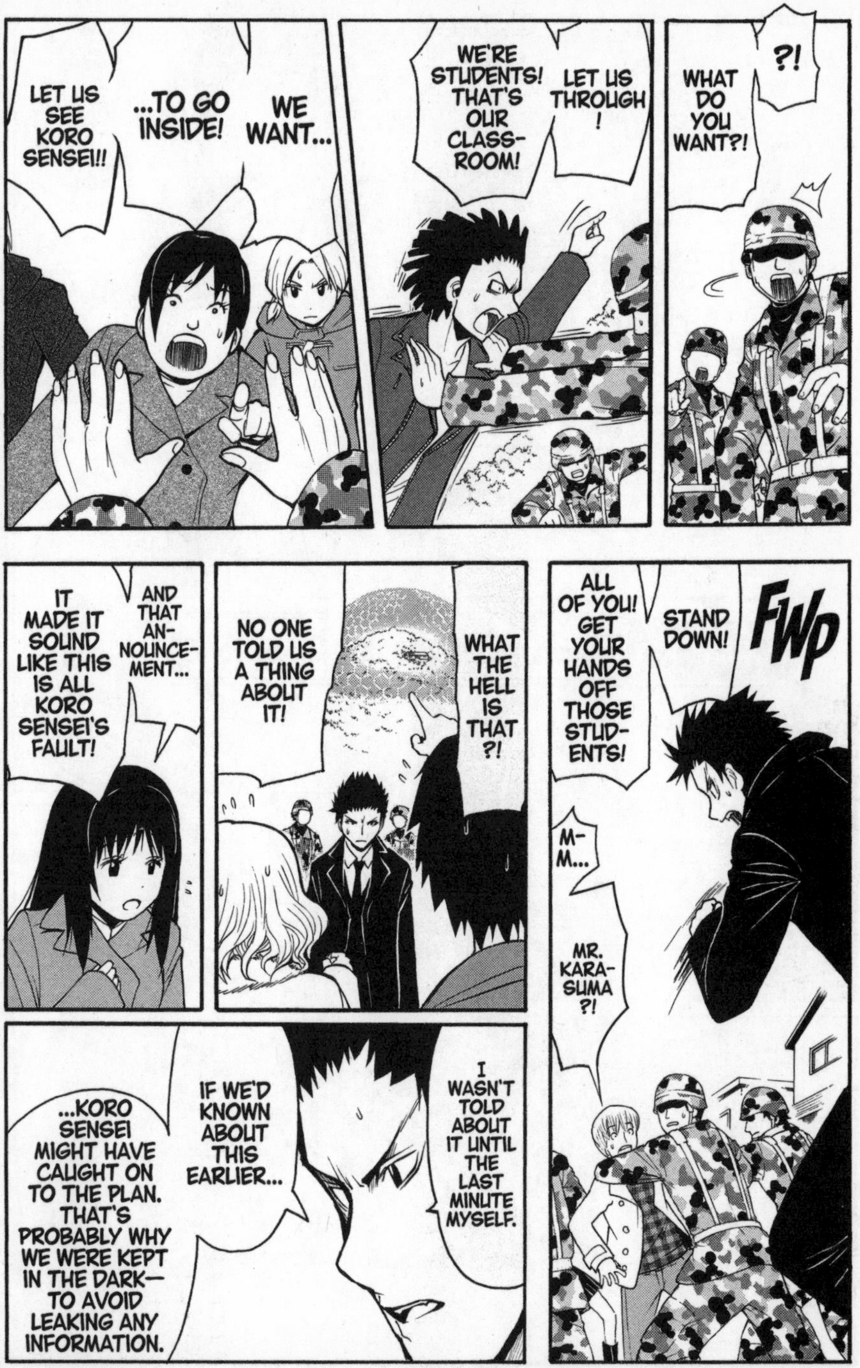
?!
WHAT DO YOU WANT?!
LET US THROUGH!
WE'RE STUDENTS! THAT'S OUR CLASSROOM!
WE WANT...
...TO GO INSIDE!
LET US SEE KORO SENSEI!!
FWP
STAND DOWN!
ALL OF YOU! GET YOUR HANDS OFF THOSE STUDENTS!
M-M...
MR. KARASUMA?!
WHAT THE HELL IS THAT?!
NO ONE TOLD US A THING ABOUT IT!
AND THAT ANNOUNCEMENT...
IT MADE IT SOUND LIKE THIS IS ALL KORO SENSEI'S FAULT!
I WASN'T TOLD ABOUT IT UNTIL THE LAST MINUTE MYSELF.
IF WE'D KNOWN ABOUT THIS EARLIER...
...KORO SENSEI MIGHT HAVE CAUGHT ON TO THE PLAN. THAT'S PROBABLY WHY WE WERE KEPT IN THE DARK—TO AVOID LEAKING ANY INFORMATION.

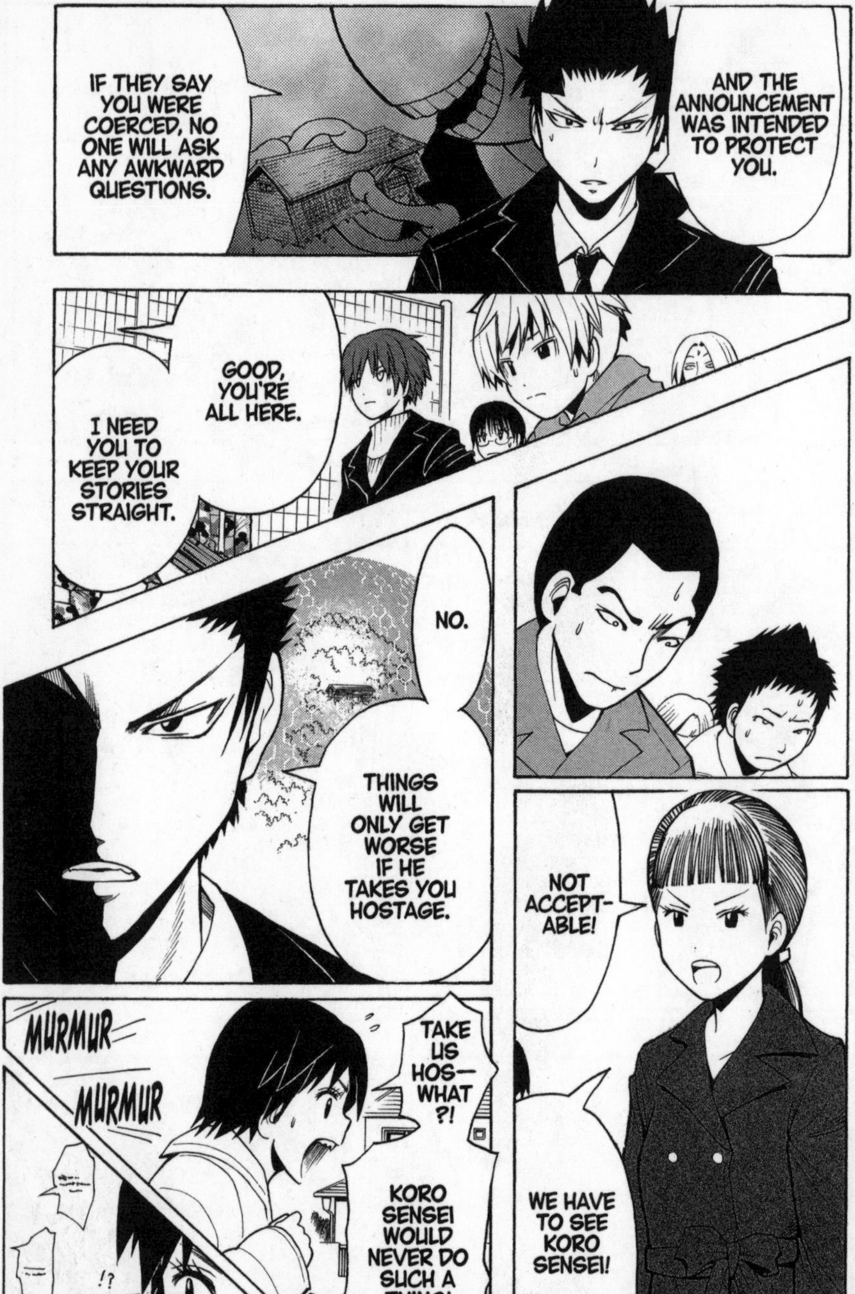
AND THE ANNOUNCEMENT WAS INTENDED TO PROTECT YOU.
IF THEY SAY YOU WERE COERCED, NO ONE WILL ASK ANY AWKWARD QUESTIONS.
GOOD, YOU'RE ALL HERE.
I NEED YOU TO KEEP YOUR STORIES STRAIGHT.
NO.
THINGS WILL ONLY GET WORSE IF HE TAKES YOU HOSTAGE.
NOT ACCEPTABLE!
WE HAVE TO SEE KORO SENSEI!
TAKE US HOS— WHAT ?!
KORO SENSEI WOULD NEVER DO SUCH A THING!
MURMUR
MURMUR
!?

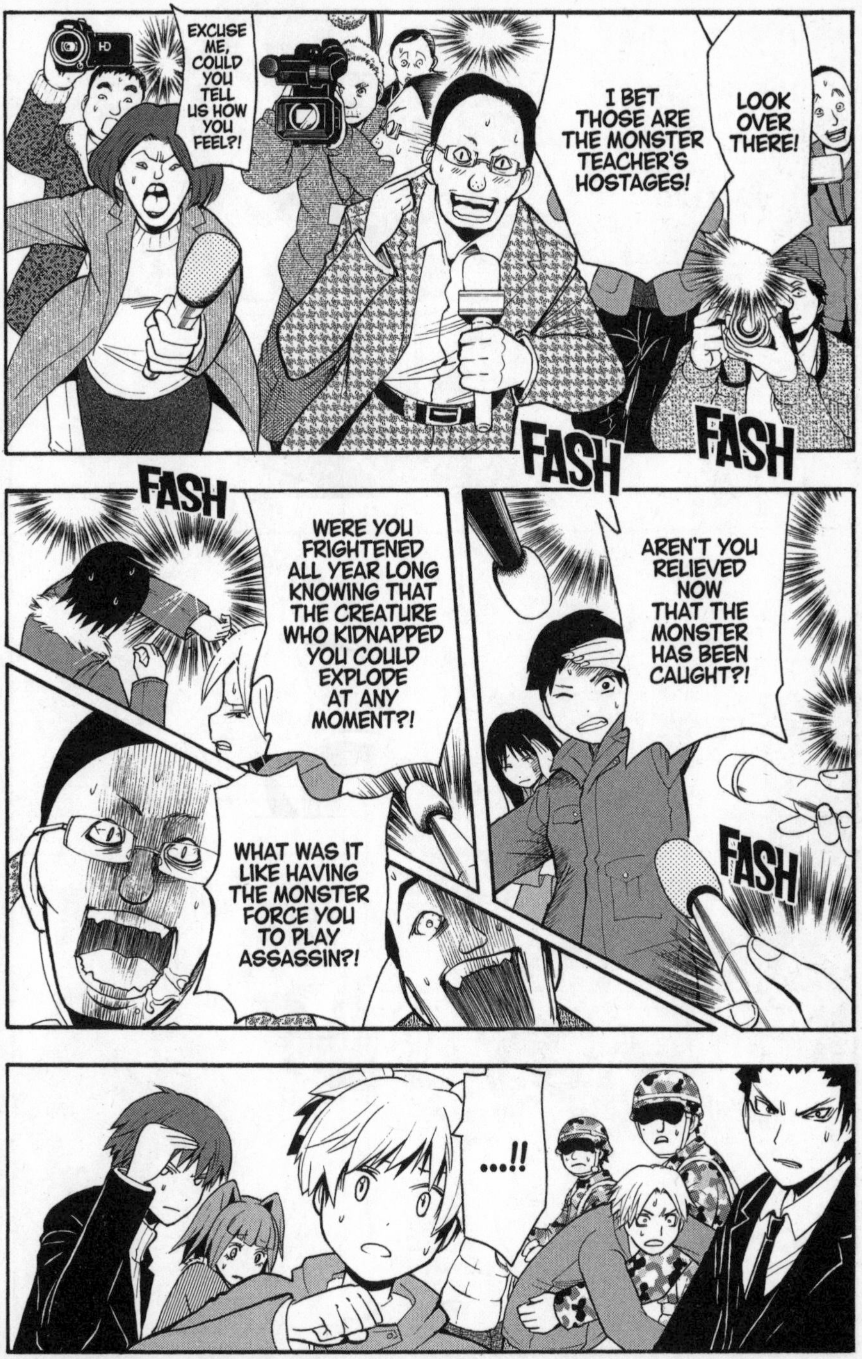
LOOK OVER THERE!
I BET THOSE ARE THE MONSTER TEACHER'S HOSTAGES!
EXCUSE ME, COULD YOU TELL US HOW YOU FEEL?!
FASH
FASH
AREN'T YOU RELIEVED NOW THAT THE MONSTER HAS BEEN CAUGHT?!
FASH
FASH
WERE YOU FRIGHTENED ALL YEAR LONG KNOWING THAT THE CREATURE WHO KIDNAPPED YOU COULD EXPLODE AT ANY MOMENT?!
WHAT WAS IT LIKE HAVING THE MONSTER FORCE YOU TO PLAY ASSASSIN?!
...!!

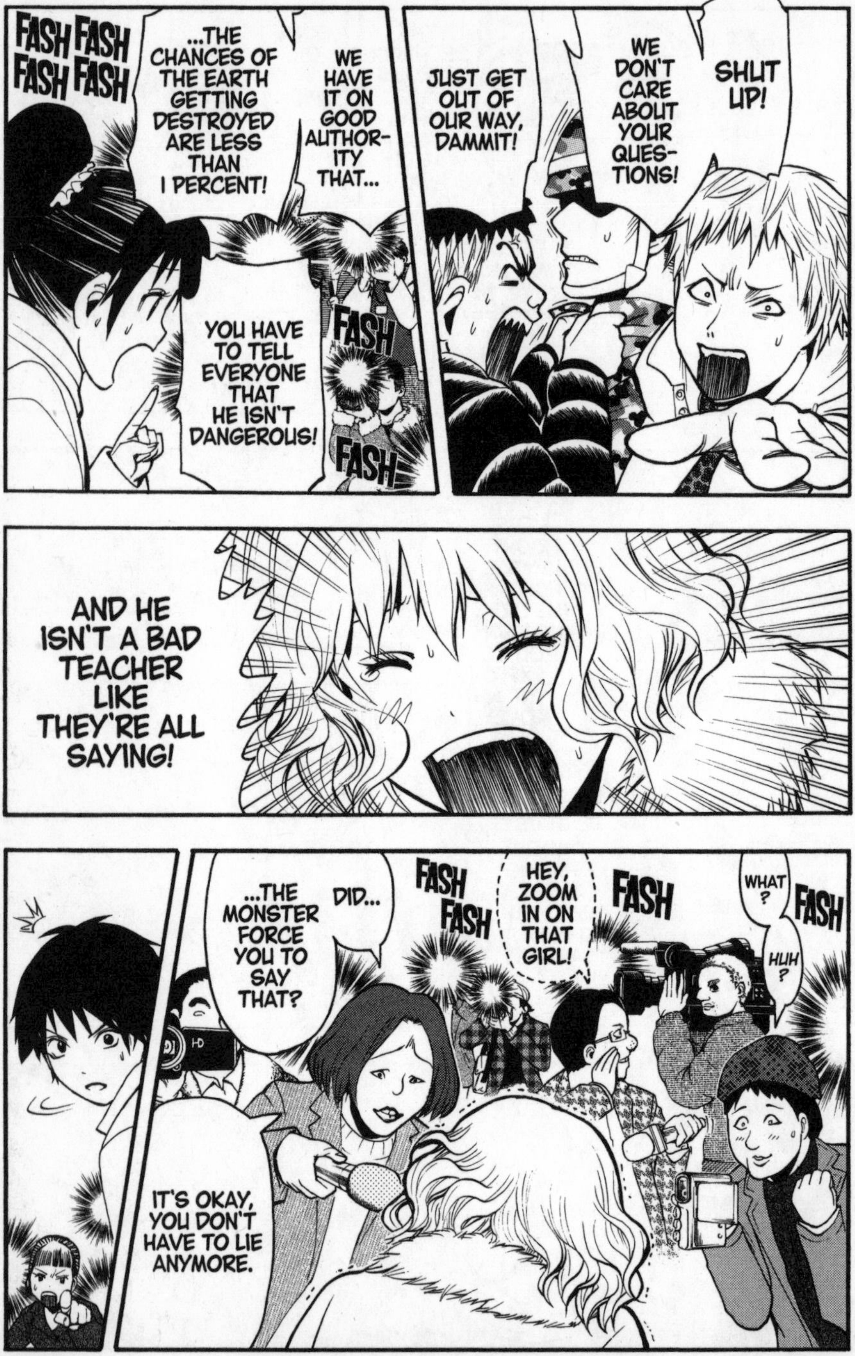
SHUT UP!
WE DON'T CARE ABOUT YOUR QUES-TIONS!
JUST GET OUT OF OUR WAY, DAMMIT!
WE HAVE IT ON GOOD AUTHOR-ITY THAT...
...THE CHANCES OF THE EARTH GETTING DESTROYED ARE LESS THAN 1 PERCENT!
FASH FASH FASH FASH
FASH
YOU HAVE TO TELL EVERYONE THAT HE ISN'T DANGEROUS!
FASH
AND HE ISN'T A BAD TEACHER LIKE THEY'RE ALL SAYING!
FASH
WHAT?
HUH?
FASH
HEY, ZOOM IN ON THAT GIRL!
FASH FASH
DID...
...THE MONSTER FORCE YOU TO SAY THAT?
IT'S OKAY, YOU DON'T HAVE TO LIE ANYMORE.

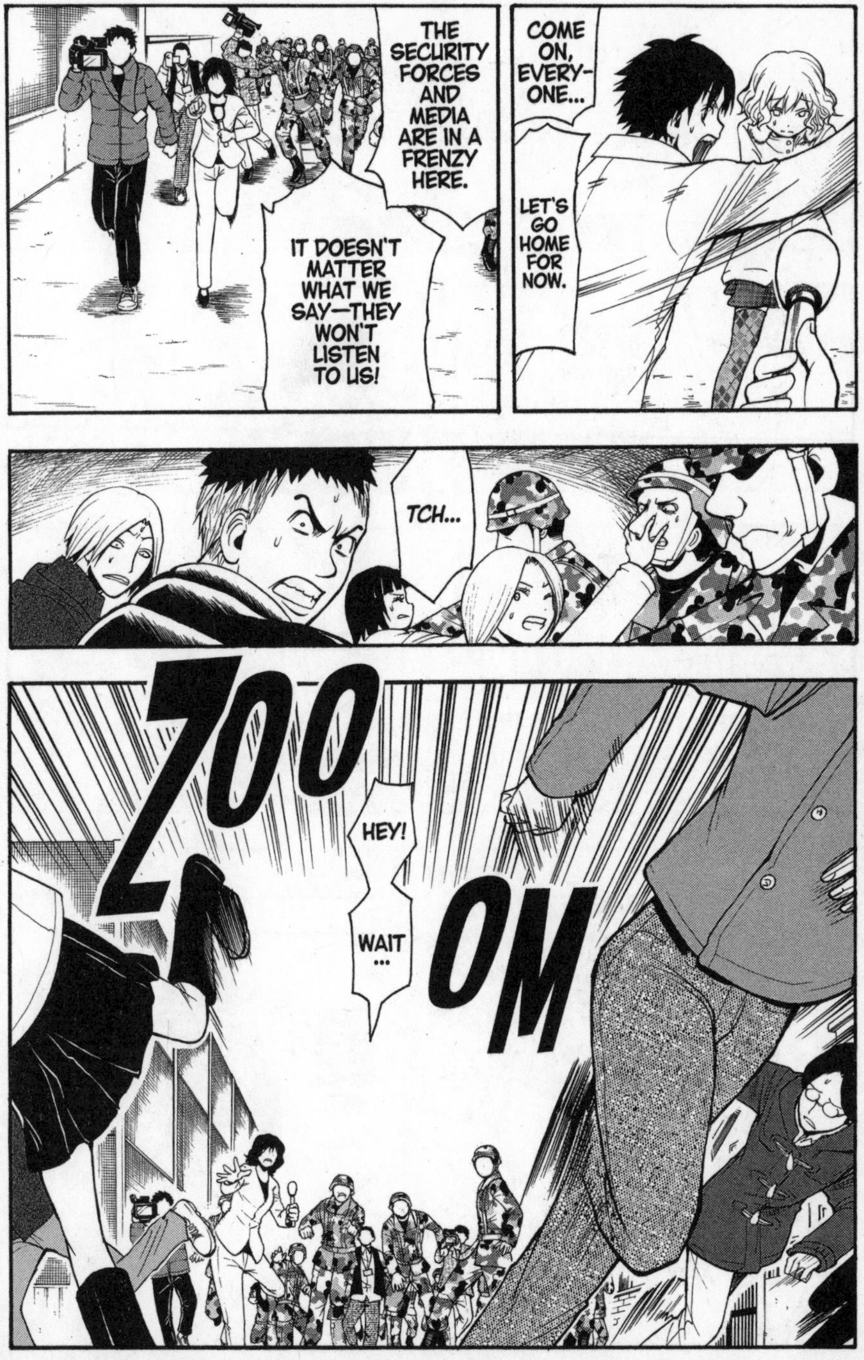
COME ON, EVERY-ONE...
LET'S GO HOME FOR NOW.
THE SECURITY FORCES AND MEDIA ARE IN A FRENZY HERE.
IT DOESN'T MATTER WHAT WE SAY—THEY WON'T LISTEN TO US!
TCH...
ZOOOM
HEY!
WAIT...

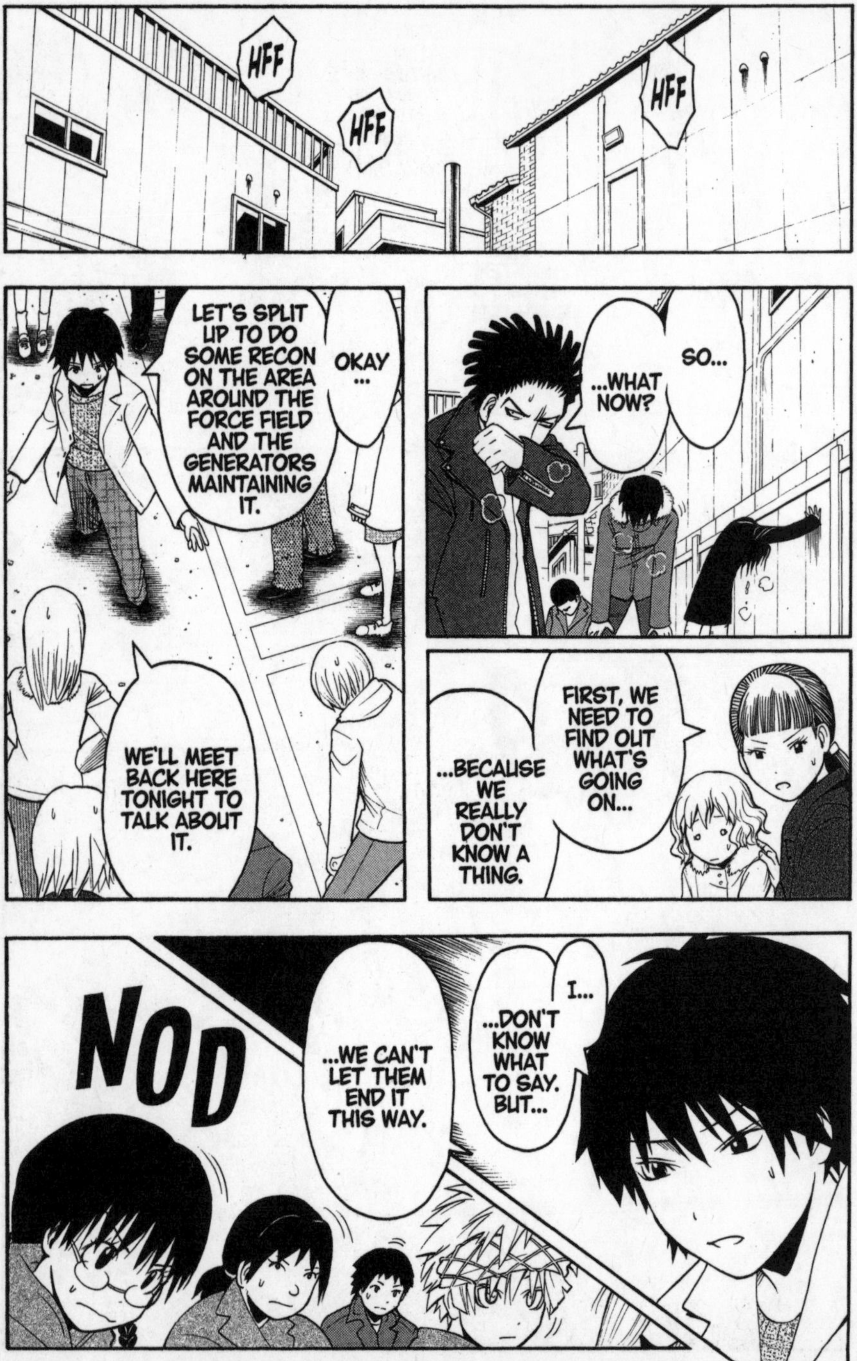
HFF
HFF
HFF
SO...
...WHAT NOW?
FIRST, WE NEED TO FIND OUT WHAT'S GOING ON...
...BECAUSE WE REALLY DON'T KNOW A THING.
LET'S SPLIT UP TO DO SOME RECON ON THE AREA AROUND THE FORCE FIELD AND THE GENERATORS MAINTAINING IT.
OKAY...
WE'LL MEET BACK HERE TONIGHT TO TALK ABOUT IT.
I...
...DON'T KNOW WHAT TO SAY. BUT...
...WE CAN'T LET THEM END IT THIS WAY.
NOD

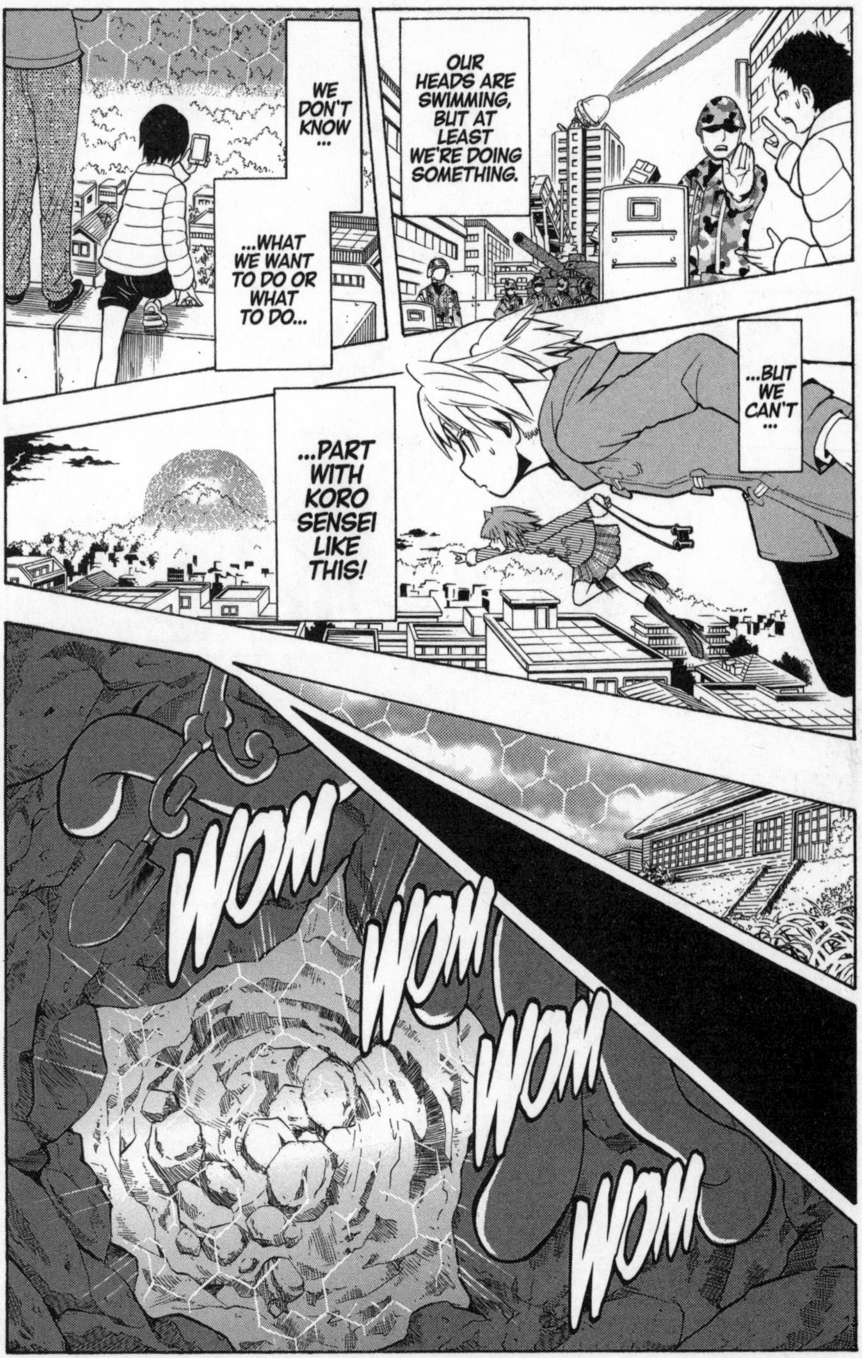
OUR HEADS ARE SWIMMING, BUT AT LEAST WE'RE DOING SOMETHING.
WE DON'T KNOW...
...WHAT WE WANT TO DO OR WHAT TO DO...
...BUT WE CAN'T...
...PART WITH KORO SENSEI LIKE THIS!
WOM
WOM
WOM
WOM

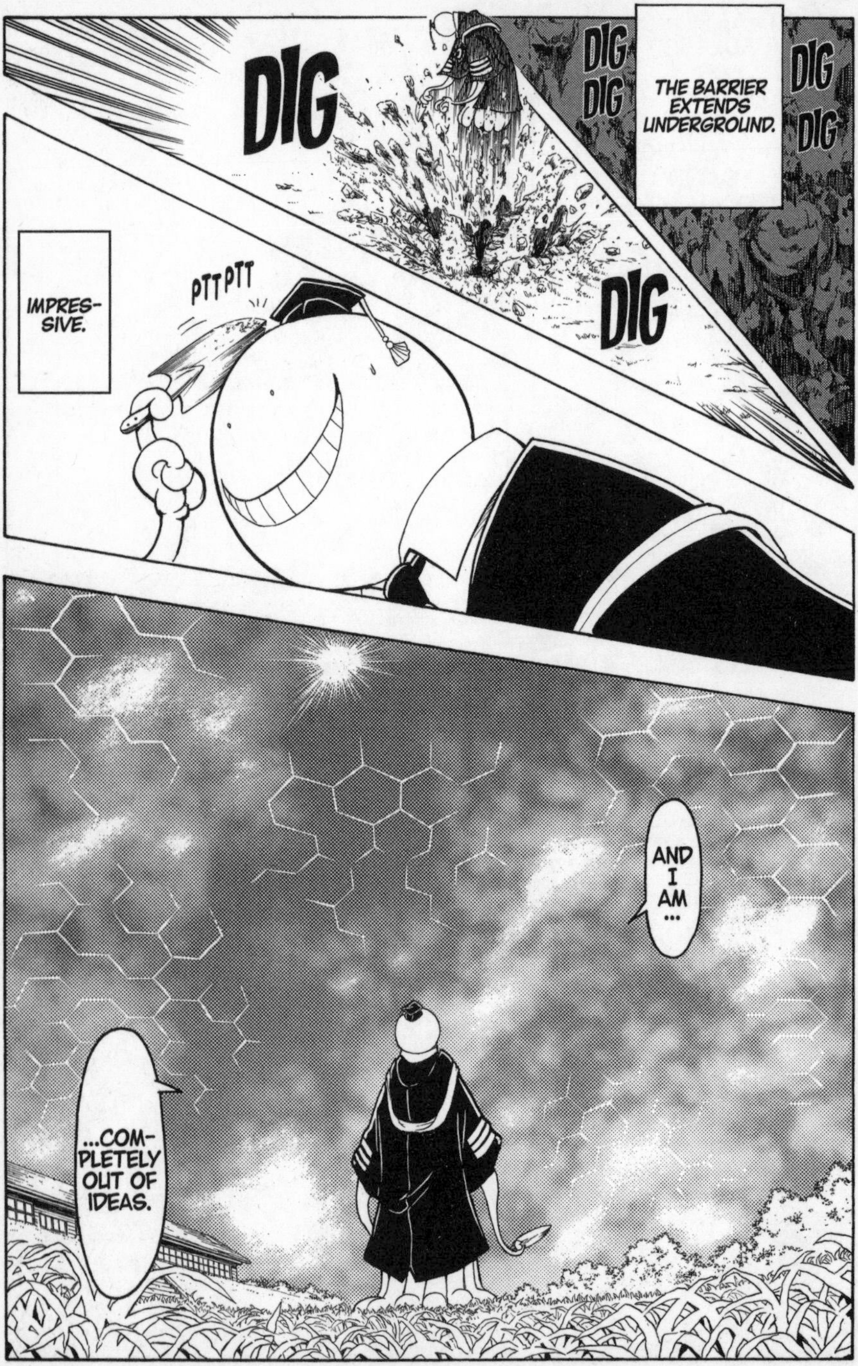
THE BARRIER EXTENDS UNDERGROUND.
DIG DIG
DIG DIG
DIG
DIG
PTT PTT
IMPRES-SIVE.
AND I AM...
...COM-PLETELY OUT OF IDEAS.

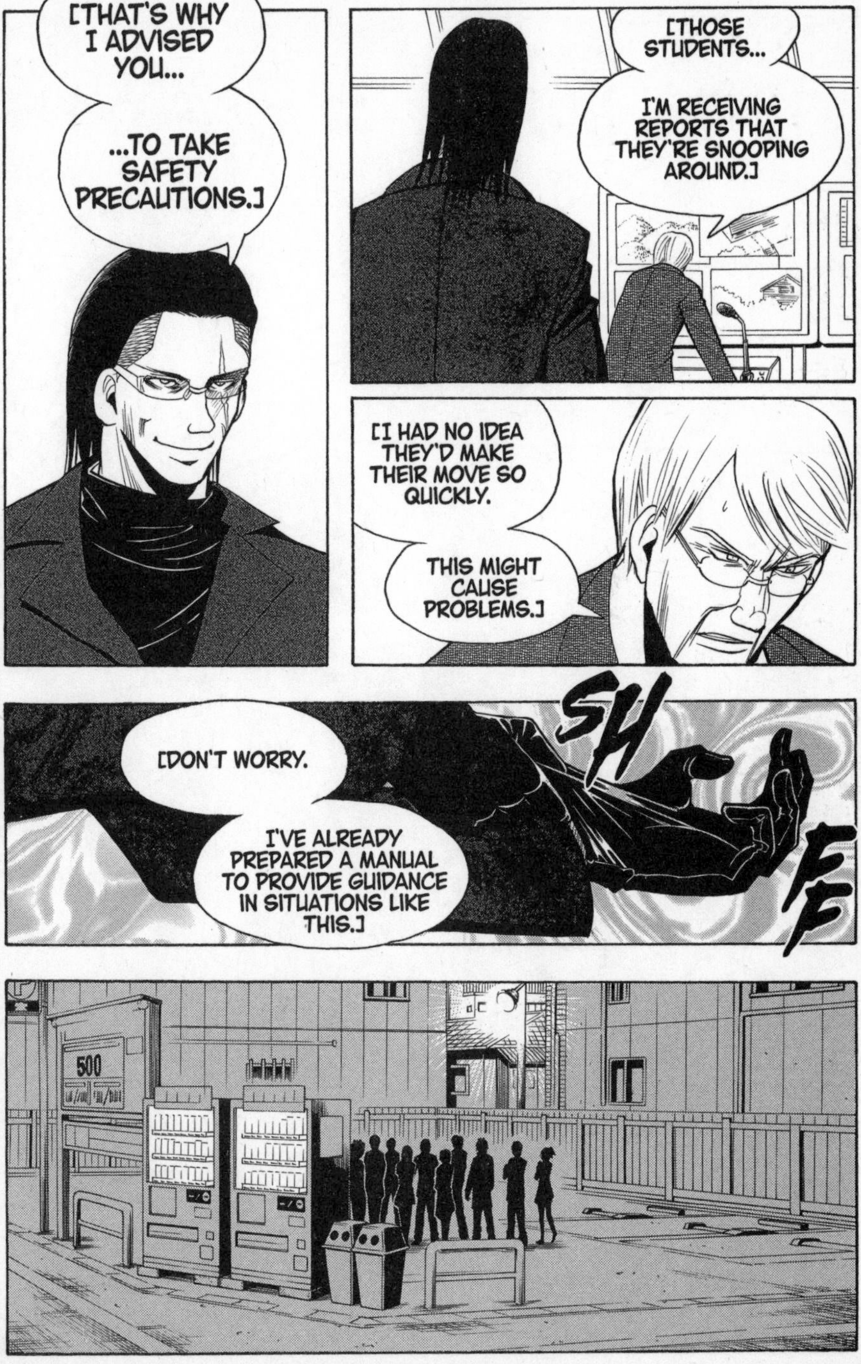
[THOSE STUDENTS...
I'M RECEIVING REPORTS THAT THEY'RE SNOOPING AROUND.]
[I HAD NO IDEA THEY'D MAKE THEIR MOVE SO QUICKLY.
THIS MIGHT CAUSE PROBLEMS.]
[THAT'S WHY I ADVISED YOU...
...TO TAKE SAFETY PRECAUTIONS.]
SHFF
[DON'T WORRY.
I'VE ALREADY PREPARED A MANUAL TO PROVIDE GUIDANCE IN SITUATIONS LIKE THIS.]
500

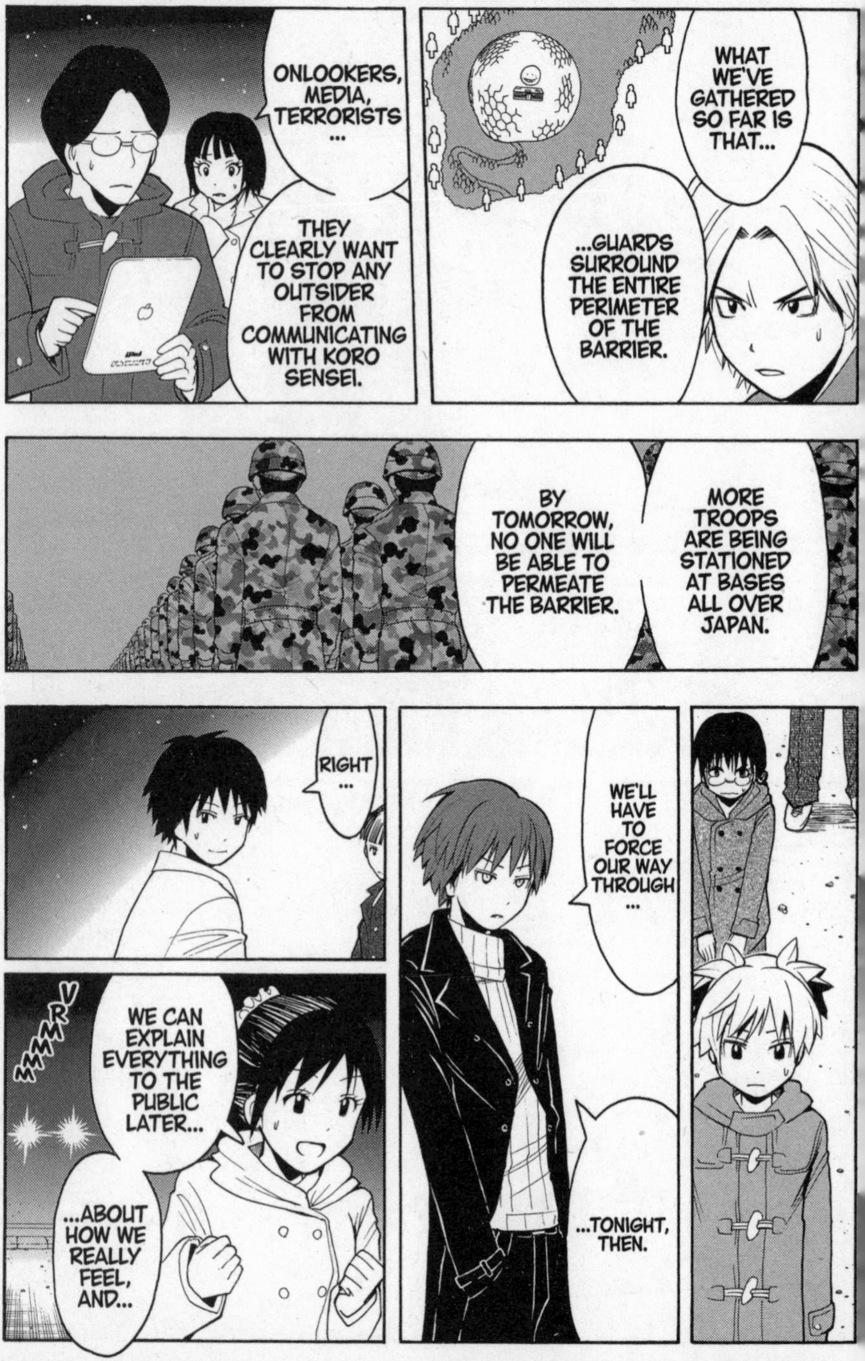
WHAT WE'VE GATHERED SO FAR IS THAT...
...GUARDS SURROUND THE ENTIRE PERIMETER OF THE BARRIER.
ONLOOKERS, MEDIA, TERRORISTS ...
THEY CLEARLY WANT TO STOP ANY OUTSIDER FROM COMMUNICATING WITH KORO SENSEI.
MORE TROOPS ARE BEING STATIONED AT BASES ALL OVER JAPAN.
BY TOMORROW, NO ONE WILL BE ABLE TO PERMEATE THE BARRIER.
WE'LL HAVE TO FORCE OUR WAY THROUGH ...
...TONIGHT, THEN.
RIGHT ...
VRMMMM
WE CAN EXPLAIN EVERYTHING TO THE PUBLIC LATER...
...ABOUT HOW WE REALLY FEEL, AND...

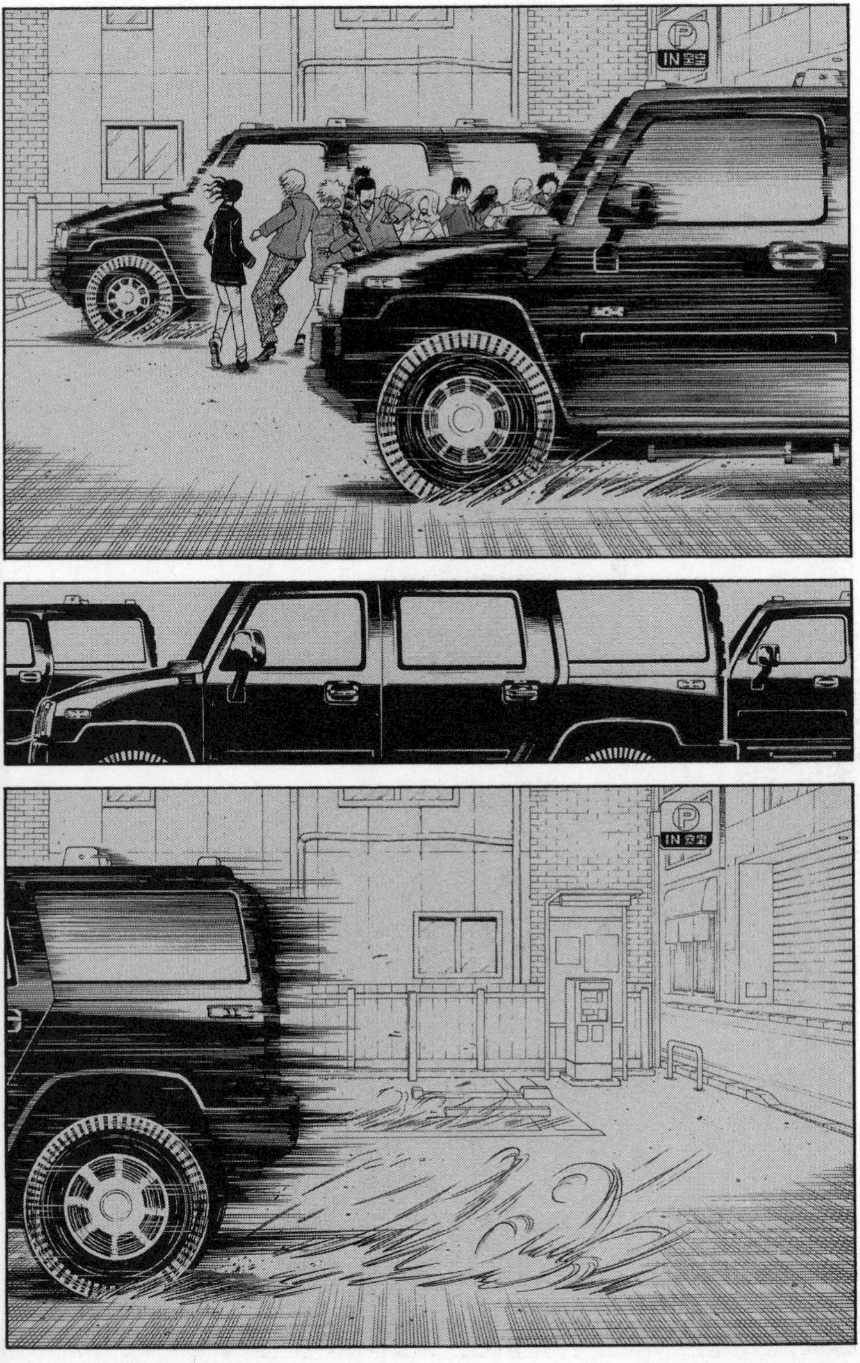
P
IN 空室

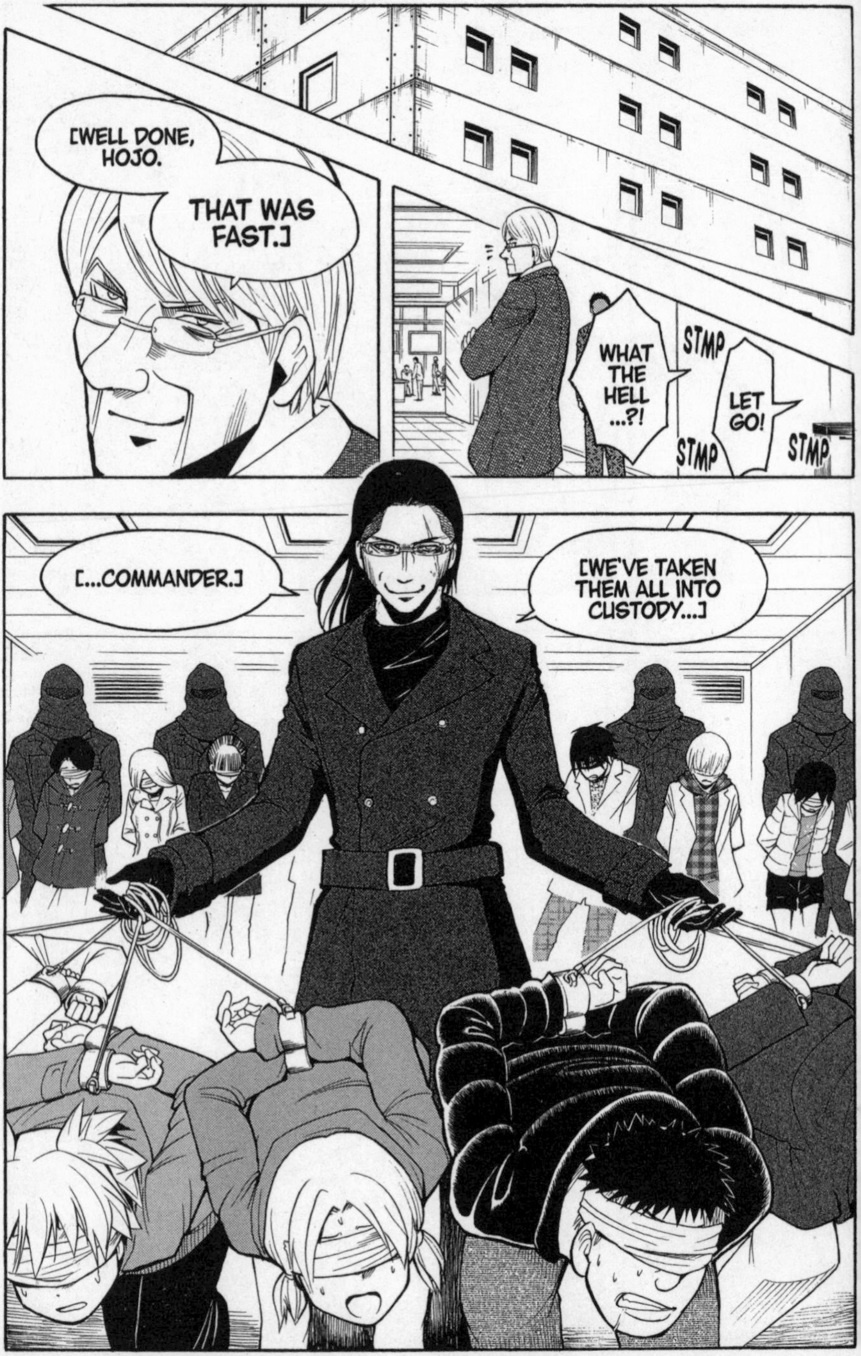
STMP
WHAT THE HELL ...?!
STMP
LET GO!
STMP
[WELL DONE, HOJO.
THAT WAS FAST.]
[WE'VE TAKEN THEM ALL INTO CUSTODY...]
[...COMMANDER.]

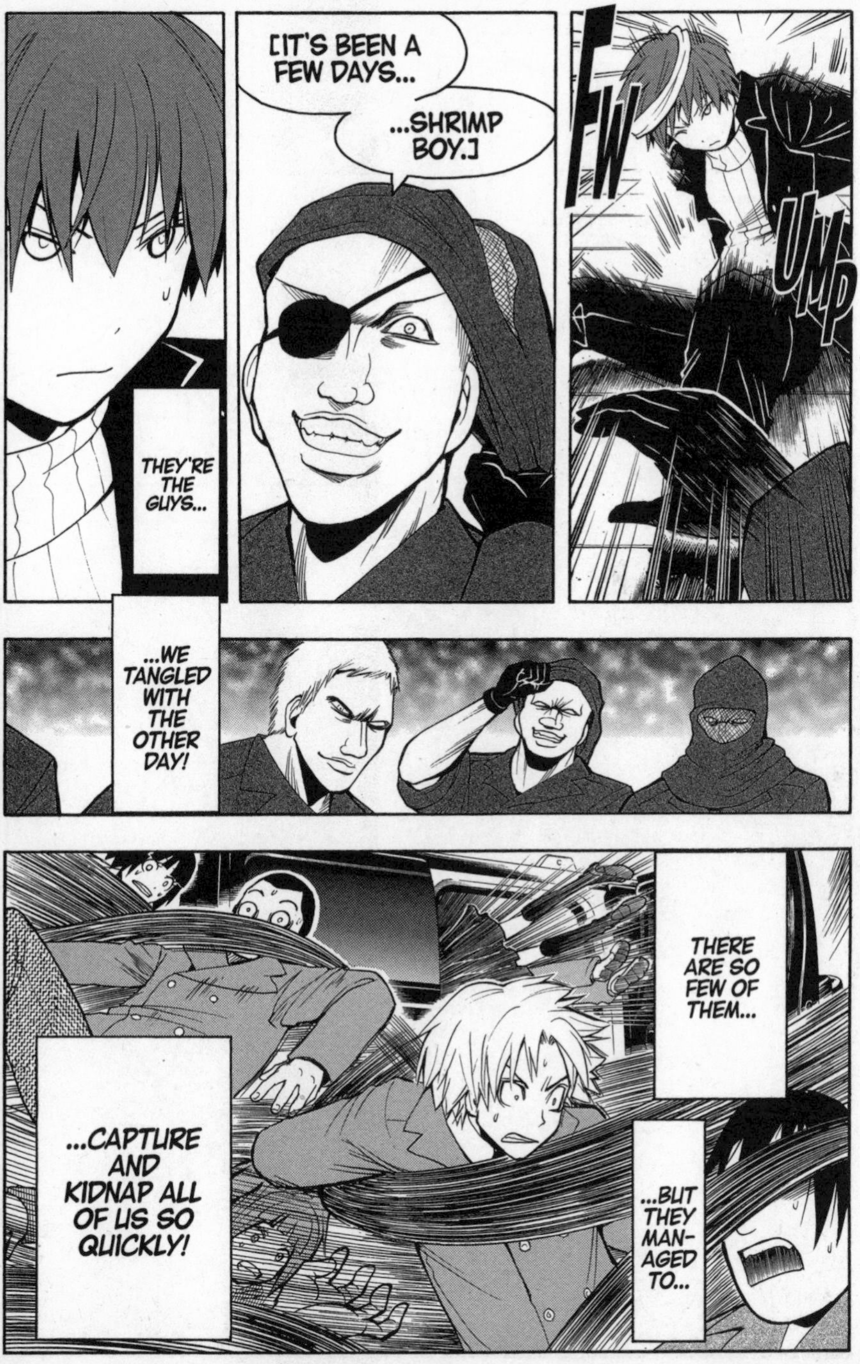
FW
UMP
[IT'S BEEN A FEW DAYS...
...SHRIMP BOY.]
THEY'RE THE GUYS...
...WE TANGLED WITH THE OTHER DAY!
THERE ARE SO FEW OF THEM...
...BUT THEY MAN-AGED TO...
...CAPTURE AND KIDNAP ALL OF US SO QUICKLY!

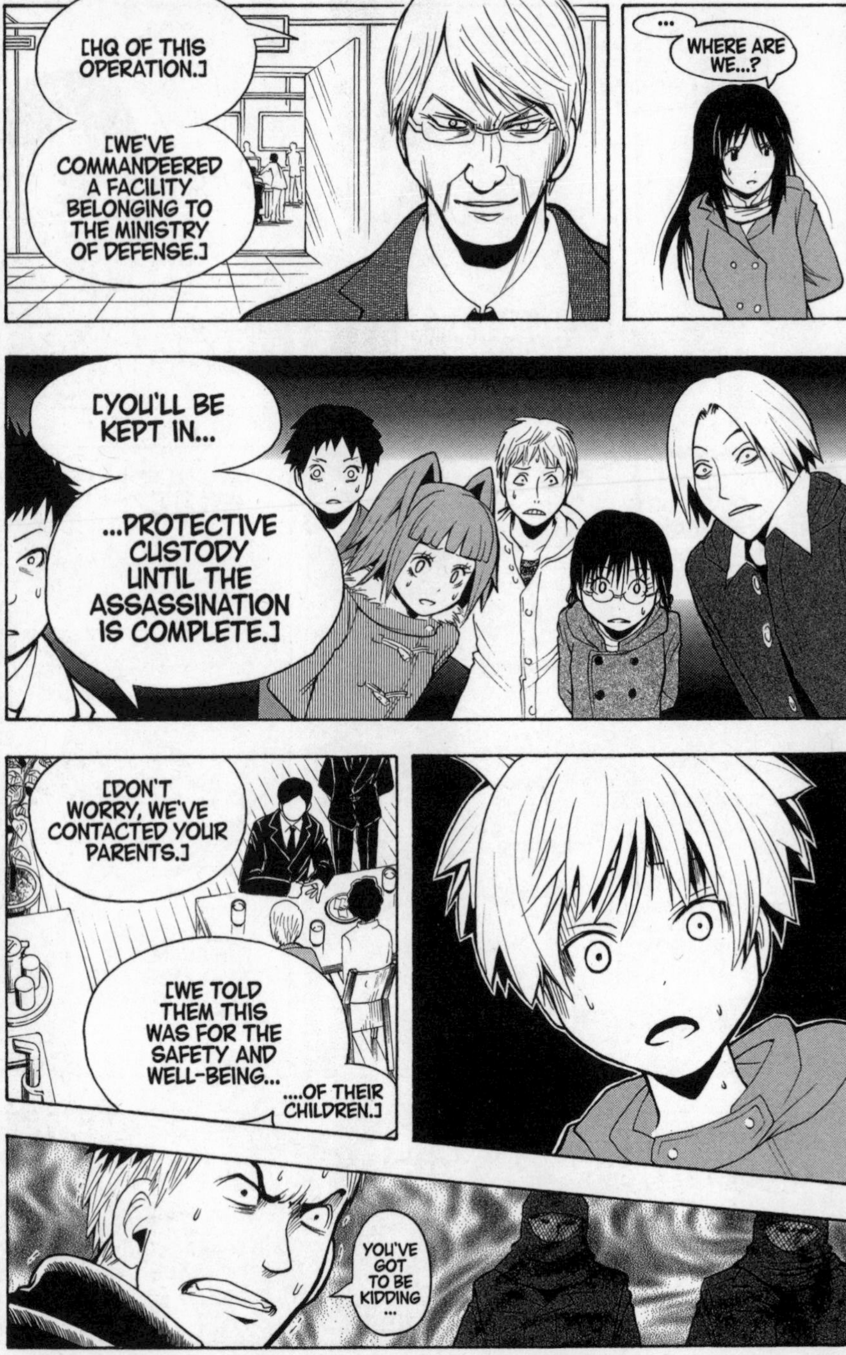
...
WHERE ARE WE...?
[HQ OF THIS OPERATION.]
[WE'VE COMMANDEERED A FACILITY BELONGING TO THE MINISTRY OF DEFENSE.]
[YOU'LL BE KEPT IN...
...PROTECTIVE CUSTODY UNTIL THE ASSASSINATION IS COMPLETE.]
[DON'T WORRY, WE'VE CONTACTED YOUR PARENTS.]
[WE TOLD THEM THIS WAS FOR THE SAFETY AND WELL-BEING...
....OF THEIR CHILDREN.]
YOU'VE GOT TO BE KIDDING...

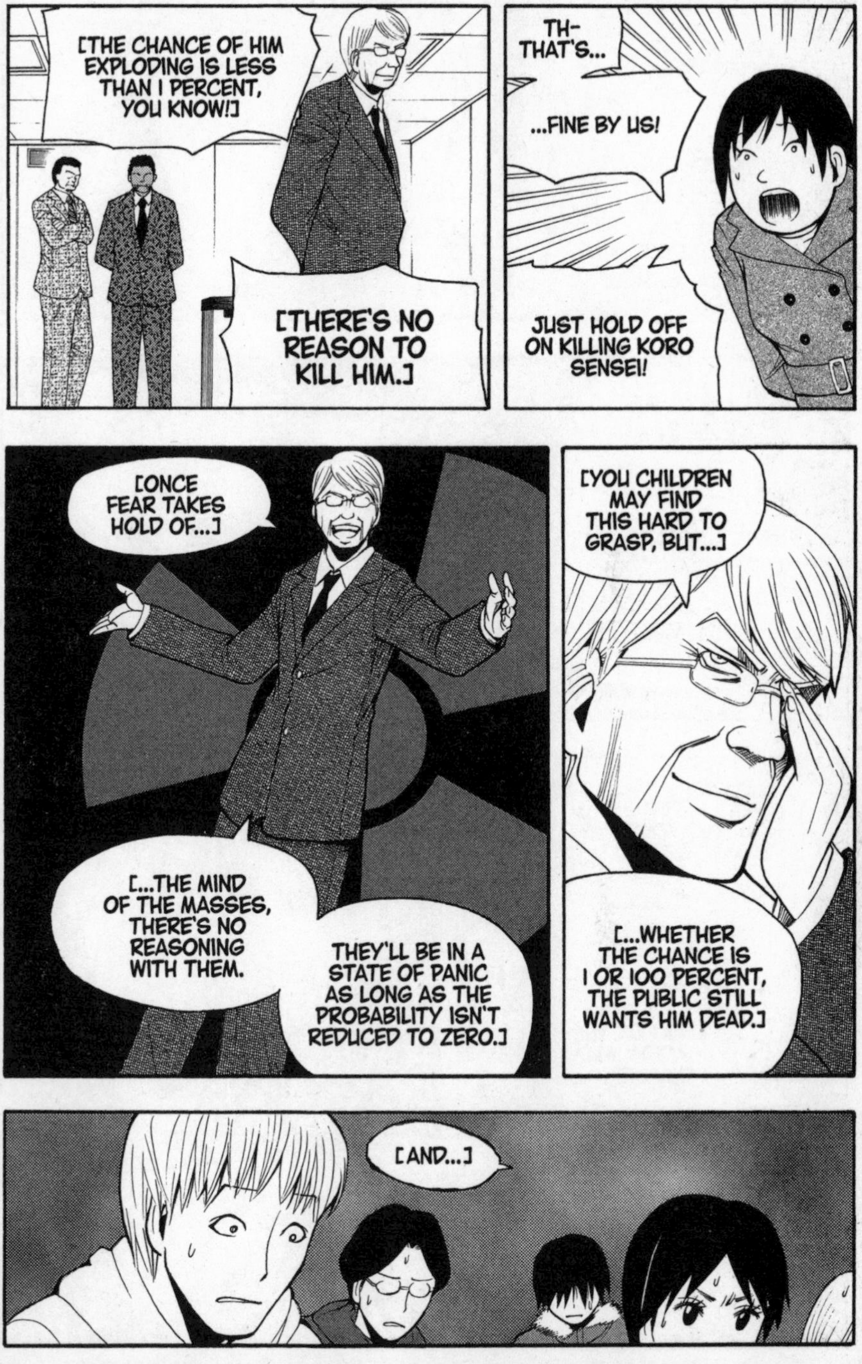
TH- THAT'S...
...FINE BY US!
JUST HOLD OFF ON KILLING KORO SENSEI!
[THE CHANCE OF HIM EXPLODING IS LESS THAN 1 PERCENT, YOU KNOW!]
[THERE'S NO REASON TO KILL HIM.]
[YOU CHILDREN MAY FIND THIS HARD TO GRASP, BUT...]
[...WHETHER THE CHANCE IS 1 OR 100 PERCENT, THE PUBLIC STILL WANTS HIM DEAD.]
[ONCE FEAR TAKES HOLD OF...]
[...THE MIND OF THE MASSES, THERE'S NO REASONING WITH THEM.
THEY'LL BE IN A STATE OF PANIC AS LONG AS THE PROBABILITY ISN'T REDUCED TO ZERO.]
[AND...]

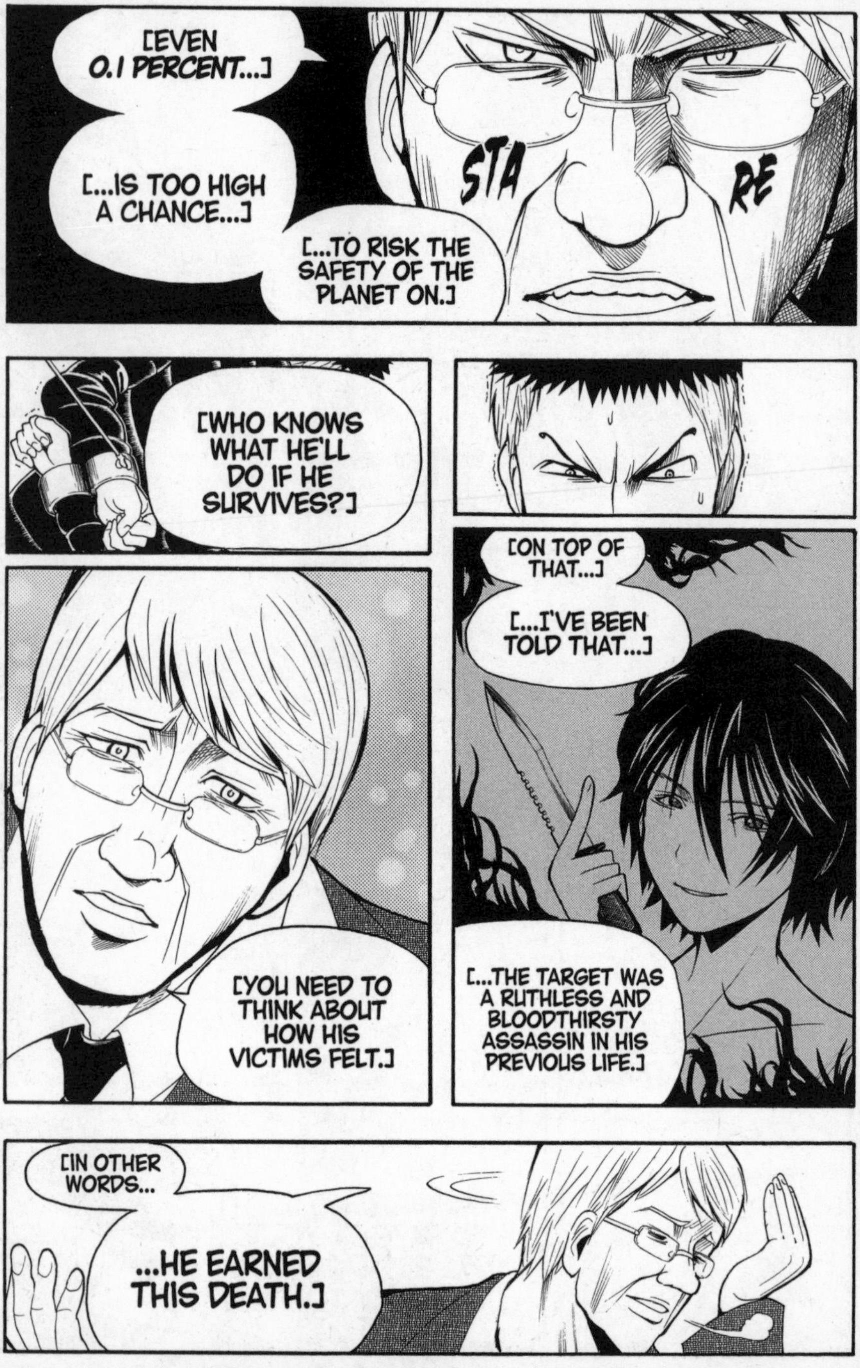
STARE
[EVEN 0.1 PERCENT...]
[...IS TOO HIGH A CHANCE...]
[...TO RISK THE SAFETY OF THE PLANET ON.]
[WHO KNOWS WHAT HE'LL DO IF HE SURVIVES?]
[ON TOP OF THAT...]
[...I'VE BEEN TOLD THAT...]
[...THE TARGET WAS A RUTHLESS AND BLOODTHIRSTY ASSASSIN IN HIS PREVIOUS LIFE.]
[YOU NEED TO THINK ABOUT HOW HIS VICTIMS FELT.]
[IN OTHER WORDS...
...HE EARNED THIS DEATH.]

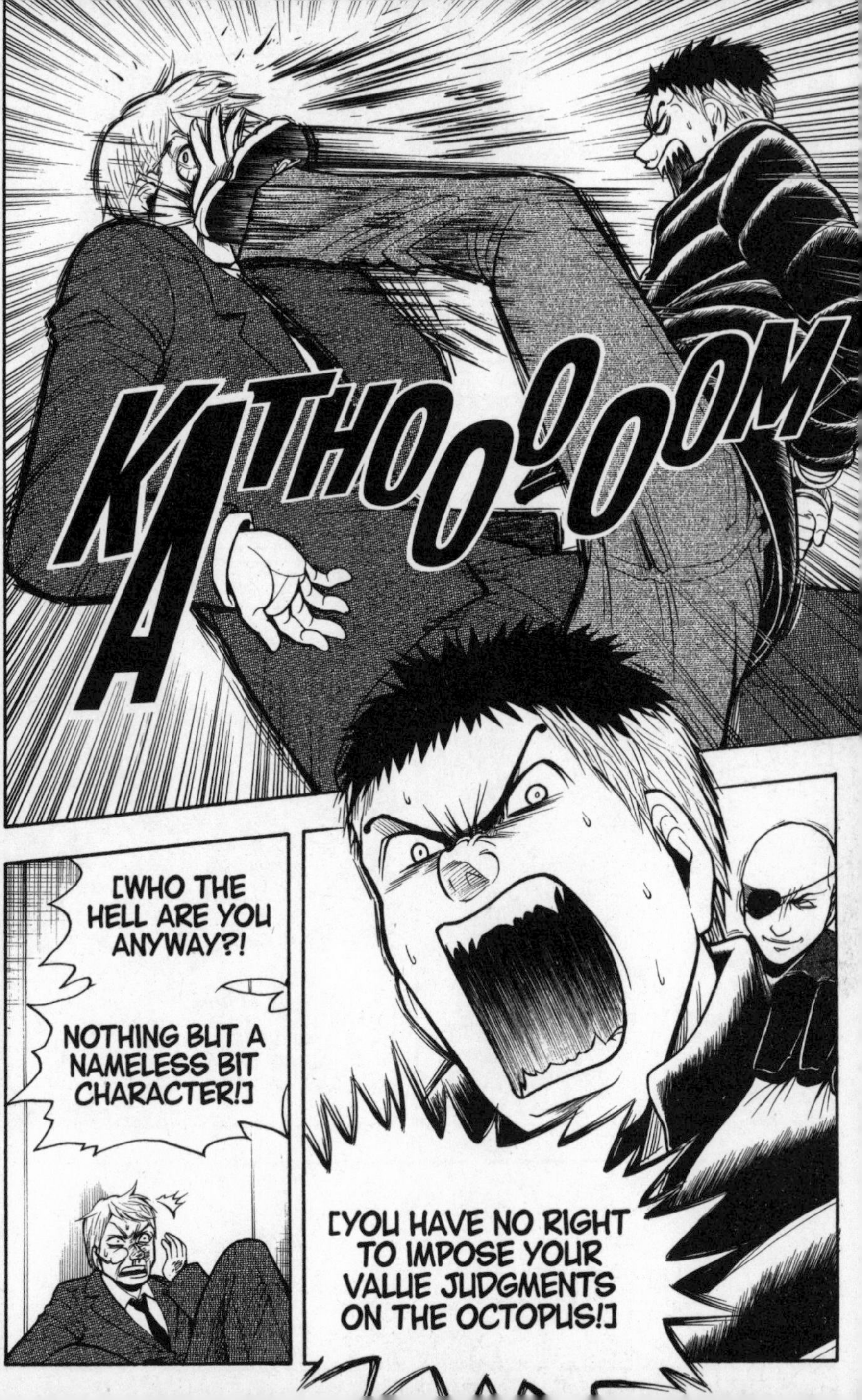
KATHOOOOOOM
[YOU HAVE NO RIGHT TO IMPOSE YOUR VALUE JUDGMENTS ON THE OCTOPUS!]
[WHO THE HELL ARE YOU ANYWAY?!
NOTHING BUT A NAMELESS BIT CHARACTER!]

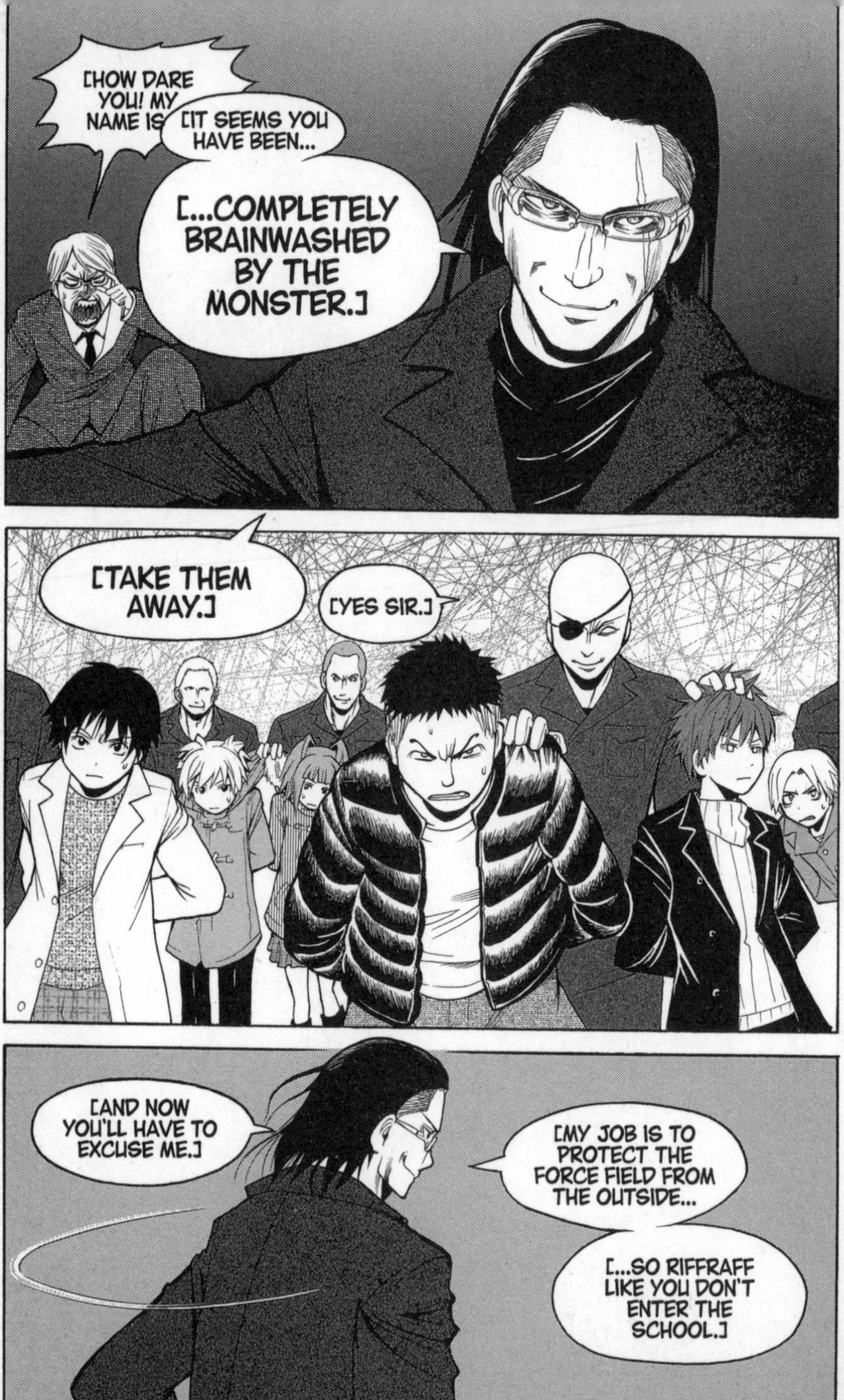
[HOW DARE YOU! MY NAME IS
[IT SEEMS YOU HAVE BEEN...
[...COMPLETELY BRAINWASHED BY THE MONSTER.]
[TAKE THEM AWAY.]
[YES SIR.]
[MY JOB IS TO PROTECT THE FORCE FIELD FROM THE OUTSIDE...
[...SO RIFFRAFF LIKE YOU DON'T ENTER THE SCHOOL.]
[AND NOW YOU'LL HAVE TO EXCUSE ME.]

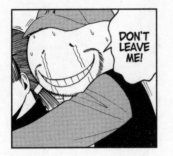

DON'T LEAVE ME!
How pathetic! This...
...has turned into this!

True Body Shaming

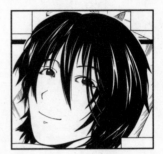

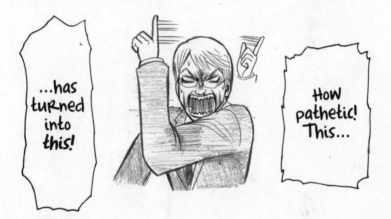

CLASS 166 TIME FOR CONFUSION

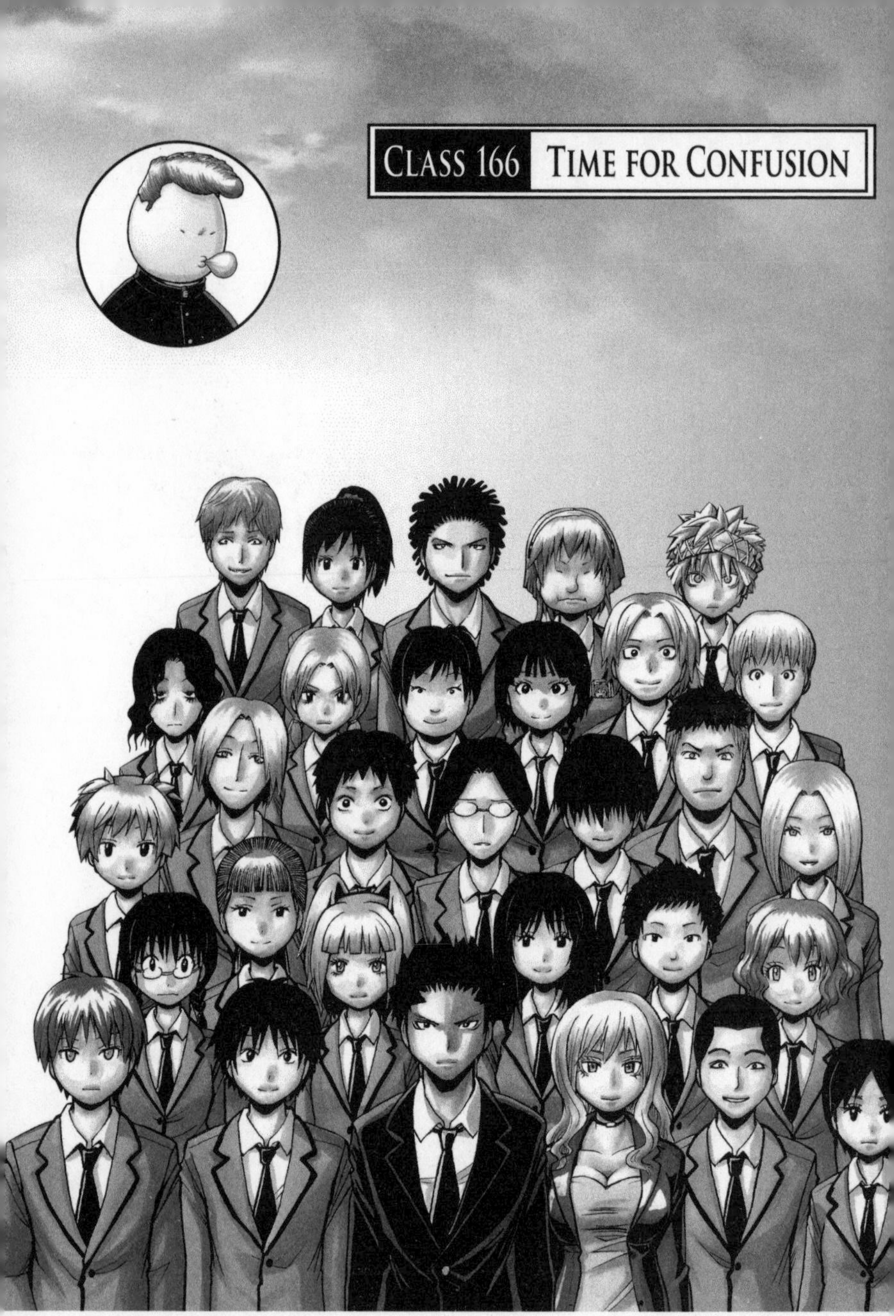

Kunugigaoka Middle School 3rd Year Class E

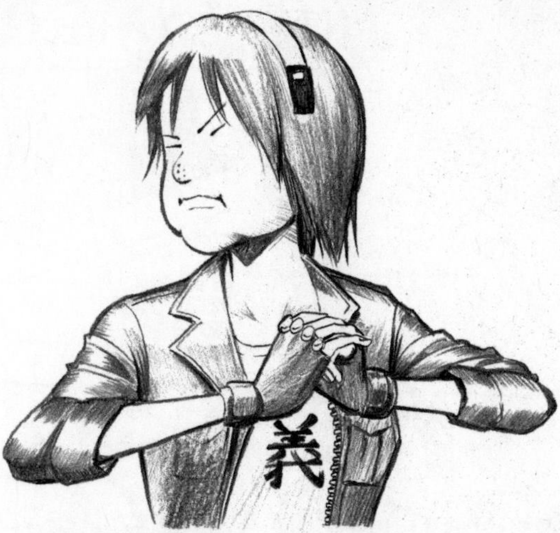

義

NISE ONAGA (FAKE RITSU)

- BIRTHDAY: FEBRUARY 4
- HEIGHT: 5' 1"
- WEIGHT: 99 LBS.
- FAVORITE SUBJECT: JAPANESE
- LEAST FAVORITE SUBJECT: MATHEMATICS
- HOBBY/SKILL: SHORINJI KEMPO
- FUTURE GOAL: MYSTERY HUNTER GAME SHOW PRESENTER
- AFTER WATCHING THE TV BROADCAST—RUSHES OUT OF THE HOUSE TO HELP CLASS E
- HER DAD NOTICES—AND TRIES TO STOP HER
- ROUND 1: NISE GETS THE UPPER HAND AFTER A REVERSE PUNCH AND RAPID ATTACK
- ROUND 2: HER FATHER COLLAPSES UNDER NISE'S ROUNDHOUSE KICK
- ROUND 3: HER FATHER CLINGS TO HER, ATTEMPTING TO CONVINCE HER TO STAY, AND NISE FINALLY GIVES IN

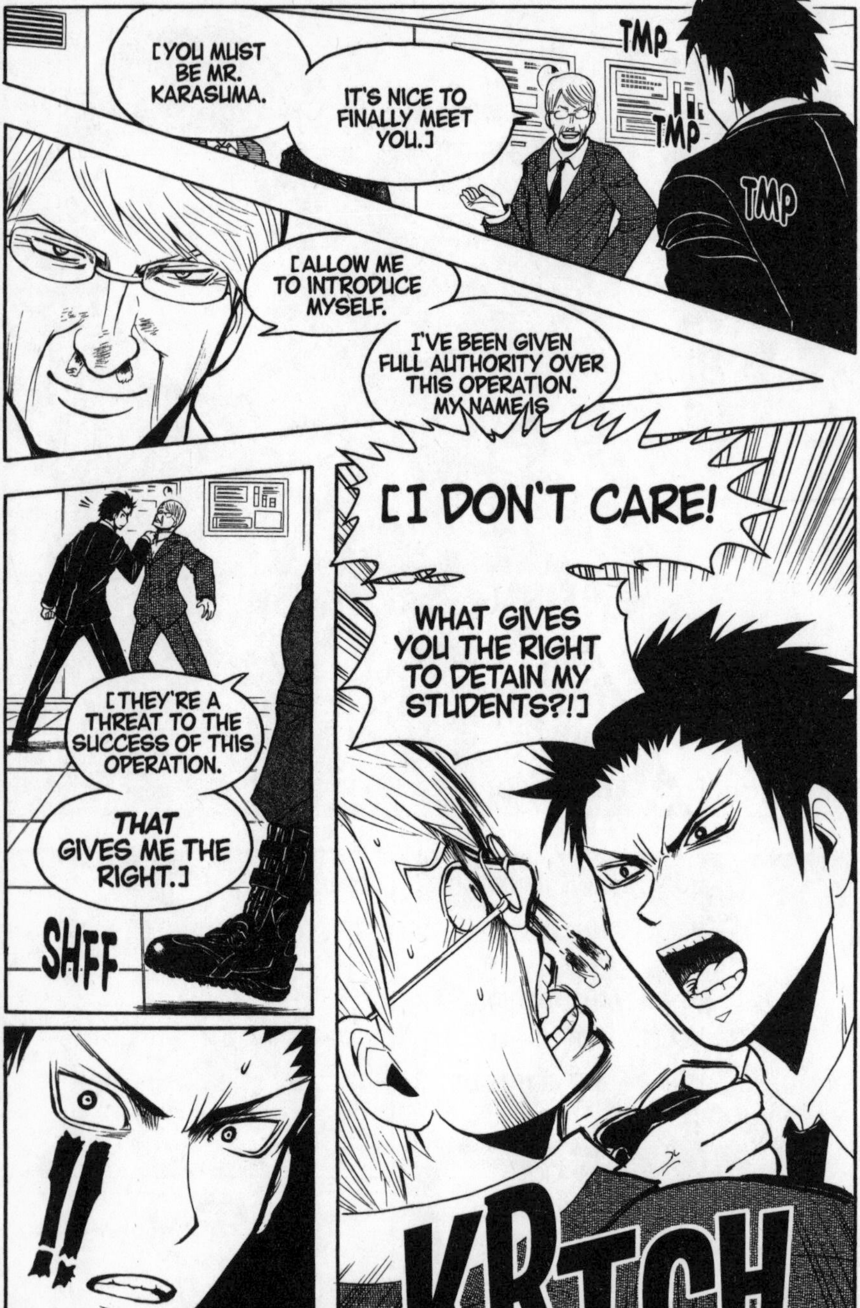
[YOU MUST BE MR. KARASUMA.
IT'S NICE TO FINALLY MEET YOU.]
TMP
TMP
TMP
[ALLOW ME TO INTRODUCE MYSELF.
I'VE BEEN GIVEN FULL AUTHORITY OVER THIS OPERATION. MY NAME IS
[I DON'T CARE!
WHAT GIVES YOU THE RIGHT TO DETAIN MY STUDENTS?!]
KRTCH
[THEY'RE A THREAT TO THE SUCCESS OF THIS OPERATION.
THAT GIVES ME THE RIGHT.]
SHFF
!!

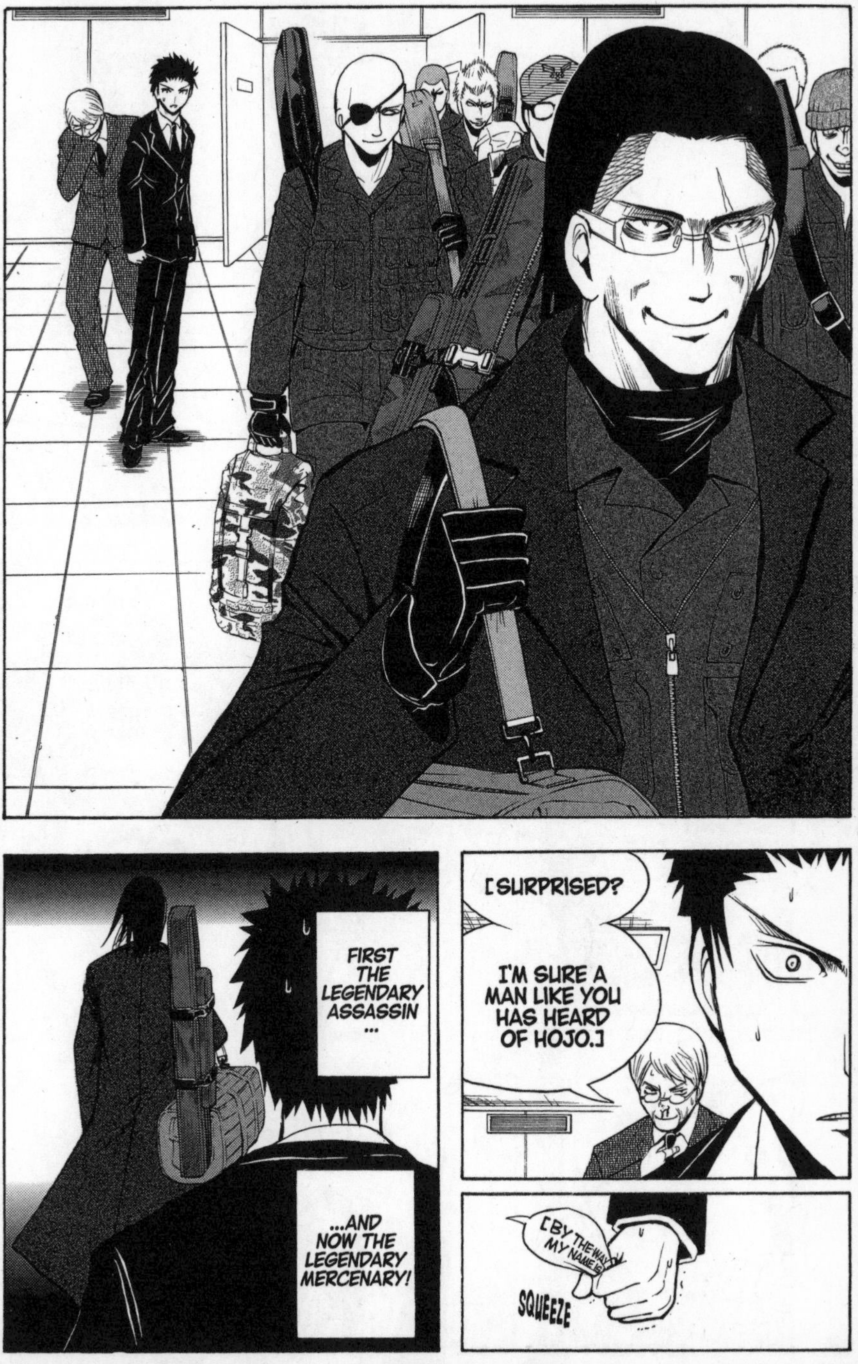
[SURPRISED?
I'M SURE A MAN LIKE YOU HAS HEARD OF HOJO.]
[BY THE WAY MY NAME IS
SQUEEZE
FIRST THE LEGENDARY ASSASSIN ...
...AND NOW THE LEGENDARY MERCENARY!

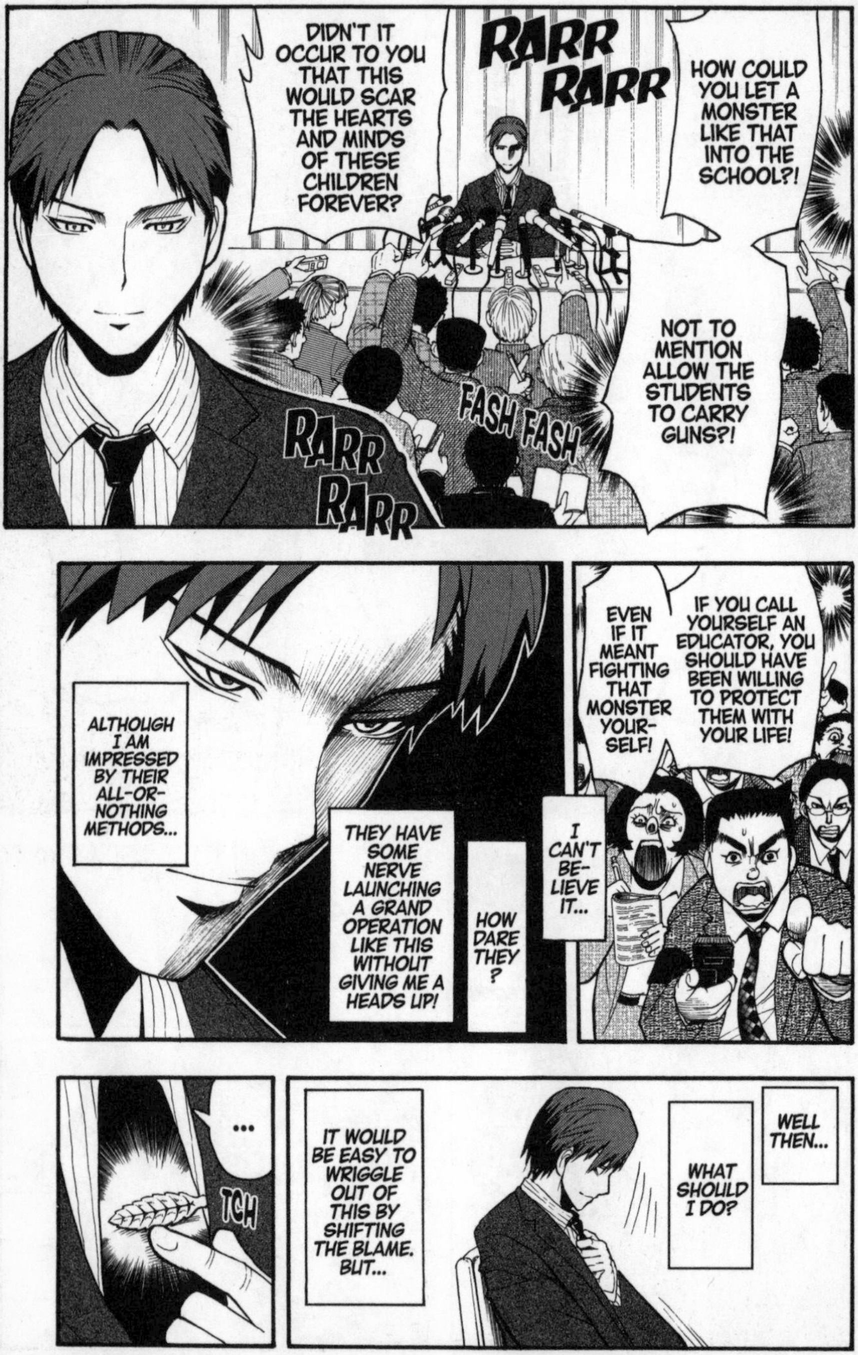
HOW COULD YOU LET A MONSTER LIKE THAT INTO THE SCHOOL?!
RARR RARR
DIDN'T IT OCCUR TO YOU THAT THIS WOULD SCAR THE HEARTS AND MINDS OF THESE CHILDREN FOREVER?
NOT TO MENTION ALLOW THE STUDENTS TO CARRY GUNS?!
FASH FASH
RARR RARR
IF YOU CALL YOURSELF AN EDUCATOR, YOU SHOULD HAVE BEEN WILLING TO PROTECT THEM WITH YOUR LIFE!
EVEN IF IT MEANT FIGHTING THAT MONSTER YOUR-SELF!
I CAN'T BE-LIEVE IT...
HOW DARE THEY?
THEY HAVE SOME NERVE LAUNCHING A GRAND OPERATION LIKE THIS WITHOUT GIVING ME A HEADS UP!
ALTHOUGH I AM IMPRESSED BY THEIR ALL-OR-NOTHING METHODS...
WELL THEN...
WHAT SHOULD I DO?
IT WOULD BE EASY TO WRIGGLE OUT OF THIS BY SHIFTING THE BLAME. BUT...
...
TCH

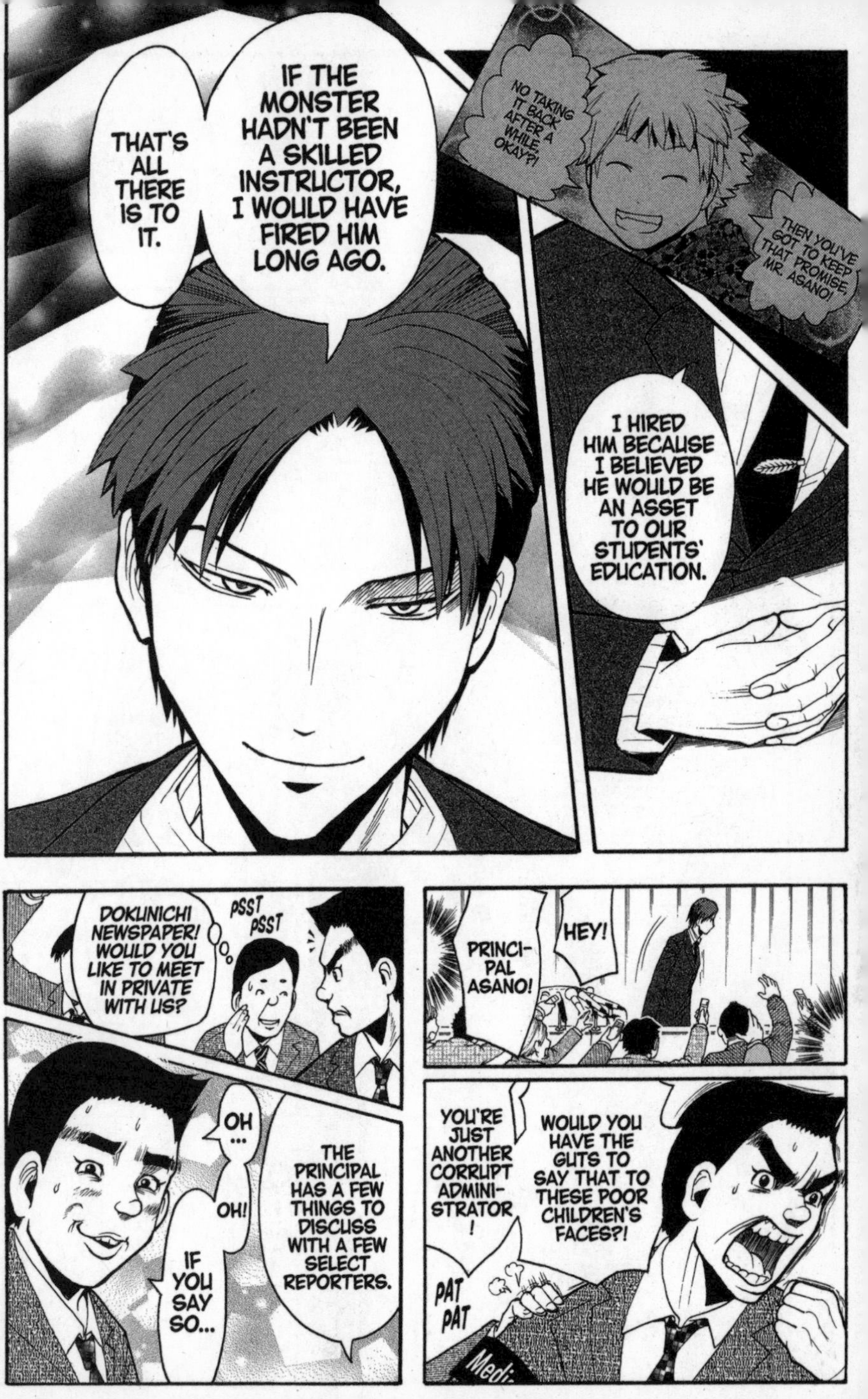
NO TAKING IT BACK AFTER A WHILE, OKAY?!
THEN YOU'VE GOT TO KEEP THAT PROMISE, MR. ASANO!
I HIRED HIM BECAUSE I BELIEVED HE WOULD BE AN ASSET TO OUR STUDENTS' EDUCATION.
IF THE MONSTER HADN'T BEEN A SKILLED INSTRUCTOR, I WOULD HAVE FIRED HIM LONG AGO.
THAT'S ALL THERE IS TO IT.
HEY!
PRINCIPAL ASANO!
WOULD YOU HAVE THE GUTS TO SAY THAT TO THESE POOR CHILDREN'S FACES?!
YOU'RE JUST ANOTHER CORRUPT ADMINISTRATOR!
PAT PAT
PSST PSST
DOKUNICHI NEWSPAPER! WOULD YOU LIKE TO MEET IN PRIVATE WITH US?
THE PRINCIPAL HAS A FEW THINGS TO DISCUSS WITH A FEW SELECT REPORTERS.
OH...
OH!
IF YOU SAY SO...

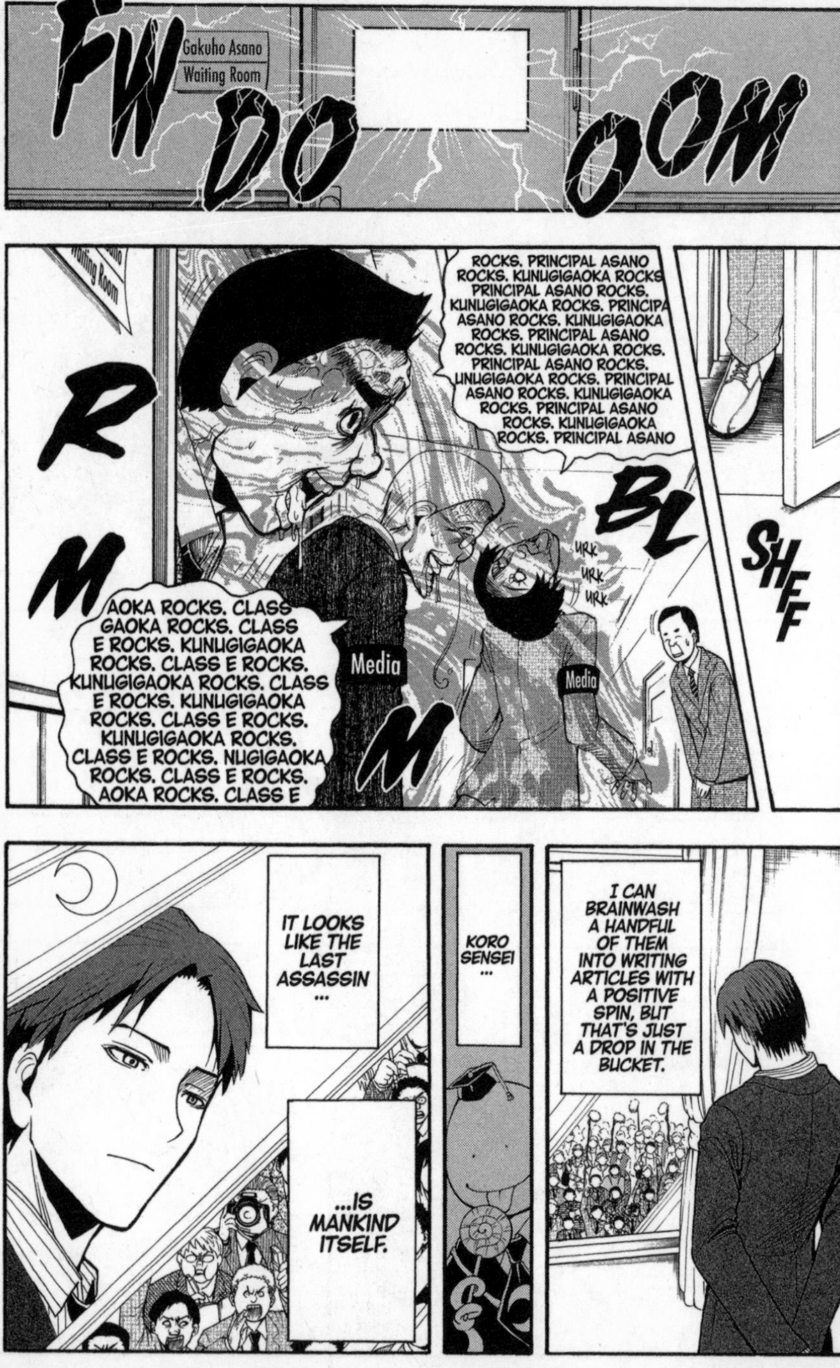
Gakuho Asano Waiting Room
FW DO OOM
SHEFF
ROCKS. PRINCIPAL ASANO ROCKS. KUNUGIGAOKA ROCKS PRINCIPAL ASANO ROCKS. KUNUGIGAOKA ROCKS. PRINCIPA ASANO ROCKS. KUNUGIGAOKA ROCKS. PRINCIPAL ASANO ROCKS. KUNUGIGAOKA ROCKS. PRINCIPAL ASANO ROCKS. UNUGIGAOKA ROCKS. PRINCIPAL ASANO ROCKS. KUNUGIGAOKA ROCKS. PRINCIPAL ASANO ROCKS. KUNUGIGAOKA ROCKS. PRINCIPAL ASANO
BL
URK URK URK
Media
Media
R M M
AOKA ROCKS. CLASS GAOKA ROCKS. CLASS E ROCKS. KUNUGIGAOKA ROCKS. CLASS E ROCKS. KUNUGIGAOKA ROCKS. CLASS E ROCKS. KUNUGIGAOKA ROCKS. CLASS E ROCKS. KUNUGIGAOKA ROCKS. CLASS E ROCKS. NUGIGAOKA ROCKS. CLASS E ROCKS. AOKA ROCKS. CLASS E
I CAN BRAINWASH A HANDFUL OF THEM INTO WRITING ARTICLES WITH A POSITIVE SPIN, BUT THAT'S JUST A DROP IN THE BUCKET.
KORO SENSEI ...
IT LOOKS LIKE THE LAST ASSASSIN ...
...IS MANKIND ITSELF.

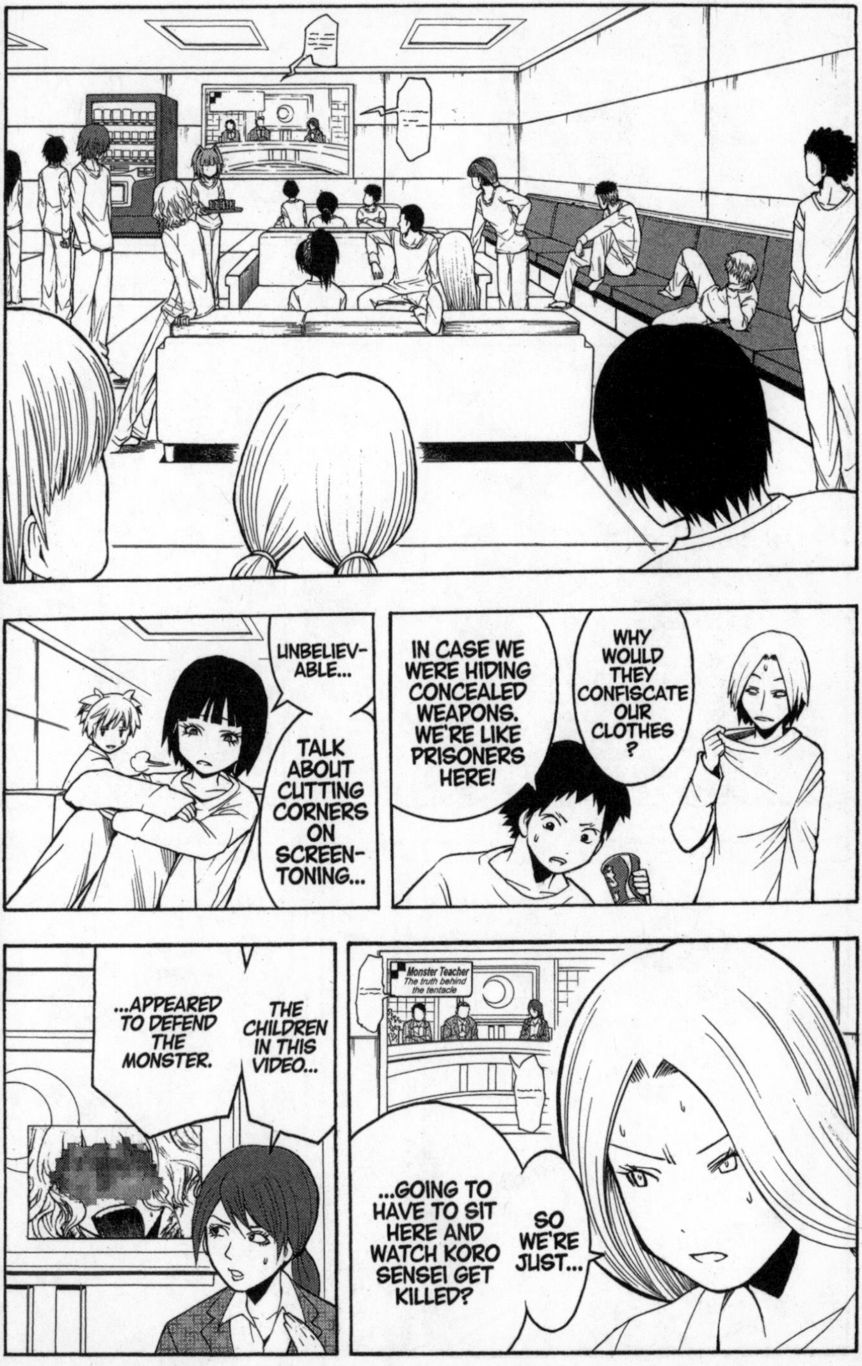
WHY WOULD THEY CONFISCATE OUR CLOTHES?
IN CASE WE WERE HIDING CONCEALED WEAPONS. WE'RE LIKE PRISONERS HERE!
UNBELIEVABLE...
TALK ABOUT CUTTING CORNERS ON SCREENTONING...
Monster Teacher
The truth behind the tentacle
SO WE'RE JUST...
...GOING TO HAVE TO SIT HERE AND WATCH KORO SENSEI GET KILLED?
THE CHILDREN IN THIS VIDEO...
...APPEARED TO DEFEND THE MONSTER.

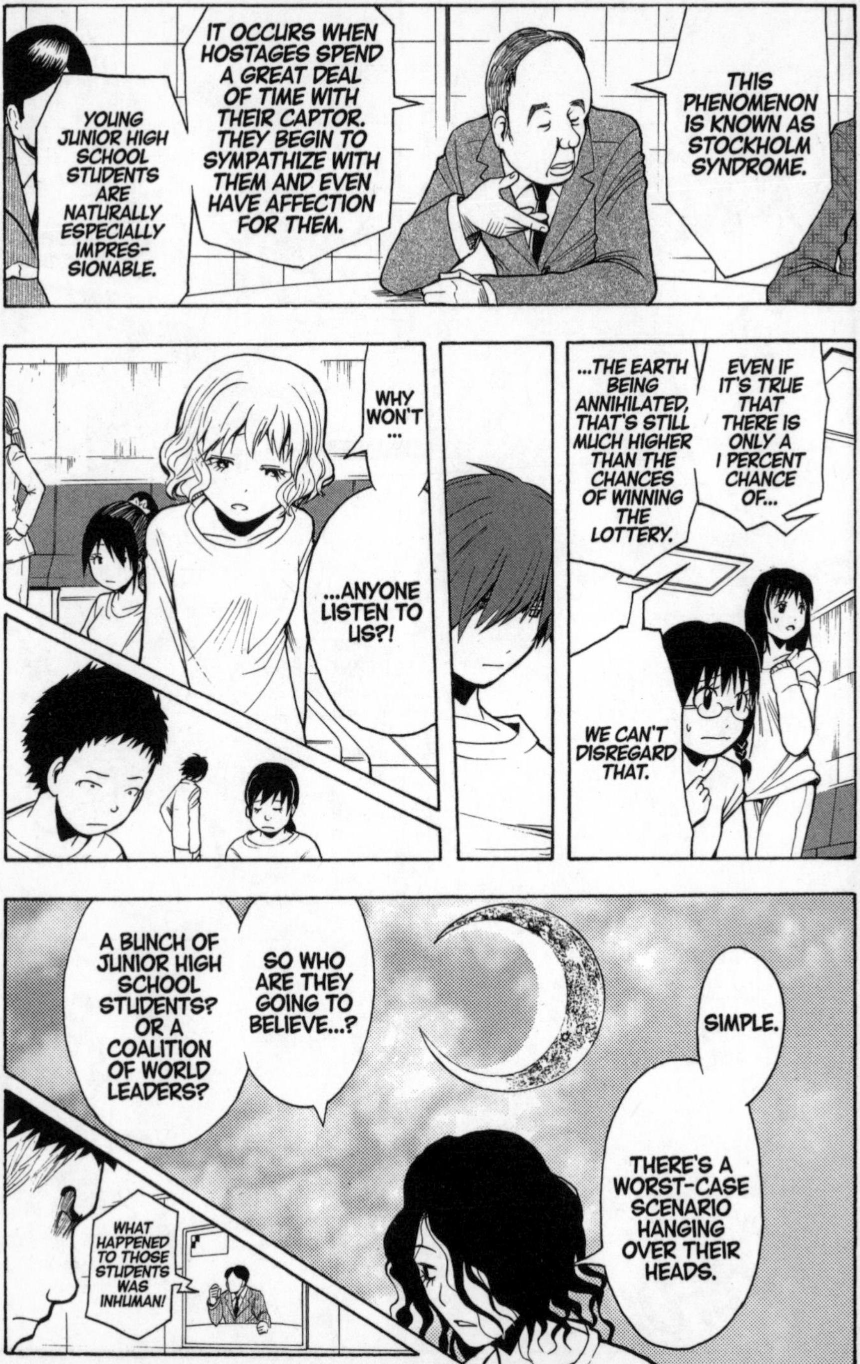
THIS PHENOMENON IS KNOWN AS STOCKHOLM SYNDROME.
IT OCCURS WHEN HOSTAGES SPEND A GREAT DEAL OF TIME WITH THEIR CAPTOR. THEY BEGIN TO SYMPATHIZE WITH THEM AND EVEN HAVE AFFECTION FOR THEM.
YOUNG JUNIOR HIGH SCHOOL STUDENTS ARE NATURALLY ESPECIALLY IMPRES-SIONABLE.
EVEN IF IT'S TRUE THAT THERE IS ONLY A 1 PERCENT CHANCE OF...
...THE EARTH BEING ANNIHILATED, THAT'S STILL MUCH HIGHER THAN THE CHANCES OF WINNING THE LOTTERY.
WE CAN'T DISREGARD THAT.
WHY WON'T ...
...ANYONE LISTEN TO US?!
SIMPLE.
SO WHO ARE THEY GOING TO BELIEVE...?
A BUNCH OF JUNIOR HIGH SCHOOL STUDENTS? OR A COALITION OF WORLD LEADERS?
THERE'S A WORST-CASE SCENARIO HANGING OVER THEIR HEADS.
WHAT HAPPENED TO THOSE STUDENTS WAS INHUMAN!

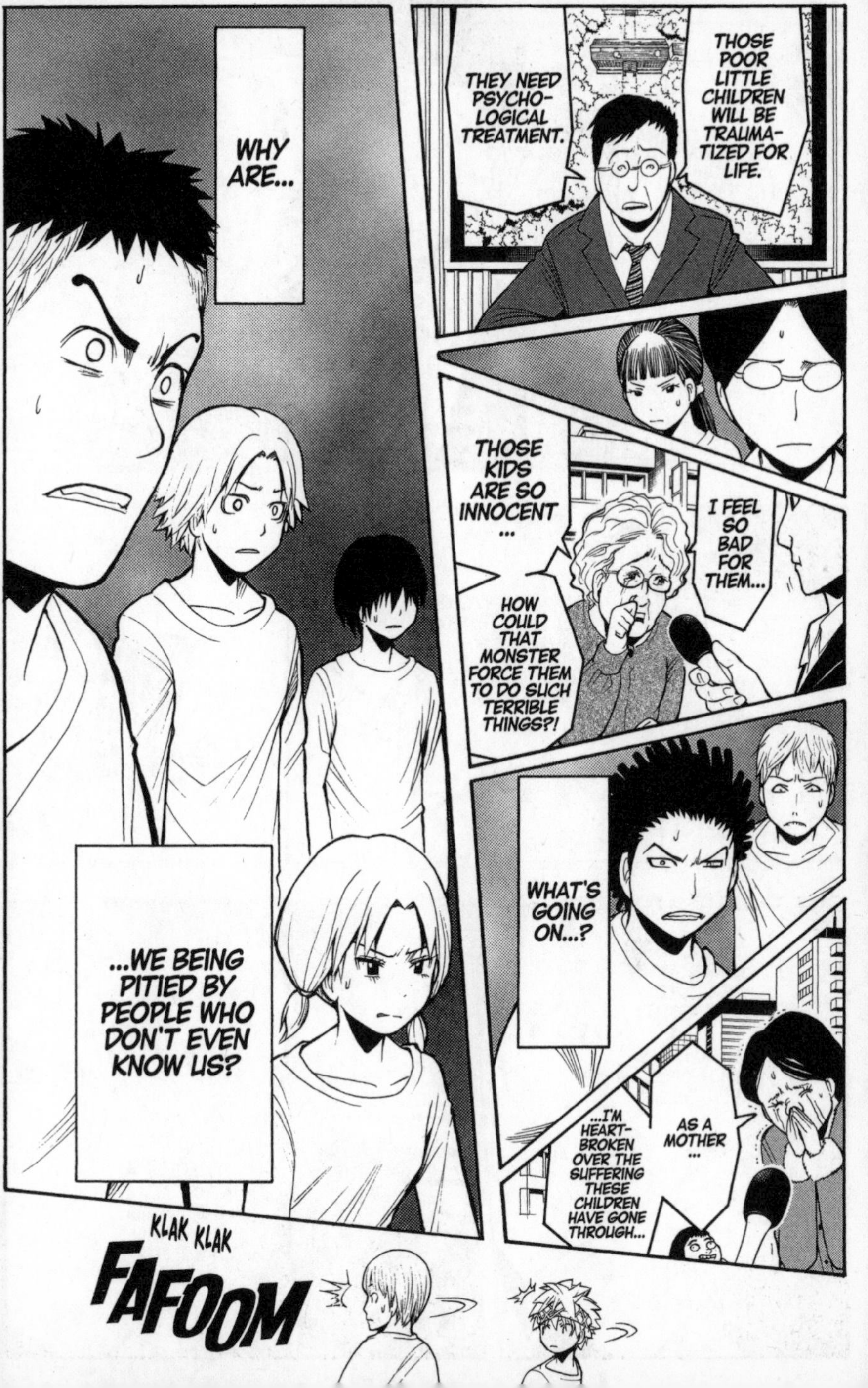
THOSE POOR LITTLE CHILDREN WILL BE TRAUMA-TIZED FOR LIFE.
THEY NEED PSYCHO-LOGICAL TREATMENT.
I FEEL SO BAD FOR THEM...
THOSE KIDS ARE SO INNOCENT ...
HOW COULD THAT MONSTER FORCE THEM TO DO SUCH TERRIBLE THINGS?!
WHAT'S GOING ON...?
AS A MOTHER ...
...I'M HEART-BROKEN OVER THE SUFFERING THESE CHILDREN HAVE GONE THROUGH...
WHY ARE...
...WE BEING PITIED BY PEOPLE WHO DON'T EVEN KNOW US?
KLAK KLAK
FAFOOM

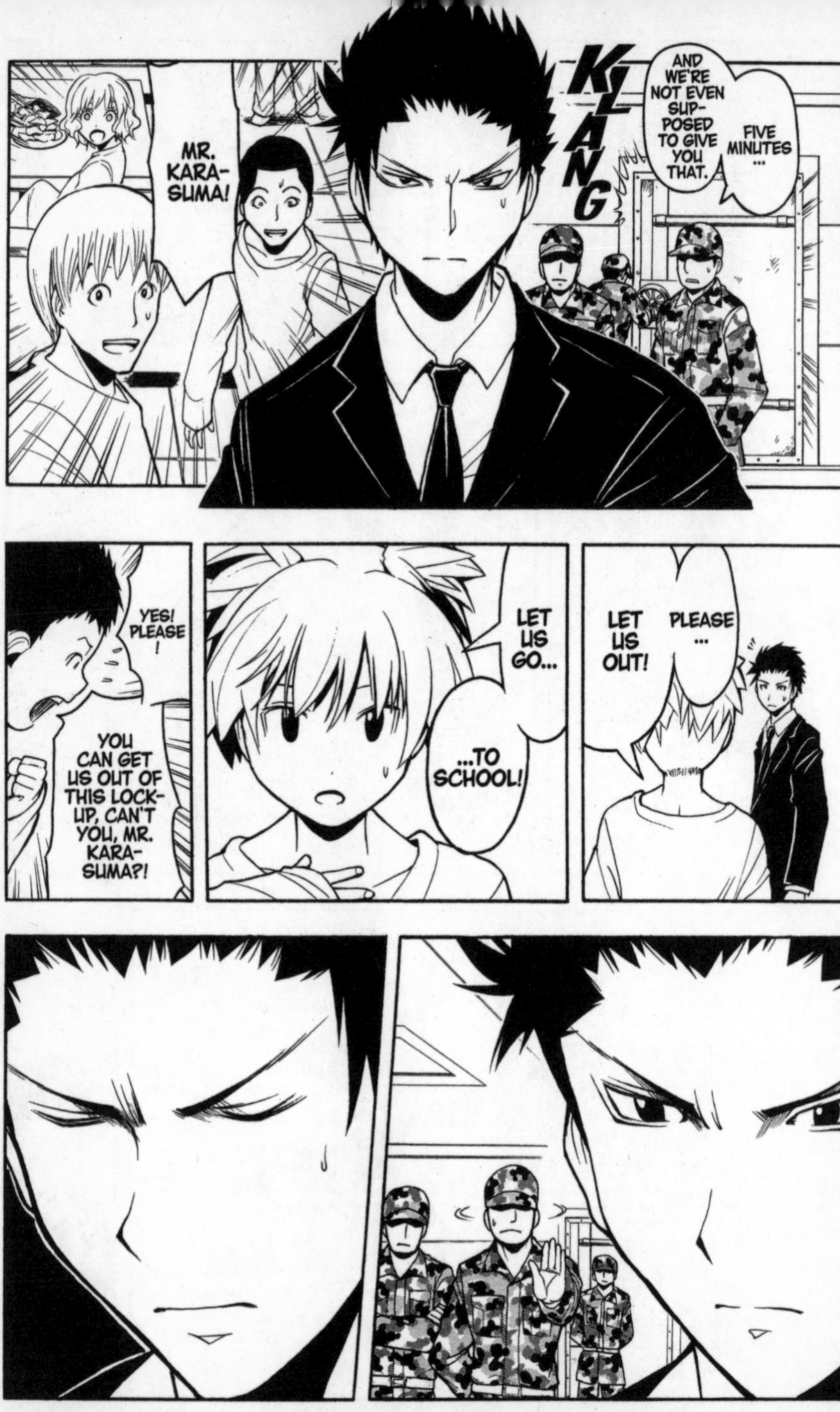

FIVE MINUTES...
AND WE'RE NOT EVEN SUPPOSED TO GIVE YOU THAT.
KLANG
MR. KARASUMA!
PLEASE...
LET US OUT!
LET US GO...
...TO SCHOOL!
YES! PLEASE!
YOU CAN GET US OUT OF THIS LOCK-UP, CAN'T YOU, MR. KARASUMA?!

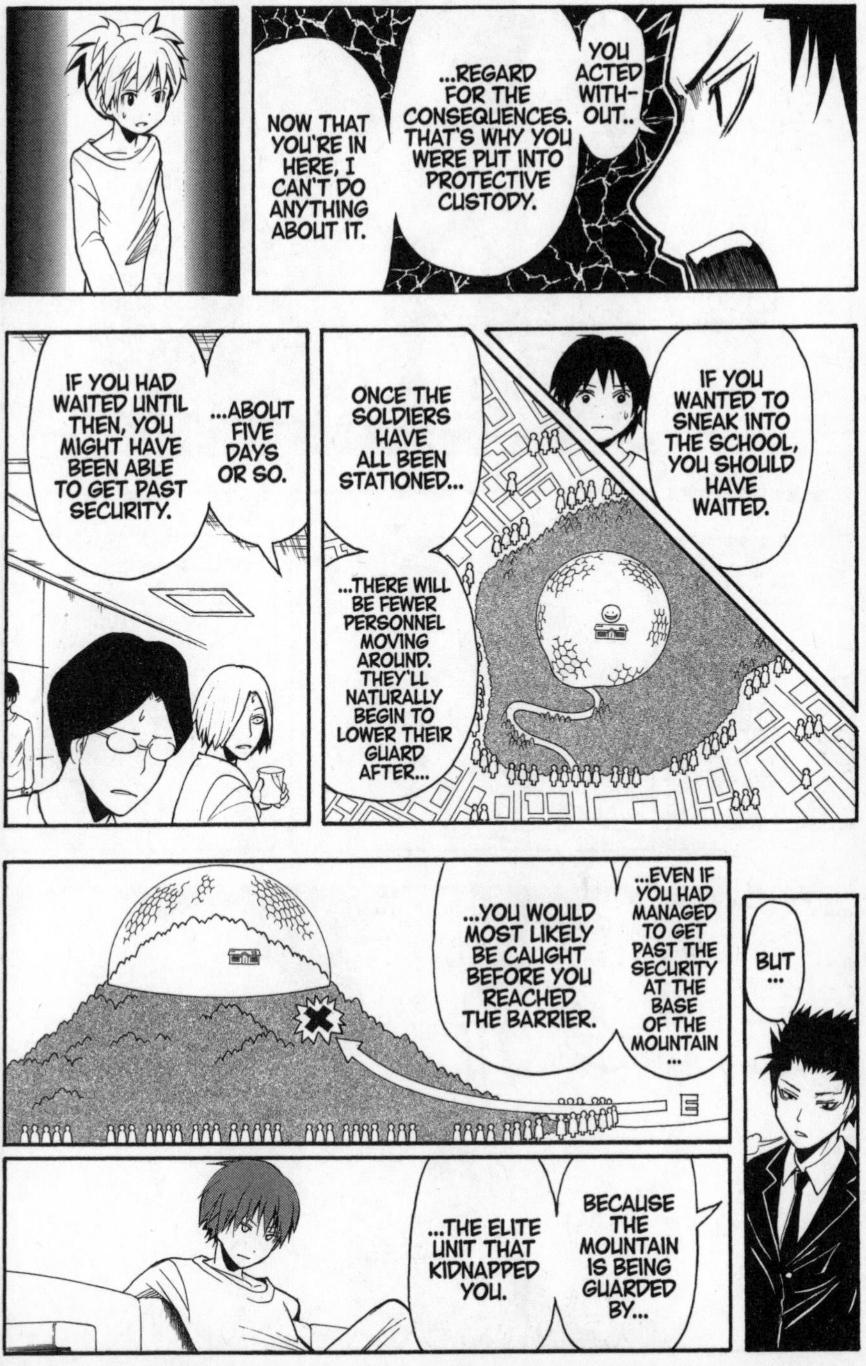
YOU ACTED WITHOUT..
...REGARD FOR THE CONSEQUENCES. THAT'S WHY YOU WERE PUT INTO PROTECTIVE CUSTODY.
NOW THAT YOU'RE IN HERE, I CAN'T DO ANYTHING ABOUT IT.
IF YOU WANTED TO SNEAK INTO THE SCHOOL, YOU SHOULD HAVE WAITED.
ONCE THE SOLDIERS HAVE ALL BEEN STATIONED...
...THERE WILL BE FEWER PERSONNEL MOVING AROUND. THEY'LL NATURALLY BEGIN TO LOWER THEIR GUARD AFTER...
...ABOUT FIVE DAYS OR SO.
IF YOU HAD WAITED UNTIL THEN, YOU MIGHT HAVE BEEN ABLE TO GET PAST SECURITY.
BUT ...
...EVEN IF YOU HAD MANAGED TO GET PAST THE SECURITY AT THE BASE OF THE MOUNTAIN ...
...YOU WOULD MOST LIKELY BE CAUGHT BEFORE YOU REACHED THE BARRIER.
BECAUSE THE MOUNTAIN IS BEING GUARDED BY...
...THE ELITE UNIT THAT KIDNAPPED YOU.

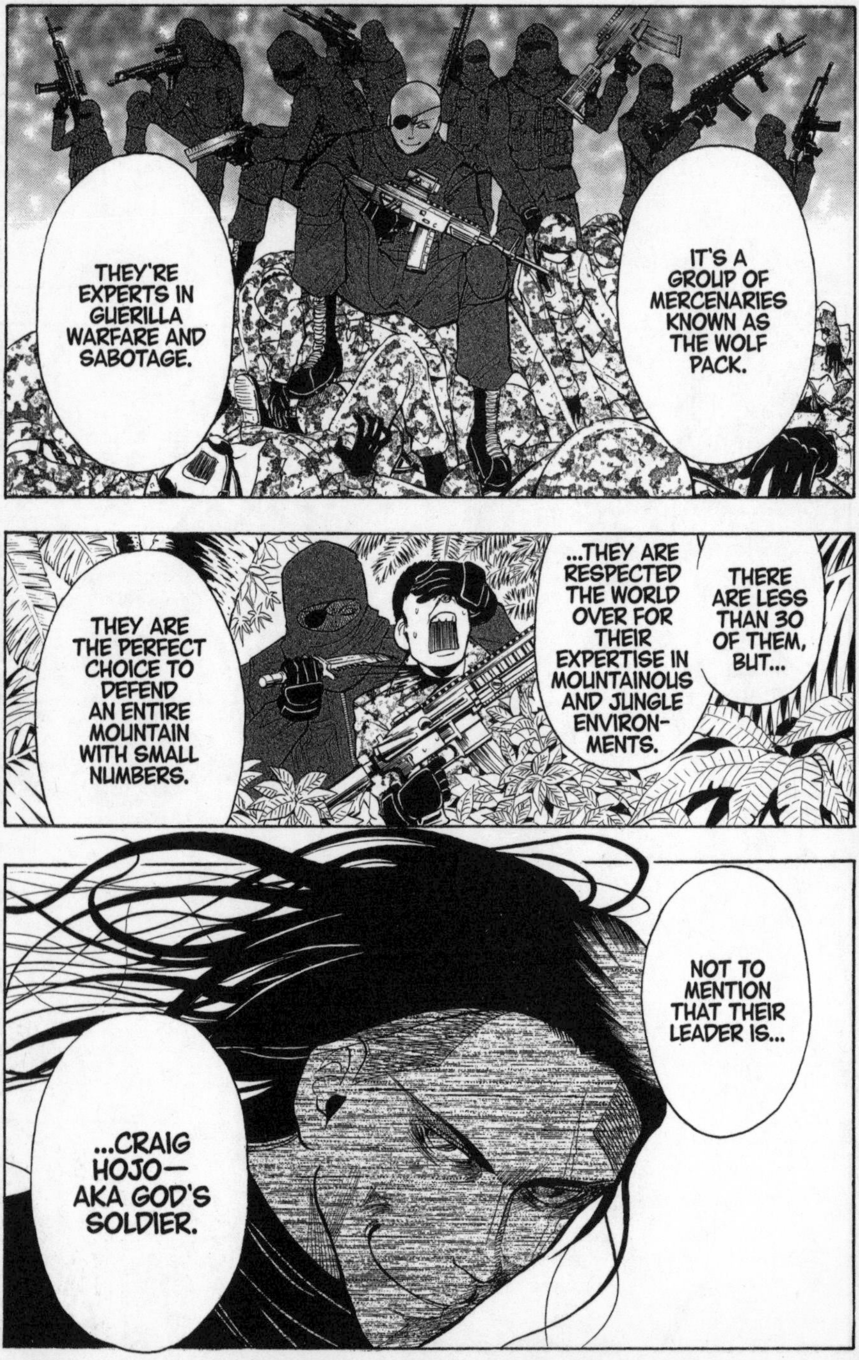
IT'S A GROUP OF MERCENARIES KNOWN AS THE WOLF PACK.
THEY'RE EXPERTS IN GUERILLA WARFARE AND SABOTAGE.
THERE ARE LESS THAN 30 OF THEM, BUT...
...THEY ARE RESPECTED THE WORLD OVER FOR THEIR EXPERTISE IN MOUNTAINOUS AND JUNGLE ENVIRON-MENTS.
THEY ARE THE PERFECT CHOICE TO DEFEND AN ENTIRE MOUNTAIN WITH SMALL NUMBERS.
NOT TO MENTION THAT THEIR LEADER IS...
...CRAIG HOJO—AKA GOD'S SOLDIER.

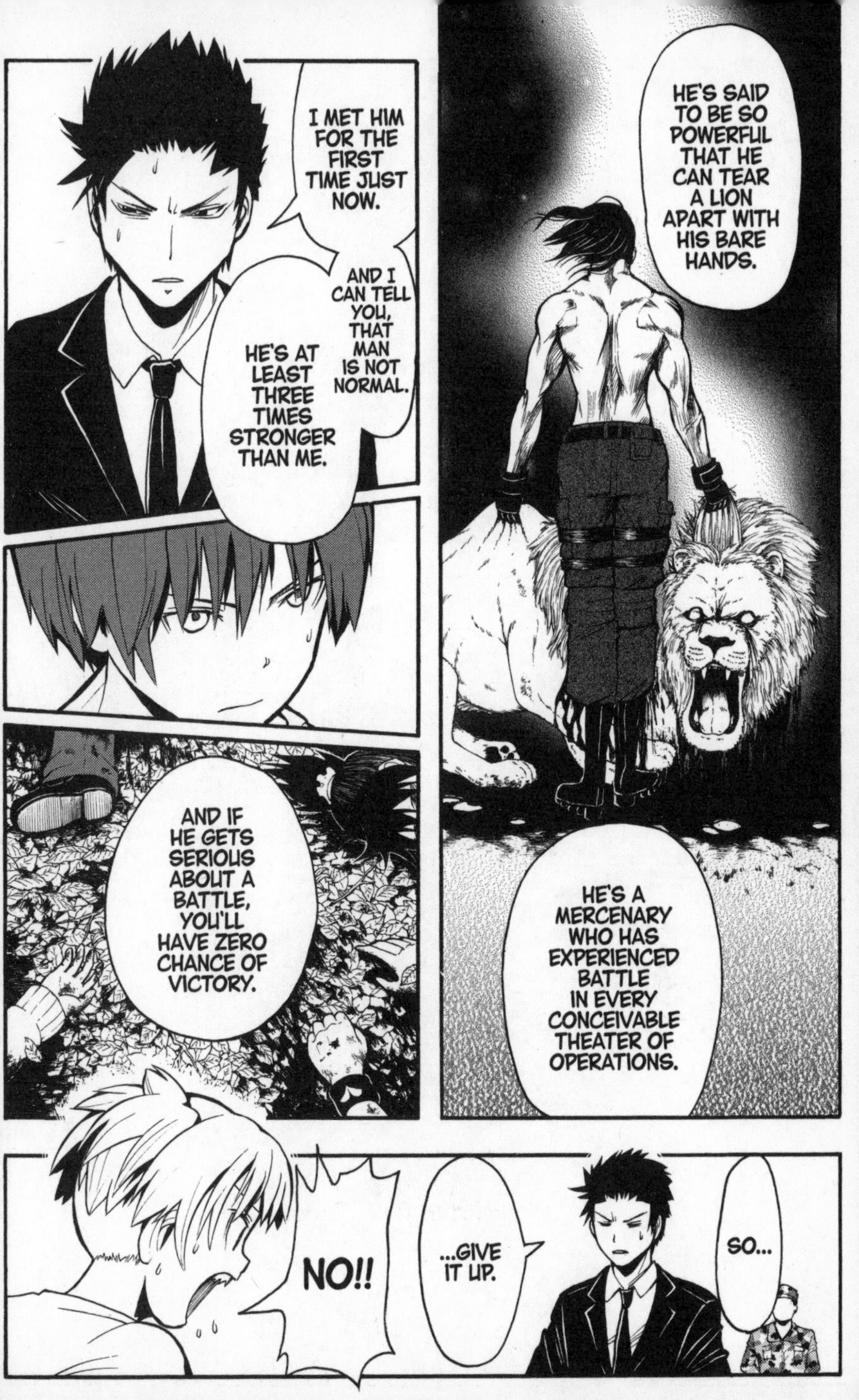
HE'S SAID TO BE SO POWERFUL THAT HE CAN TEAR A LION APART WITH HIS BARE HANDS.
HE'S A MERCENARY WHO HAS EXPERIENCED BATTLE IN EVERY CONCEIVABLE THEATER OF OPERATIONS.
I MET HIM FOR THE FIRST TIME JUST NOW.
AND I CAN TELL YOU, THAT MAN IS NOT NORMAL.
HE'S AT LEAST THREE TIMES STRONGER THAN ME.
AND IF HE GETS SERIOUS ABOUT A BATTLE, YOU'LL HAVE ZERO CHANCE OF VICTORY.
SO...
...GIVE IT UP.
NO!!

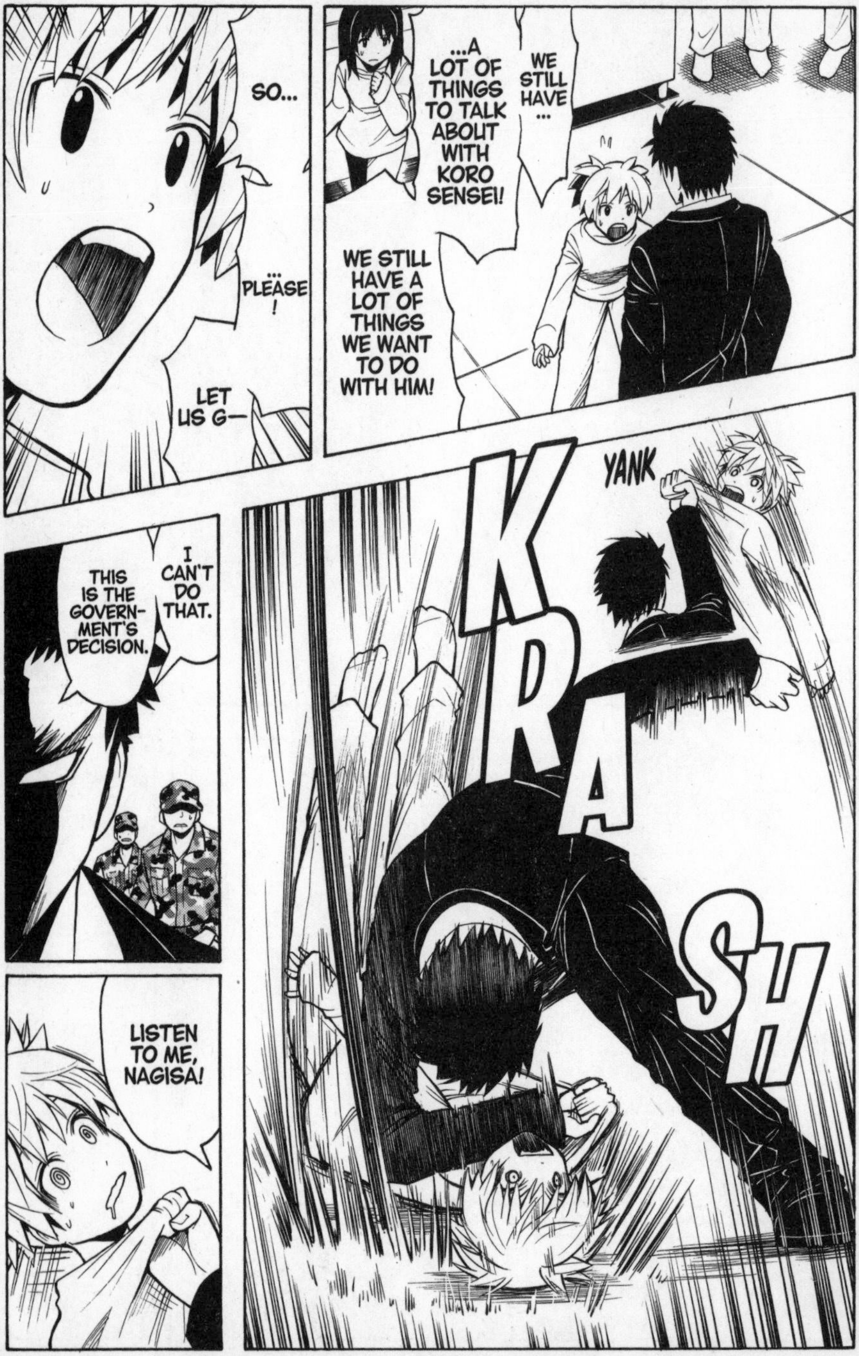

WE STILL HAVE ...
...A LOT OF THINGS TO TALK ABOUT WITH KORO SENSEI!
WE STILL HAVE A LOT OF THINGS WE WANT TO DO WITH HIM!
SO...
...PLEASE!
LET US G—
YANK
KRASH
I CAN'T DO THAT.
THIS IS THE GOVERNMENT'S DECISION.
LISTEN TO ME, NAGISA!

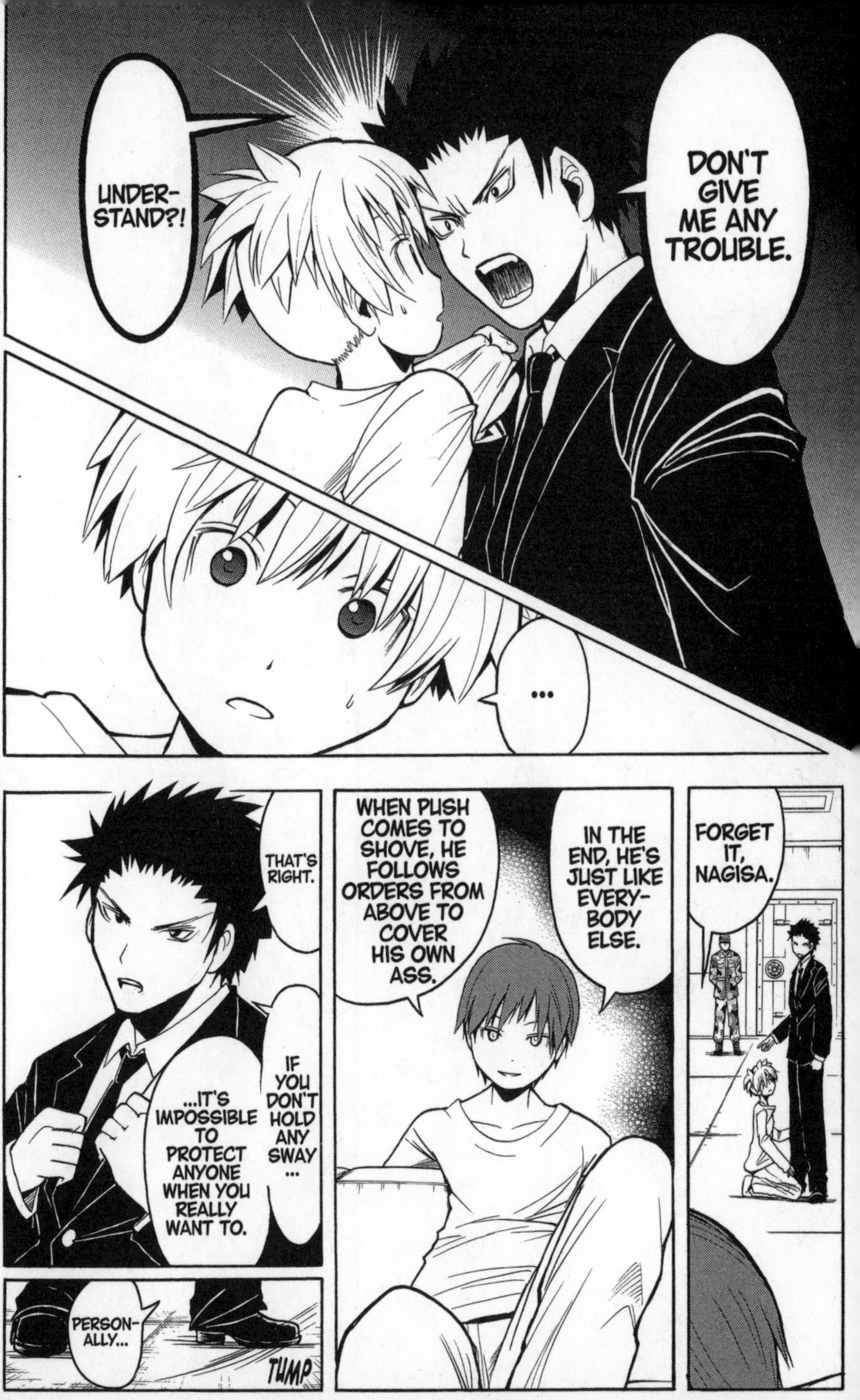
DON'T GIVE ME ANY TROUBLE.
UNDER-STAND?!
...
FORGET IT, NAGISA.
IN THE END, HE'S JUST LIKE EVERY-BODY ELSE.
WHEN PUSH COMES TO SHOVE, HE FOLLOWS ORDERS FROM ABOVE TO COVER HIS OWN ASS.
THAT'S RIGHT.
IF YOU DON'T HOLD ANY SWAY...
...IT'S IMPOSSIBLE TO PROTECT ANYONE WHEN YOU REALLY WANT TO.
PERSON-ALLY...
TUMP

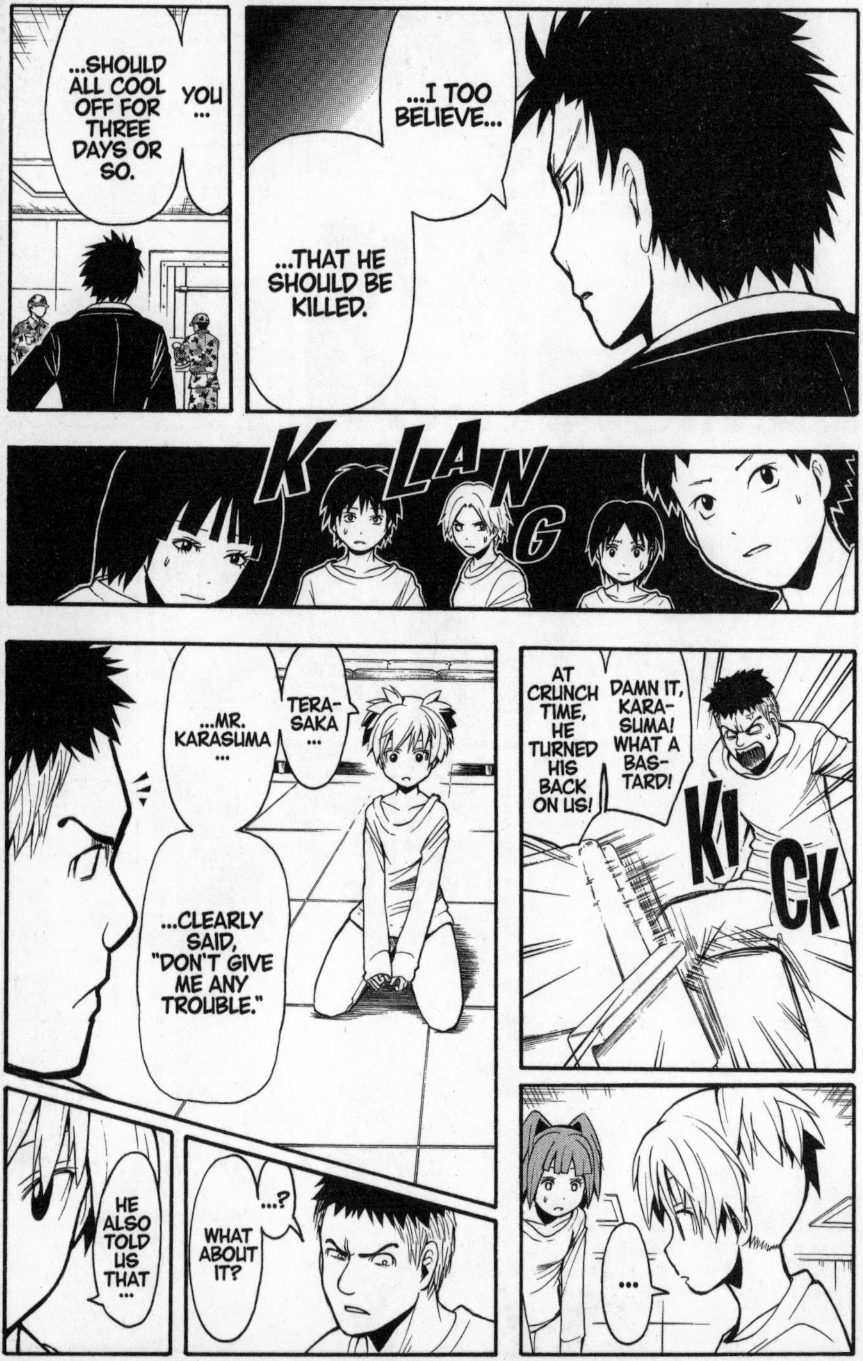
...I TOO BELIEVE...
...THAT HE SHOULD BE KILLED.
YOU ...
...SHOULD ALL COOL OFF FOR THREE DAYS OR SO.
KLANG
DAMN IT, KARASUMA! WHAT A BASTARD!
AT CRUNCH TIME, HE TURNED HIS BACK ON US!
KICK
TERASAKA ...
...MR. KARASUMA ...
...CLEARLY SAID, "DON'T GIVE ME ANY TROUBLE."
...
...?
WHAT ABOUT IT?
HE ALSO TOLD US THAT ...

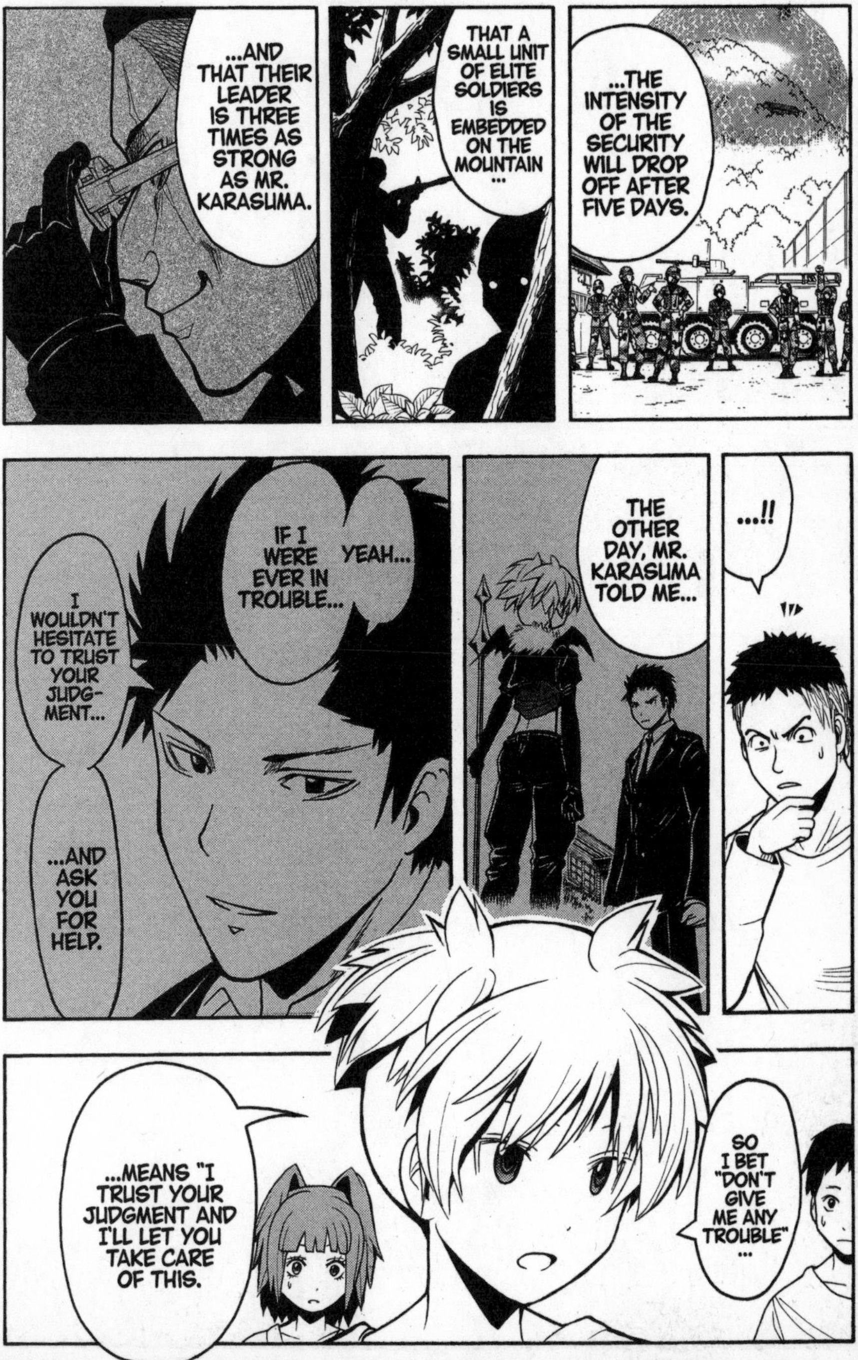
...THE INTENSITY OF THE SECURITY WILL DROP OFF AFTER FIVE DAYS.
THAT A SMALL UNIT OF ELITE SOLDIERS IS EMBEDDED ON THE MOUNTAIN ...
...AND THAT THEIR LEADER IS THREE TIMES AS STRONG AS MR. KARASUMA.
...!!
THE OTHER DAY, MR. KARASUMA TOLD ME...
YEAH...
IF I WERE EVER IN TROUBLE...
I WOULDN'T HESITATE TO TRUST YOUR JUDG-MENT...
...AND ASK YOU FOR HELP.
SO I BET "DON'T GIVE ME ANY TROUBLE" ...
...MEANS "I TRUST YOUR JUDGMENT AND I'LL LET YOU TAKE CARE OF THIS.

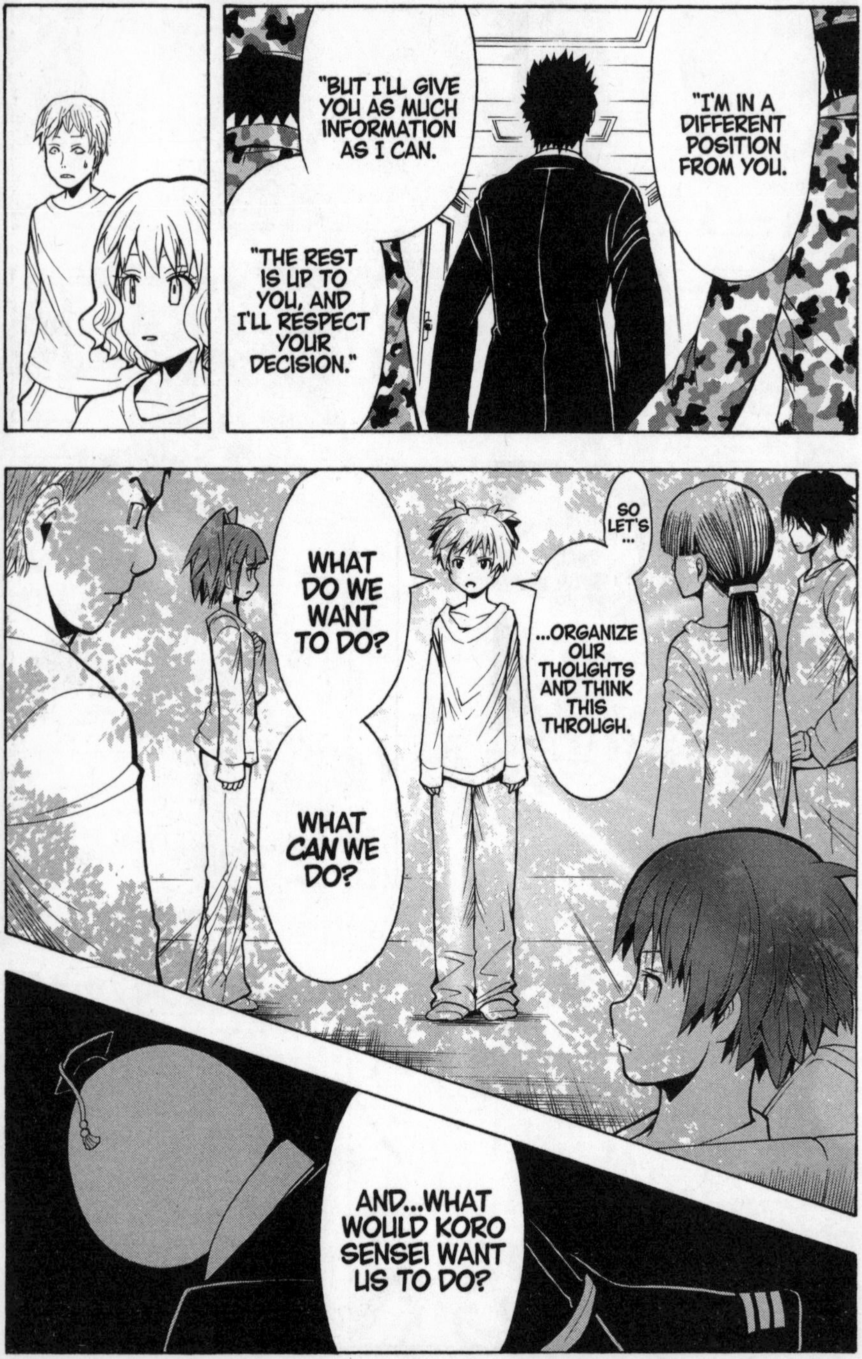
"I'M IN A DIFFERENT POSITION FROM YOU.
"BUT I'LL GIVE YOU AS MUCH INFORMATION AS I CAN.
"THE REST IS UP TO YOU, AND I'LL RESPECT YOUR DECISION."
SO LET'S...
...ORGANIZE OUR THOUGHTS AND THINK THIS THROUGH.
WHAT DO WE WANT TO DO?
WHAT CAN WE DO?
AND...WHAT WOULD KORO SENSEI WANT US TO DO?

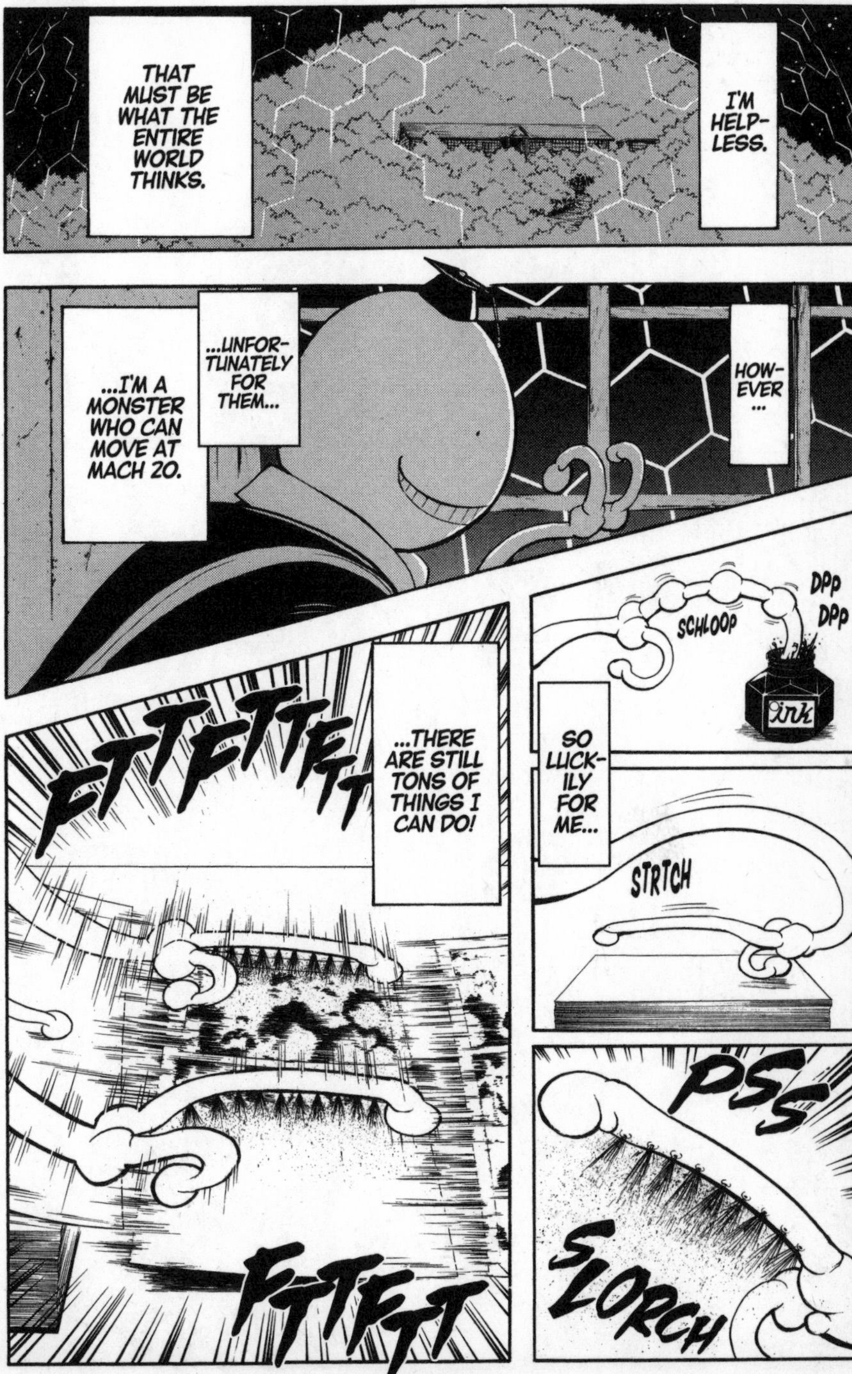
I'M HELP-LESS.
THAT MUST BE WHAT THE ENTIRE WORLD THINKS.
HOW-EVER...
...UNFOR-TUNATELY FOR THEM...
...I'M A MONSTER WHO CAN MOVE AT MACH 20.
DPP DPP
SCHLOOP
ink
SO LUCK-ILY FOR ME...
STRTCH
PSS
SLORCH
FTTFTTFTTT
...THERE ARE STILL TONS OF THINGS I CAN DO!
FTTFTT

Class 167 Time for Trust

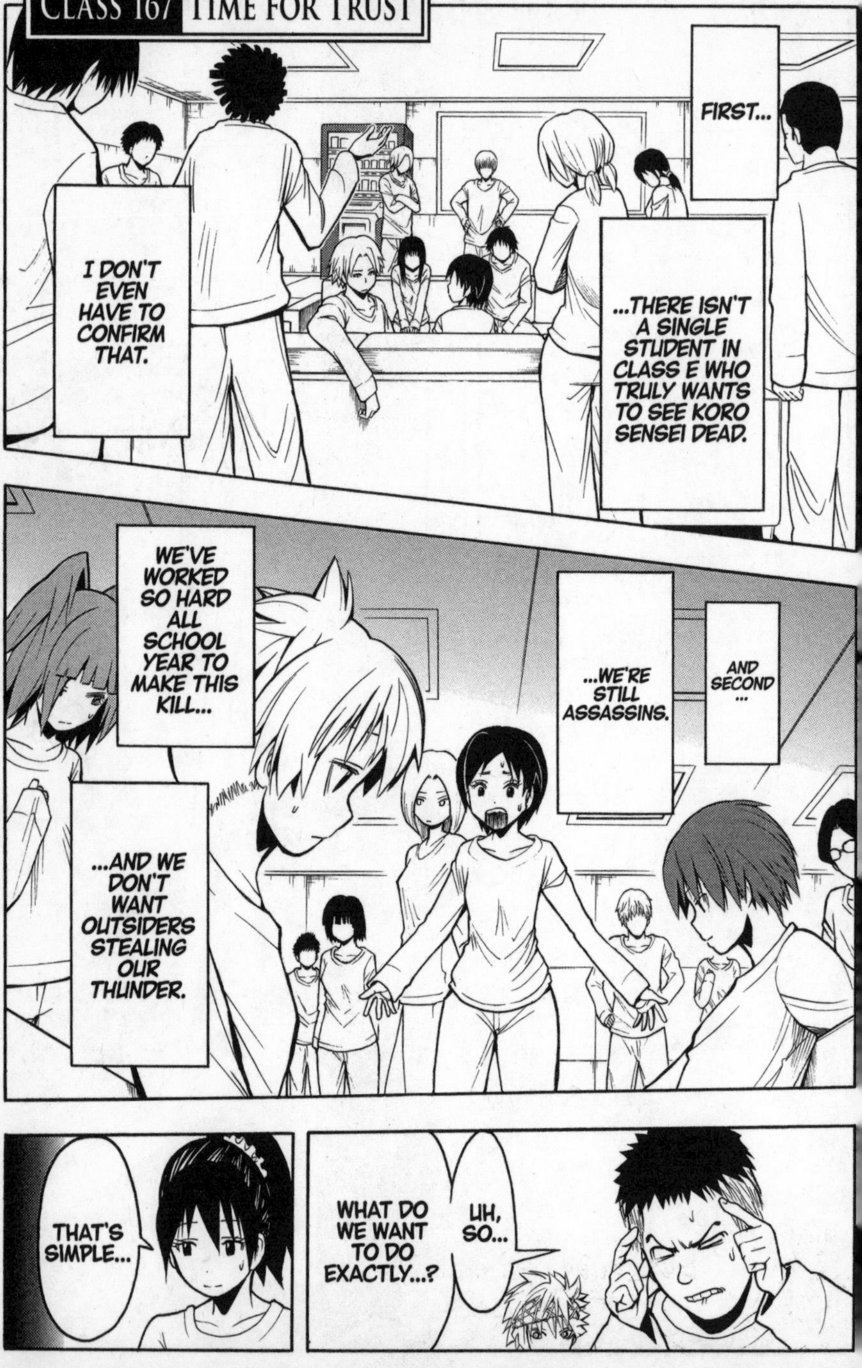
FIRST...
...THERE ISN'T A SINGLE STUDENT IN CLASS E WHO TRULY WANTS TO SEE KORO SENSEI DEAD.
I DON'T EVEN HAVE TO CONFIRM THAT.
AND SECOND...
...WE'RE STILL ASSASSINS.
WE'VE WORKED SO HARD ALL SCHOOL YEAR TO MAKE THIS KILL...
...AND WE DON'T WANT OUTSIDERS STEALING OUR THUNDER.
UH, SO...
WHAT DO WE WANT TO DO EXACTLY...?
THAT'S SIMPLE...

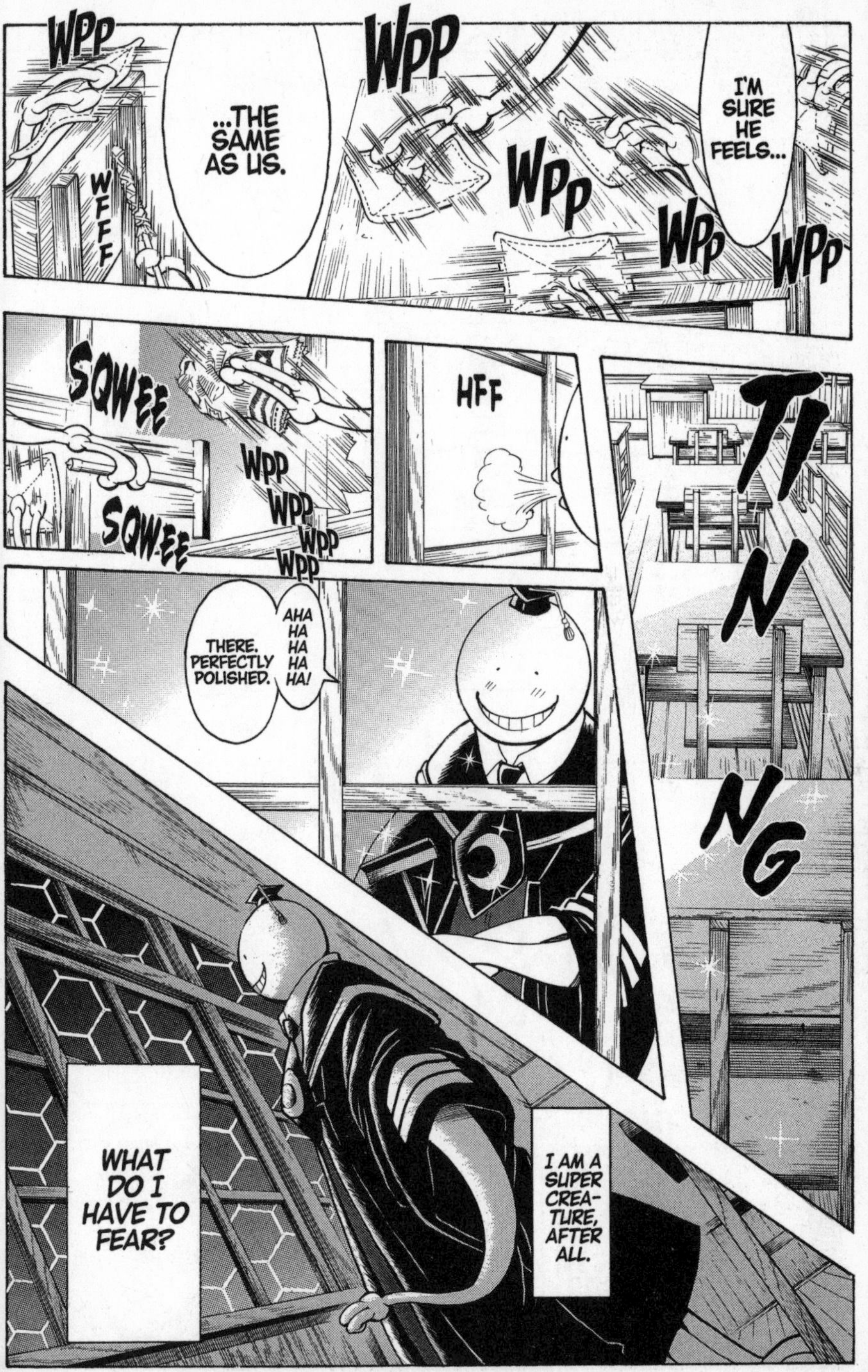

WPP
I'M SURE HE FEELS...
WPP
WPP
WPP
WPP
...THE SAME AS US.
WFFF
WPP
TINNNG
HFF
SQWEE
WPP
WPP
SQWEE
WPP
WPP
AHA HA HA HA HA!
THERE. PERFECTLY POLISHED.
I AM A SUPER CREA-TURE, AFTER ALL.
WHAT DO I HAVE TO FEAR?

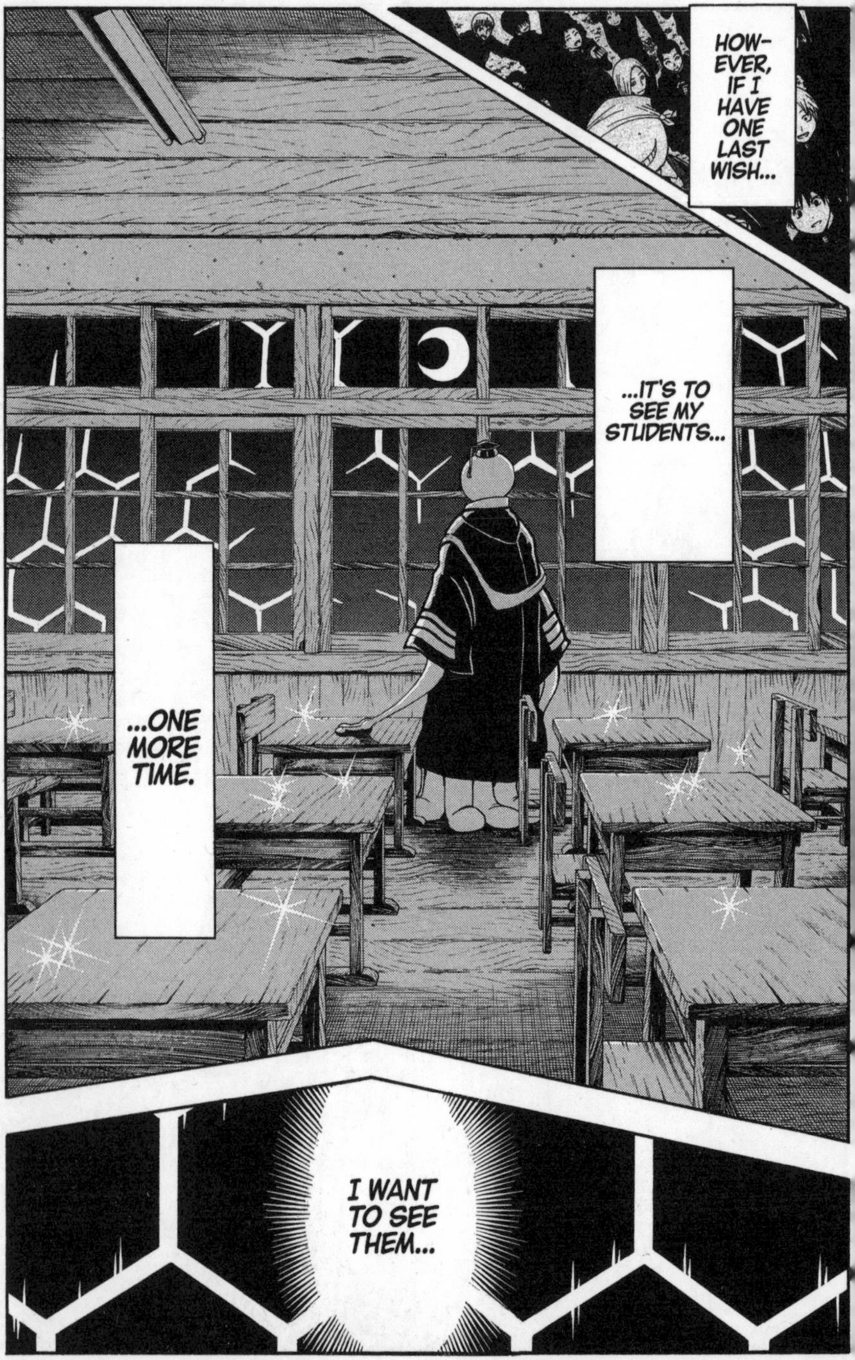
HOW-EVER, IF I HAVE ONE LAST WISH...
...IT'S TO SEE MY STUDENTS...
...ONE MORE TIME.
I WANT TO SEE THEM...

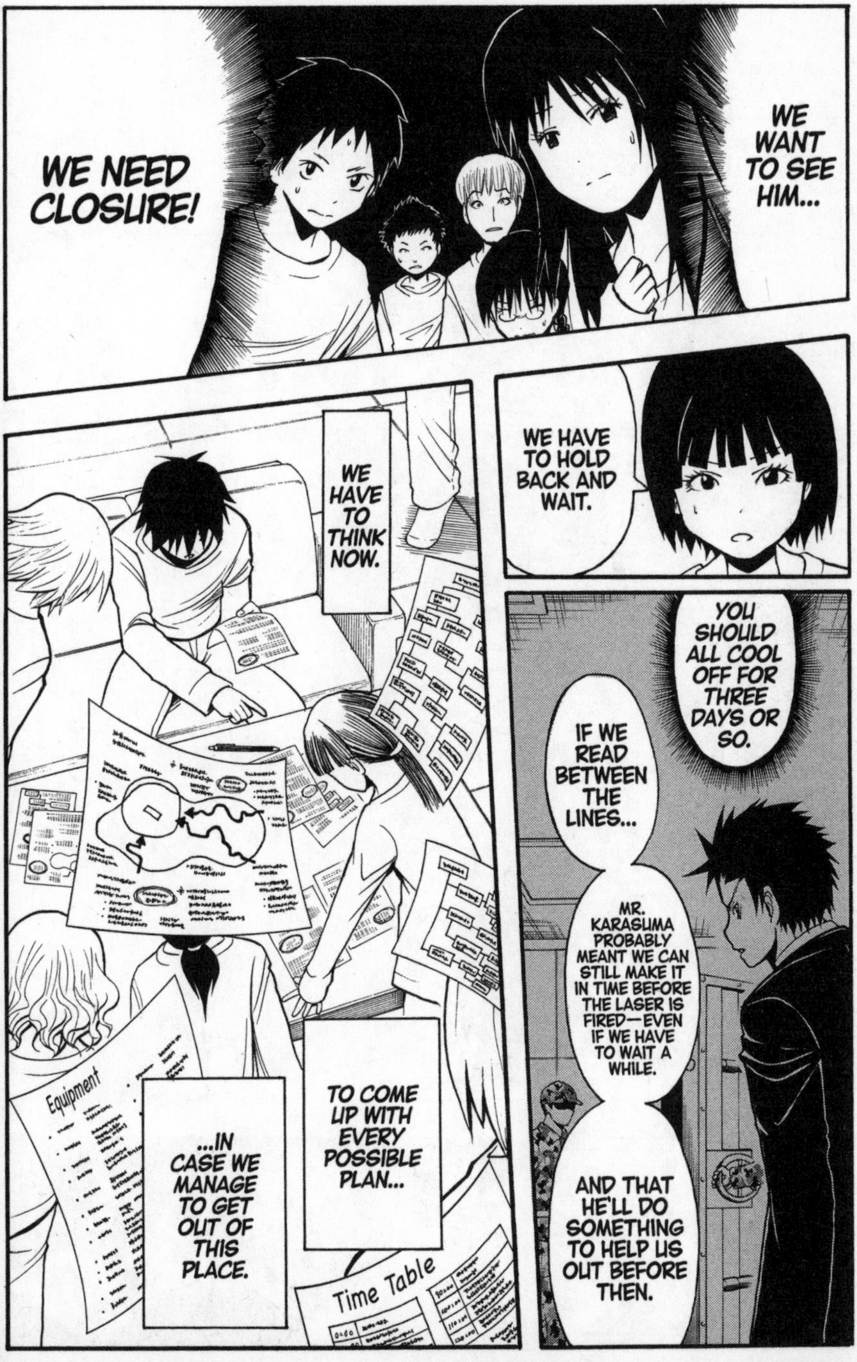
WE WANT TO SEE HIM...
WE NEED CLOSURE!
WE HAVE TO HOLD BACK AND WAIT.
YOU SHOULD ALL COOL OFF FOR THREE DAYS OR SO.
IF WE READ BETWEEN THE LINES...
MR. KARASUMA PROBABLY MEANT WE CAN STILL MAKE IT IN TIME BEFORE THE LASER IS FIRED—EVEN IF WE HAVE TO WAIT A WHILE.
AND THAT HE'LL DO SOMETHING TO HELP US OUT BEFORE THEN.
WE HAVE TO THINK NOW.
TO COME UP WITH EVERY POSSIBLE PLAN...
...IN CASE WE MANAGE TO GET OUT OF THIS PLACE.
Equipment
Time Table

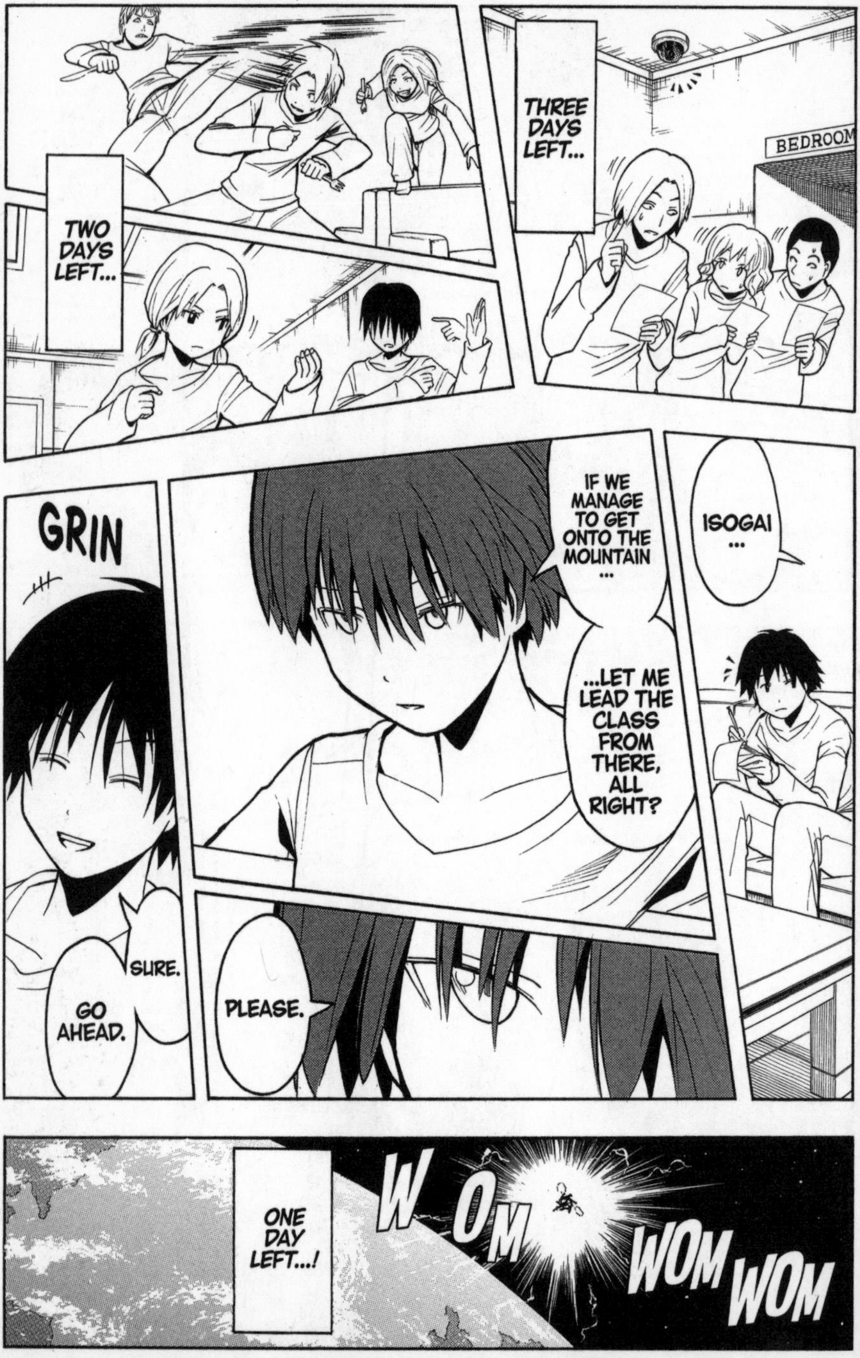
BEDROOM
THREE DAYS LEFT...
TWO DAYS LEFT...
ISOGAI...
IF WE MANAGE TO GET ONTO THE MOUNTAIN...
...LET ME LEAD THE CLASS FROM THERE, ALL RIGHT?
PLEASE.
GRIN
SURE.
GO AHEAD.
ONE DAY LEFT...!
WOM
WOM WOM

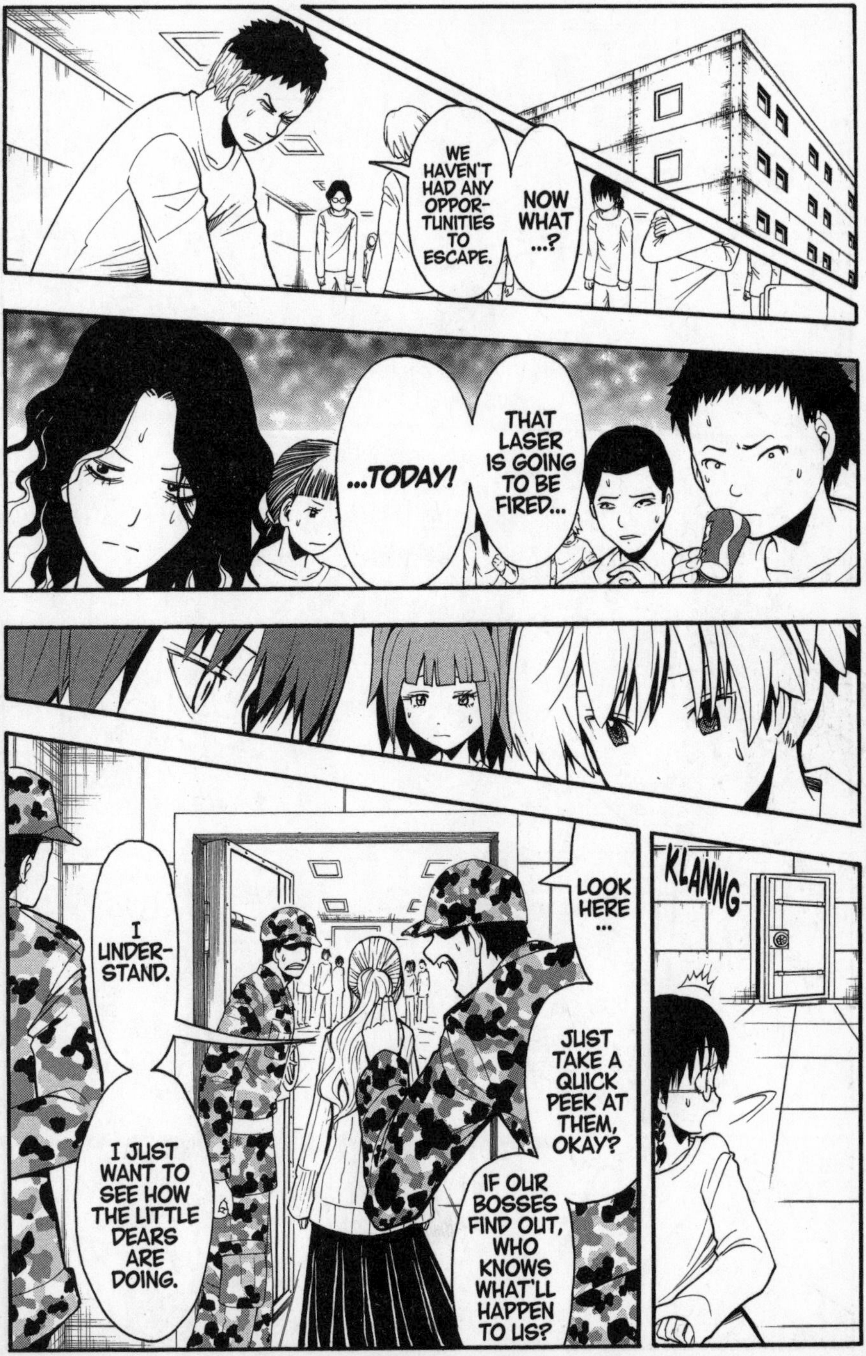
NOW WHAT ...?
WE HAVEN'T HAD ANY OPPOR-TUNITIES TO ESCAPE.
THAT LASER IS GOING TO BE FIRED...
...TODAY!
KLANNG
LOOK HERE ...
JUST TAKE A QUICK PEEK AT THEM, OKAY?
IF OUR BOSSES FIND OUT, WHO KNOWS WHAT'LL HAPPEN TO US?
I UNDER-STAND.
I JUST WANT TO SEE HOW THE LITTLE DEARS ARE DOING.

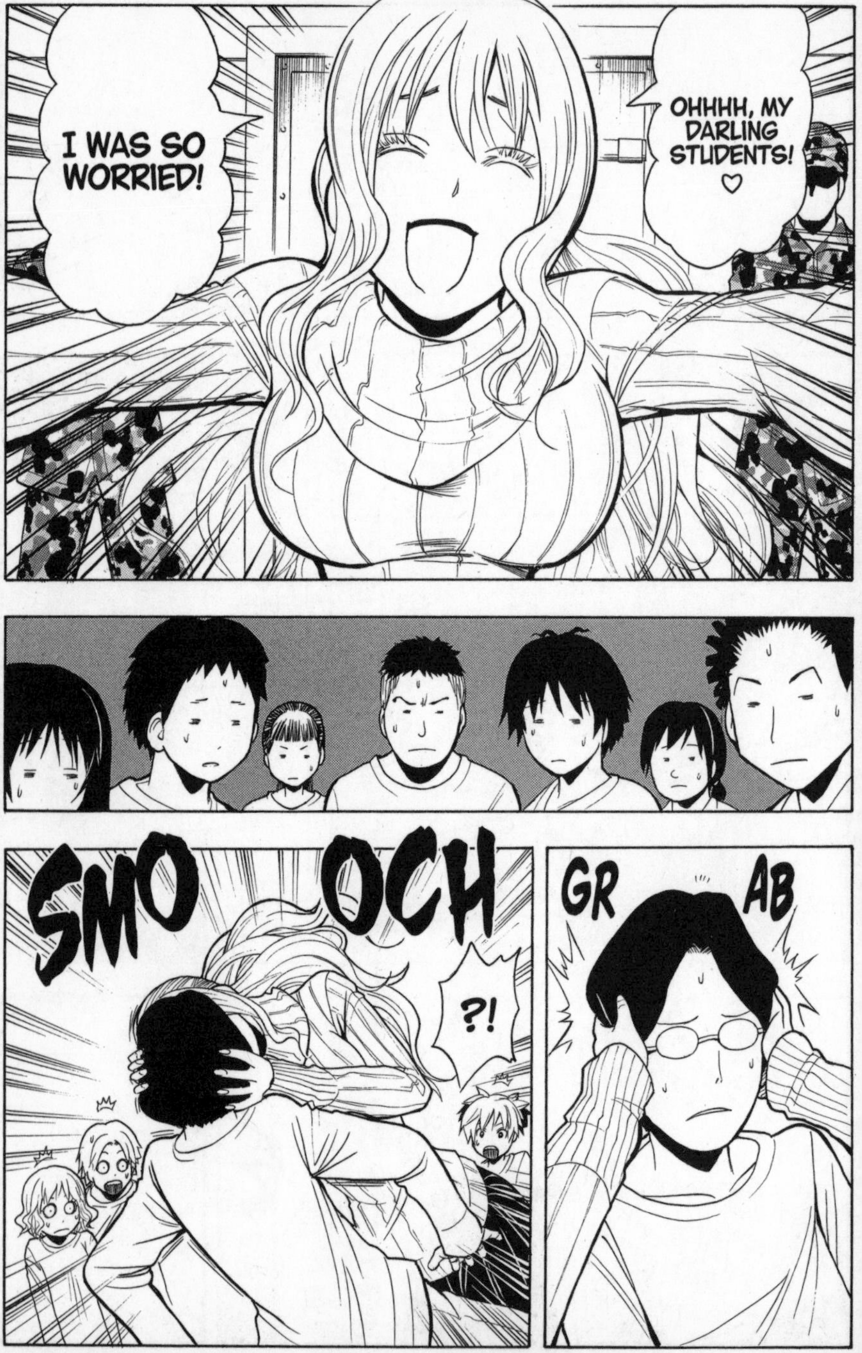
OHHHH, MY DARLING STUDENTS! ♡
I WAS SO WORRIED!
GRAB
SMOOCH
?!

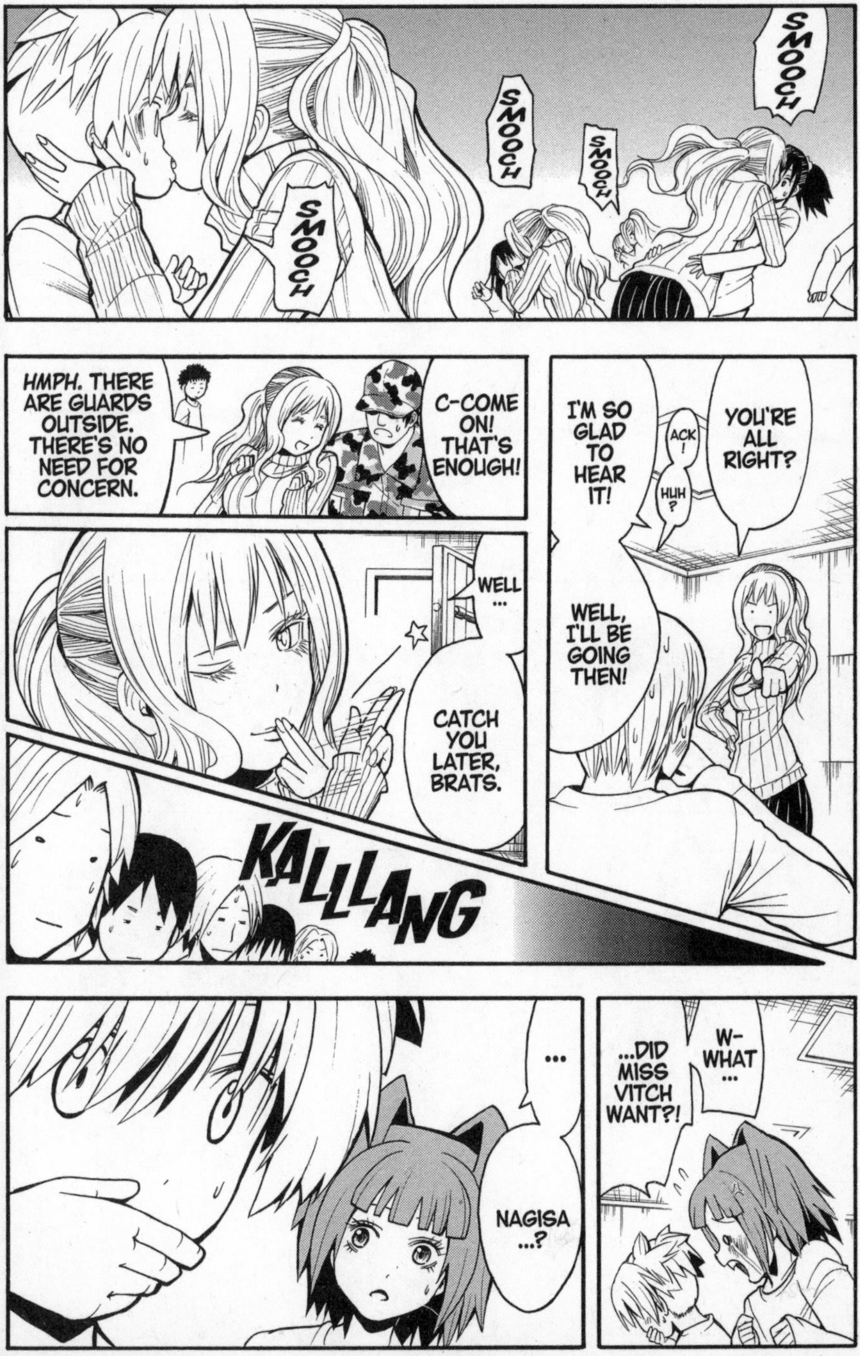
SMOOCH
SMOOCH
SMOOCH
SMOOCH
YOU'RE ALL RIGHT?
ACK!
HUH?
I'M SO GLAD TO HEAR IT!
WELL, I'LL BE GOING THEN!
C-COME ON! THAT'S ENOUGH!
HMPH. THERE ARE GUARDS OUTSIDE. THERE'S NO NEED FOR CONCERN.
WELL...
CATCH YOU LATER, BRATS.
KALLLANG
W-WHAT...
...DID MISS VITCH WANT?!
...
NAGISA...?

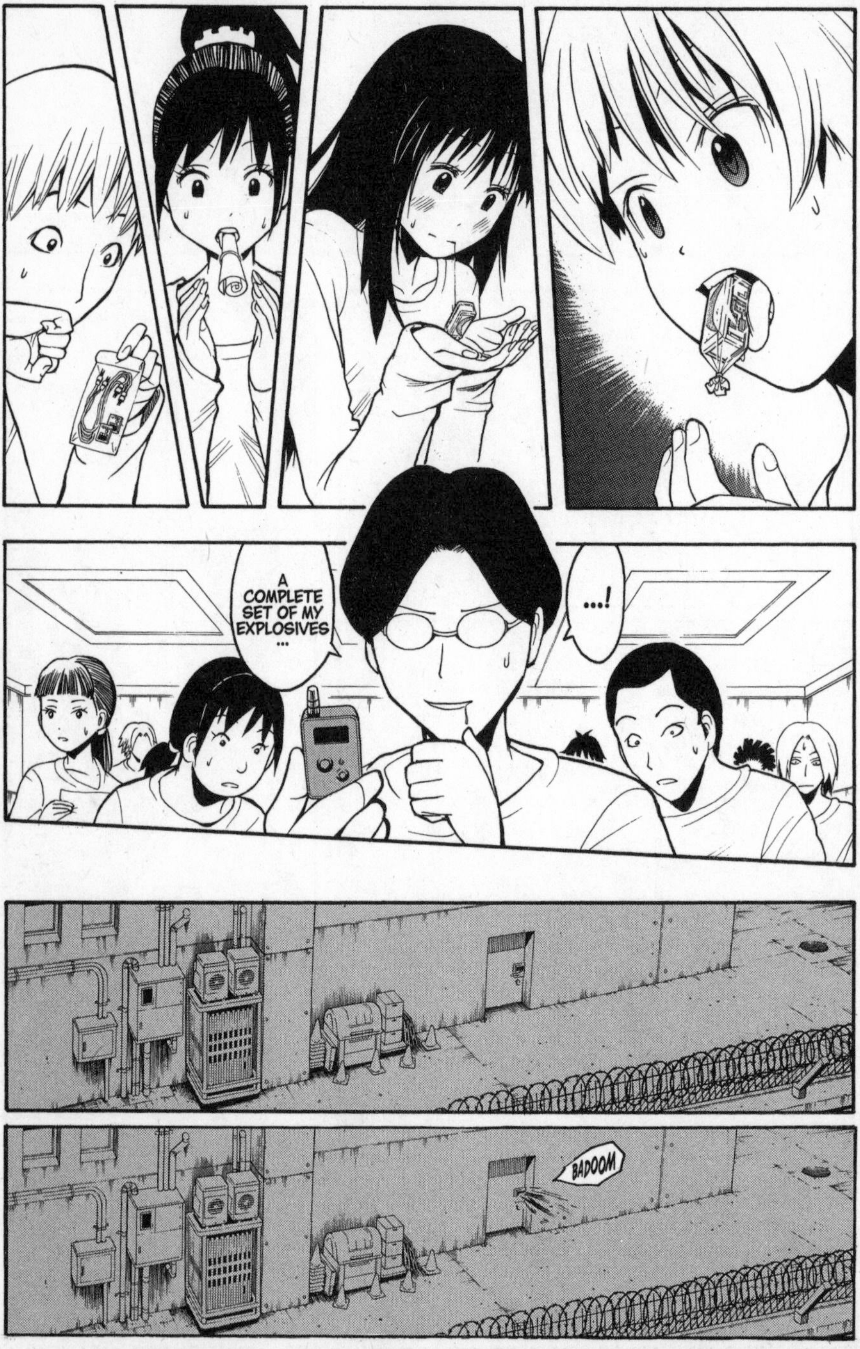
...!
A COMPLETE SET OF MY EXPLOSIVES ...
BADOOM

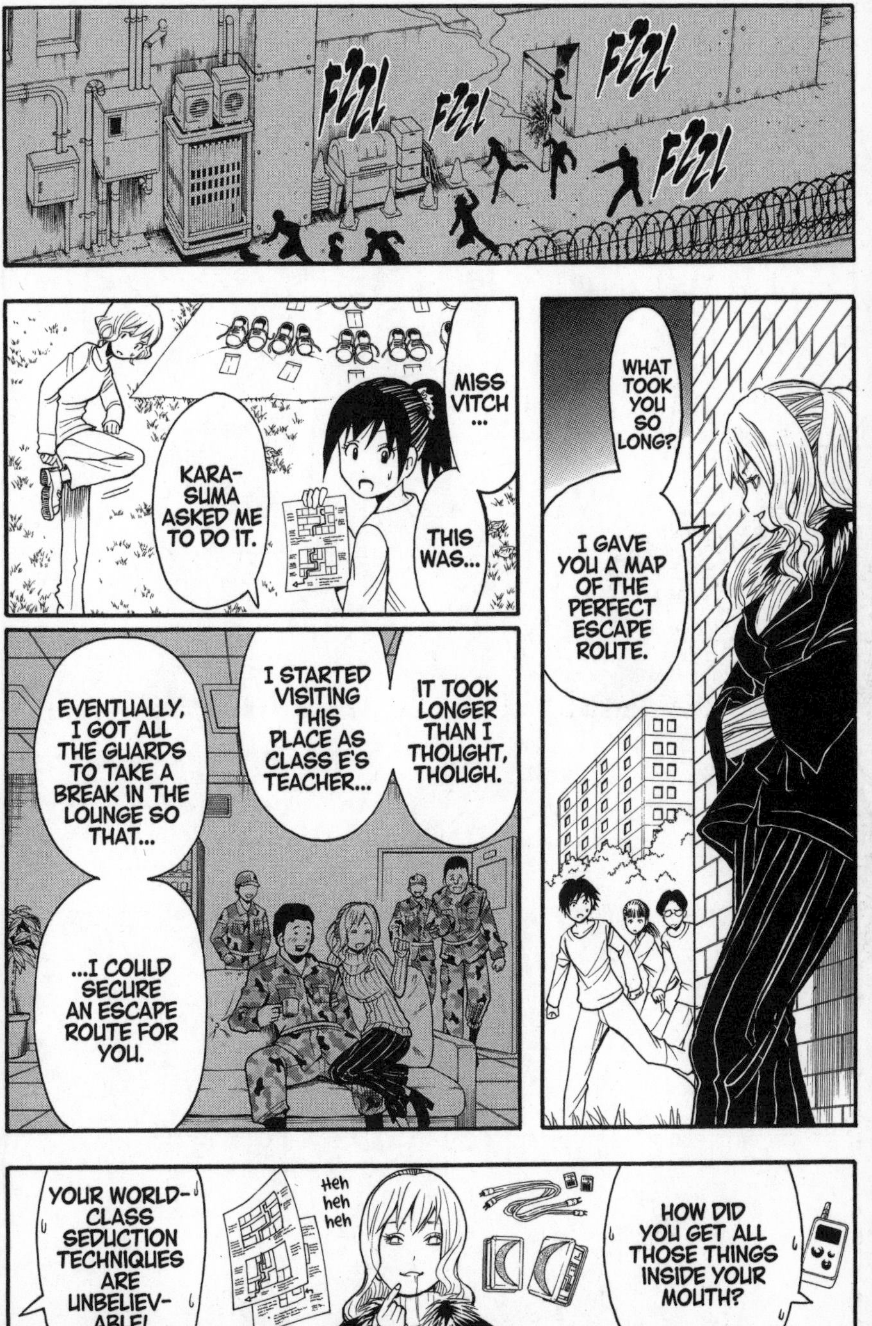
FZZL
FZZL
FZZL
FZZL
WHAT TOOK YOU SO LONG?
I GAVE YOU A MAP OF THE PERFECT ESCAPE ROUTE.
MISS VITCH...
THIS WAS...
KARA-SUMA ASKED ME TO DO IT.
IT TOOK LONGER THAN I THOUGHT, THOUGH.
I STARTED VISITING THIS PLACE AS CLASS E'S TEACHER...
EVENTUALLY, I GOT ALL THE GUARDS TO TAKE A BREAK IN THE LOUNGE SO THAT...
...I COULD SECURE AN ESCAPE ROUTE FOR YOU.
HOW DID YOU GET ALL THOSE THINGS INSIDE YOUR MOUTH?
Heh heh heh
YOUR WORLD-CLASS SEDUCTION TECHNIQUES ARE UNBELIEV-ABLE!

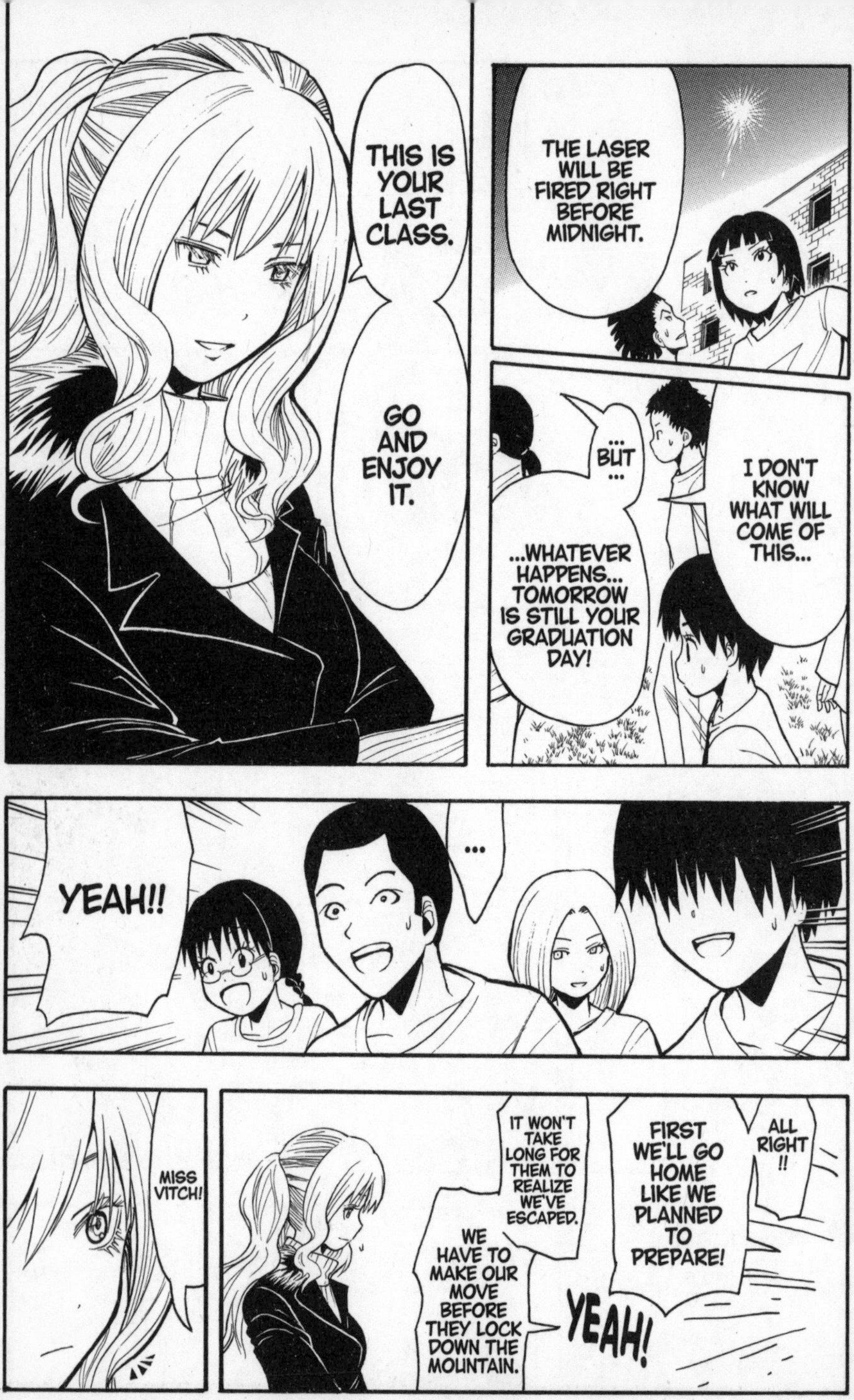
THE LASER WILL BE FIRED RIGHT BEFORE MIDNIGHT.
I DON'T KNOW WHAT WILL COME OF THIS...
...BUT...
...WHATEVER HAPPENS... TOMORROW IS STILL YOUR GRADUATION DAY!
THIS IS YOUR LAST CLASS.
GO AND ENJOY IT.
...
YEAH!!
ALL RIGHT!!
FIRST WE'LL GO HOME LIKE WE PLANNED TO PREPARE!
IT WON'T TAKE LONG FOR THEM TO REALIZE WE'VE ESCAPED.
WE HAVE TO MAKE OUR MOVE BEFORE THEY LOCK DOWN THE MOUNTAIN.
YEAH!
MISS VITCH!

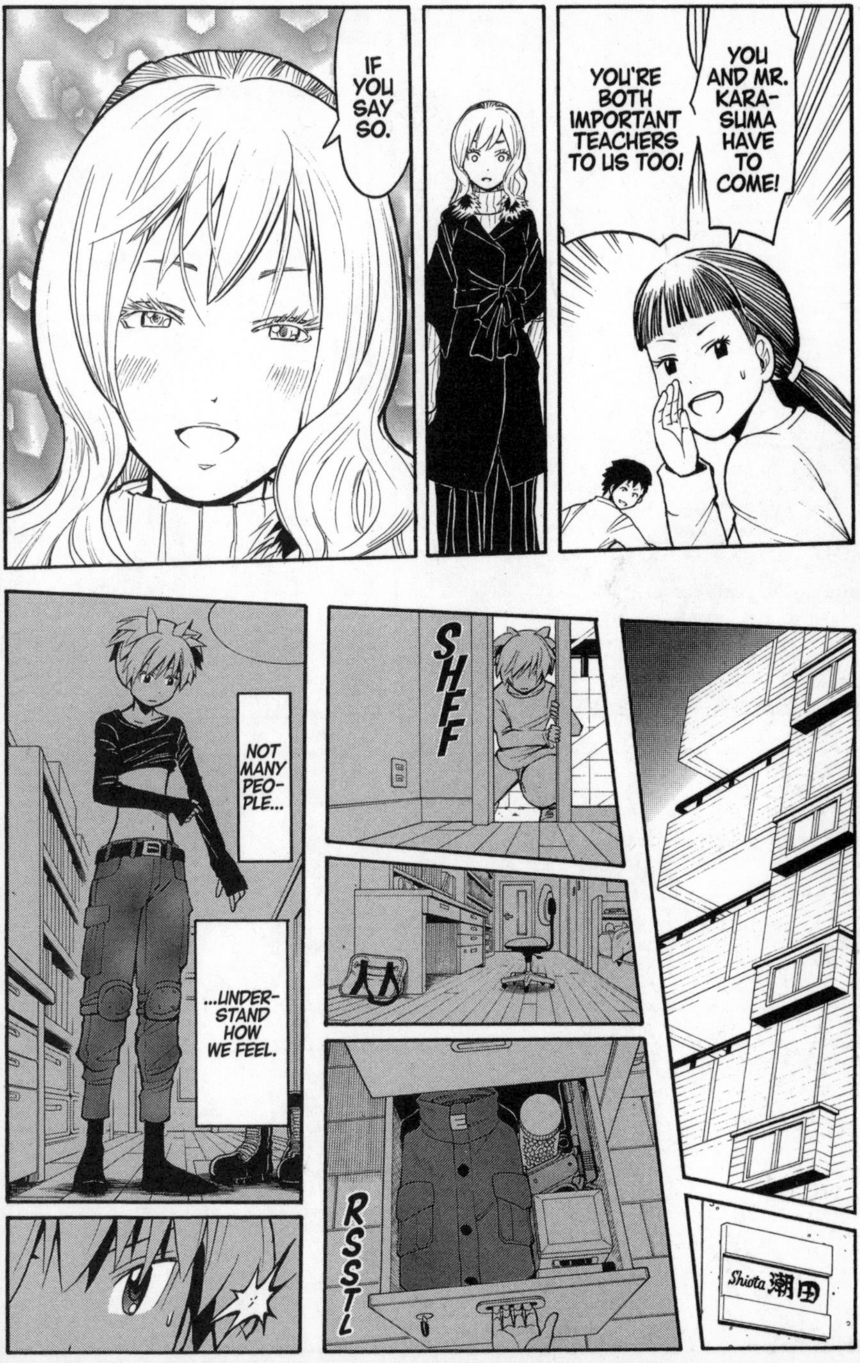
YOU AND MR. KARA-SUMA HAVE TO COME!
YOU'RE BOTH IMPORTANT TEACHERS TO US TOO!
IF YOU SAY SO.
Shiota 潮田
SHFF
RSSTL
NOT MANY PEO-PLE...
...UNDER-STAND HOW WE FEEL.

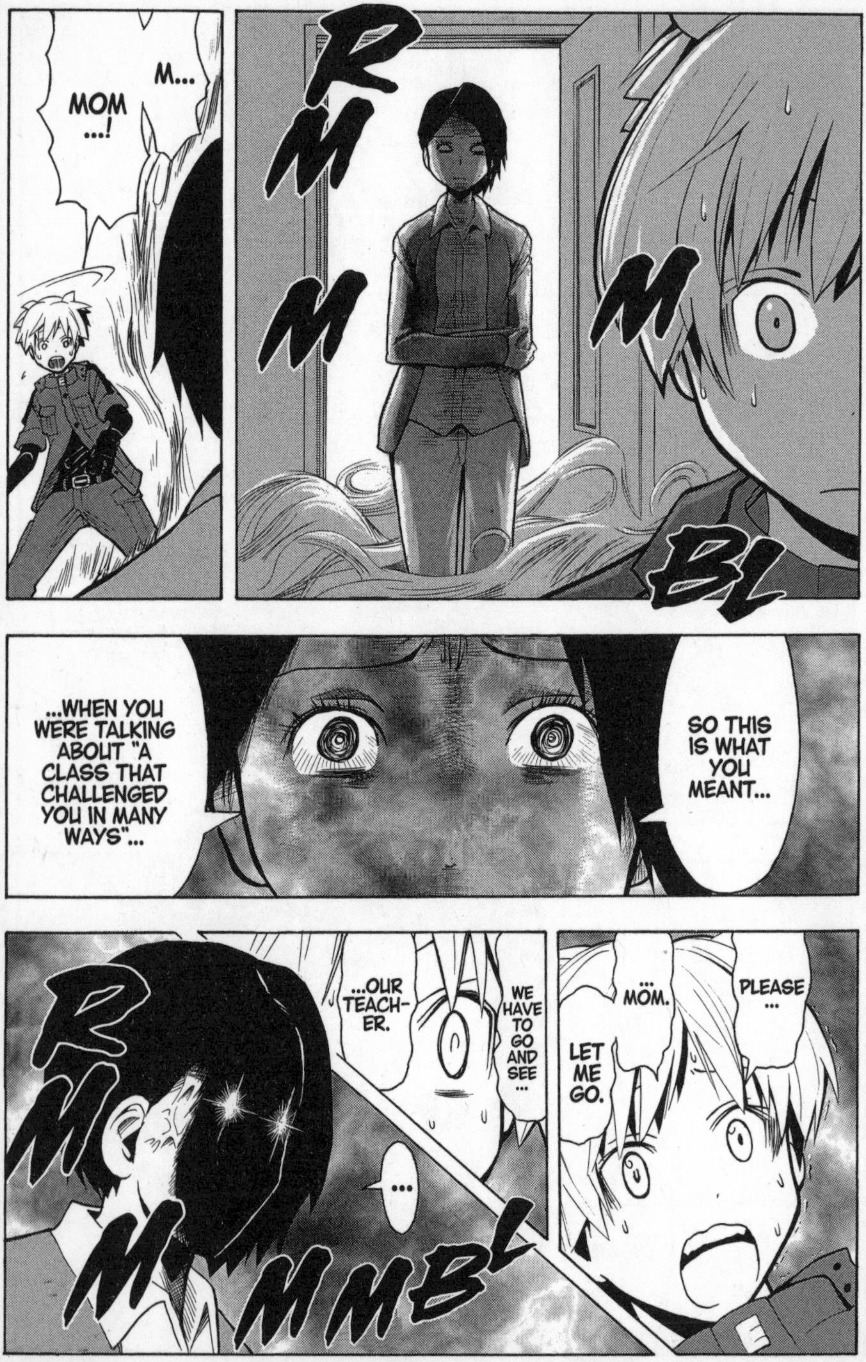
RMMMMBL
M...
MOM ...!
SO THIS IS WHAT YOU MEANT...
...WHEN YOU WERE TALKING ABOUT "A CLASS THAT CHALLENGED YOU IN MANY WAYS"...
PLEASE ...
... MOM.
LET ME GO.
WE HAVE TO GO AND SEE ...
...OUR TEACHER.
...
RMMMMB!

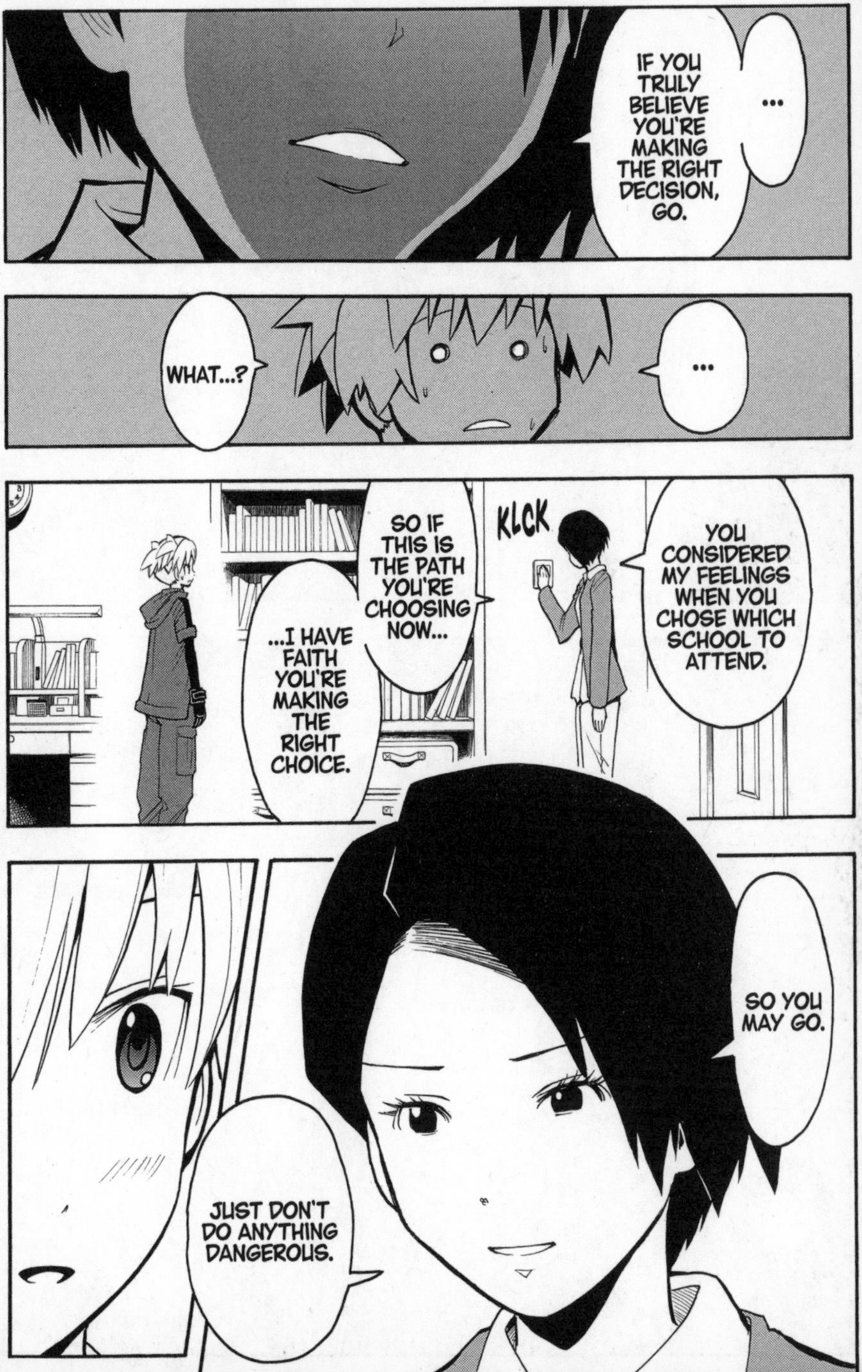
...
IF YOU TRULY BELIEVE YOU'RE MAKING THE RIGHT DECISION, GO.
...
WHAT...?
YOU CONSIDERED MY FEELINGS WHEN YOU CHOSE WHICH SCHOOL TO ATTEND.
KLCK
SO IF THIS IS THE PATH YOU'RE CHOOSING NOW...
...I HAVE FAITH YOU'RE MAKING THE RIGHT CHOICE.
SO YOU MAY GO.
JUST DON'T DO ANYTHING DANGEROUS.

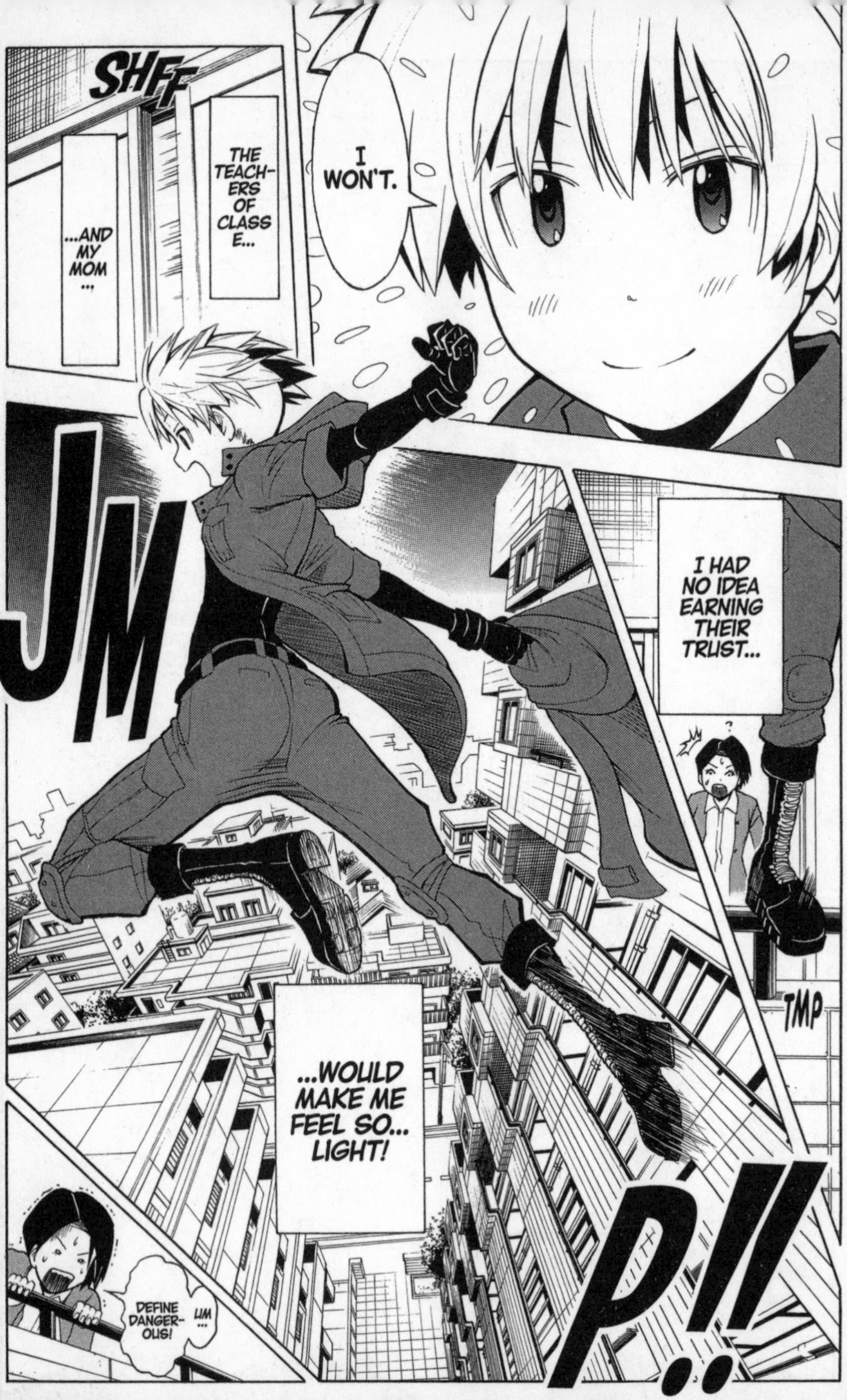
I WON'T.
SHFF
THE TEACHERS OF CLASS E...
...AND MY MOM...
I HAD NO IDEA EARNING THEIR TRUST...
?
TMP
JM
...WOULD MAKE ME FEEL SO... LIGHT!
P!!
UM ...
DEFINE DANGEROUS!

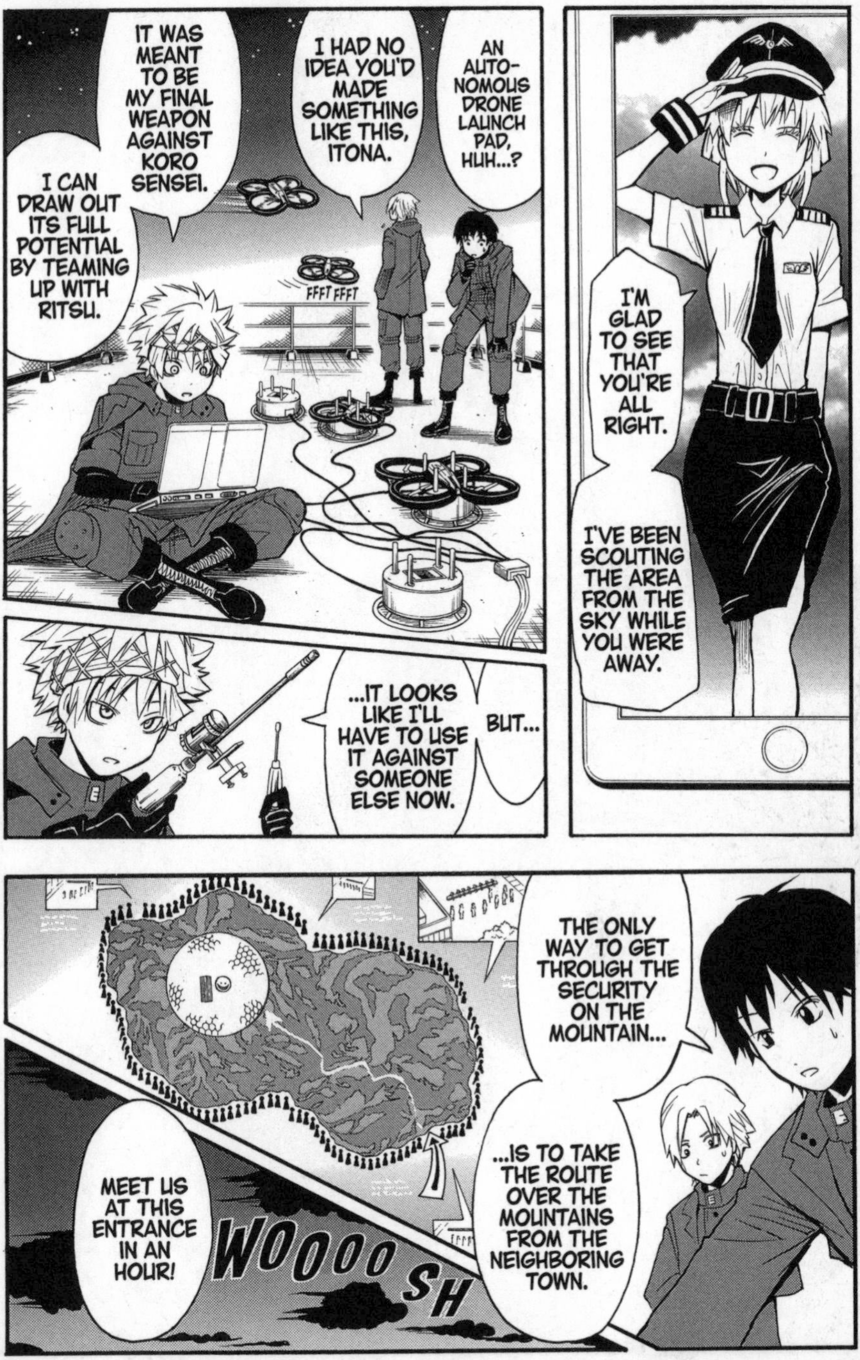
I'M GLAD TO SEE THAT YOU'RE ALL RIGHT.
I'VE BEEN SCOUTING THE AREA FROM THE SKY WHILE YOU WERE AWAY.
AN AUTONOMOUS DRONE LAUNCH PAD, HUH...?
I HAD NO IDEA YOU'D MADE SOMETHING LIKE THIS, ITONA.
IT WAS MEANT TO BE MY FINAL WEAPON AGAINST KORO SENSEI.
I CAN DRAW OUT ITS FULL POTENTIAL BY TEAMING UP WITH RITSU.
FFFT FFFT
BUT...
...IT LOOKS LIKE I'LL HAVE TO USE IT AGAINST SOMEONE ELSE NOW.
THE ONLY WAY TO GET THROUGH THE SECURITY ON THE MOUNTAIN...
...IS TO TAKE THE ROUTE OVER THE MOUNTAINS FROM THE NEIGHBORING TOWN.
MEET US AT THIS ENTRANCE IN AN HOUR!
WOOOOSH

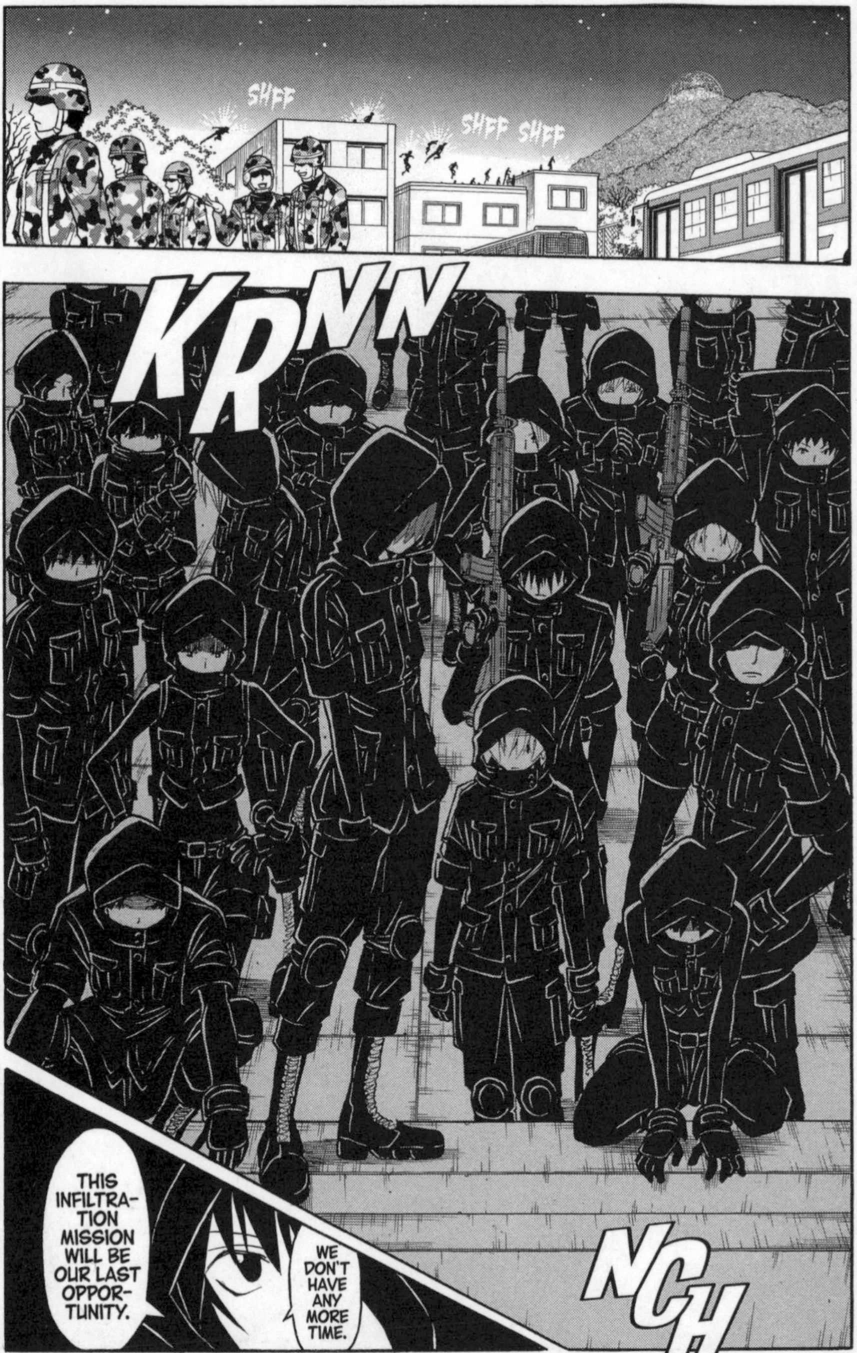
SHFF
SHFF SHFF
KRNNN
NCH
WE DON'T HAVE ANY MORE TIME.
THIS INFILTRATION MISSION WILL BE OUR LAST OPPORTUNITY.

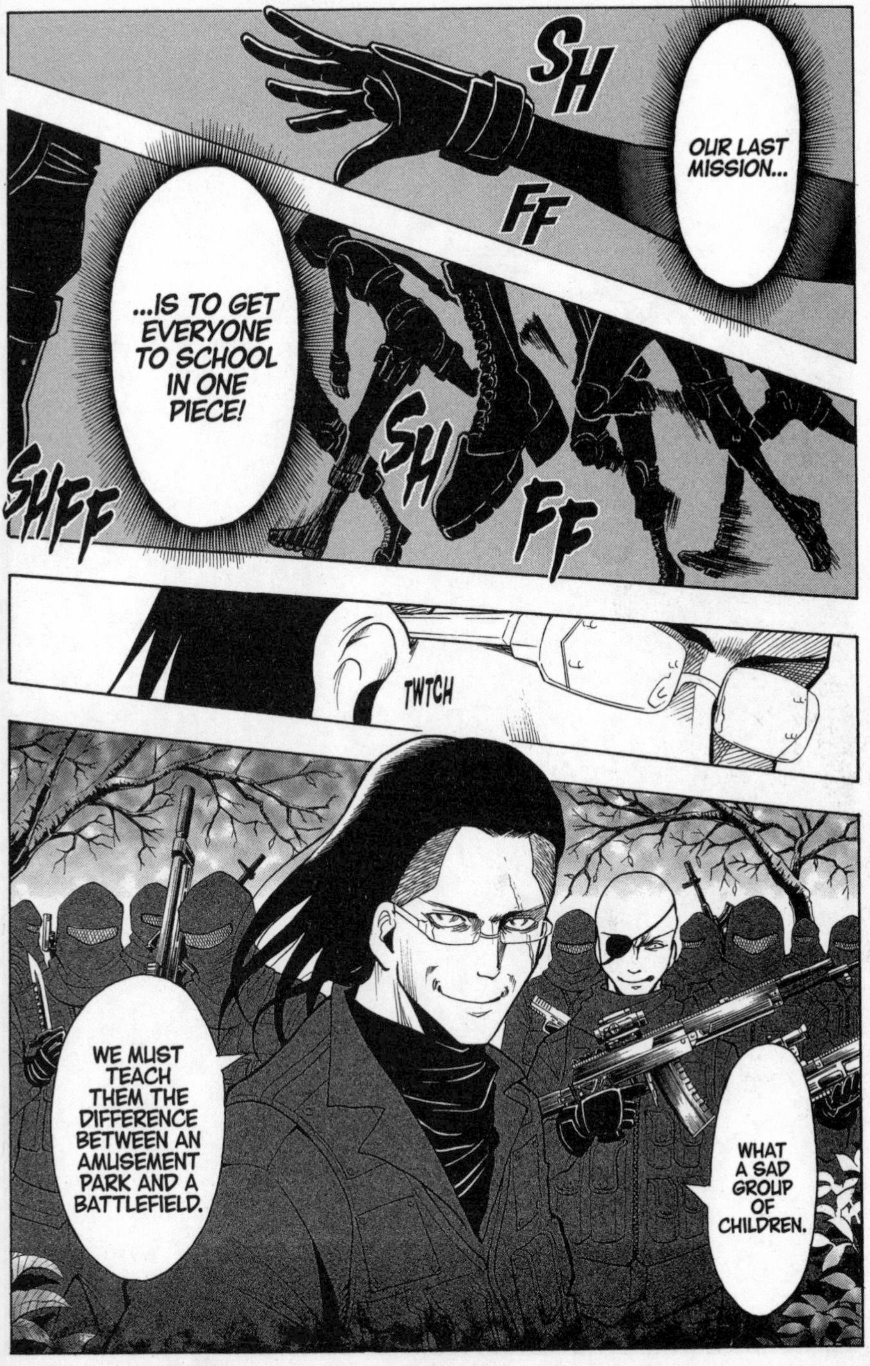
SHFF
OUR LAST MISSION...
...IS TO GET EVERYONE TO SCHOOL IN ONE PIECE!
SHFF
SHFF
TWTCH
WHAT A SAD GROUP OF CHILDREN.
WE MUST TEACH THEM THE DIFFERENCE BETWEEN AN AMUSEMENT PARK AND A BATTLEFIELD.

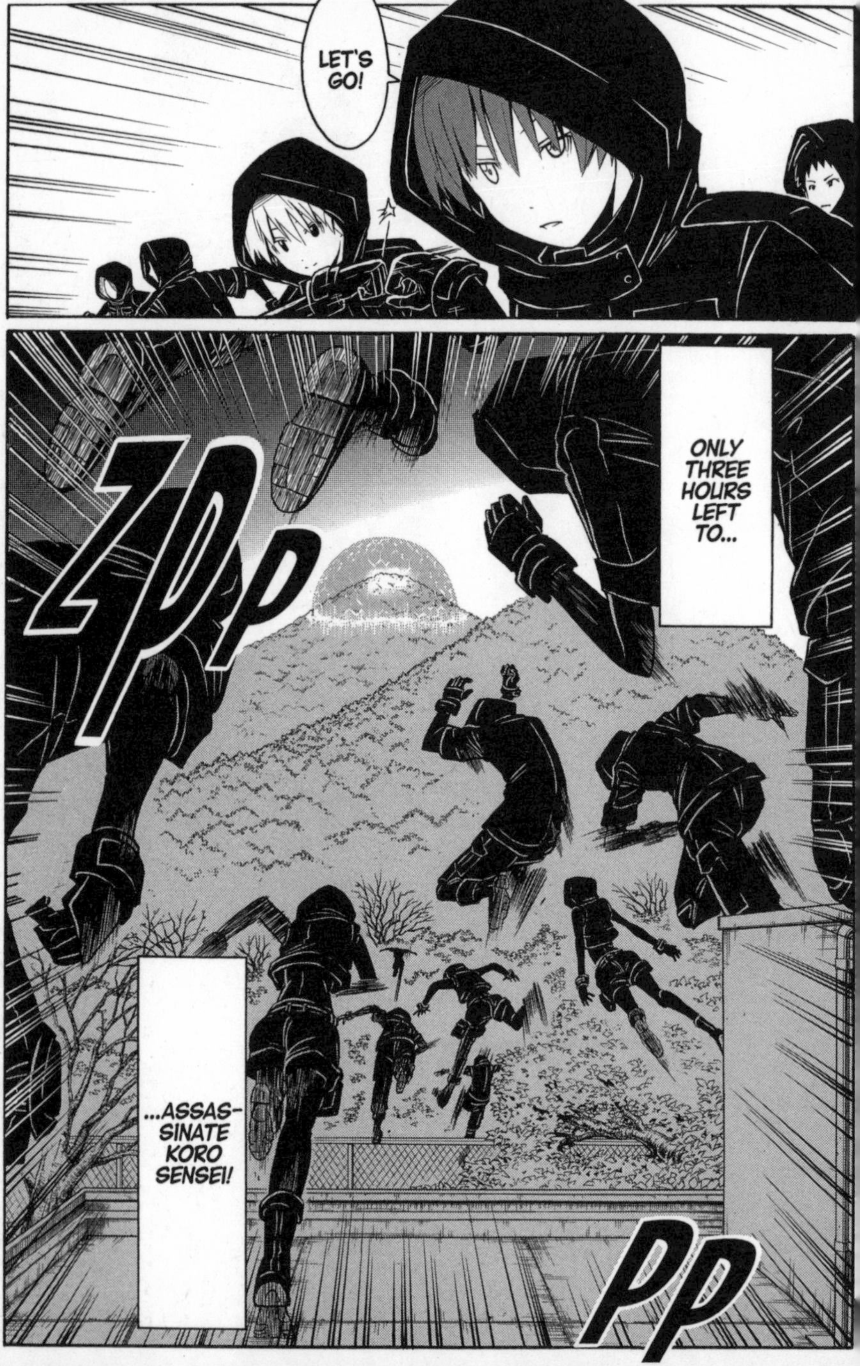
LET'S GO!
ONLY THREE HOURS LEFT TO...
ZIPP
...ASSAS-SINATE KORO SENSEI!
PP

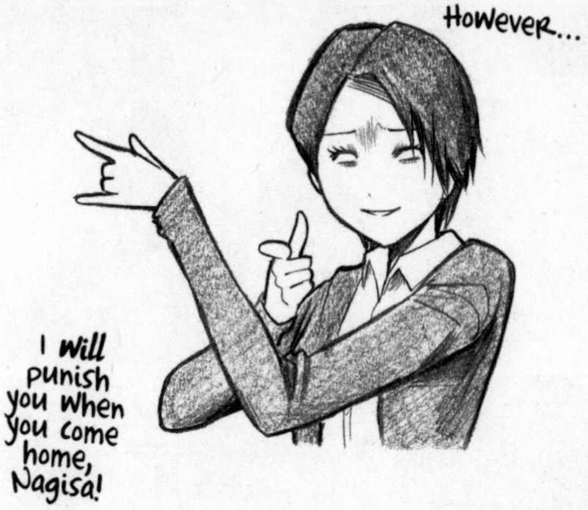
However...
I will punish you when you come home, Nagisa!

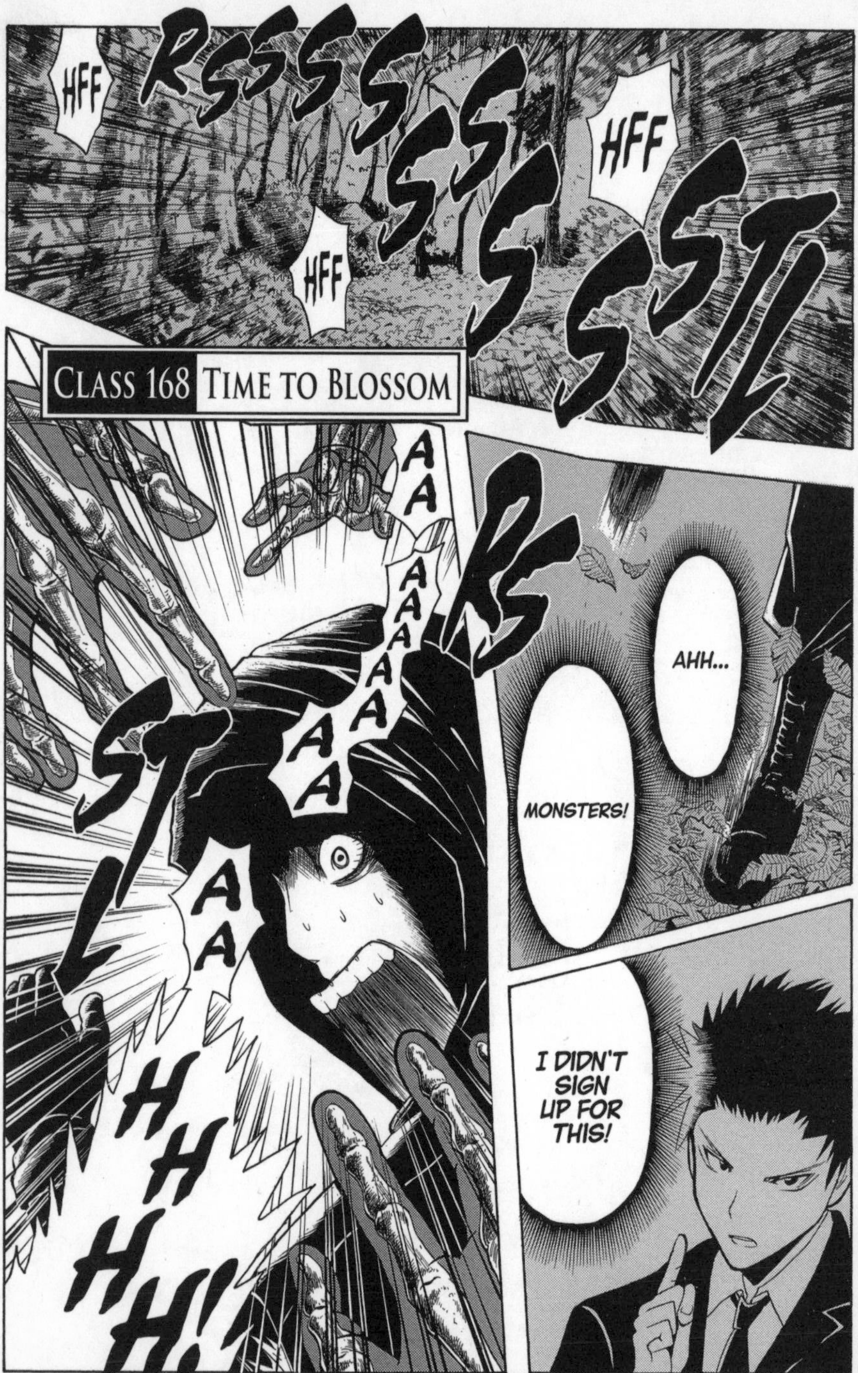
HFF
RSSSSSSSSSST
HFF
HFF
CLASS 168 TIME TO BLOSSOM
RS
AHH...
MONSTERS!
I DIDN'T SIGN UP FOR THIS!
AAAAAAAAAAAAAHHHHHH!
STL

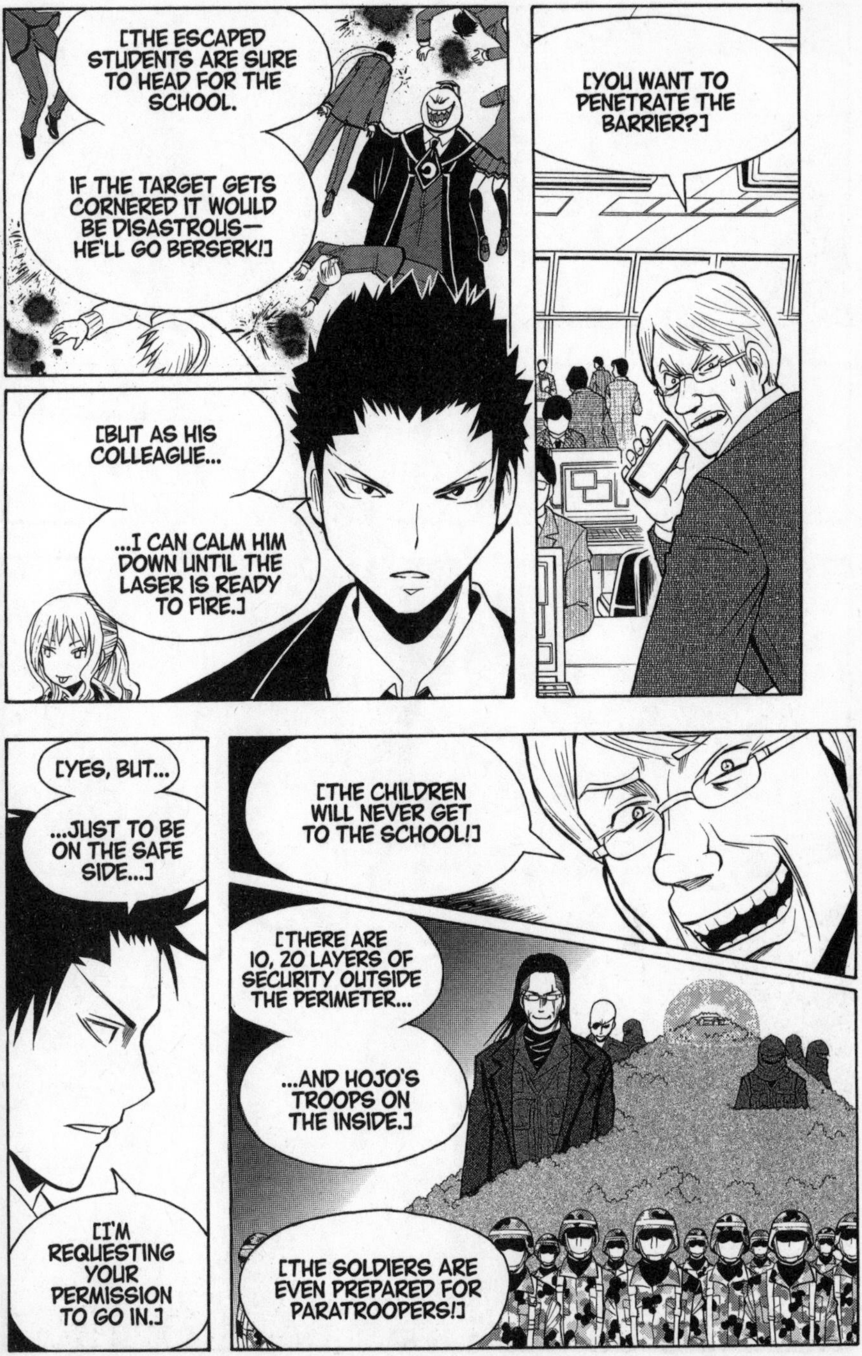
[YOU WANT TO PENETRATE THE BARRIER?]
[THE ESCAPED STUDENTS ARE SURE TO HEAD FOR THE SCHOOL.
IF THE TARGET GETS CORNERED IT WOULD BE DISASTROUS—HE'LL GO BERSERK!]
[BUT AS HIS COLLEAGUE...
...I CAN CALM HIM DOWN UNTIL THE LASER IS READY TO FIRE.]
[THE CHILDREN WILL NEVER GET TO THE SCHOOL!]
[THERE ARE 10, 20 LAYERS OF SECURITY OUTSIDE THE PERIMETER...
...AND HOJO'S TROOPS ON THE INSIDE.]
[THE SOLDIERS ARE EVEN PREPARED FOR PARATROOPERS!]
[YES, BUT...
...JUST TO BE ON THE SAFE SIDE...]
[I'M REQUESTING YOUR PERMISSION TO GO IN.]

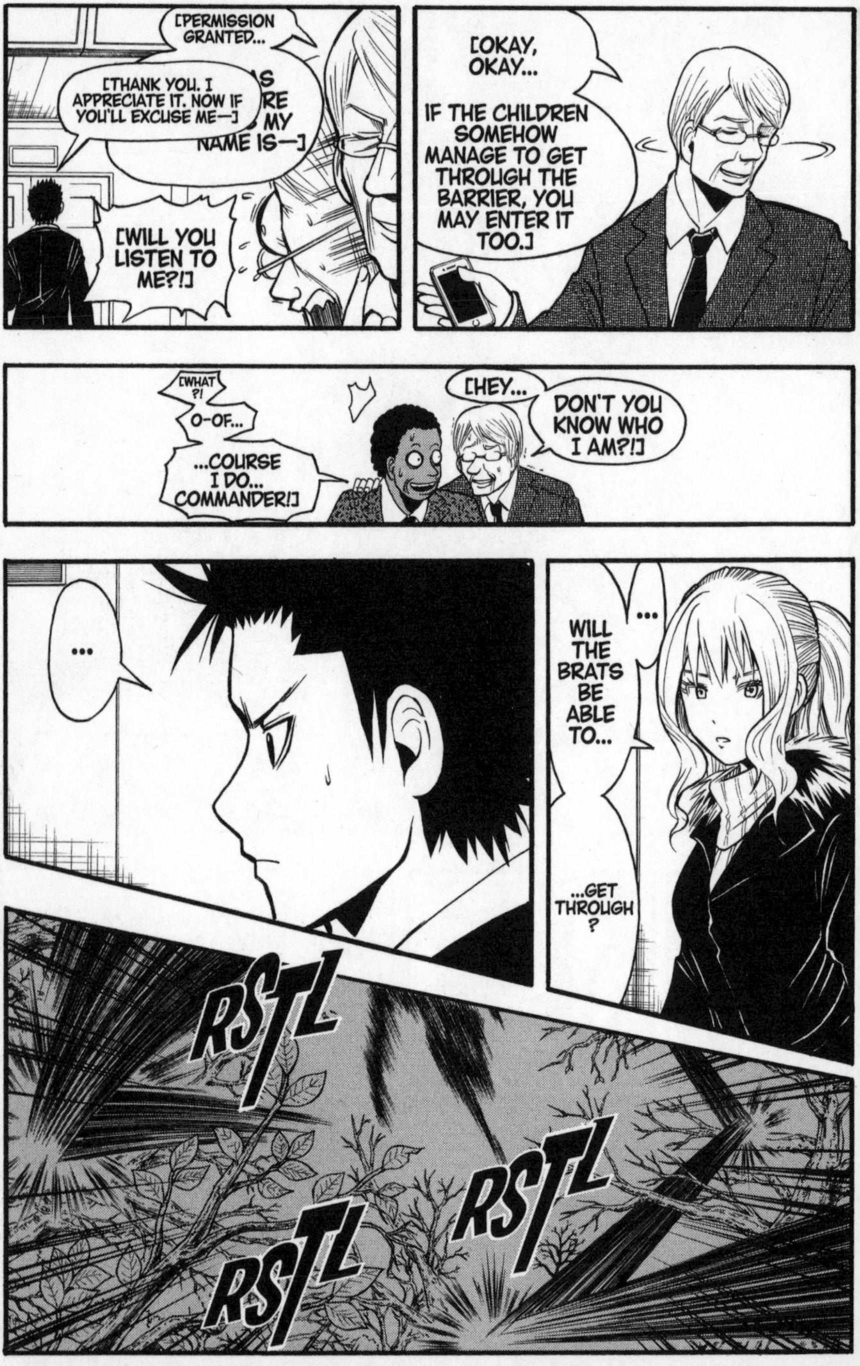
[OKAY, OKAY...
IF THE CHILDREN SOMEHOW MANAGE TO GET THROUGH THE BARRIER, YOU MAY ENTER IT TOO.]
[PERMISSION GRANTED...
NAME IS—]
[THANK YOU. I APPRECIATE IT. NOW IF YOU'LL EXCUSE ME—]
[WILL YOU LISTEN TO ME?!]
[HEY...
DON'T YOU KNOW WHO I AM?!]
[WHAT ?!
O-OF...
...COURSE I DO... COMMANDER!]
...
WILL THE BRATS BE ABLE TO...
...GET THROUGH ?
...
RSTL
RSTL
RSTL

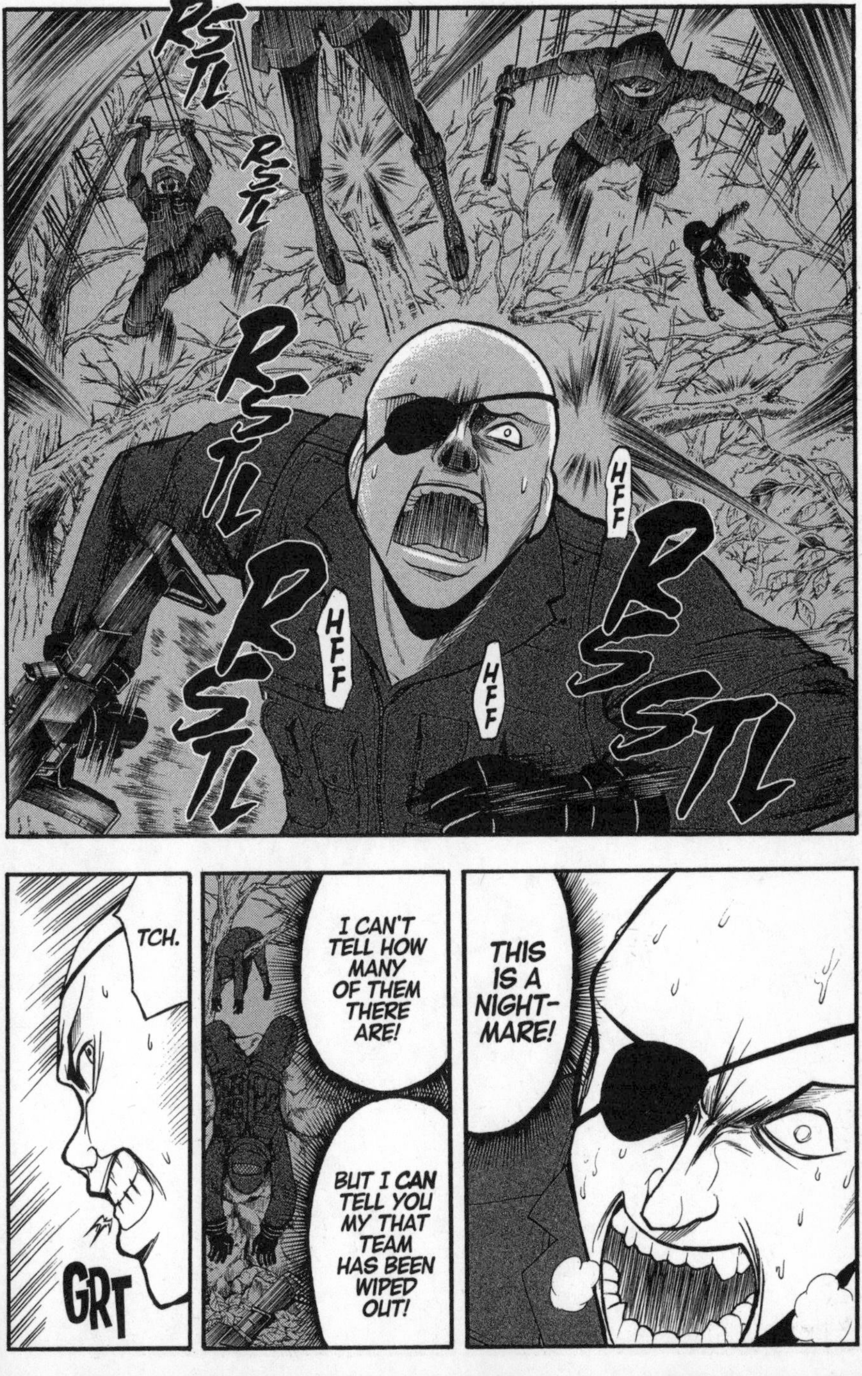
RSTL
RSTL
RSTL
HFF
HFF
HFF
RSTL
RSTL
THIS IS A NIGHT-MARE!
I CAN'T TELL HOW MANY OF THEM THERE ARE!
BUT I CAN TELL YOU MY THAT TEAM HAS BEEN WIPED OUT!
TCH.
GRT

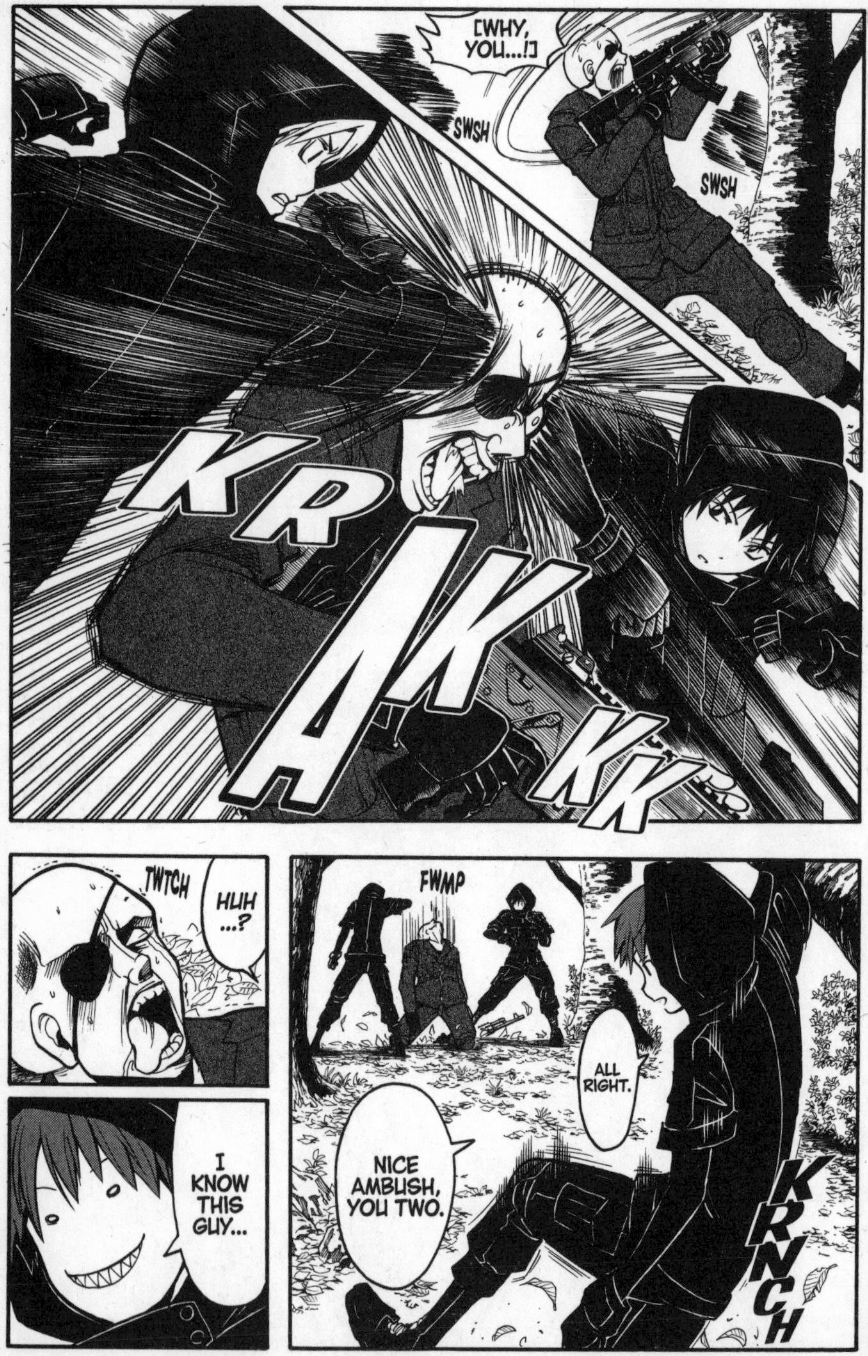
[WHY, YOU...!]
SWSH
SWSH
KRAKKK
FWMP
ALL RIGHT.
NICE AMBUSH, YOU TWO.
KRNCH
TWTCH
HUH ...?
I KNOW THIS GUY...

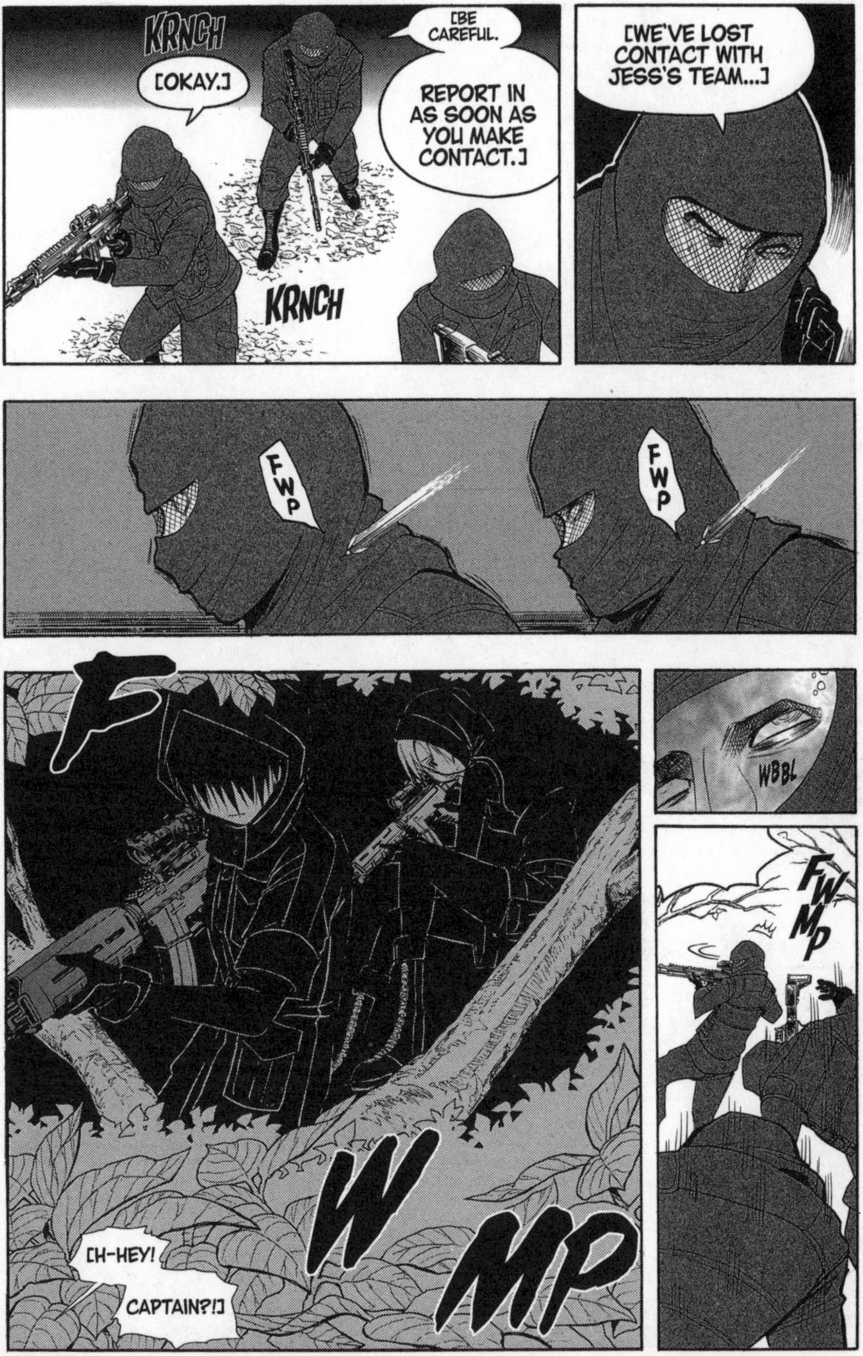
[WE'VE LOST CONTACT WITH JESS'S TEAM...]
[BE CAREFUL.
REPORT IN AS SOON AS YOU MAKE CONTACT.]
KRNCH
[OKAY.]
KRNCH
FWP
FWP
WBBL
FWMP
F
WMP
[H-HEY!
CAPTAIN?!]

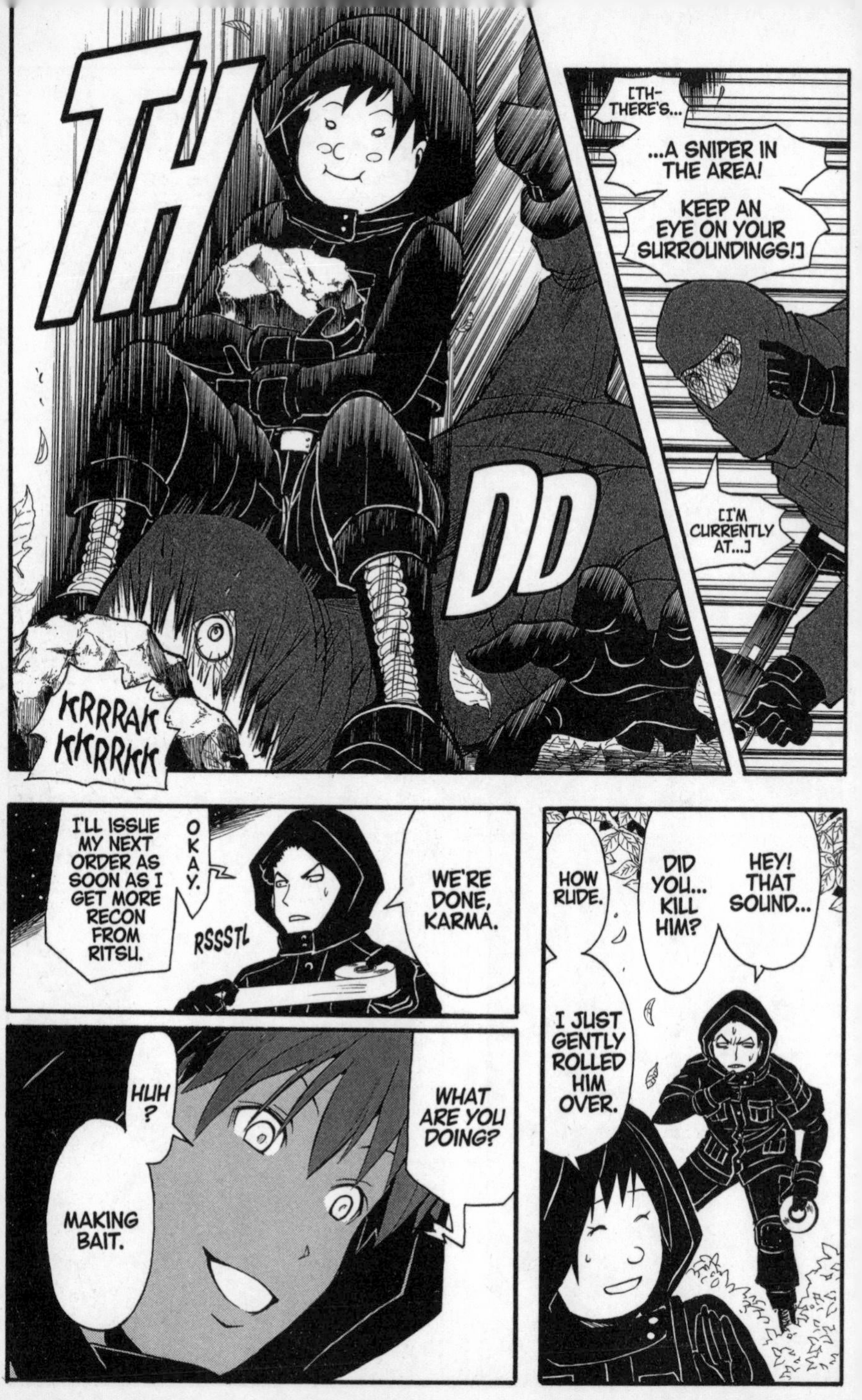
[TH-THERE'S...
...A SNIPER IN THE AREA!
KEEP AN EYE ON YOUR SURROUNDINGS!]
[I'M CURRENTLY AT...]
THDD
KRRRAK KKRRKK
HEY! THAT SOUND...
DID YOU... KILL HIM?
HOW RUDE.
I JUST GENTLY ROLLED HIM OVER.
WE'RE DONE, KARMA.
OKAY.
I'LL ISSUE MY NEXT ORDER AS SOON AS I GET MORE RECON FROM RITSU.
RSSSTL
WHAT ARE YOU DOING?
HUH?
MAKING BAIT.

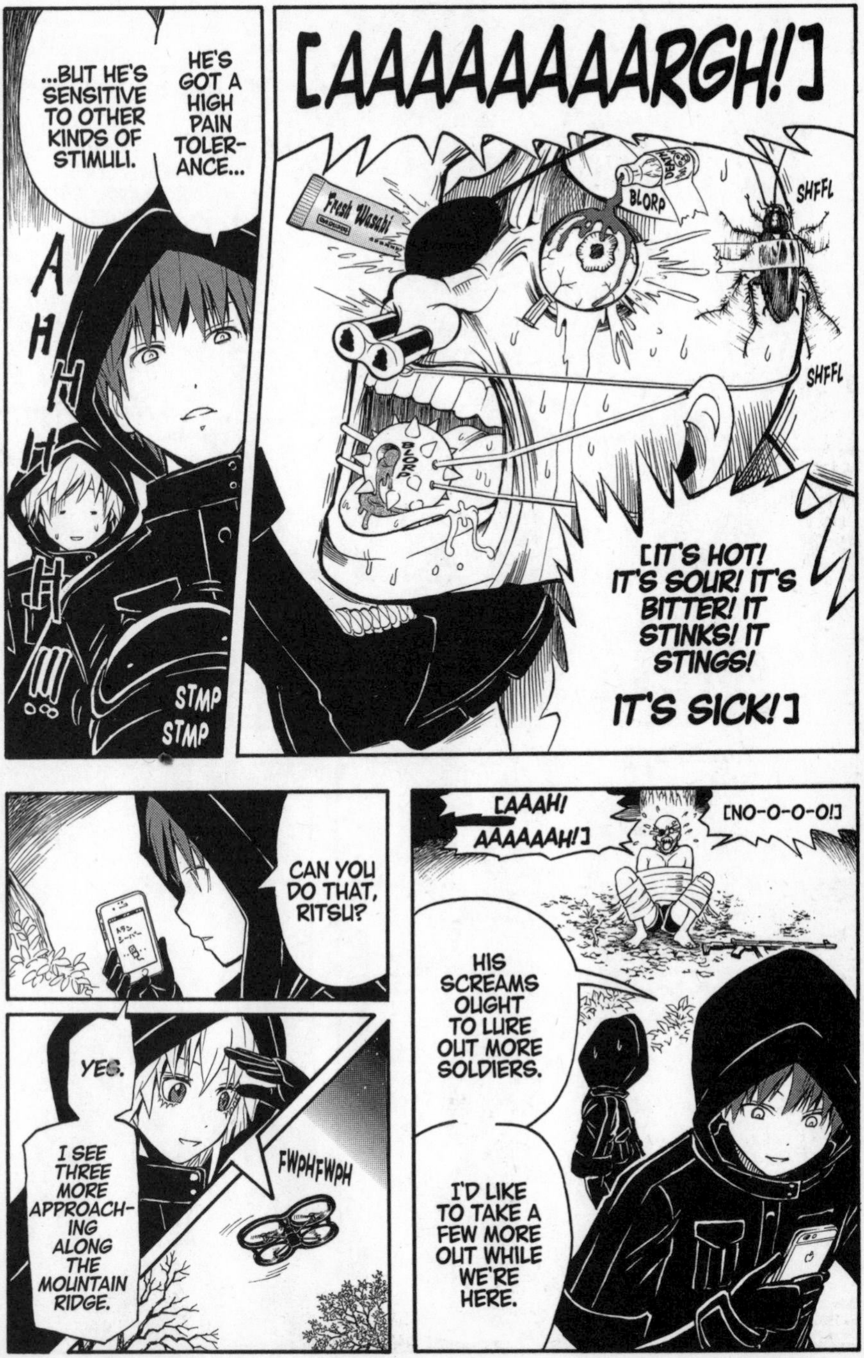
[AAAAAAAARGH!]
Fresh Wasabi
DEATH
BLORP
SHFFL
SHFFL
BLORP
[IT'S HOT! IT'S SOUR! IT'S BITTER! IT STINKS! IT STINGS!
IT'S SICK!]
HE'S GOT A HIGH PAIN TOLERANCE...
...BUT HE'S SENSITIVE TO OTHER KINDS OF STIMULI.
AHHHHHH!!!
STMP STMP
[NO-O-O-O!]
[AAAH! AAAAAAH!]
HIS SCREAMS OUGHT TO LURE OUT MORE SOLDIERS.
I'D LIKE TO TAKE A FEW MORE OUT WHILE WE'RE HERE.
CAN YOU DO THAT, RITSU?
YES.
I SEE THREE MORE APPROACHING ALONG THE MOUNTAIN RIDGE.
FWPHFWPH

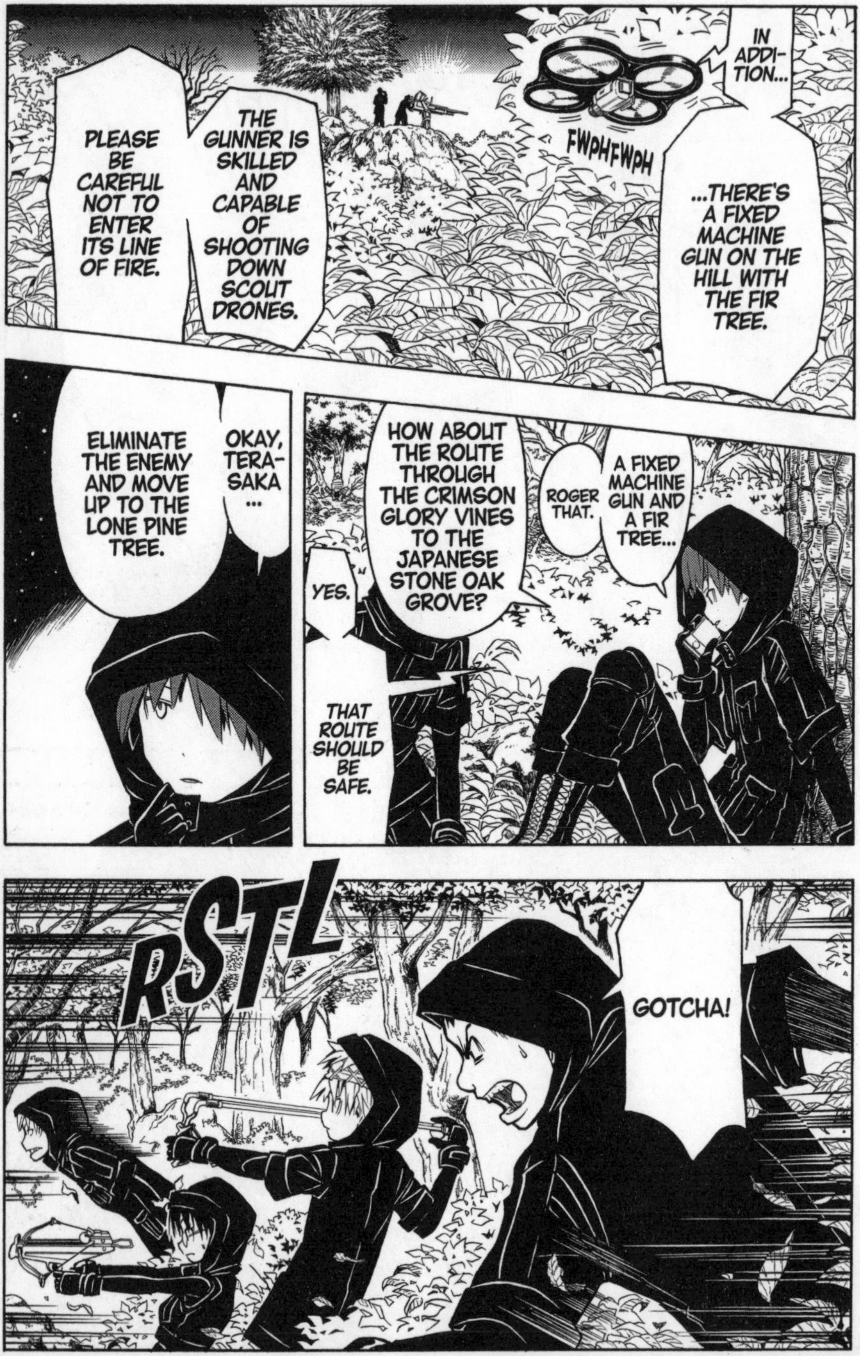
IN ADDITION...
FWPHFWPH
...THERE'S A FIXED MACHINE GUN ON THE HILL WITH THE FIR TREE.
THE GUNNER IS SKILLED AND CAPABLE OF SHOOTING DOWN SCOUT DRONES.
PLEASE BE CAREFUL NOT TO ENTER ITS LINE OF FIRE.
A FIXED MACHINE GUN AND A FIR TREE...
ROGER THAT.
HOW ABOUT THE ROUTE THROUGH THE CRIMSON GLORY VINES TO THE JAPANESE STONE OAK GROVE?
YES.
THAT ROUTE SHOULD BE SAFE.
OKAY, TERASAKA...
ELIMINATE THE ENEMY AND MOVE UP TO THE LONE PINE TREE.
GOTCHA!
RSTL

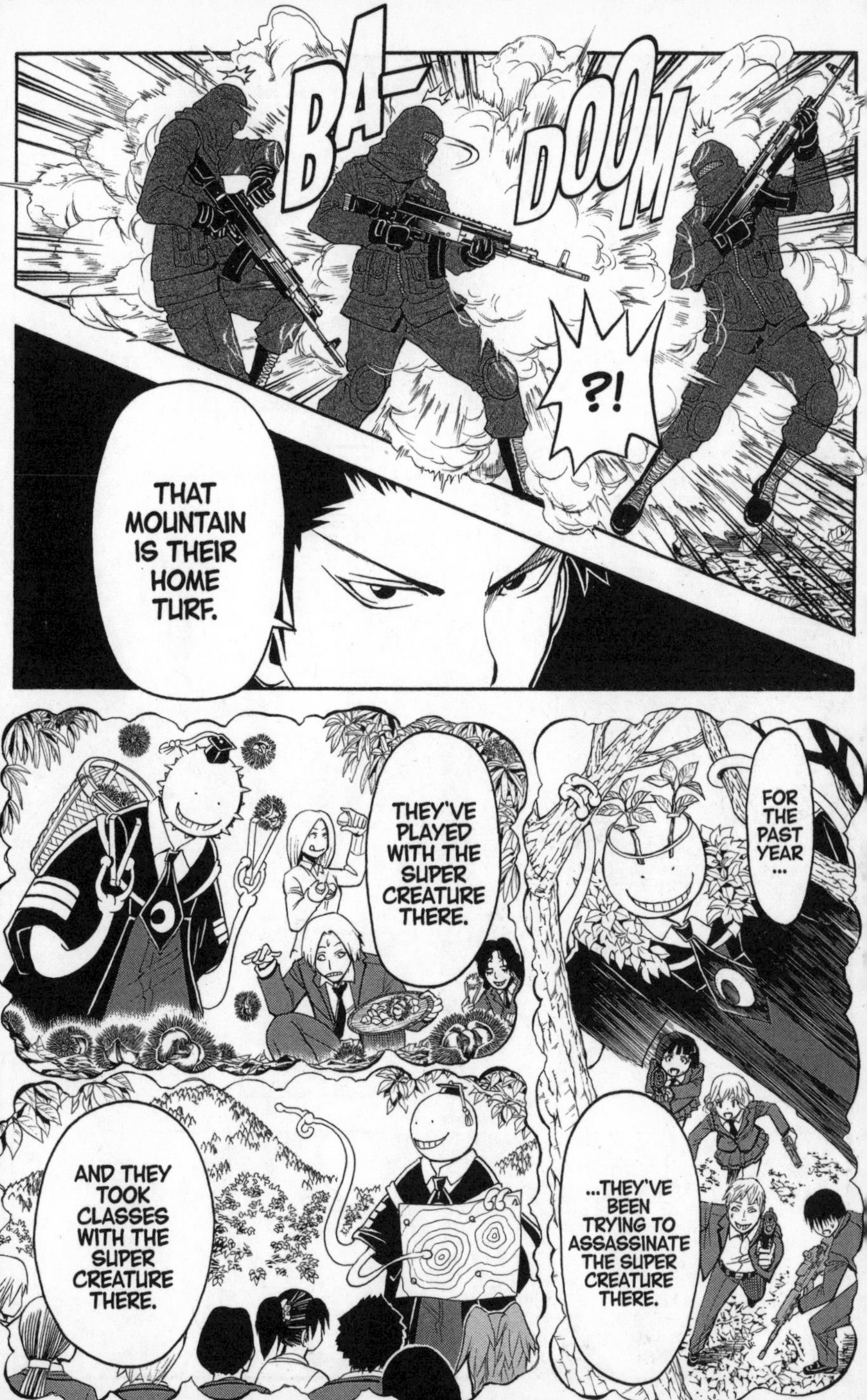
BA-DOOM
?!
THAT MOUNTAIN IS THEIR HOME TURF.
FOR THE PAST YEAR...
...THEY'VE BEEN TRYING TO ASSASSINATE THE SUPER CREATURE THERE.
THEY'VE PLAYED WITH THE SUPER CREATURE THERE.
AND THEY TOOK CLASSES WITH THE SUPER CREATURE THERE.

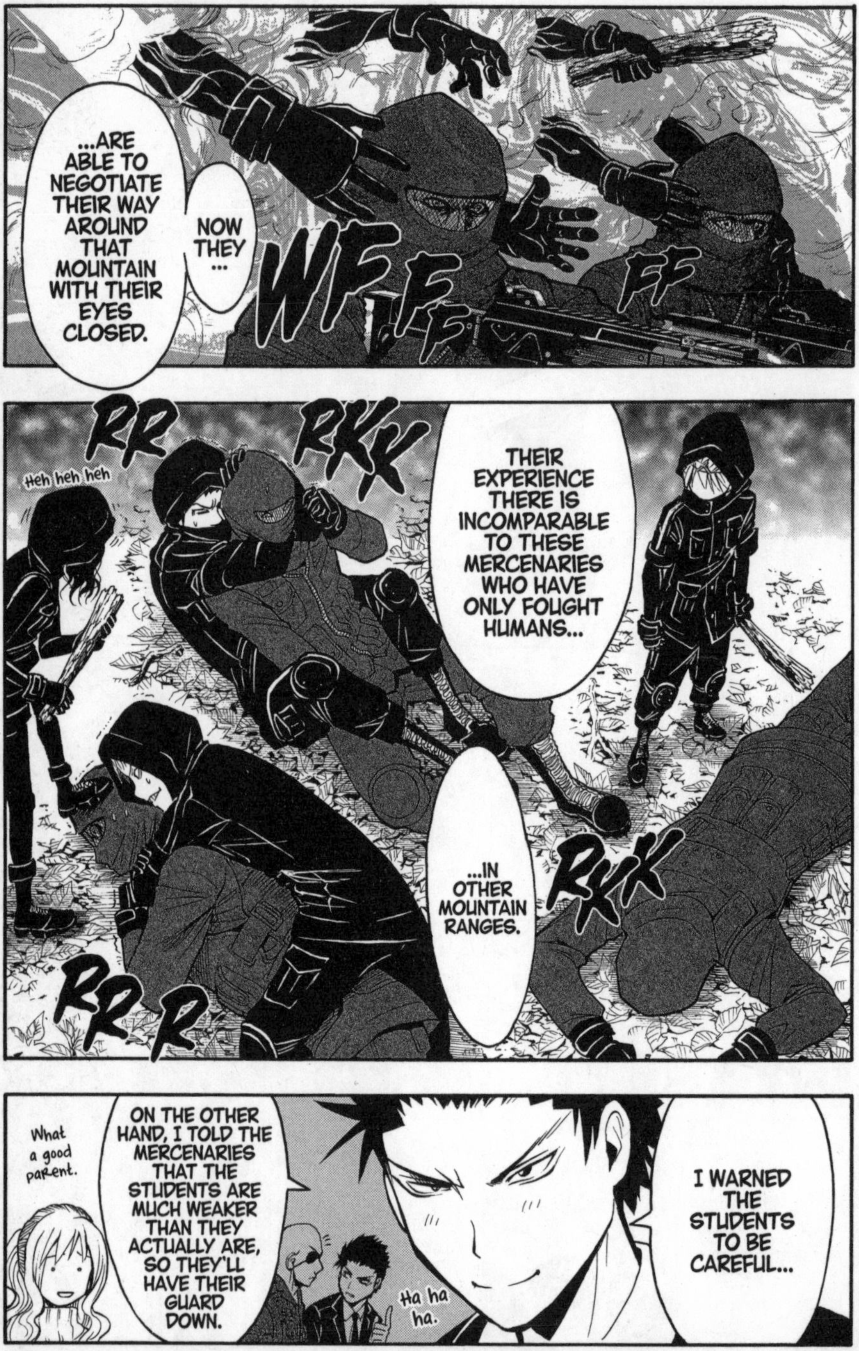
FF
WFFF
NOW THEY...
...ARE ABLE TO NEGOTIATE THEIR WAY AROUND THAT MOUNTAIN WITH THEIR EYES CLOSED.
THEIR EXPERIENCE THERE IS INCOMPARABLE TO THESE MERCENARIES WHO HAVE ONLY FOUGHT HUMANS...
RKK
RR
Heh heh heh
RKK
...IN OTHER MOUNTAIN RANGES.
RRR
I WARNED THE STUDENTS TO BE CAREFUL...
Ha ha ha.
ON THE OTHER HAND, I TOLD THE MERCENARIES THAT THE STUDENTS ARE MUCH WEAKER THAN THEY ACTUALLY ARE, SO THEY'LL HAVE THEIR GUARD DOWN.
What a good parent.

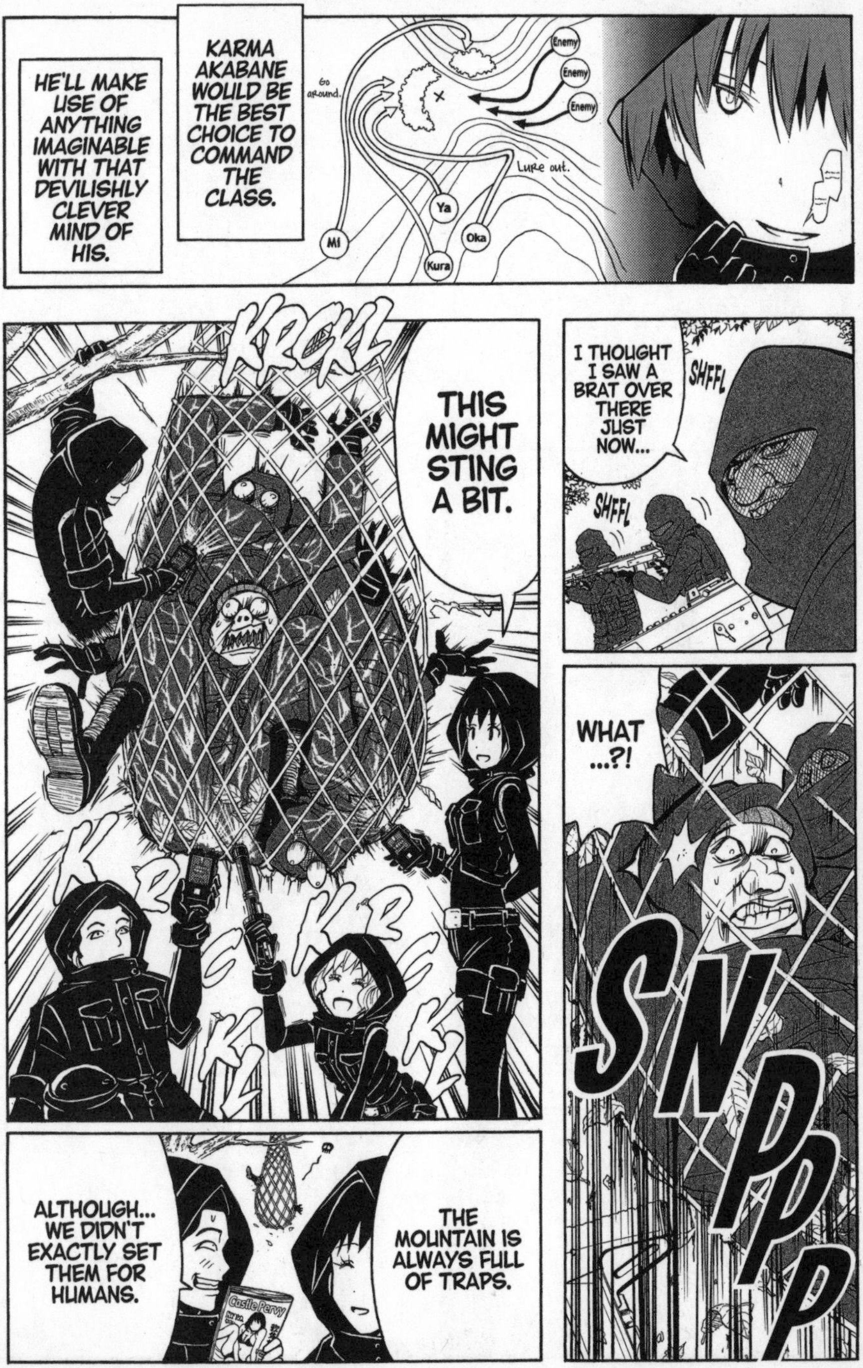
Enemy
Enemy
Enemy
Go around.
Lure out.
Ya
Oka
Mi
Kura
KARMA AKABANE WOULD BE THE BEST CHOICE TO COMMAND THE CLASS.
HE'LL MAKE USE OF ANYTHING IMAGINABLE WITH THAT DEVILISHLY CLEVER MIND OF HIS.
I THOUGHT I SAW A BRAT OVER THERE JUST NOW...
SHFFL
SHFFL
WHAT ...?!
SNPPP
KRCKL
THIS MIGHT STING A BIT.
KRCKL
KRCKL
THE MOUNTAIN IS ALWAYS FULL OF TRAPS.
ALTHOUGH... WE DIDN'T EXACTLY SET THEM FOR HUMANS.
Castle Pervy

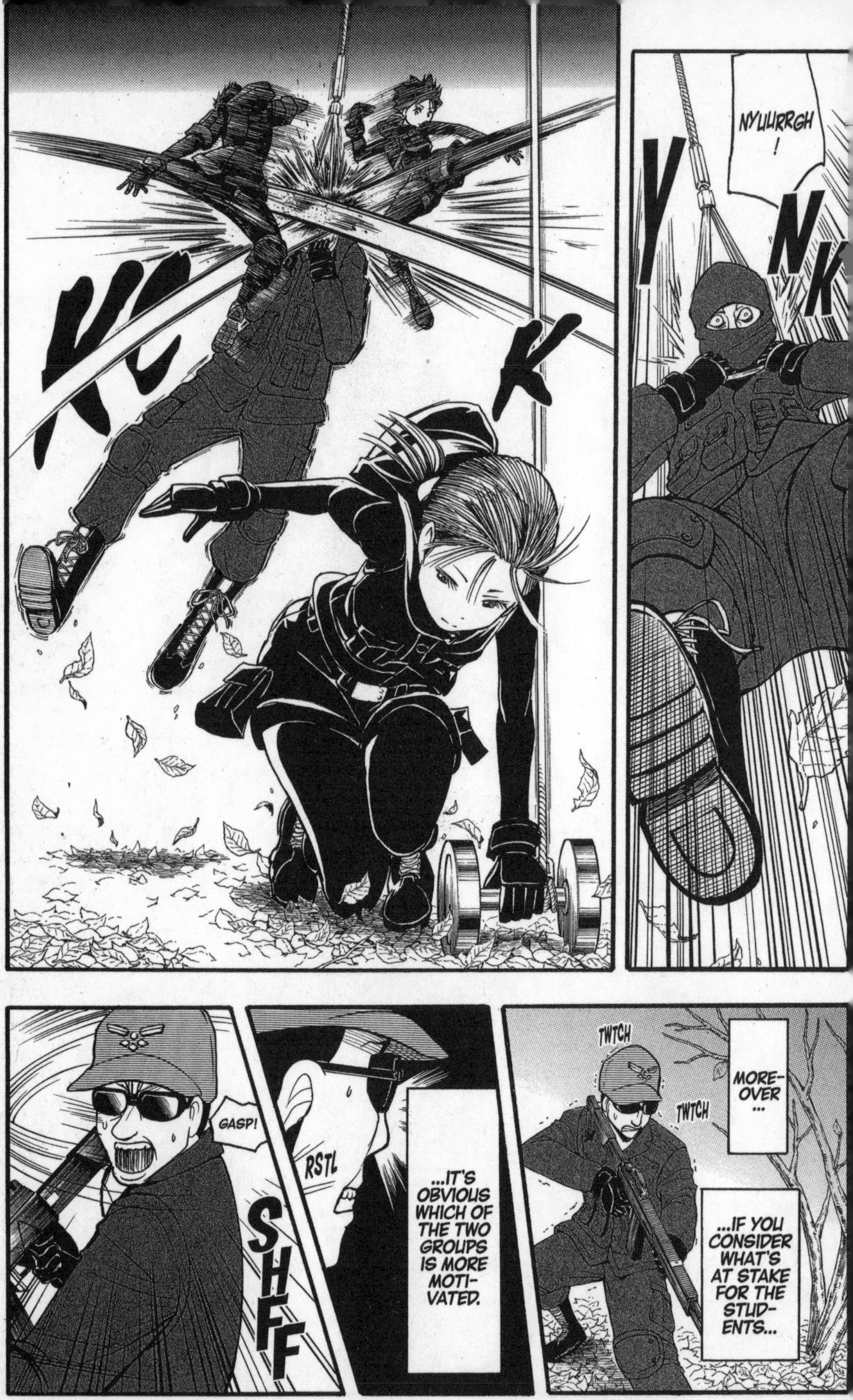
NYUURRGH!
YNK
MORE-OVER...
TWTCH
TWTCH
...IF YOU CONSIDER WHAT'S AT STAKE FOR THE STUDENTS...
...IT'S OBVIOUS WHICH OF THE TWO GROUPS IS MORE MOTIVATED.
RSTL
SHFF
GASP!

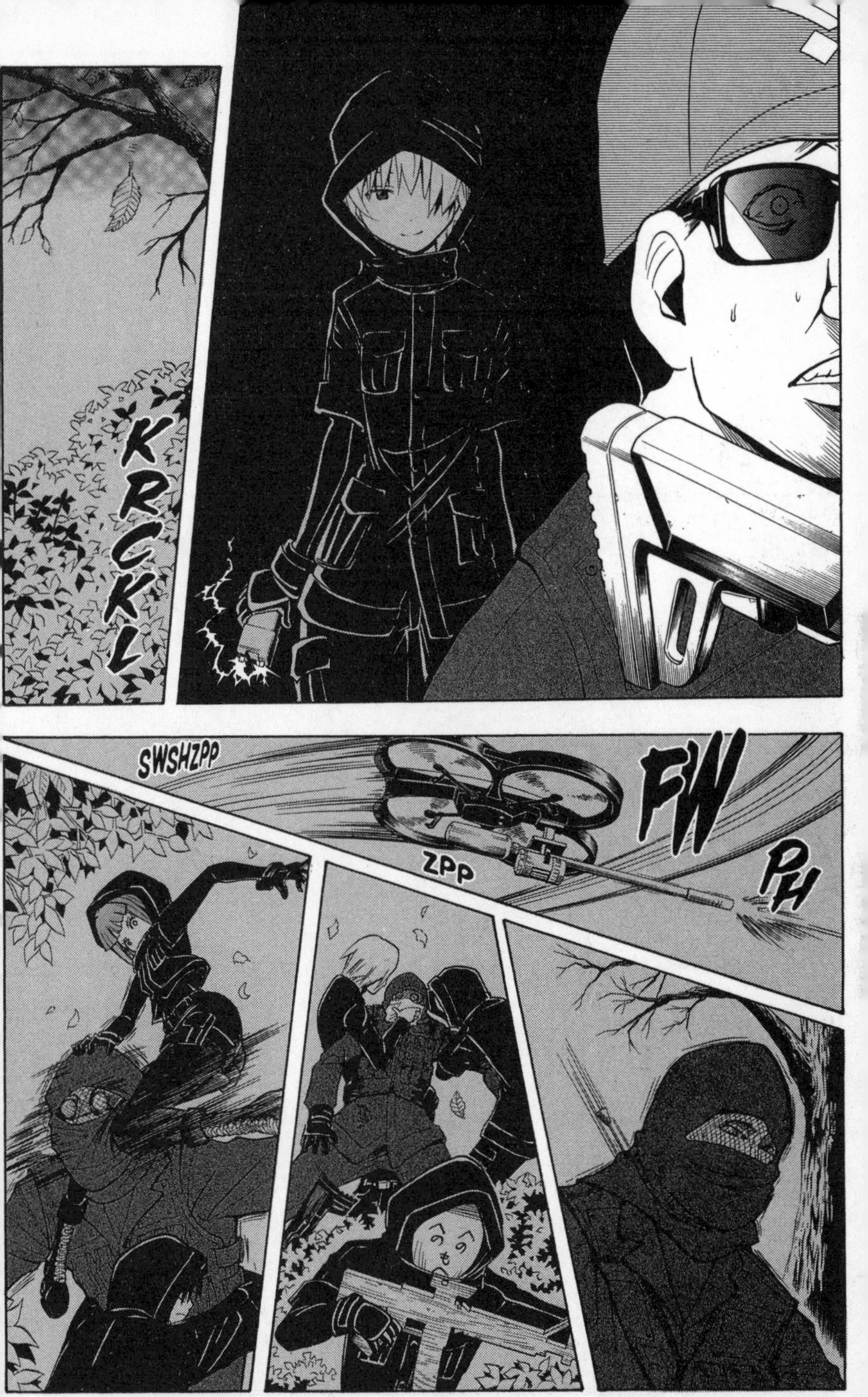
KRCKL
FW
PH
ZPP
SWSHZPP

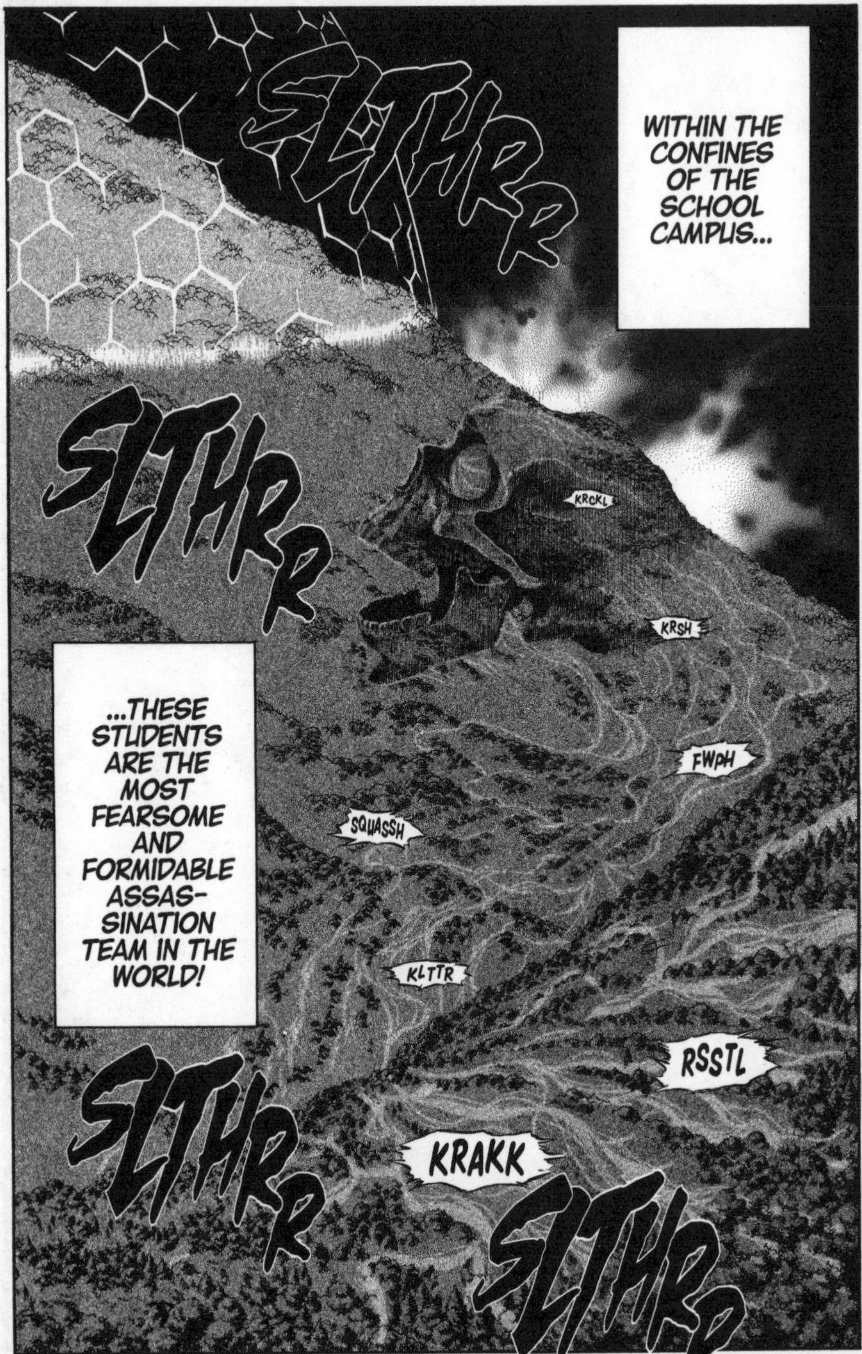
WITHIN THE CONFINES OF THE SCHOOL CAMPUS...
SLITHRR
SLITHRR
KRCKL
KRSH
FWPH
...THESE STUDENTS ARE THE MOST FEARSOME AND FORMIDABLE ASSAS-SINATION TEAM IN THE WORLD!
SQUASSH
KLTTR
RSSTL
KRAKK
SLITHRR
SLITHRR

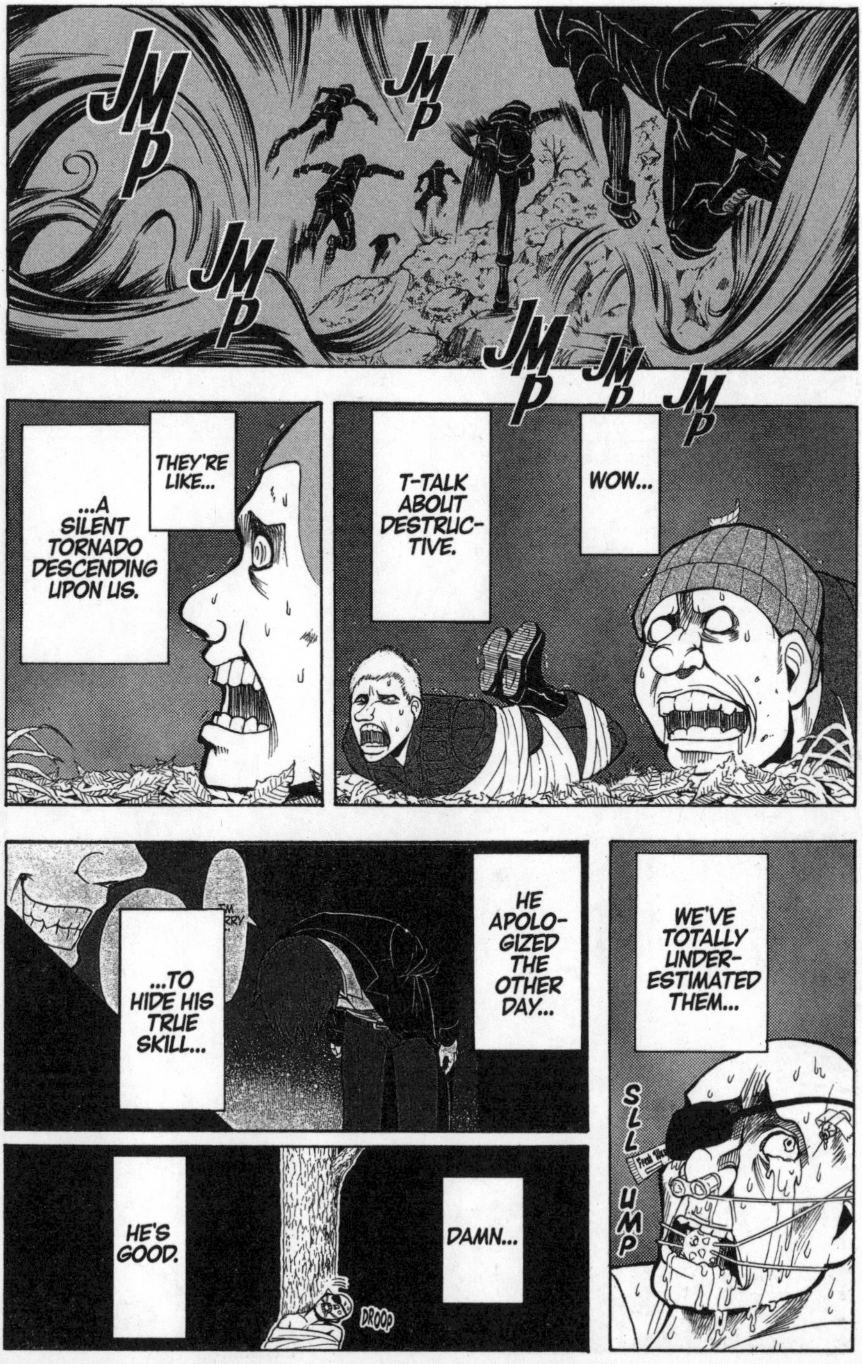
JMP
JMP
JMP
JMP
JMP
JMP
WOW...
T-TALK ABOUT DESTRUC-TIVE.
THEY'RE LIKE...
...A SILENT TORNADO DESCENDING UPON US.
WE'VE TOTALLY UNDER-ESTIMATED THEM...
SLLUMP
HE APOLO-GIZED THE OTHER DAY...
...TO HIDE HIS TRUE SKILL...
DAMN...
HE'S GOOD.
DROOP

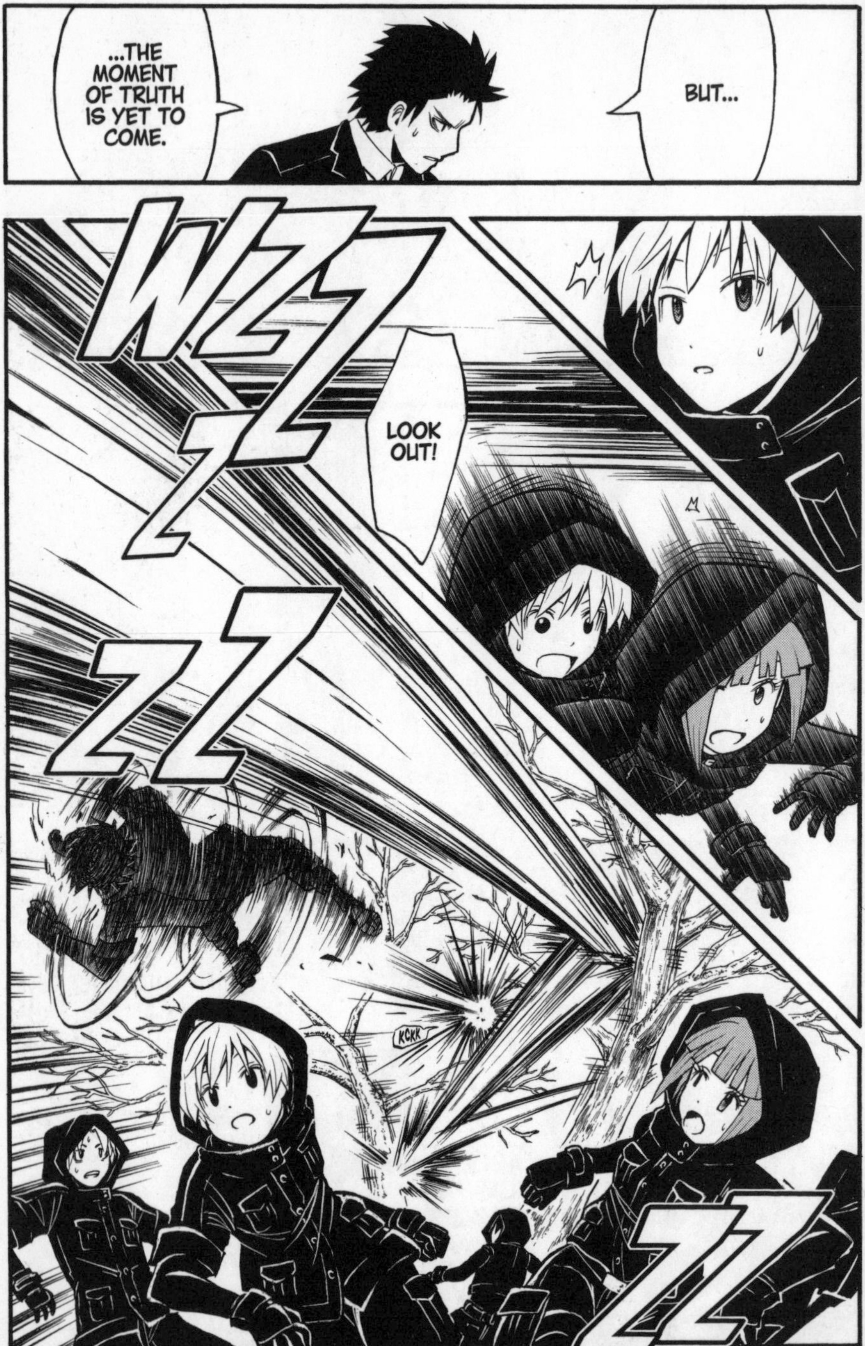
BUT...
...THE MOMENT OF TRUTH IS YET TO COME.
WHZZ
LOOK OUT!
ZZ
KCKK
ZZ

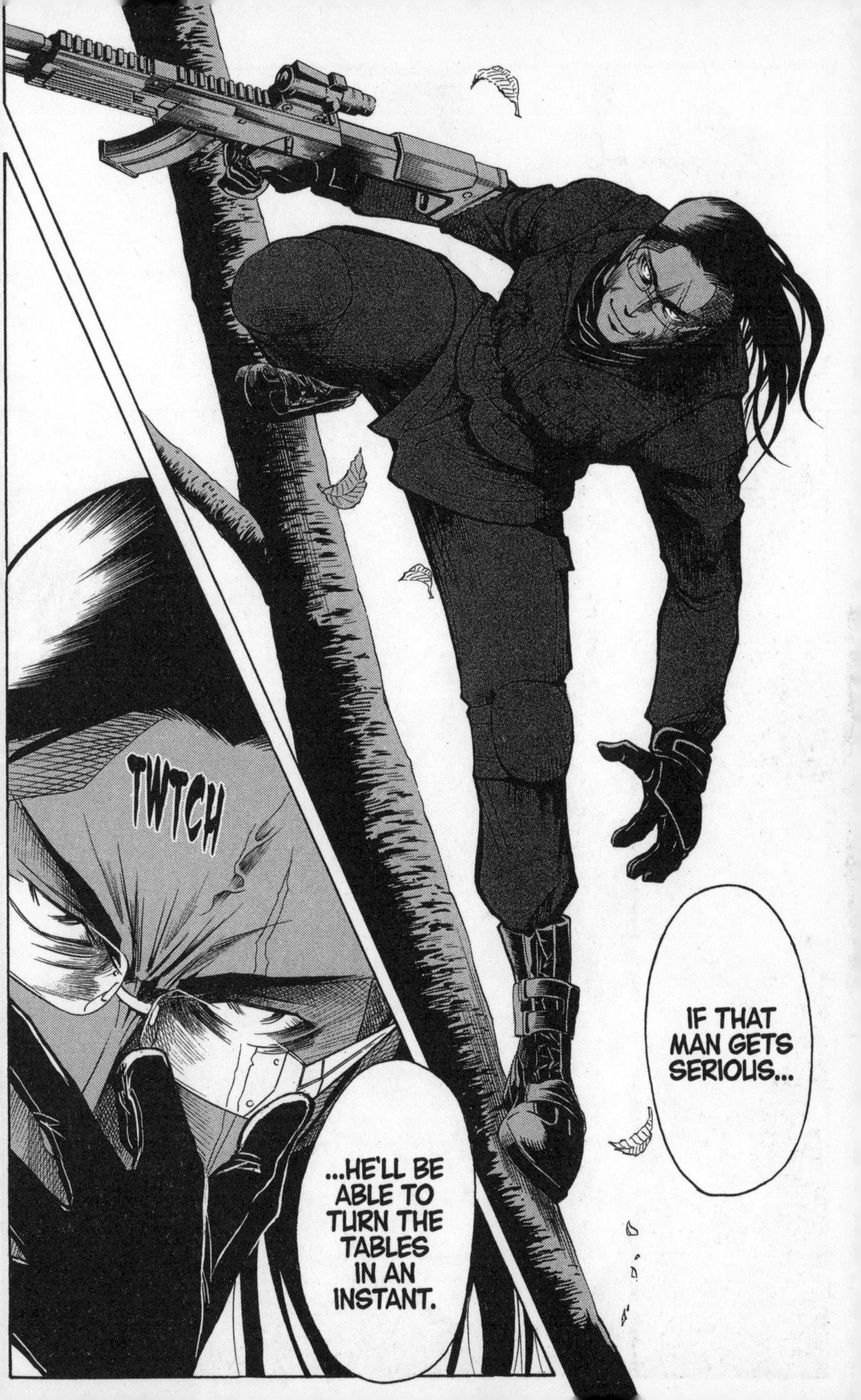
IF THAT MAN GETS SERIOUS...
TWTCH
...HE'LL BE ABLE TO TURN THE TABLES IN AN INSTANT.

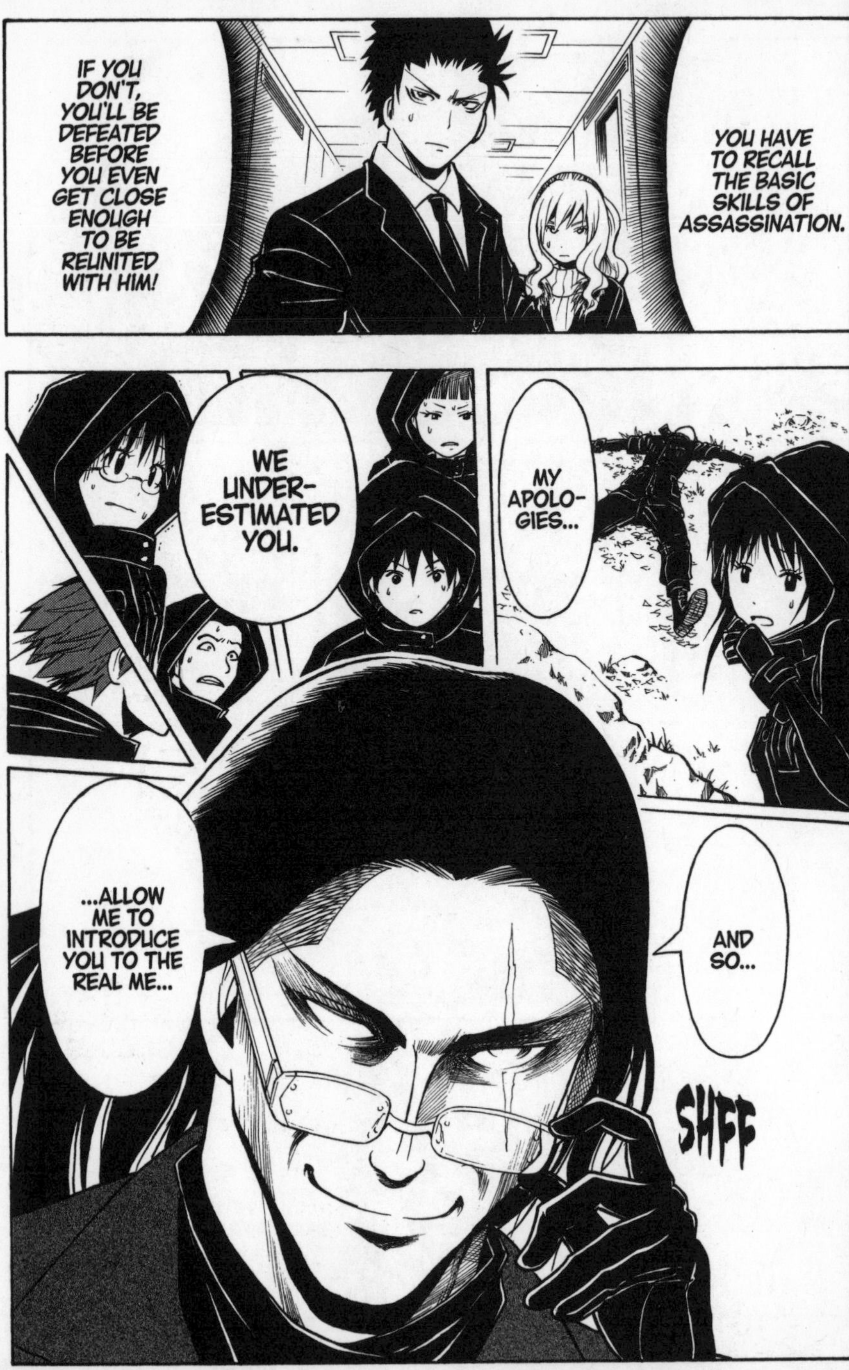
YOU HAVE TO RECALL THE BASIC SKILLS OF ASSASSINATION.
IF YOU DON'T, YOU'LL BE DEFEATED BEFORE YOU EVEN GET CLOSE ENOUGH TO BE REUNITED WITH HIM!
MY APOLO-GIES...
WE UNDER-ESTIMATED YOU.
AND SO...
...ALLOW ME TO INTRODUCE YOU TO THE REAL ME...
SHFF

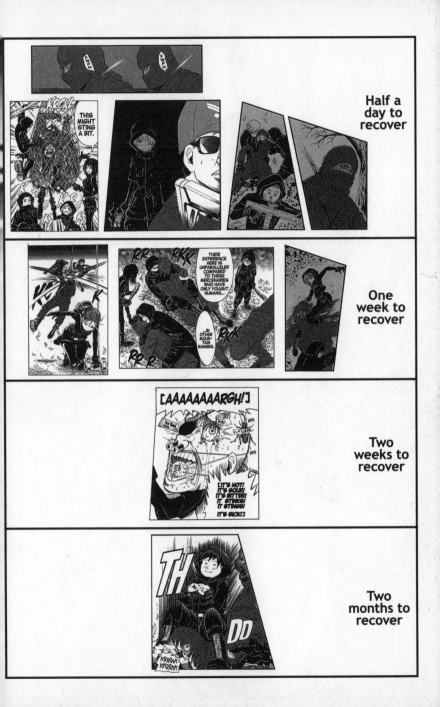

Half a day to recover

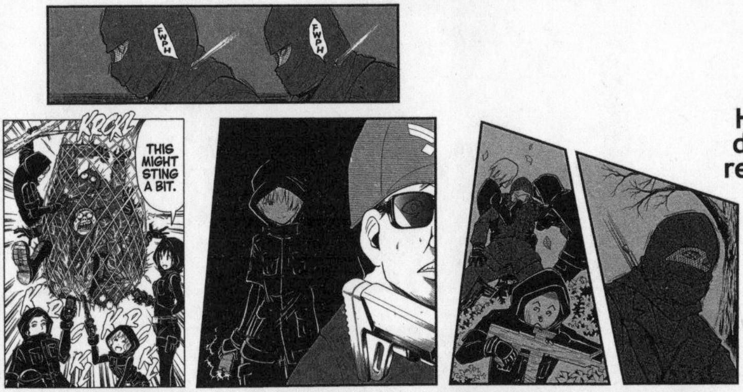
FWPH
FWPH
KRCKL
THIS MIGHT STING A BIT.

One week to recover

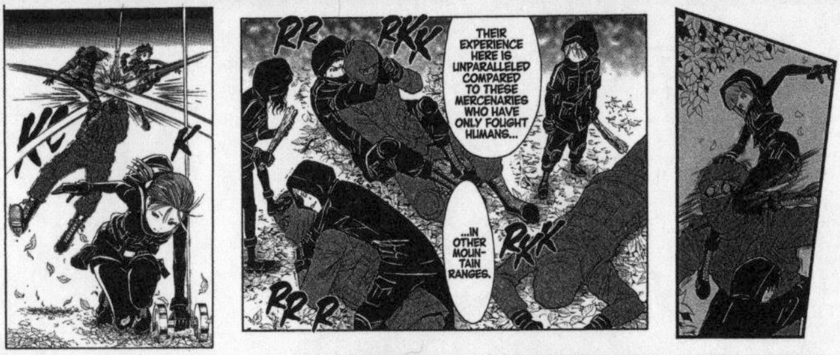
RR
RKK
THEIR EXPERIENCE HERE IS UNPARALLELED COMPARED TO THESE MERCENARIES WHO HAVE ONLY FOUGHT HUMANS...
...IN OTHER MOUNTAIN RANGES.
RKK
RR
R

Two weeks to recover

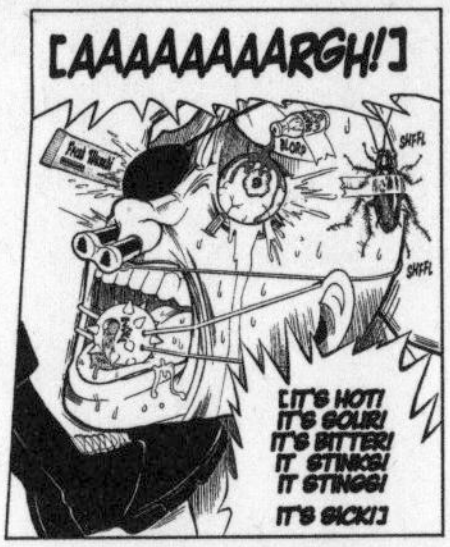
[AAAAAAAARGH!]
SHFF
SHFF
[IT'S HOT! IT'S SOUR! IT'S BITTER! IT STINKS! IT STINGS! IT'S SICK!]

Two months to recover

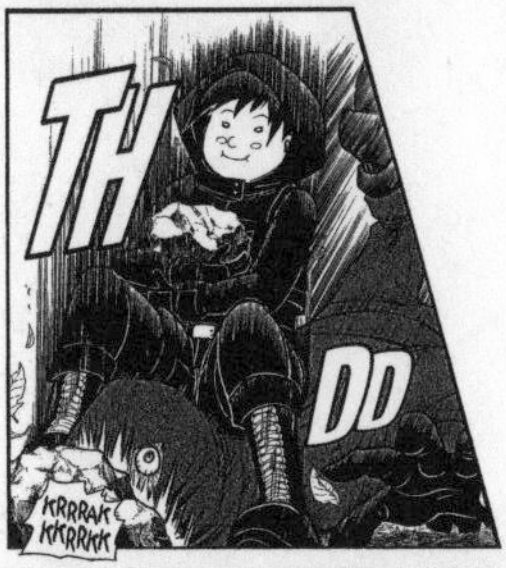
TH
DD
KRRRAK KKRRKK

Class 169 | Time to go to School

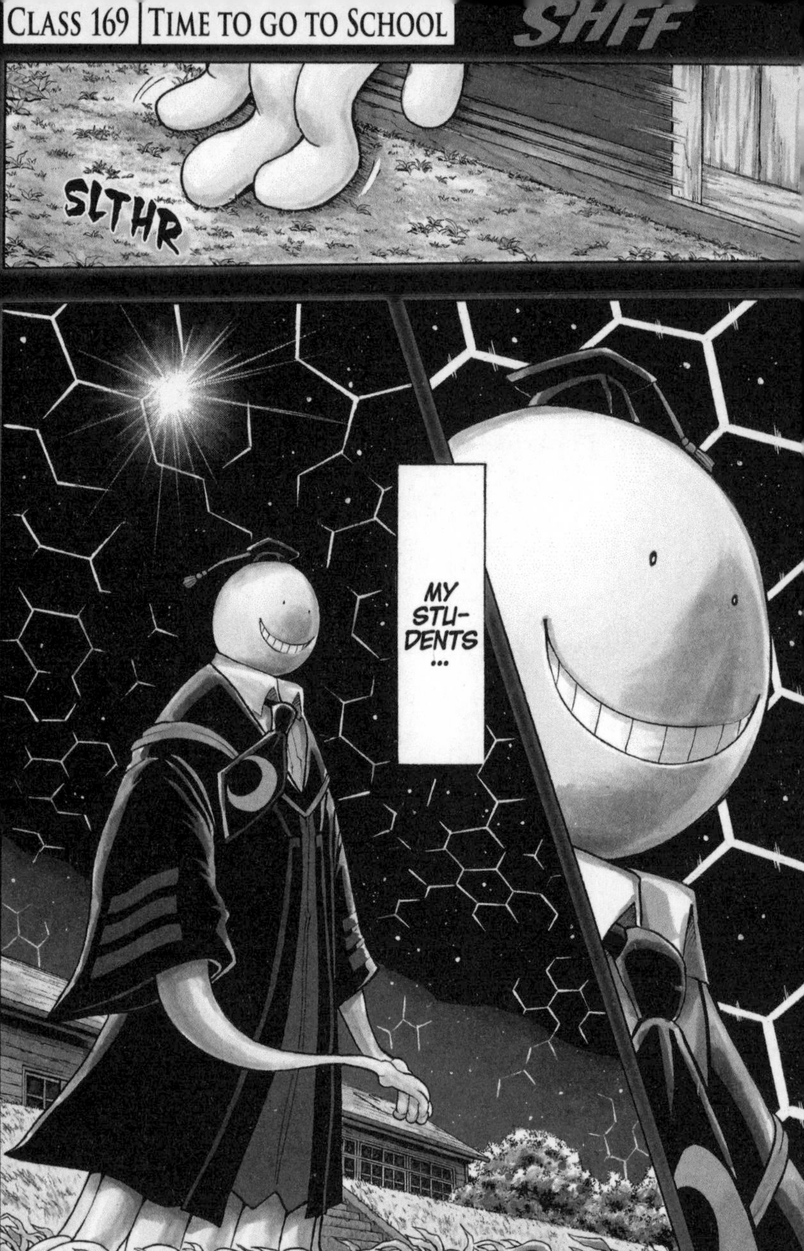
SHFF
SLTHR
MY STUDENTS...

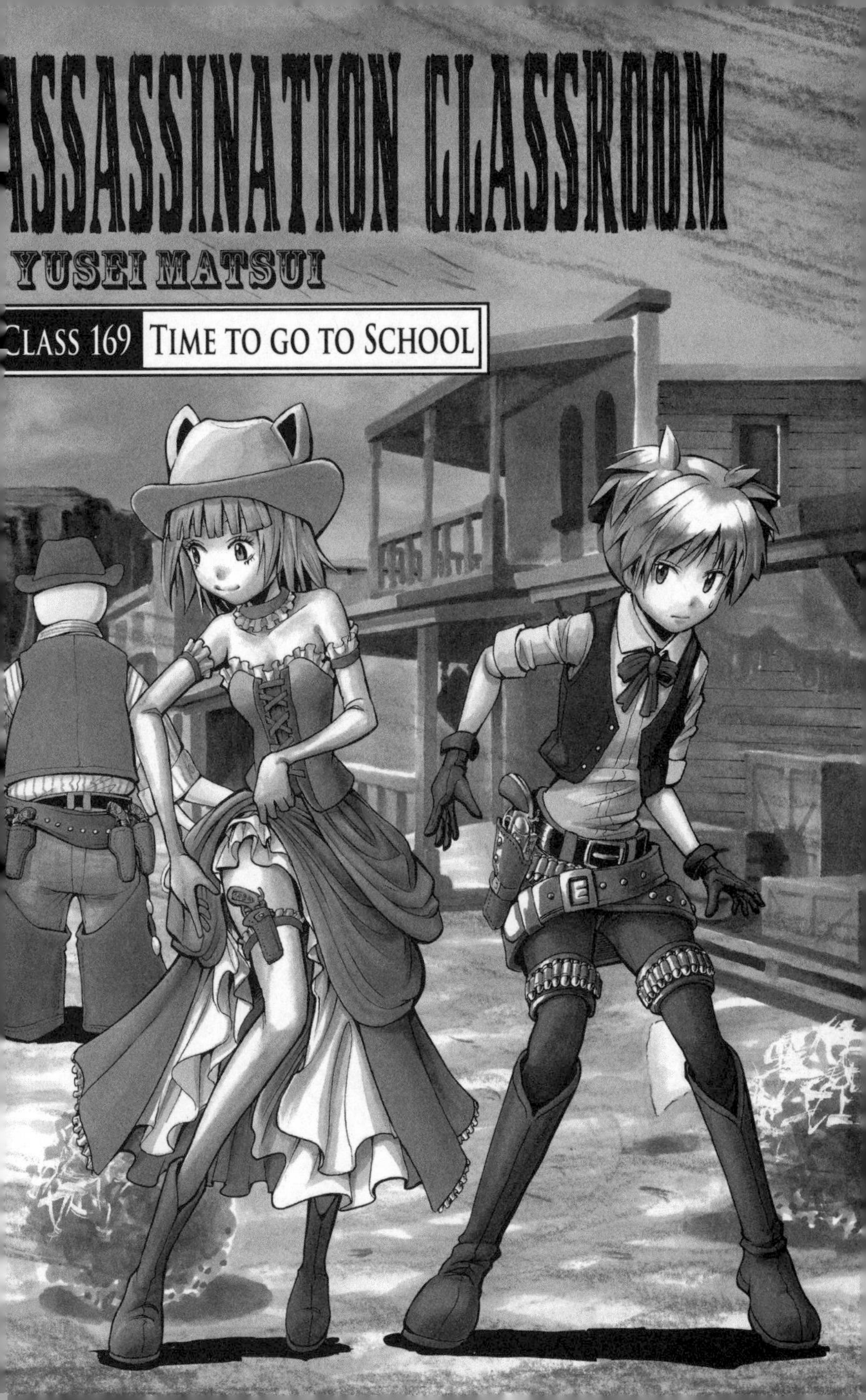
ASSASSINATION CLASSROOM
YUSEI MATSUI
CLASS 169 TIME TO GO TO SCHOOL

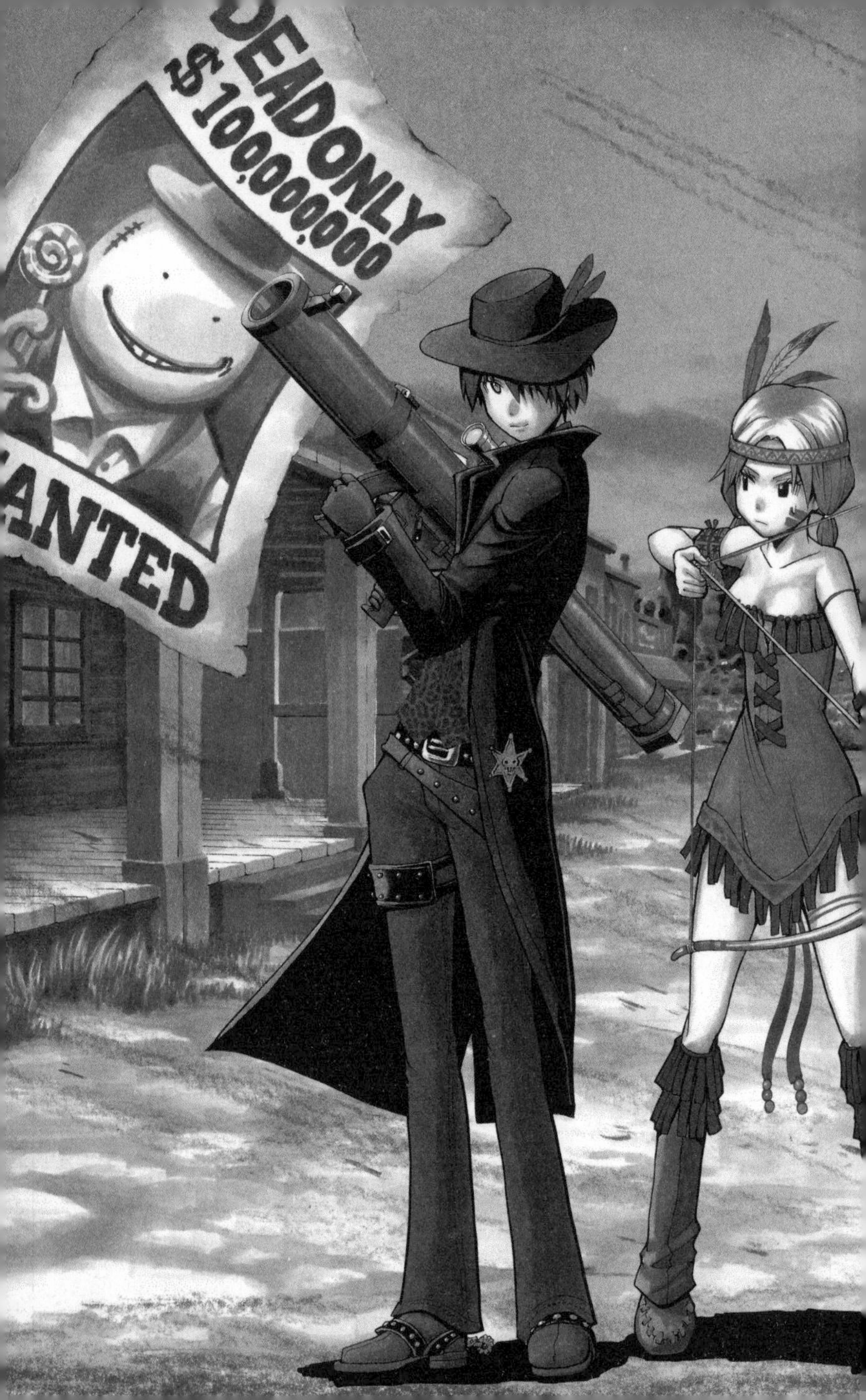
DEAD ONLY
$ 10,000,000
ANTED

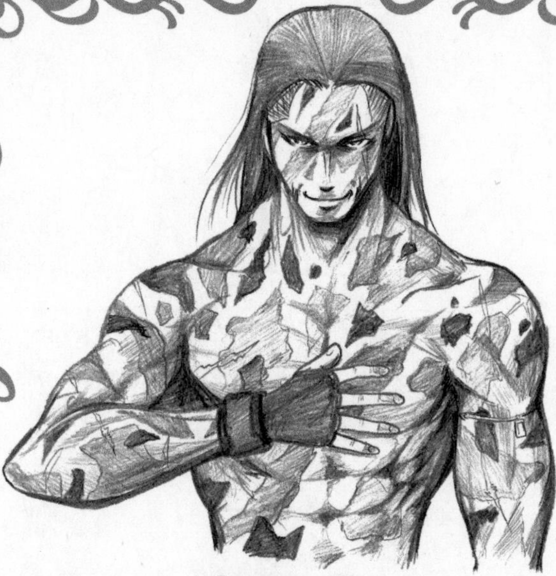

CRAIG HOJO

- BIRTHDAY: SEPTEMBER 1 (42 YEARS OLD)
- HEIGHT: 6' 5"
- WEIGHT: 265 LBS.
- CAREER HISTORY: GREEN BERETS → PRIVATE MILITARY COMPANY → FREELANCE
- HOBBY/SKILL: WAR
- MOTTO: WAR IS THE SCIENCE OF DESTRUCTION
- TOTAL NUMBER OF BATTLES: OVER 5,000
- AFFINITY FOR WARFARE: WAR IS ALL HE THINKS ABOUT WHETHER HE'S AWAKE OR ASLEEP
- HE LIKES WAR SO MUCH THAT THE CD HE BOUGHT IN JAPAN THE MOMENT HE SAW THE COVER WAS: *WOW, WAR TONIGHT*!*

*A 2003 POP SONG THAT HAS NOTHING TO DO WITH WAR

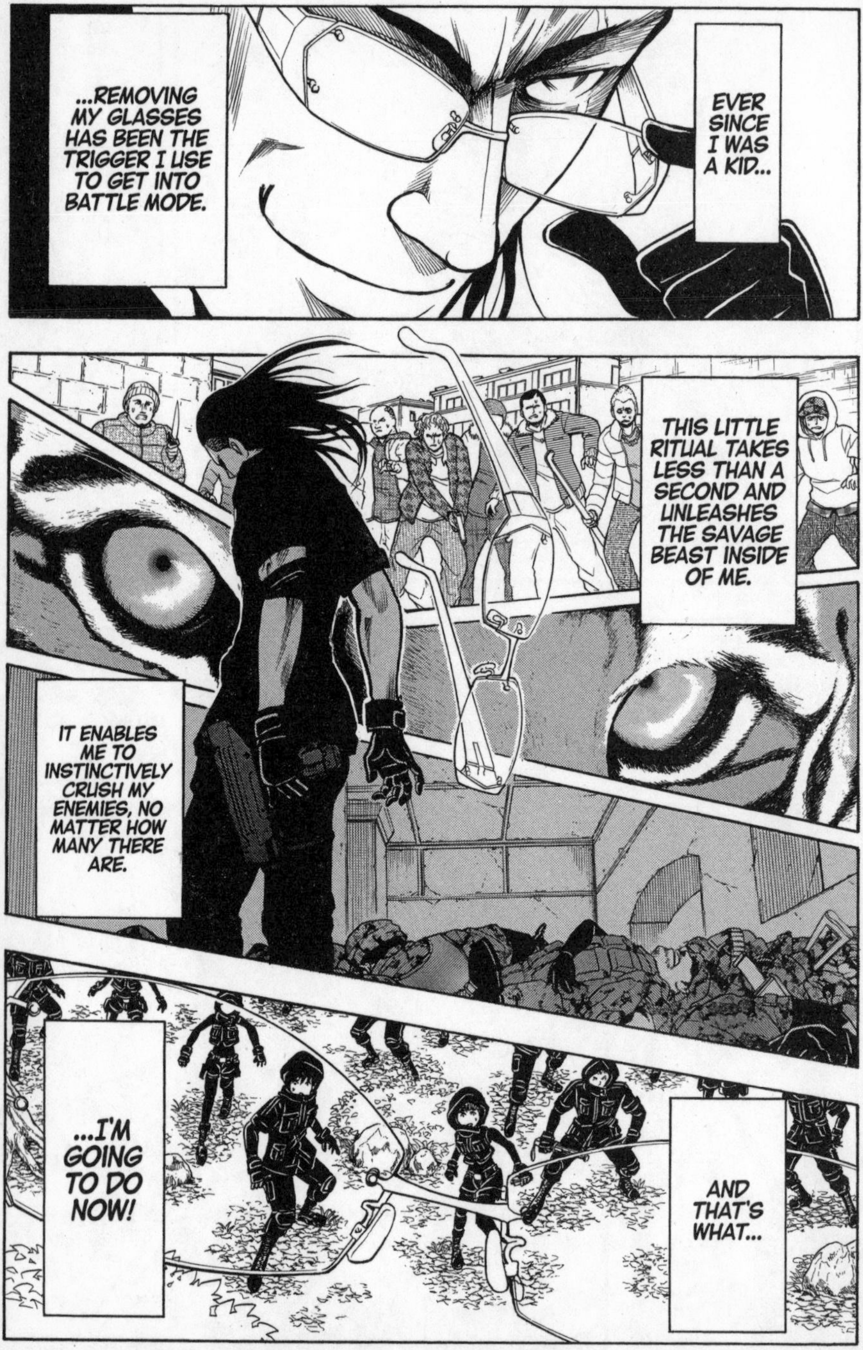
EVER SINCE I WAS A KID...
...REMOVING MY GLASSES HAS BEEN THE TRIGGER I USE TO GET INTO BATTLE MODE.
THIS LITTLE RITUAL TAKES LESS THAN A SECOND AND UNLEASHES THE SAVAGE BEAST INSIDE OF ME.
IT ENABLES ME TO INSTINCTIVELY CRUSH MY ENEMIES, NO MATTER HOW MANY THERE ARE.
AND THAT'S WHAT...
...I'M GOING TO DO NOW!

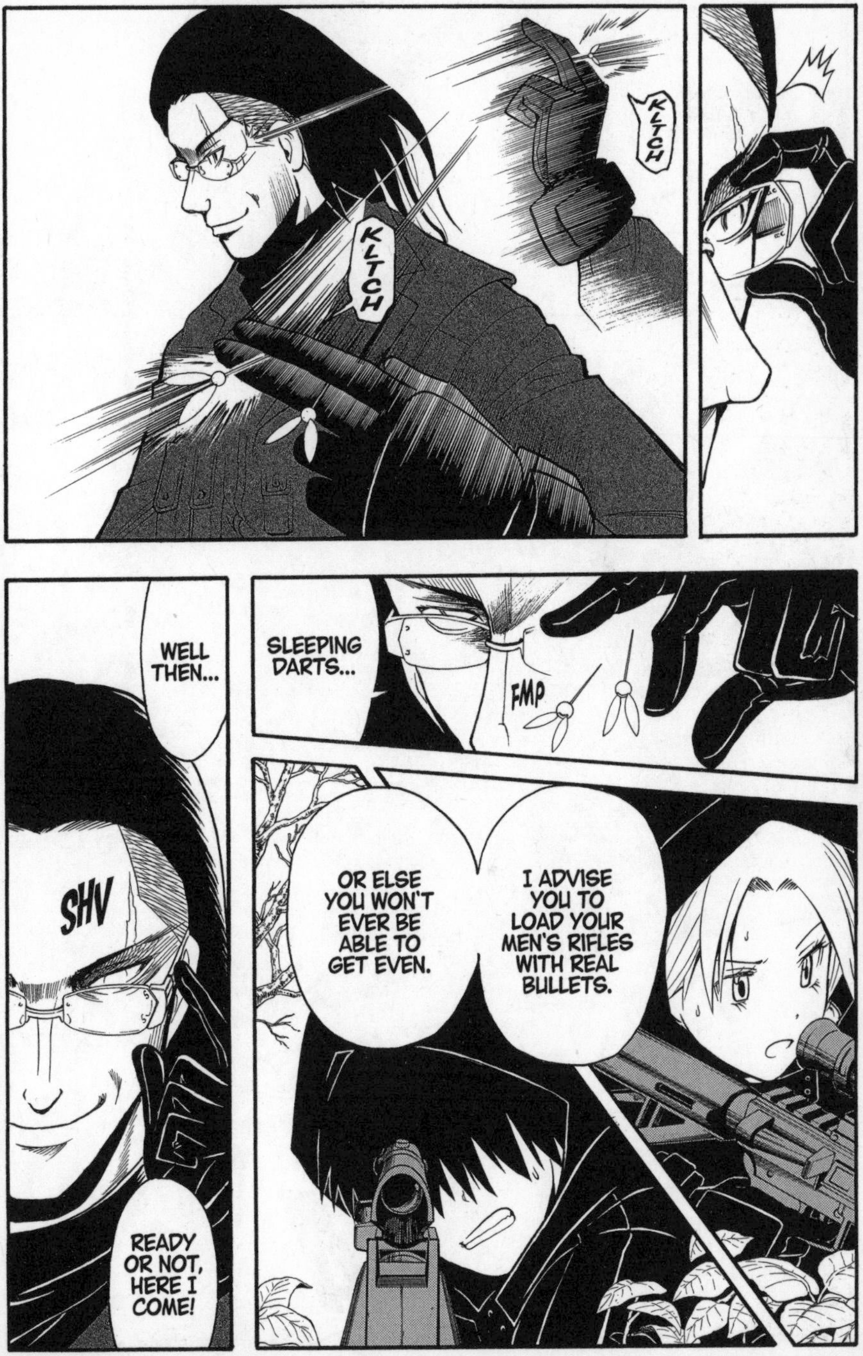
KLTCH
KLTCH
SLEEPING DARTS...
FMP
I ADVISE YOU TO LOAD YOUR MEN'S RIFLES WITH REAL BULLETS.
OR ELSE YOU WON'T EVER BE ABLE TO GET EVEN.
WELL THEN...
SHV
READY OR NOT, HERE I COME!

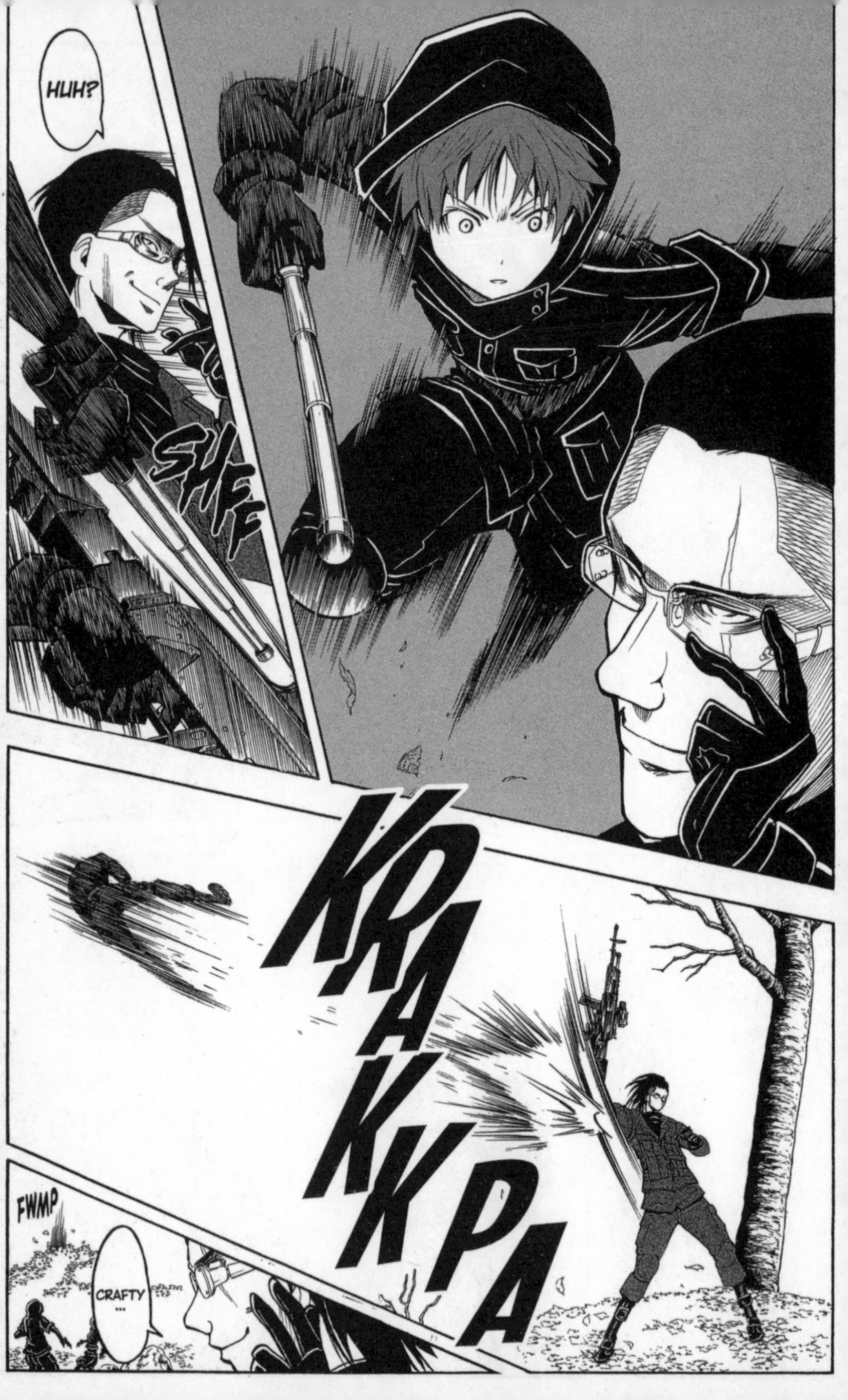
HUH?
SHFF
KRAKKPA
FWMP
CRAFTY...

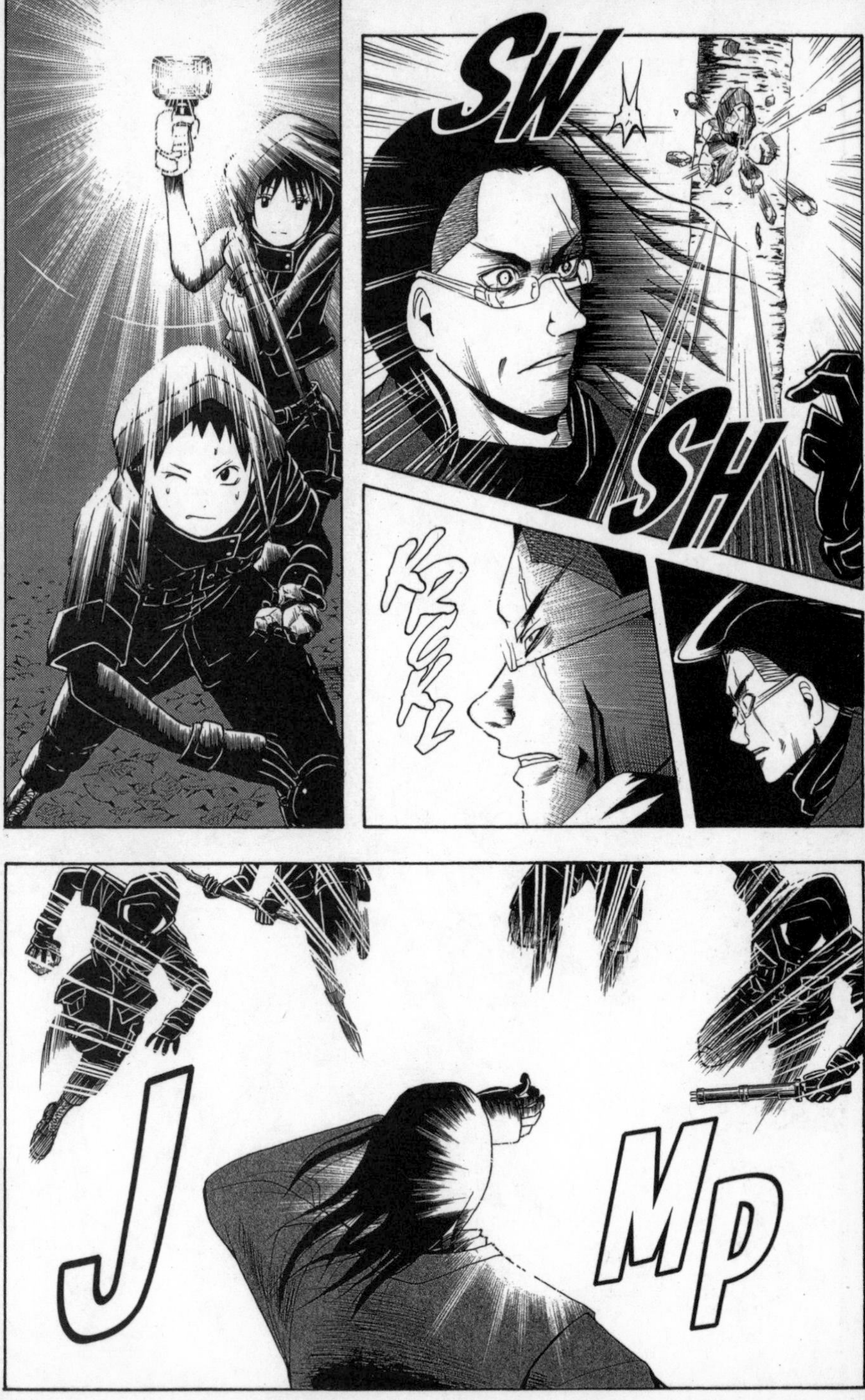
SW
SH
KRUNK
J
Mp

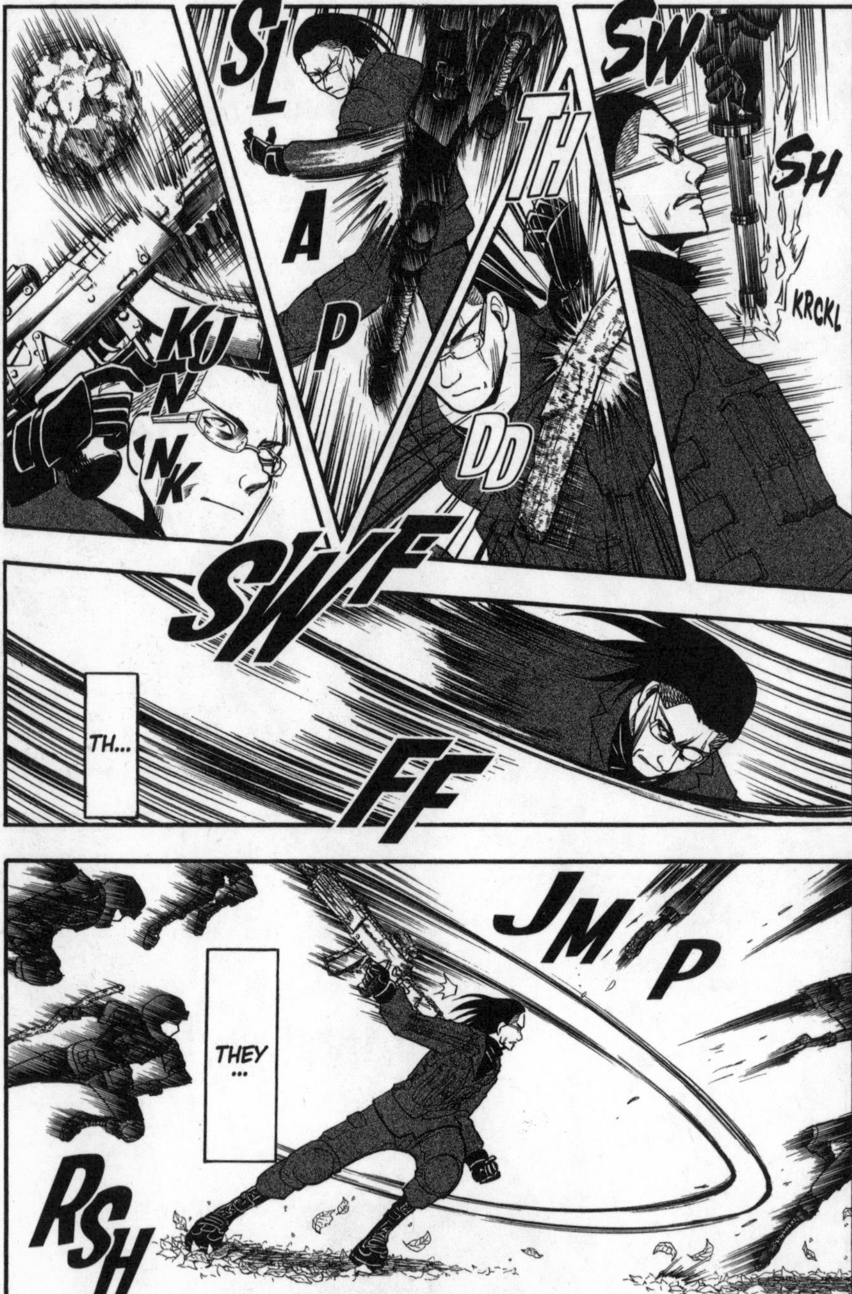
SW
SH
KRCKL
TH
DD
SLAP
KUNNK
SWFF
TH...
JMP
THEY...
RSH

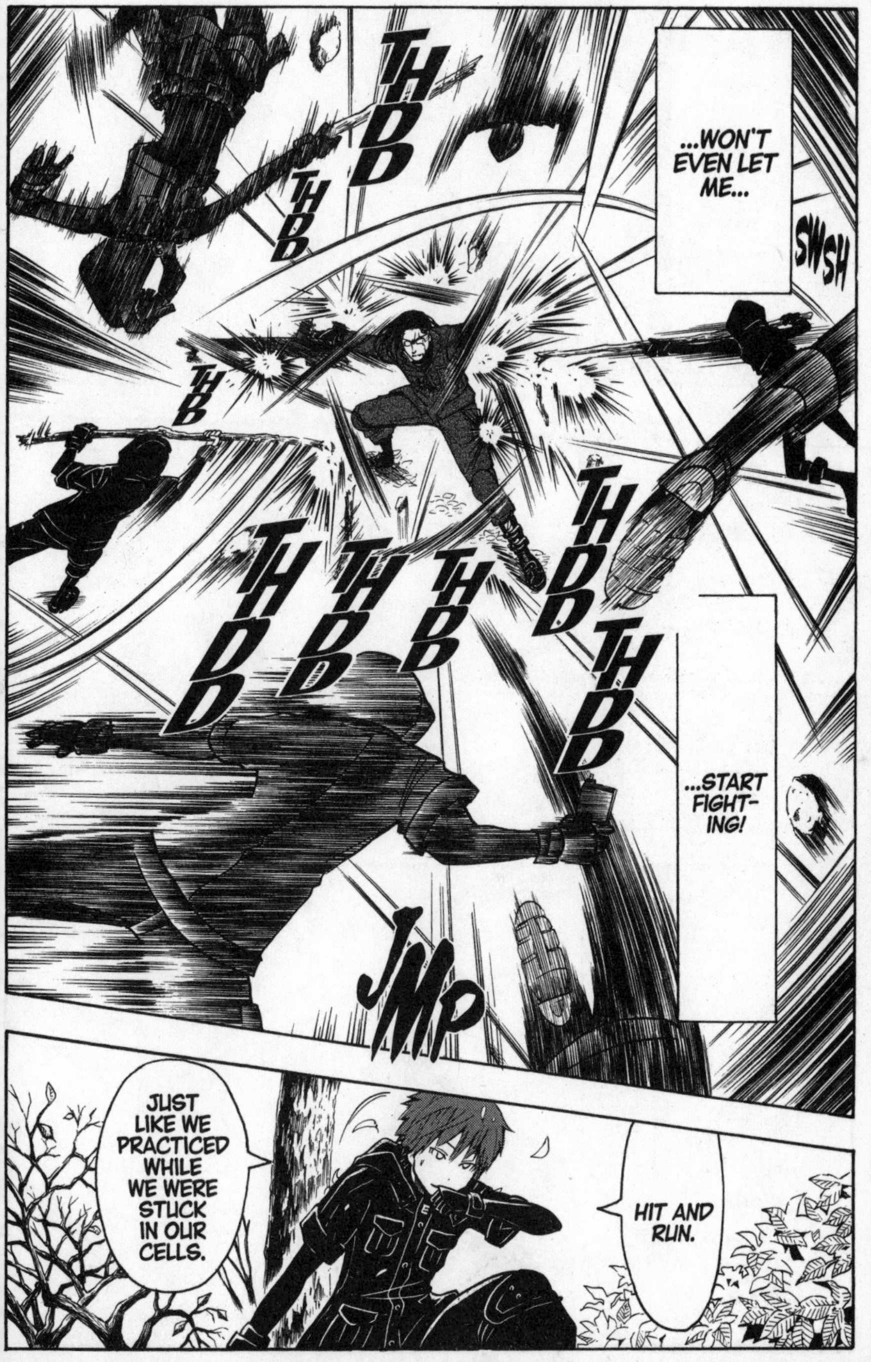
...WON'T EVEN LET ME...
SWSH
THDD
THDD
THDD
THDD
THDD
THDD
THDD
THDD
THDD
...START FIGHT-ING!
JMP
HIT AND RUN.
JUST LIKE WE PRACTICED WHILE WE WERE STUCK IN OUR CELLS.

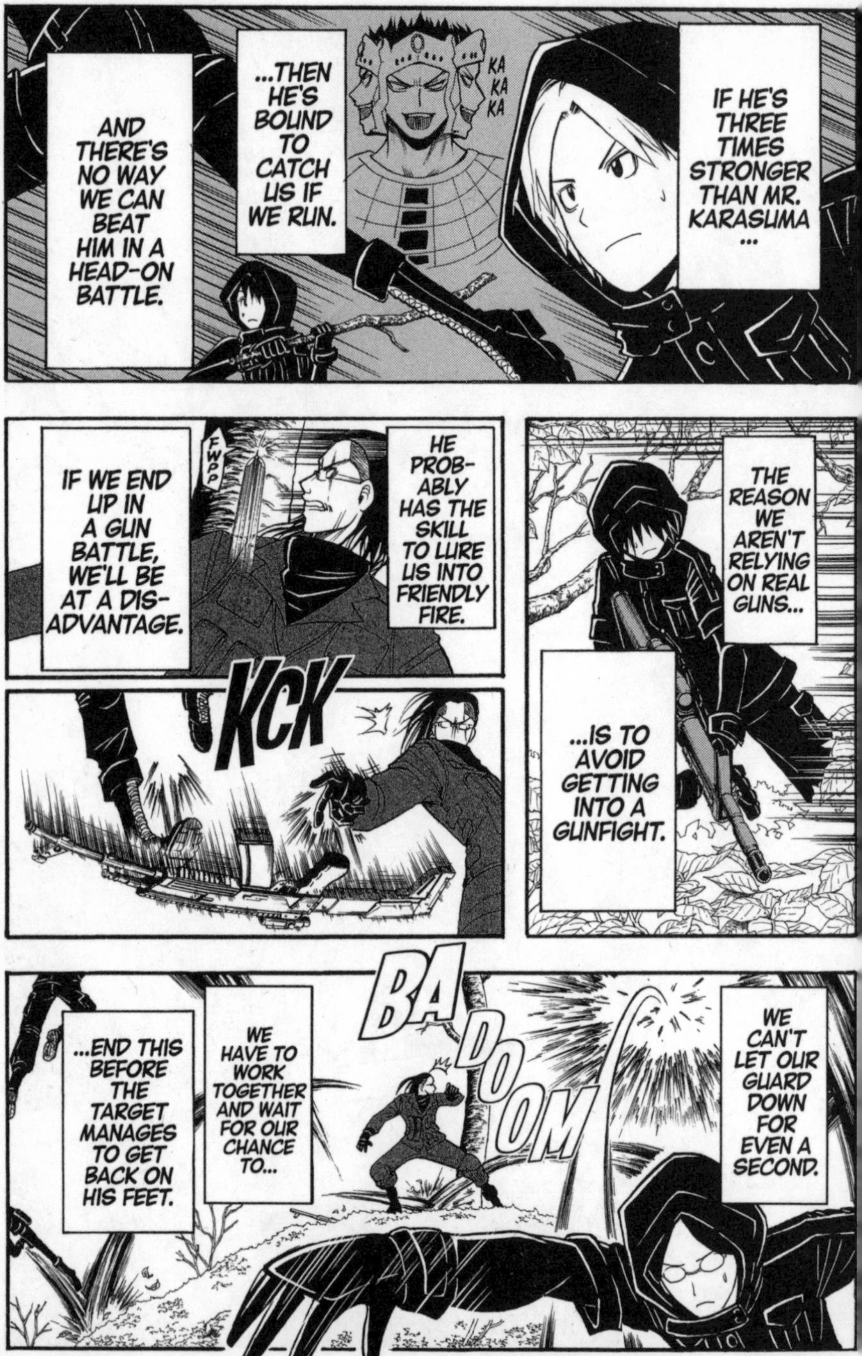
IF HE'S THREE TIMES STRONGER THAN MR. KARASUMA...
KA KA KA
...THEN HE'S BOUND TO CATCH US IF WE RUN.
AND THERE'S NO WAY WE CAN BEAT HIM IN A HEAD-ON BATTLE.
THE REASON WE AREN'T RELYING ON REAL GUNS...
...IS TO AVOID GETTING INTO A GUNFIGHT.
HE PROBABLY HAS THE SKILL TO LURE US INTO FRIENDLY FIRE.
FWPP
IF WE END UP IN A GUN BATTLE, WE'LL BE AT A DISADVANTAGE.
KCK
WE CAN'T LET OUR GUARD DOWN FOR EVEN A SECOND.
BADOOM
WE HAVE TO WORK TOGETHER AND WAIT FOR OUR CHANCE TO...
...END THIS BEFORE THE TARGET MANAGES TO GET BACK ON HIS FEET.

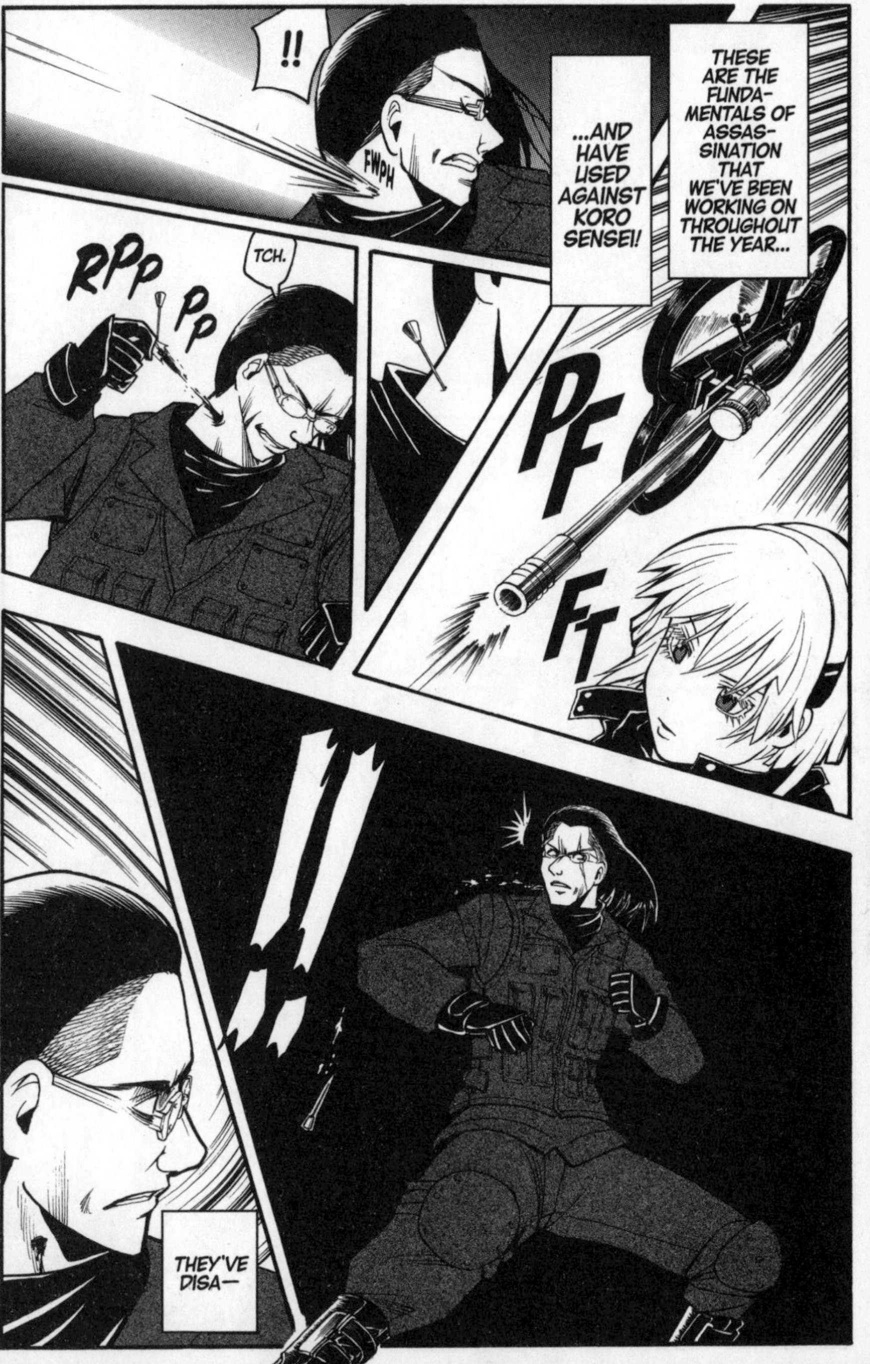
THESE ARE THE FUNDA-MENTALS OF ASSAS-SINATION THAT WE'VE BEEN WORKING ON THROUGHOUT THE YEAR...
...AND HAVE USED AGAINST KORO SENSEI!
!!
FWPH
PFFT
TCH.
RPPPP
THEY'VE DISA—

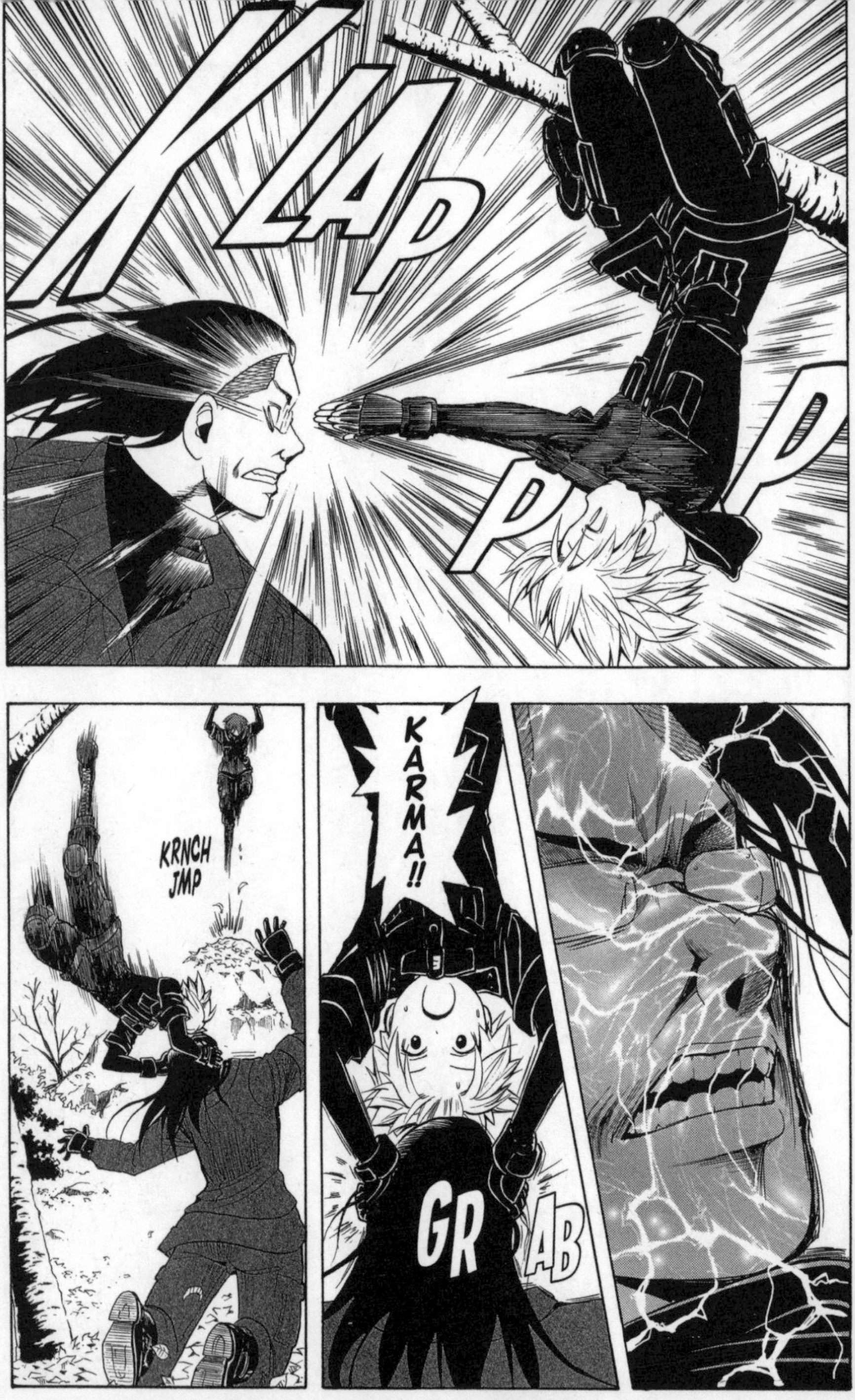
KLAPPP
KARMA!!
GR AB
KRNCH
JMP

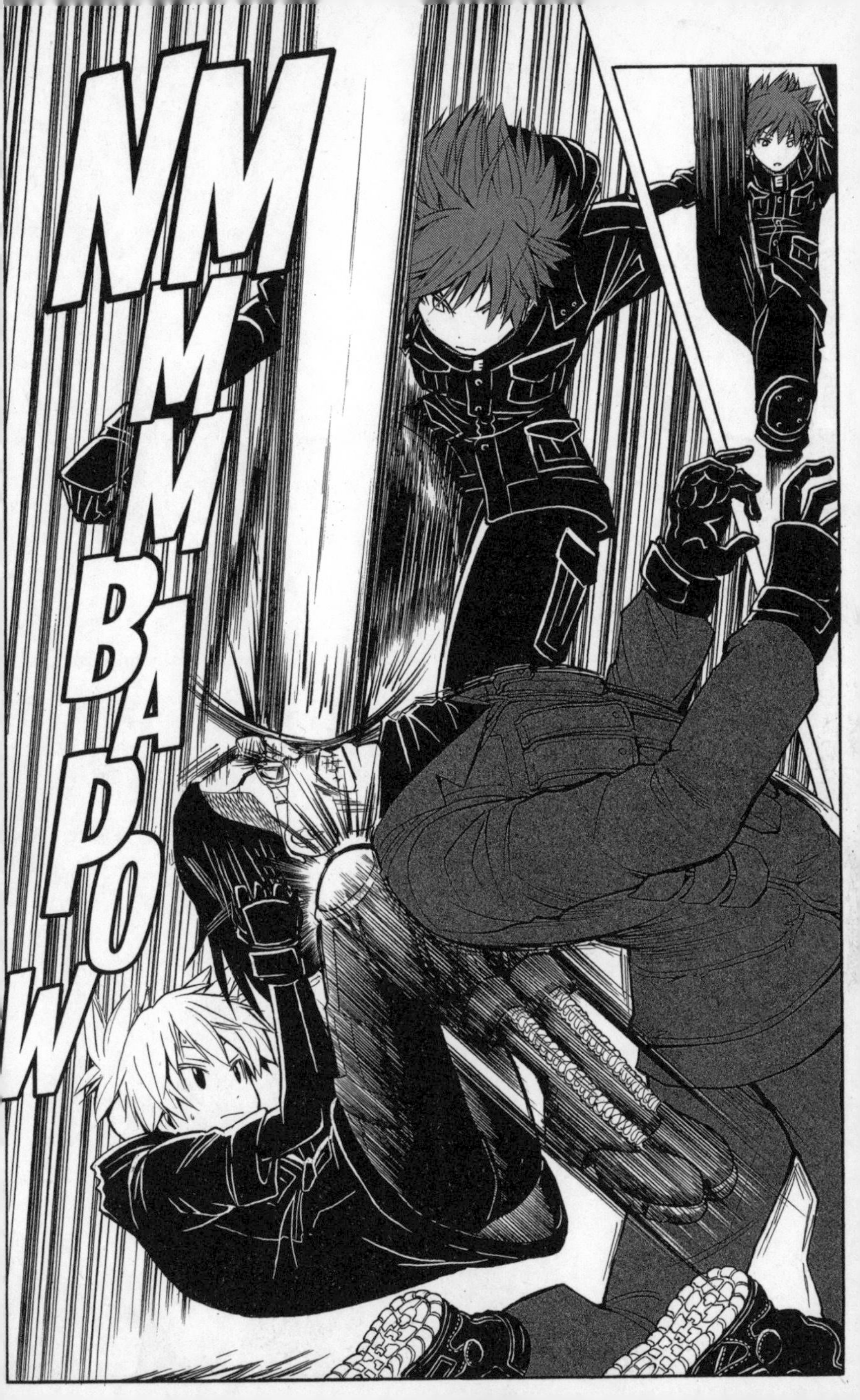
NNMMMBAPOW

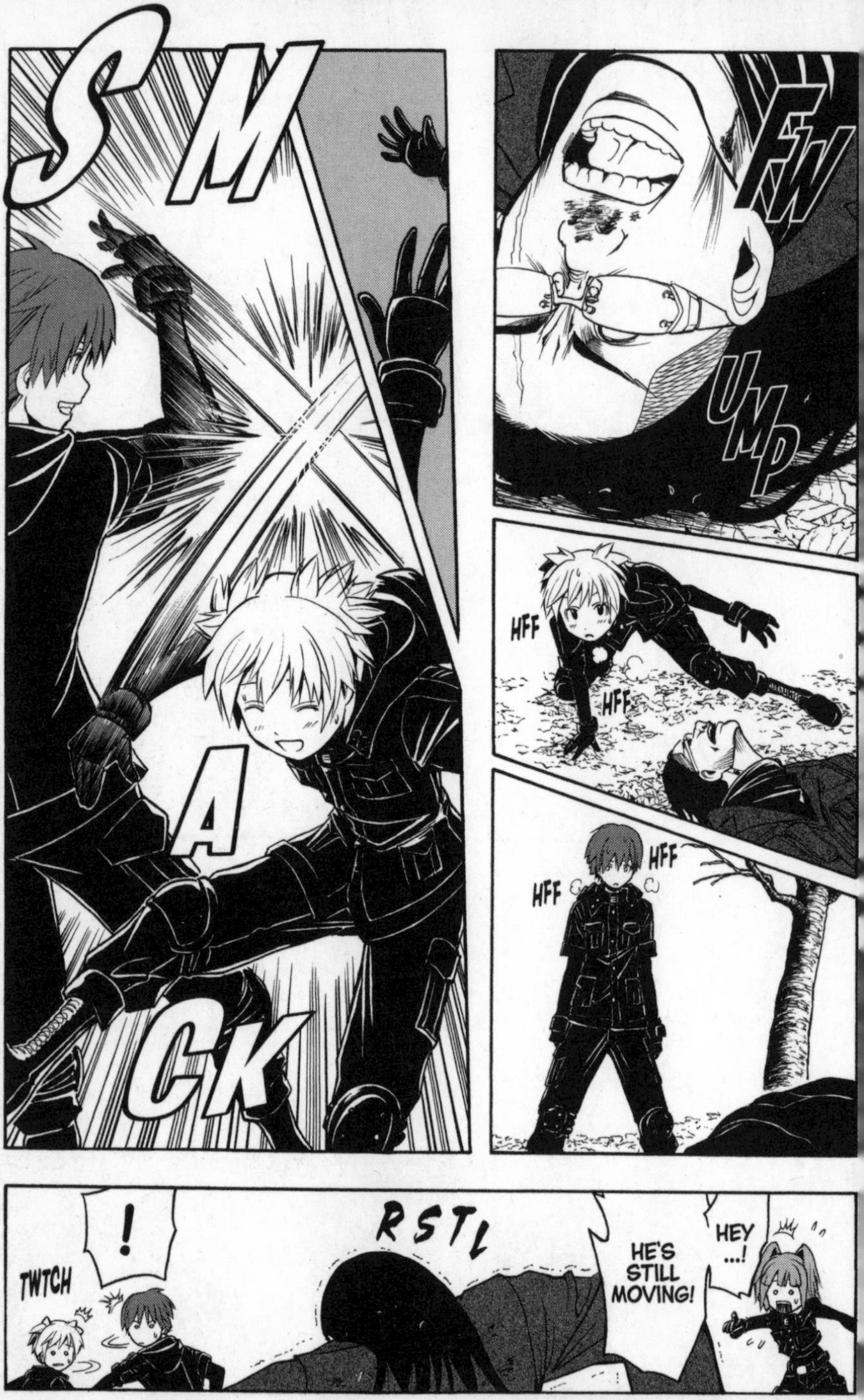
FWUMP
HFF
HFF
HFF
HFF
SMACK
HEY ...!
HE'S STILL MOVING!
RSTL
!
TWTCH

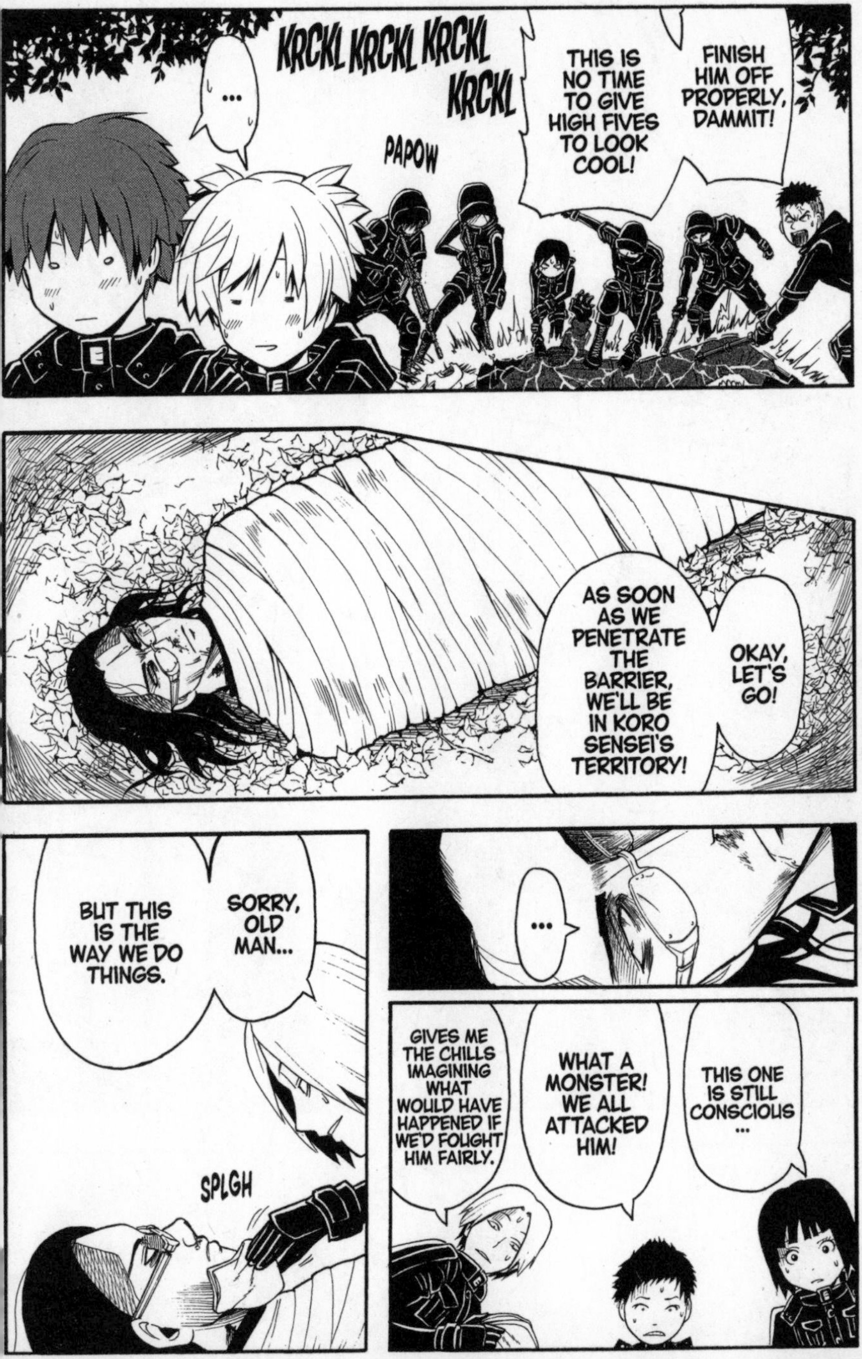
FINISH HIM OFF PROPERLY, DAMMIT!
THIS IS NO TIME TO GIVE HIGH FIVES TO LOOK COOL!
KRCKL KRCKL KRCKL KRCKL
PAPOW
...
OKAY, LET'S GO!
AS SOON AS WE PENETRATE THE BARRIER, WE'LL BE IN KORO SENSEI'S TERRITORY!
...
THIS ONE IS STILL CONSCIOUS ...
WHAT A MONSTER! WE ALL ATTACKED HIM!
GIVES ME THE CHILLS IMAGINING WHAT WOULD HAVE HAPPENED IF WE'D FOUGHT HIM FAIRLY.
SORRY, OLD MAN...
BUT THIS IS THE WAY WE DO THINGS.
SPLGH

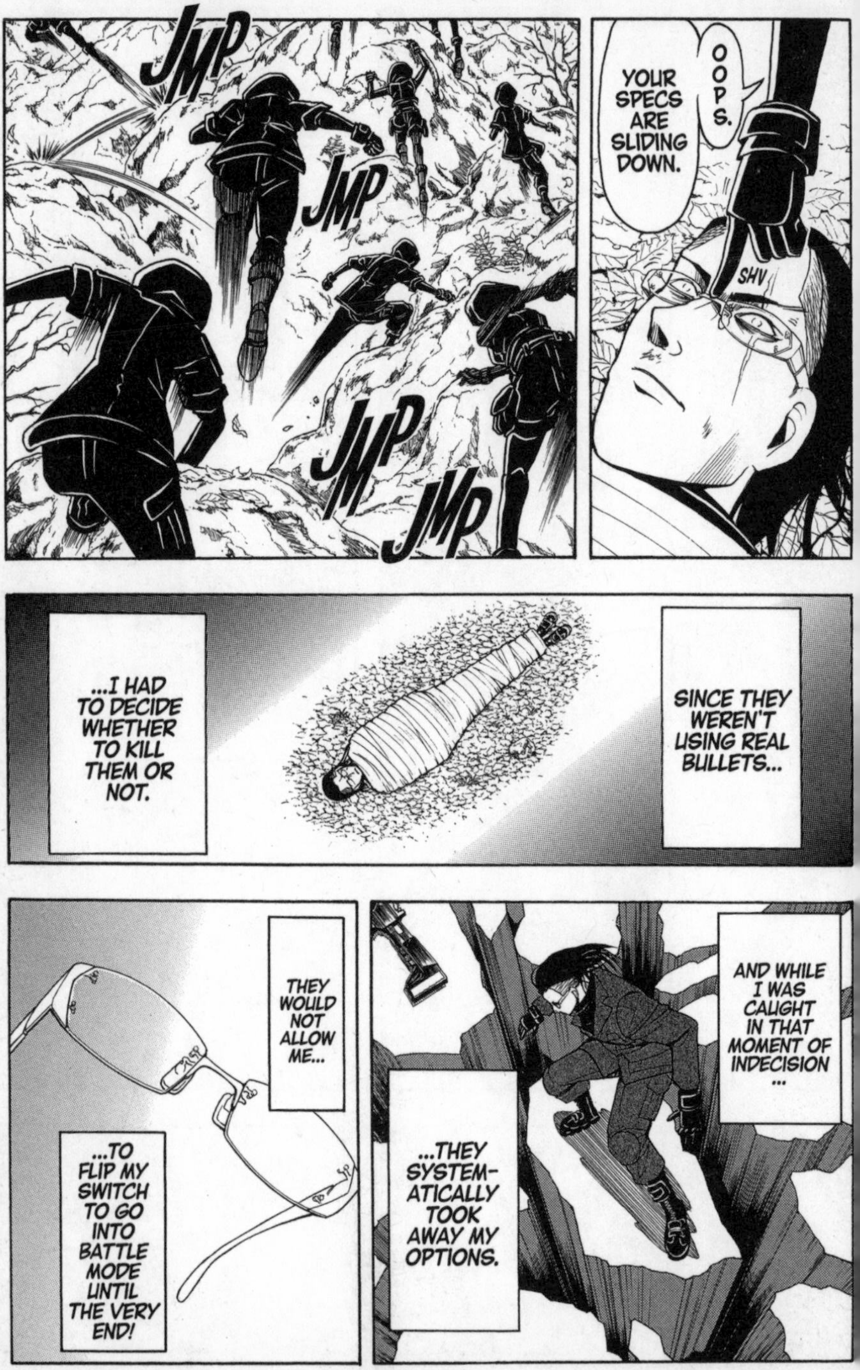
OOPS.
YOUR SPECS ARE SLIDING DOWN.
SHV
JMP
JMP
JMP
JMP
SINCE THEY WEREN'T USING REAL BULLETS...
...I HAD TO DECIDE WHETHER TO KILL THEM OR NOT.
AND WHILE I WAS CAUGHT IN THAT MOMENT OF INDECISION ...
...THEY SYSTEM-ATICALLY TOOK AWAY MY OPTIONS.
THEY WOULD NOT ALLOW ME...
...TO FLIP MY SWITCH TO GO INTO BATTLE MODE UNTIL THE VERY END!

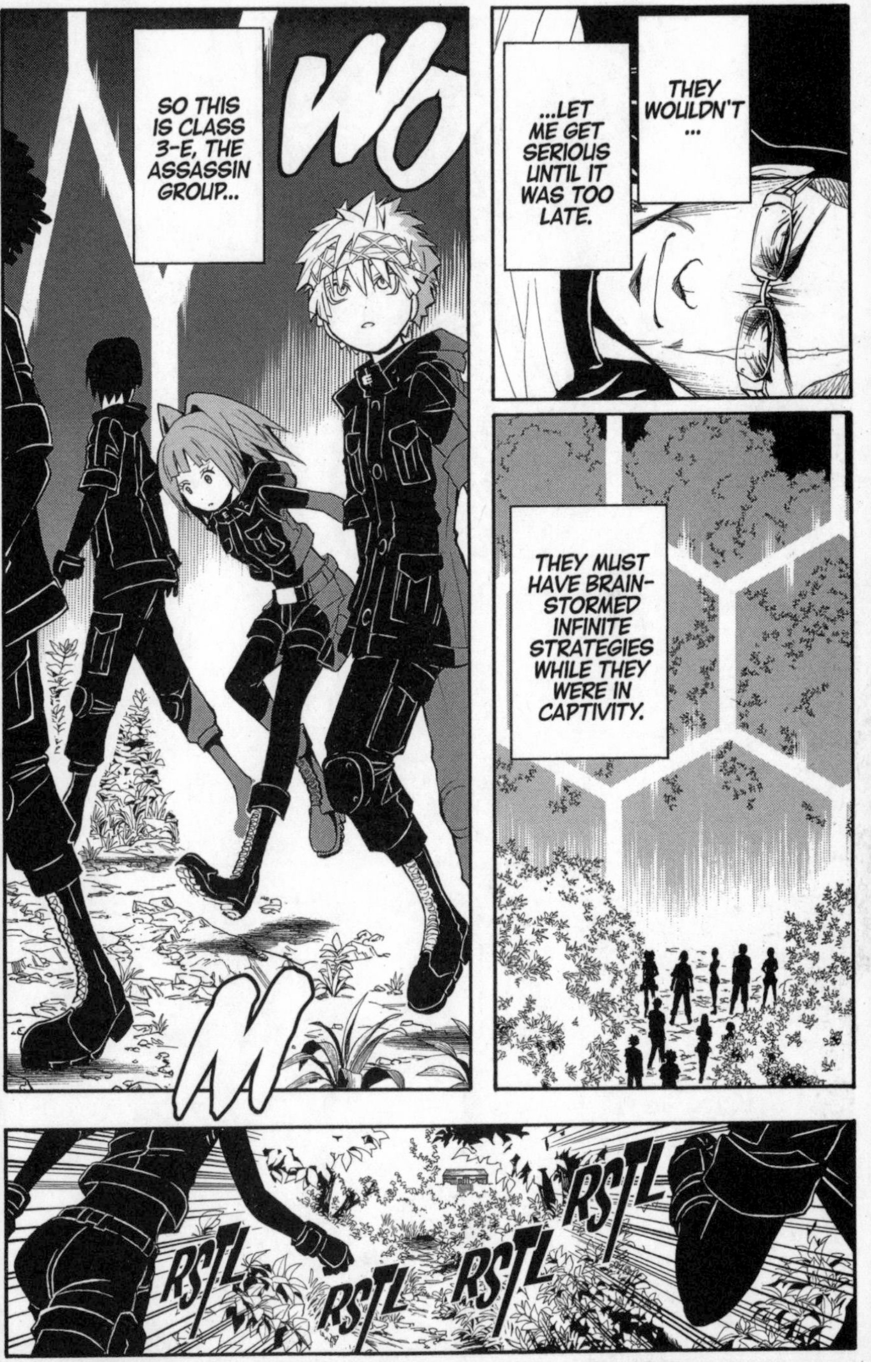
THEY WOULDN'T ...
...LET ME GET SERIOUS UNTIL IT WAS TOO LATE.
THEY MUST HAVE BRAIN-STORMED INFINITE STRATEGIES WHILE THEY WERE IN CAPTIVITY.
SO THIS IS CLASS 3-E, THE ASSASSIN GROUP...
WOM
RSTL
RSTL
RSTL
RSTL
RSTL

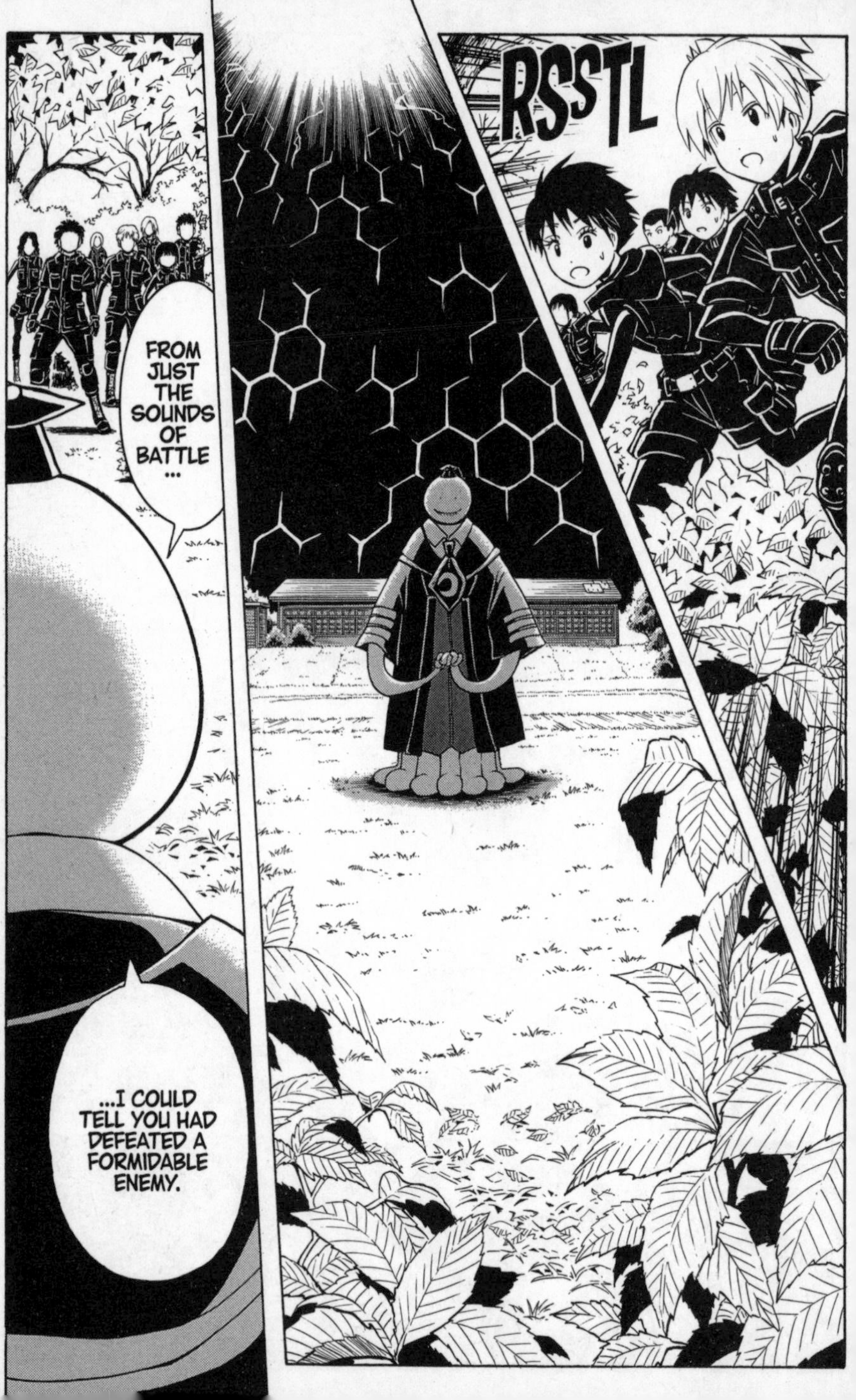
RSSTL
FROM JUST THE SOUNDS OF BATTLE ...
...I COULD TELL YOU HAD DEFEATED A FORMIDABLE ENEMY.

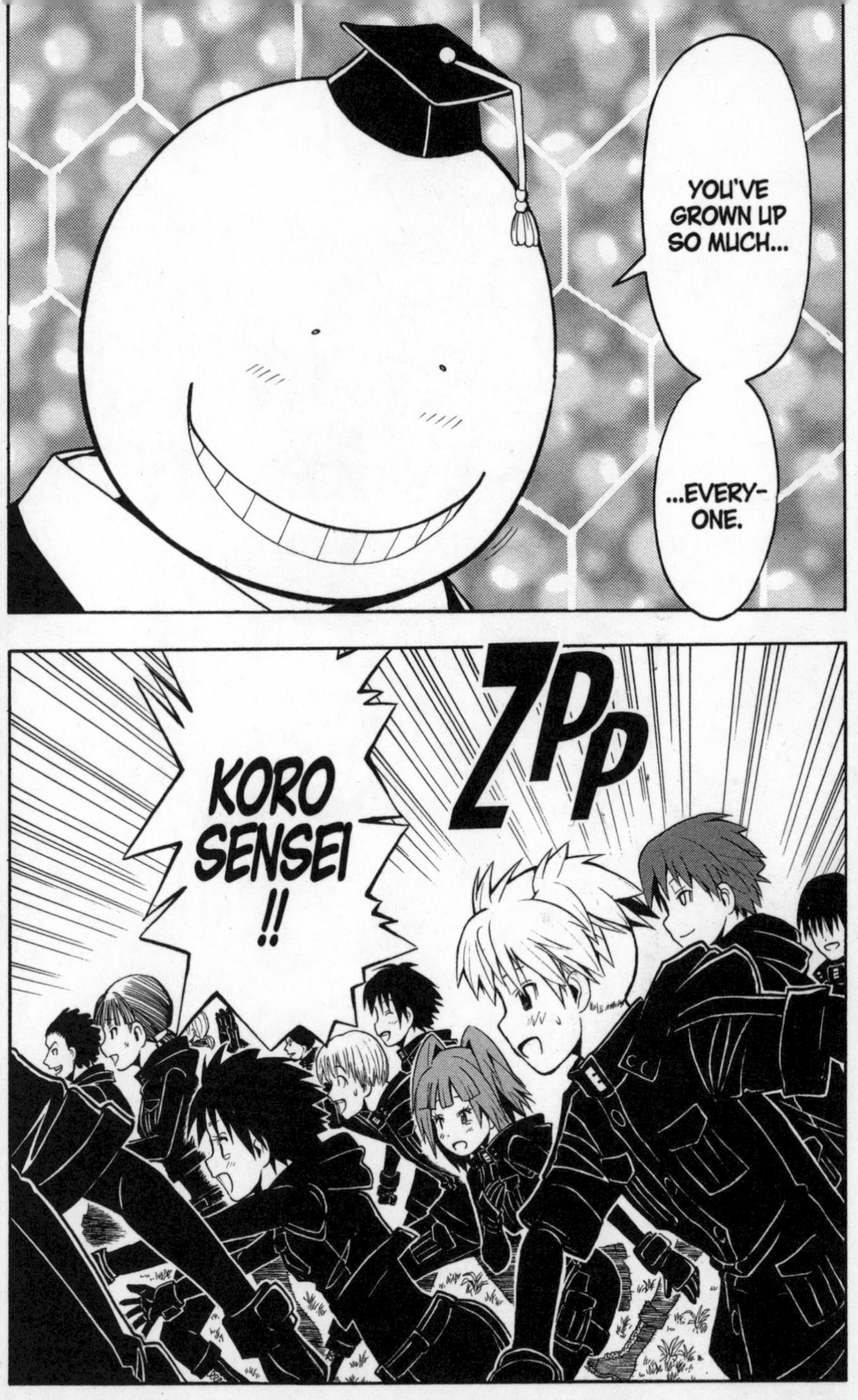
YOU'VE GROWN UP SO MUCH...
...EVERY-ONE.
ZPP
KORO SENSEI !!

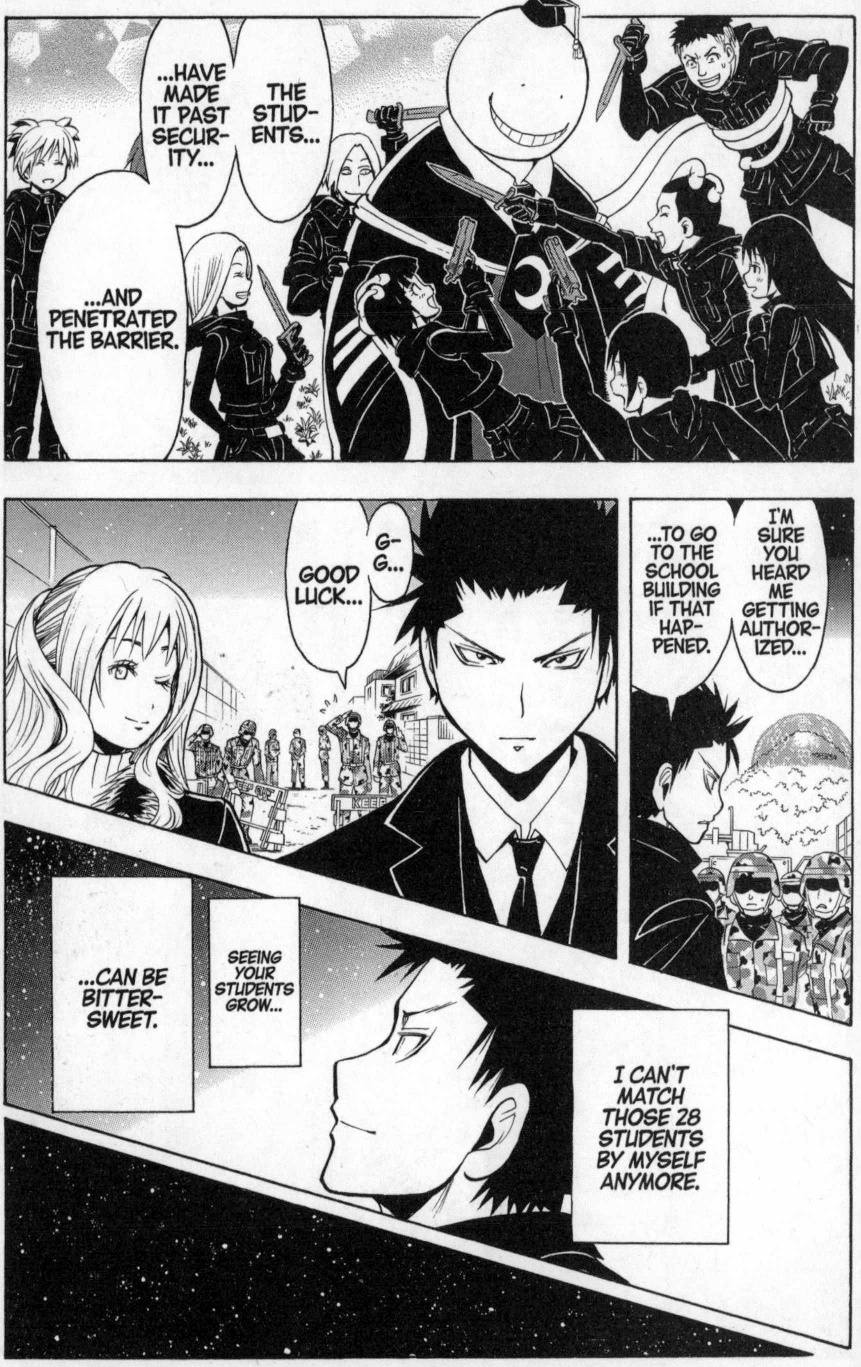
THE STUDENTS...
...HAVE MADE IT PAST SECURITY...
...AND PENETRATED THE BARRIER.
I'M SURE YOU HEARD ME GETTING AUTHORIZED...
...TO GO TO THE SCHOOL BUILDING IF THAT HAPPENED.
G-G...
GOOD LUCK...
I CAN'T MATCH THOSE 28 STUDENTS BY MYSELF ANYMORE.
SEEING YOUR STUDENTS GROW...
...CAN BE BITTERSWEET.

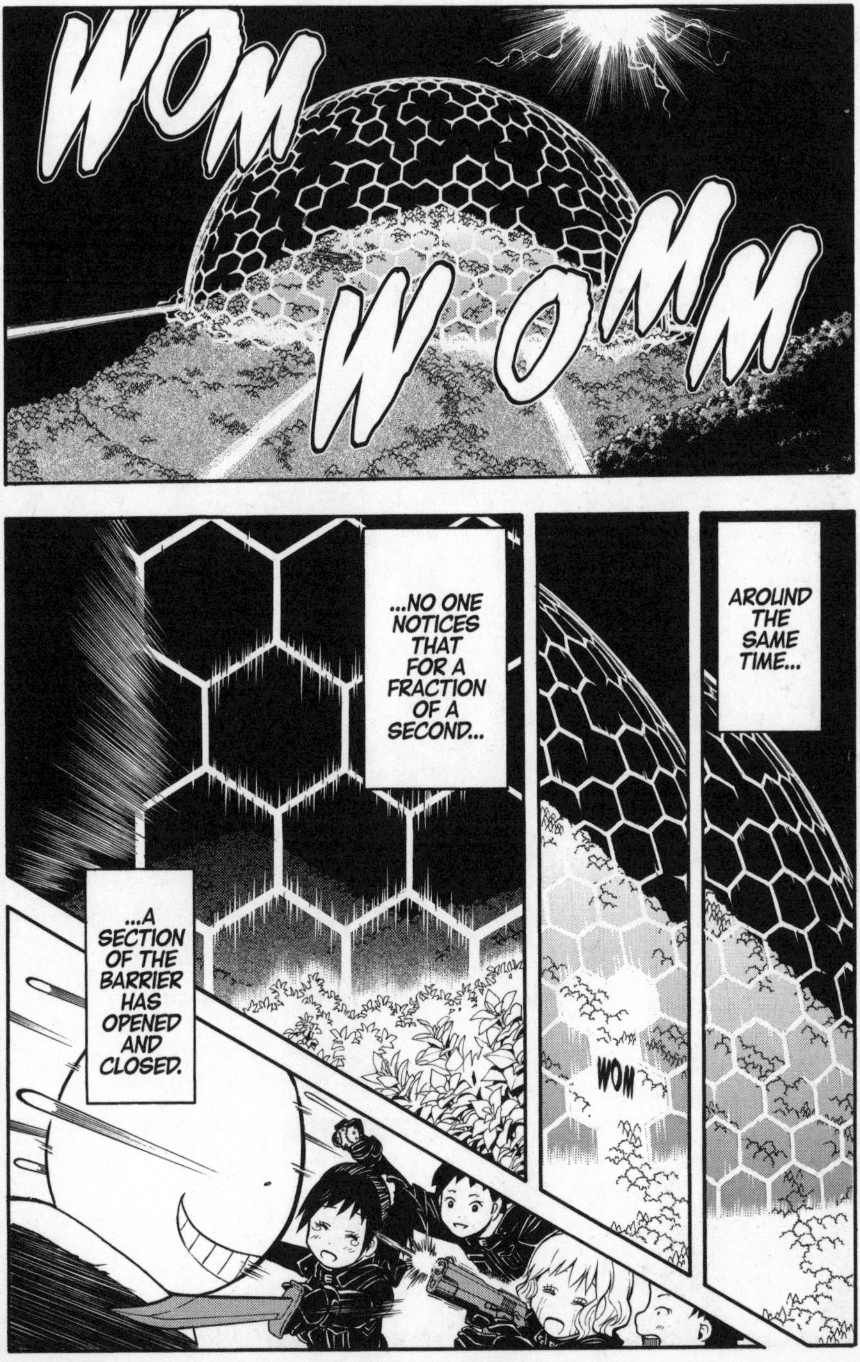
WOM
WOMM
AROUND THE SAME TIME...
WOM
...NO ONE NOTICES THAT FOR A FRACTION OF A SECOND...
...A SECTION OF THE BARRIER HAS OPENED AND CLOSED.

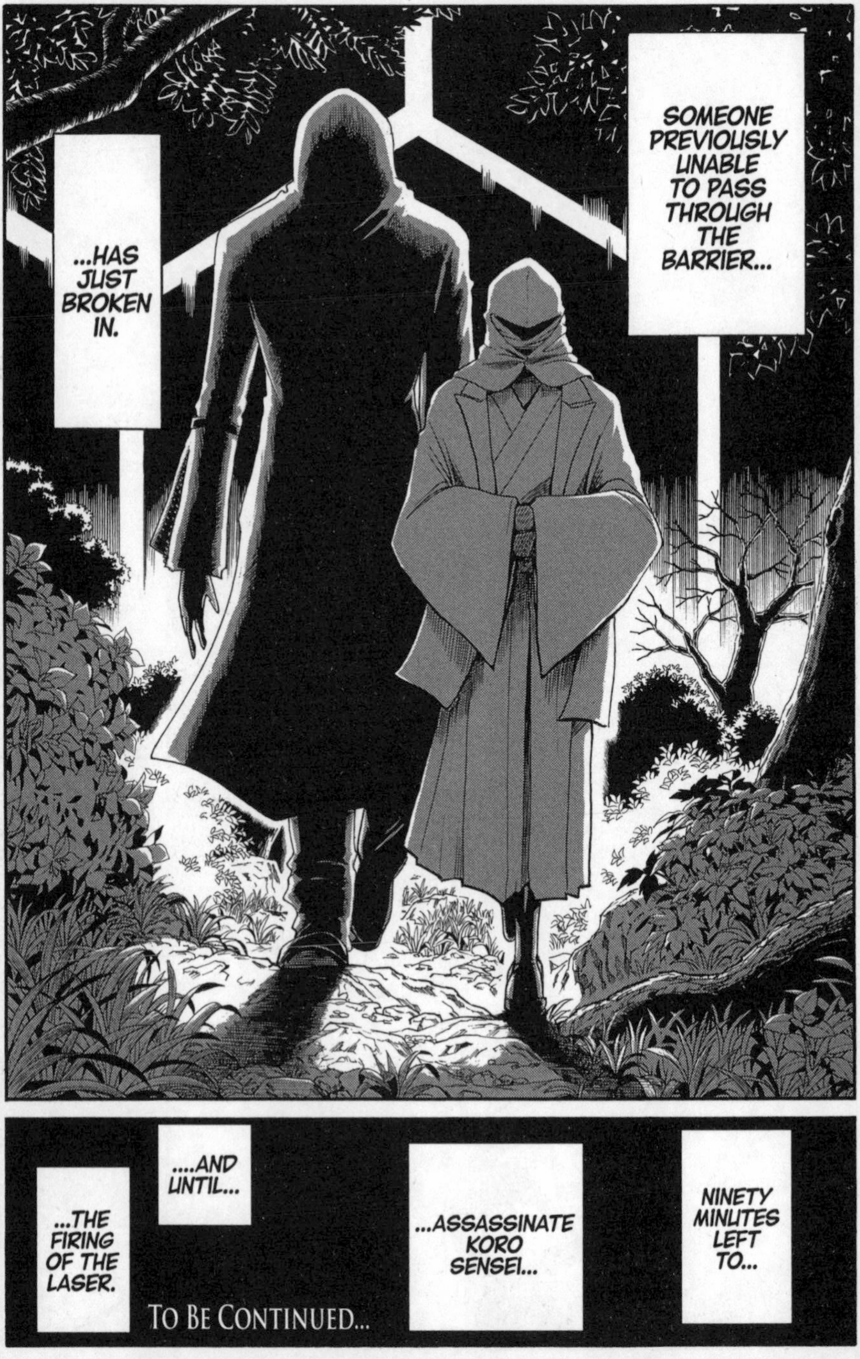
SOMEONE PREVIOUSLY UNABLE TO PASS THROUGH THE BARRIER...
...HAS JUST BROKEN IN.
NINETY MINUTES LEFT TO...
...ASSASSINATE KORO SENSEI...
....AND UNTIL...
...THE FIRING OF THE LASER.
TO BE CONTINUED...

One of the best things about working on this series is that I've had the privilege of meeting so many people I would never have otherwise met.

I met people for interviews and various projects. I met people for the live-action movie and anime.

Some my age and some even younger were the leading experts in their profession. And they all had such super-human talent and ideas.

Even though I'm pretty laid-back, talking with them made me think, "I still have a long way to go" and wonder, "Is there something I can steal from them?" It made me feel young again.

I think it's encounters like this with creative people that help prolong my life as a manga artist.

—Yusei Matsui

Yusei Matsui was born on the last day of January in Saitama Prefecture, Japan. He has been drawing manga since elementary school. Some of his favorite manga series are *Bobobo-bo Bo-bobo*, *JoJo's Bizarre Adventure* and *Ultimate Muscle*. Matsui learned his trade working as an assistant to manga artist Yoshio Sawai, creator of *Bobobo-bo Bo-bobo*. In 2005, Matsui debuted his original manga *Neuro: Supernatural Detective* in *Weekly Shonen Jump*. In 2007, *Neuro* was adapted into an anime. In 2012, *Assassination Classroom* began serialization in *Weekly Shonen Jump*.

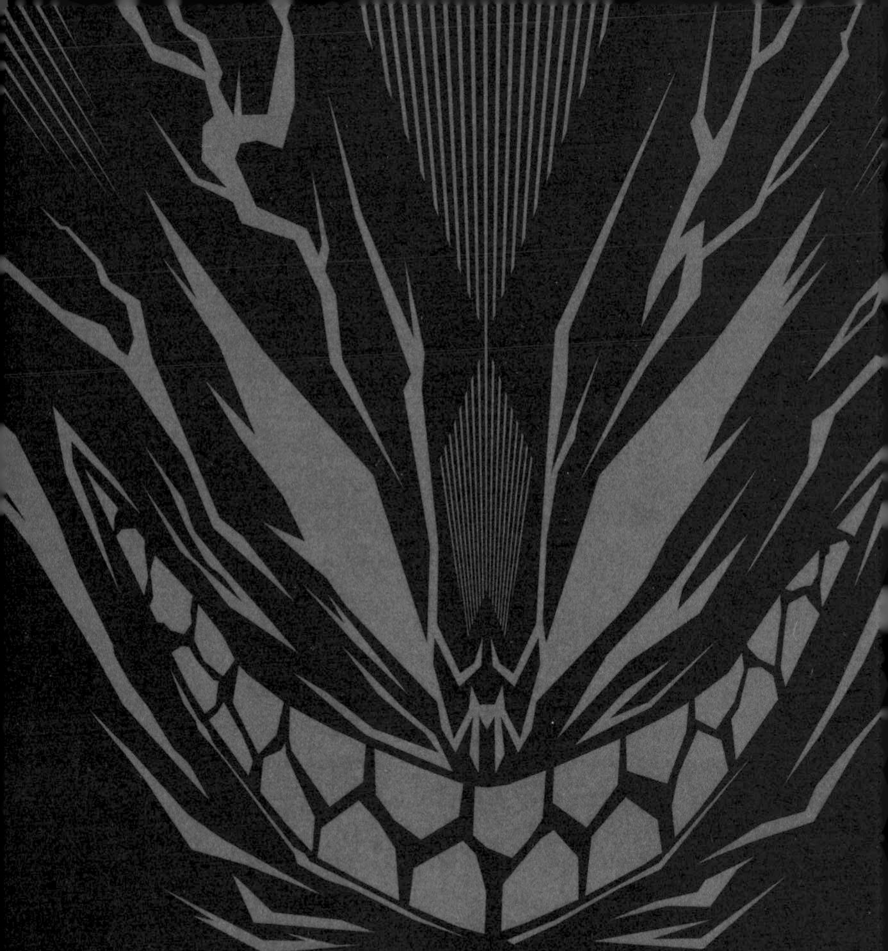

Pitch-black is Koro Sensei's color when he is enraged. But this "Koro gunmetal" in gray color is mixed into it, so he isn't totally beside himself with anger here. He appears furious purely for educational purposes.

ASSASSINATION CLASSROOM

YUSEI MATSUI

19

TIME TO GO TO SCHOOL

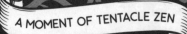

A MOMENT OF TENTACLE ZEN

Time has passed.
Dark wars have occurred.
Slime slimey slime.

– Nakakoro Chuya